IBM

MW01705114

IBM's Official

OS/2 WARP Connect PowerPC Edition

Operating in the New Frontier

Ken CHRISTOPHER

Scott WINTERS

Mary Pollak WRIGHT

An IBM Press Book

IDG Books Worldwide, Inc.
An International Data Group Company

Foster City, CA ♦ Chicago, IL ♦ Indianapolis, IN ♦ Braintree, MA ♦ Dallas, TX

IBM's Official OS/2 WARP Connect PowerPC Edition: Operating in the New Frontier

An IBM Press Book

Published by
IDG Books Worldwide, Inc.
An International Data Group Company
919 E. Hillsdale Blvd.
Suite 400
Foster City, CA 94404

Library of Congress Catalog Card No.: 95-78782

ISBN: 1-56884-458-1

Printed in the United States of America

10 9 8 7 6 5 4 3 2 1

1E/SX/RQ/ZV

Distributed in the United States by IDG Books Worldwide, Inc.

Distributed by Macmillan Canada for Canada; by Computer and Technical Books for the Caribbean Basin; by Contemporanea de Ediciones for Venezuela; by Distribuidora Cuspide for Argentina; by CITEC for Brazil; by Ediciones ZETA S.C.R. Ltda. for Peru; by Editorial Limusa SA for Mexico; by Transworld Publishers Limited in the United Kingdom and Europe; by Al-Maiman Publishers & Distributors for Saudi Arabia; by Simron Pty. Ltd. for South Africa; by IDG Communications (HK) Ltd. for Hong Kong; by Toppan Company Ltd. for Japan; by Addison Wesley Publishing Company for Korea; by Longman Singapore Publishers Ltd. for Singapore, Malaysia, Thailand, and Indonesia; by Unalis Corporation for Taiwan; by WS Computer Publishing Company, Inc. for the Philippines; by WoodsLane Pty. Ltd. for Australia; by WoodsLane Enterprises Ltd. for New Zealand.

For general information on IDG Books Worldwide's books in the U.S., please call our Consumer Customer Service department at 800-762-2974. For reseller information, including discounts and premium sales, please call our Reseller Customer Service department at 800-434-3422.

For information on where to purchase IDG Books Worldwide's books outside the U.S., contact IDG Books Worldwide at 415-655-3021 or fax 415-655-3295.

For information on translations, contact Marc Jeffrey Mikulich, Director, Foreign & Subsidiary Rights, at IDG Books Worldwide, 415-655-3018 or fax 415-655-3295.

For sales inquiries and special prices for bulk quantities, write to the address above or call IDG Books Worldwide at 415-655-3200.

For information on using IDG Books Worldwide's books in the classroom, or ordering examination copies, contact Jim Kelly at 800-434-2086.

About the Authors

Kenneth W. Christopher Jr., Program Director of Operating Systems Development in IBM's Boca Raton Laboratory, is responsible for the development of the OS/2 Warp operating system for the Intel and PowerPC architectures. Previously, Ken managed OS/2 subsystem development groups as well as the performance and usability teams for OS/2 2.1. During the DOS 4.0 project, he was the Development Programming Manager. He is the coauthor of four technical books on DOS and holds four U.S. Patents on PC software. He is a graduate of the University of Central Florida.

Scott L. Winters, a Senior Technical Staff Member, and the Manager of Operating Systems Strategy for the IBM Boca Raton Laboratory, is the technical leader of Architecture and Development for OS/2 Warp Connect (PowerPC Edition). Previously, Scott was the Lead Architect in the OS/2 Multimedia Systems Software group where the Multimedia Presentation Manager/2 (MMPM/2) product was created. He has published many magazine articles on operating systems and holds U.S. Patents on systems software algorithms. He received a Bachelor of Science degree in Computer Science from the University of Florida.

Mary Pollak Wright is the Technical Editor for the IBM OS/2 Warp Technical Library. She has received a number of awards from IBM, including an *Outstanding Technical Achievement* for her contribution to the OS/2 Toolkit and Technical Library. Mary has extensive programming and writing credentials. She is a former OS/2 developer who has written numerous technical articles for the *OS/2 Developer* magazine and *OS/2 Notebooks*. She has a Bachelor of Arts degree in Mathematics and Russian and a Master of Arts degree in Russian from Case Western Reserve University, Cleveland, Ohio.

Contributing Authors

Maria Azua, Advisory Programmer, works on the Systems Software Architecture team. She has extensive experience developing and architecting software products for UNIX, Windows, and OS/2. Her area of expertise includes device drivers, databases, and operating system design. She has a Bachelor of Science degree in Physics and Math and a Master of Science degree in Computer Science.

Bill Bodin, Senior Programmer, is the Video Team Lead and the Video Architect for the Graphics Device Driver Development team. Bill has several software patents, as well as IBM *Outstanding Technical Achievement* awards for OEM Video Support and Industry Standard Video Subsystem Design. His broad knowledge of all aspects of OS/2 has earned him recognition as the expert on the OS/2 Video subsystems and Base Video architecture.

Allen Gilbert, Senior Programmer, works on the Systems Software Architecture team. He has a wealth of knowledge about OS/2 and most recently shared his expertise on PowerPC Shared Services at the IBM Technical Interchange in New Orleans. He has a Bachelor of Science in Biology from the State University of New York at Stony Brook and a Master of Science degree in Genetics from the University of California.

Keith Kelly, Senior Programmer, works on the Multimedia Architecture and Strategy team. Keith has over 10 years of multimedia experience. He holds a patent related to multimedia and has received an *Outstanding Technical Achievement* award for his work on OS/2 Warp. He has a Bachelor of Science degree in Electrical Engineering from Clarkson.

Kelvin Lawrence, Senior Programmer, is the Lead Architect for the Presentation Services and Graphics Software subsystems. Kelvin is a speaker at many major OS/2 conferences and other computer industry events. He was instrumental in helping define and implement the OS/2 Presentation Manager in 1986. He has written numerous magazine articles and papers about OS/2 Presentation Services, including a paper on using the OS/2 Graphical Programming Interface that he presented at the 1994 Software Development Conference. Kelvin has an Honours degree in Computer Science from Brighton Polytechnic in England.

Ingrid Rodriguez, Senior Programming Manager of OS/2 Systems Technology Planning, joined IBM in 1989. Ingrid has held various roles including programming, software architecture, and management positions. She has a Bachelor of Science degree in Chemistry from the University of the Sacred Heart in Puerto Rico and a Bachelor of Science degree in Computer Engineering from the University of Florida.

James Schoech, Advisory Programmer, has worked for IBM for almost 15 years and has worked on OS/2 since 1988. He has several software patents related to his area of expertise–File Systems.

Helen Smith, Advisory Programming Manager, is responsible for the development of the MVM Subsystem. Helen has been with IBM for 10 years, holding a variety of positions in application and operating system software development. She has a Bachelor of Arts degree from the State University of New York at Potsdam and is pursuing a Master of Science degree in Computer Engineering from Syracuse University.

James Taylor, Senior Programmer, currently works in the OpenDoc Support department in Austin, Texas. He was a key member of the Workplace Shell Development team in Boca Raton, Florida.

Jay Tunkel, Senior Programmer, works on the OS/2 Development Tools team. He joined IBM in 1968 and has worked on a wide variety of mainframe and desktop software projects. He has been active in the design of OS/2 since 1985 and is the author of several articles and book chapters pertaining to OS/2 application development. He has a Master of Business Administration degree from the University of Connecticut and a Master of Science degree from the State University of New York at Binghamton.

Robert Tycast, Advisory Programmer, works on the OpenDoc for OS/2 team. He joined IBM in 1989 as a member of the OS/2 Toolkit Development Team. He was also a member of the team that worked on distributed Presentation Manager technology, which allows interoperation of PM programs and X Window System servers. He has a Bachelor of Science degree from MIT and has completed graduate work at MIT in the Computer Science department.

About IBM Press

IBM Press is committed to bringing you high-quality books about IBM products and technologies. You can count on IBM Press to provide books that are of interest to all computer users—home and office users, network and systems administrators, application developers and programmers.

It is a great pleasure to present *OS/2 Warp Connect (PowerPC Edition): Operating in the New Frontier*. This book is the first and only authorized preview guide for OS/2 Warp Connect (PowerPC Edition).

Inside these pages, you will learn about the benefits that OS/2 Warp Connect (PowerPC Edition) can bring to your business and your home. This preview guide provides an *inside look* at the development of the next-generation 32-bit operating system for the PowerPC computer.

During the development of this book, our new IBM Press Home Page was also under construction. By the time you read this book, construction should be completed. You can use the IBM Press Home Page to find out what books are currently available and how to order those books, or simply to converse with us. We'd enjoy hearing from you.

You can also use our *What's New* icon to find out what books we are planning to publish in the near future. For example, if you used the *What's New* icon today, you would find out that a user's guide for OS/2 Warp Connect (PowerPC Edition) and a 4-volume set of programming books for OS/2 Warp are under development right now and should be available later in the year.

Our Internet address is: http://www.austin.ibm.com/ibmpress

Beth Tripi
Imprint Manager
International Business Machines Corporation

ABOUT IDG BOOKS WORLDWIDE

Welcome to the world of IDG Books Worldwide.

IDG Books Worldwide, Inc., is a subsidiary of International Data Group, the world's largest publisher of computer-related information and the leading global provider of information services on information technology. IDG was founded more than 25 years ago and now employs more than 7,700 people worldwide. IDG publishes more than 250 computer publications in 67 countries (see listing below). More than 70 million people read one or more IDG publications each month.

Launched in 1990, IDG Books Worldwide is today the #1 publisher of best-selling computer books in the United States. We are proud to have received 8 awards from the Computer Press Association in recognition of editorial excellence and three from Computer Currents' First Annual Readers' Choice Awards, and our best-selling *...For Dummies*® series has more than 19 million copies in print with translations in 28 languages. IDG Books Worldwide, through a joint venture with IDG's Hi-Tech Beijing, became the first U.S. publisher to publish a computer book in the People's Republic of China. In record time, IDG Books Worldwide has become the first choice for millions of readers around the world who want to learn how to better manage their businesses.

Our mission is simple: Every IDG and IBM Press book is designed to bring extra value and skill-building instructions to the reader. Our books are written by experts who understand and care about our readers. The knowledge base of our editorial staff comes from years of experience in publishing, education, and journalism — experience which we use to produce books for the '90s. In short, we care about books, so we attract the best people. We devote special attention to details such as audience, interior design, use of icons, and illustrations. And because we use an efficient process of authoring, editing, and desktop publishing our books electronically, we can spend more time ensuring superior content and spend less time on the technicalities of making books.

You can count on our commitment to deliver high-quality books at competitive prices on topics you want to read about. At IDG Books Worldwide, we continue in the IDG tradition of delivering quality for more than 25 years. You'll find no better book on a subject than one from IDG Books Worldwide.

John Kilcullen
President and CEO
IDG Books Worldwide, Inc.

VIII
WINNER
Eighth Annual Computer Press Awards 1992

IX
WINNER
Ninth Annual Computer Press Awards 1993

IDG Books Worldwide, Inc., is a publication of International Data Group, the world's largest publisher of computer-related information and the leading global provider of information services on information technology. International Data Group publishes over 250 computer publications in 67 countries. Seventy million people read one or more International Data Group publications each month. International Data Group's publications include: **ARGENTINA:** Computerworld Argentina, GamePro, Infoworld, PC World Argentina; **AUSTRALIA:** Australian Macworld, Client/Server Journal, Computer Living, Computerworld, Digital News, Network World, PC World, Publishing Essentials, Reseller; **AUSTRIA:** Computerwelt, PC TEST; **BELARUS:** PC World Belarus; **BELGIUM:** Data News; **BRAZIL:** Annuário de Informática, Computerworld Brazil, Connections, Super Game Power, Macworld, PC World Brazil, Publish Brazil, SUPERGAME; **BULGARIA:** Computerworld Bulgaria, Networkworld/Bulgaria, PC & MacWorld Bulgaria; **CANADA:** CIO Canada, ComputerWorld Canada, InfoCanada, Network World Canada, Reseller World; **CHILE:** Computerworld Chile, GamePro, PC World Chile; **COLUMBIA:** Computerworld Colombia, GamePro, PC World Colombia; **COSTA RICA:** PC World Costa Rica/Nicaragua; **THE CZECH AND SLOVAK REPUBLICS:** Computerworld Czechoslovakia, Elektronika Czechoslovakia, PC World Czechoslovakia; **DENMARK:** Communications World, Computerworld Danmark, Macworld Danmark, PC World Danmark, PC World Danmark Supplements, TECH World; **DOMINICAN REPUBLIC:** PC World Republica Dominicana; **ECUADOR:** PC World Ecuador, GamePro; **EGYPT:** Computerworld Middle East, PC World Middle East; **EL SALVADOR:** PC World Centro America; **FINLAND:** MikroPC, Tietoverkko, Tietoviikko; **FRANCE:** Distributique, Golden, Info PC, Le Guide du Monde Informatique, Le Monde Informatique, Reseaux & Telecoms; **GERMANY:** Computer Business, Computerwoche, Computerwoche Extra, Computerwoche Focus, Electronic Entertainment, GamePro, I/M Information Management, Macwelt, PC Welt; **GREECE:** GamePro, Macworld & Publish; **GUATEMALA:** PC World Centro America; **HONDURAS:** PC World Centro America; **HONG KONG:** Computerworld Hong Kong, PCWorld Hong Kong, Publish in Asia; **HUNGARY:** ABCD CD-ROM, Computerworld Szamitastechnika, PC & Mac World Hungary, PC-X Magazine; **INDIA:** Computerworld India, PC World India, Publish in Asia; **INDONESIA:** InfoKomputer PC World, Komputek Computerworld, Publish in Asia; **IRELAND':** ComputerScope, PC Live!; **ISRAEL:** PC World 32 BIT, People & Computers; **ITALY:** Computerworld Italia, Computerworld Italia Special Editions, Lotus Italia, Macworld Italia, Networking Italia, PC Shopping, PC World Italia, PC World/Walt Disney; **JAPAN:** Macworld Japan, Nikkei Personal Computing, SunWorld Japan, Windows World Japan; **KENYA:** East African Computer News; **KOREA:** Hi-Tech Information/Computerworld, Macworld Korea, PC World Korea; **MACEDONIA:** PC World Macedonia; **MALAYSIA:** Computerworld Malaysia, PC World Malaysia, Publish in Asia; **MEXICO:** Computerworld Mexico, GamePro, Macworld, PC World Mexico; **MYANMAR:** PC World Myanmar; **NETHERLANDS:** Computable, Computer! Totaal, LAN Magazine, Macworld, Net Magazine; **NEW ZEALAND:** Computer Buyer, Computerworld New Zealand, MTB, Network World, PC World New Zealand; **NICARAGUA:** PC World Costa Rica/Nicaragua; **NIGERIA:** PC World Africa; **NORWAY:** Computerworld Norge, Computerworld Privat, CW Rapport Klient/Tjener, CW Rapport Nettverk & Telecom, CW Rapport Offentlig Sektor, IDG's KURSGUIDE, Macworld Norge, Multimedia World, PC World Ekspress, PC World Nettverk, PC World Norge, PC World's Produktguide, Windows Spesial; **PAKISTAN:** Computerworld Pakistan, PC World Pakistan; **PANAMA:** GamePro, PC World Panama; **PARAGUAY:** PC World Paraguay; **P. R. OF CHINA:** China Computerworld, China Infoworld, Computer & Communication, Electronic Product World, Electronics Today, Game Camp, PC World China, Popular Computer Week, Software World, Telecom Product World; **PERU:** Computerworld Peru, GamePro, PC World Profesional Peru, PC World Peru; **POLAND:** Computerworld Poland, Computerworld Special Report, Macworld, Networld, PC World Komputer; **PHILIPPINES:** Computerworld Philippines, PC Digest, Publish in Asia; **PORTUGAL:** Cerebro/PC World, Correio Informático/Computerworld, Mac•In/PC•In Portugal; **PUERTO RICO:** PC World Puerto Rico; **ROMANIA:** Computerworld Romania, PC World Romania, Telecom Romania; **RUSSIA:** Computerworld Rossiya, Network World Russia, PC World Russia; **SINGAPORE:** Computerworld Singapore, PC World Singapore, Publish in Asia; **SLOVENIA:** MONITOR; **SOUTH AFRICA:** Computing S.A., Network World S.A., Software World; **SPAIN:** Computerworld España, COMUNICACIONES WORLD, Dealer World, Macworld España, PC World España; **SWEDEN:** CAP&Design, Computer Sweden, Corporate Computing, MacWorld, Maxi Data, MikroDatorn, Nätverk & Kommunikation, PC/Aktiv, PC World, Windows World; **SWITZERLAND:** Computerworld Schweiz, Macworld Schweiz, PCtip; **TAIWAN:** Computerworld Taiwan, Macworld Taiwan, PC World Taiwan, Publish Taiwan, Windows World; **THAILAND:** Thai Computerworld, Publish in Asia; **TURKEY:** Computerworld Monitör, MACWORLD Turkiye, PC WORLD Turkiye; **UKRAINE:** Computerworld Kiev, Computers & Software Magazine, PC World Ukraine; **UNITED KINGDOM:** Acorn User, Amiga Action, Amiga Computing, Amiga, Appletalk, CD Powerplay, CD-ROM Now, Computing, Connexion, GamePro, Lotus Magazine, Macaction, Macworld, Open Computing, Parents and Computers, PC Home, PC Works, The WEB; **UNITED STATES:** Cable in the Classroom, CD Review, CIO Magazine, Computerworld, Computerworld Client/Server Journal, Digital Video Magazine, DOS World, Electronic, InfoWorld, I-Way, Macworld, Maximize, MULTIMEDIA WORLD, Network World, PC World, PUBLISH, SWATPro Magazine, Video Event, WebMaster; **URUGUAY:** PC World Uruguay; **VENEZUELA:** Computerworld Venezuela, GamePro, PC World Venezuela; and **VIETNAM:** PC World Vietnam 10/16/95

IDG BOOKS WORLDWIDE

Dedication

Ken wishes to dedicate this book to his wife, Milena, and daughters, Christina and Jacquelyn, for their support throughout this demanding project.

Scott wishes to dedicate this book to his wife, Honey, and children, Matthew and Stephanie, for the love and support they give him at home and to his parents, Ann and Hy, for all that they did to get him this far. He additionally would like to dedicate this book to Mark T. and Franz W. for helping him fulfill a career dream.

Mary wishes to dedicate this book to her husband, David (for all his patience and support), to her parents, Matilda and Frank Pollak (for their lifelong encouragement), and to her children, Victoria, Neal, and Michael (for their future).

Acknowledgments

We have been involved with this project for over 30 months. During that time, many people have interacted with us. They have left a significant mark on the architecture, design, development, test, documentation, and management of the effort now known as OS/2 Warp Connect (PowerPC Edition). We wish to acknowledge and thank all of these people (far too many to list) for their dedication and hard work.

We would like to acknowledge Larry Loucks, IBM Fellow and Vice President of Technology, for his vision, his leadership, and his mentorship. The building blocks of our architecture were his vision. We are proud to implement it for him. We would also like to acknowledge the two IBM Vice Presidents who have led the delivery of this product. Our best wishes go to Guy Harrison, who started us up, and whose charismatic leadership brought us through to the first Beta release. To John Schwarz, who now has the most difficult task of overseeing the completion of our work, we thank you for a "cool head" in a chaotic and stressful time. It is a pleasure to work for executives who have the "hands-on" knowledge of software development. We also thank Lee Reiswig, Dave Schleicher, and Jim Cannavino for their inspiration and commitment to us. Many times they were pressured by alternate strategies; they stayed with us.

A number of people have significantly contributed toward the completion of this book. We would like to acknowledge our contributing authors in alphabetical order, with the exception of Allen Gilbert, whose personal vitality and contribution were outstanding. Thanks to Allen, Maria Azua, Bill Bodin, Keith Kelly, Kelvin Lawrence, Ingrid Rodriguez, James Schoech, Helen Smith, James Taylor, Jay Tunkel, and Robert Tycast.

We would also like to thank Adam Jollans, who originally conceived the circular diagrams used in this book, and Suzanne Baird, Miles Barel, Diane Baron, Arnold Bramnick, Ralph Dafoe, Jeri Dube, Mary Forlenza, Paul Giangarra, Richard Hoffman, Mike Kiehl, Dorothy Kruger, Cheryl Leone, Eric Lund, Martin McElroy, D'Ann Ostrom, Cliff Reeves, John Wilson, and Steve Wuest for their support.

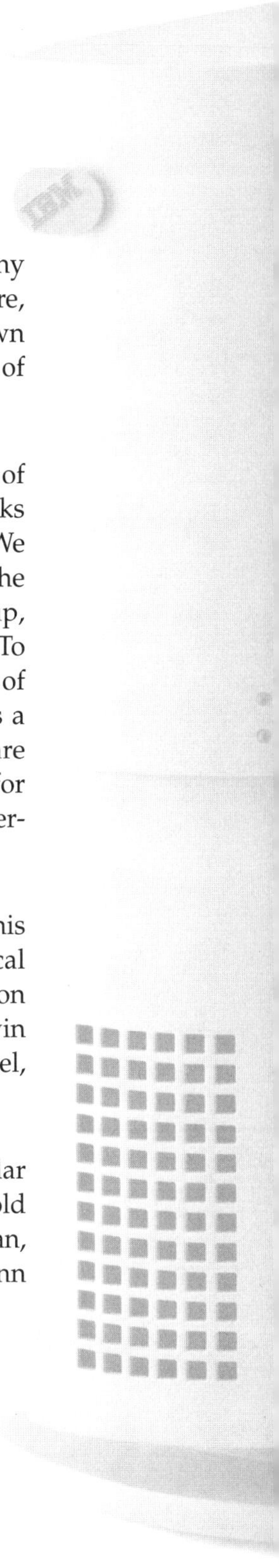

The authors would like to thank the IBM Press, because without Beth Tripi this book would never have been completed. She is one of the world's fastest decision makers. We would also like to thank the IBM Press staff, especially the editors and graphic designers, for their great skill and diligence.

Lastly, we like to give a special thanks to Eric Stone and John Kilcullen of IDG Books for this opportunity.

(The publisher would like to give special thanks to Patrick J. McGovern, without whom this book would not have been possible.)

Credits

IBM Press Staff

Imprint Manager
Beth Tripi

Acquisitions Manager
Diane Walewski

Editors
Elizabeth Jean
Tracey Marcelo

Cover Designer
Jeffrey Lewis

Cover Illustrator
Kevin McMahon

Book and Illustration Designer
Shirley Kuan

Production Coordinator
Ginny Black

Technical Coordinator
Eugene Ignatowski

Desktop Publishing Specialist
John Mangrum

Graphic Design Specialist
Cathy Card

IDG Staff

Vice President and Publisher
Brenda McLaughlin

Publishing Director
John Osborne

Brand Manager
Pradeepa Siva

Associate Developmental Editor
Amy Marks

Production Director
Beth Jenkins

Supervisor of Project Coordination
Cindy L. Phipps

Supervisor of Page Layout
Kathie S. Schnorr

Production Systems Specialist
Steve Peake

Associate Project Coordinator
Sherry Gomoll

Production Staff
Todd Klemme
Laura Puranen
Mark Owens
Patricia Reynolds

Proofreaders
Betty Kish
Gwenette Gaddis
Dwight Ramsey
Robert Springer

Table of Chapters

Table of Contents

OS/2 Warp Connect (PowerPC Edition) consist of the following programs:

1. OS/2 Warp Version 3 for the PowerPC
2. The IBM Microkernal Product
3. The BonusPak for the PowerPC
4. Networking products from IBM and other parties
5. As well as other additional products

Foreword

I believe that to be competitive and, therefore, successful, customers need an operating system that satisfies and simplifies long-range computing needs and that is as dynamic as emerging new software and hardware technologies. It is essential that such an operating system support an increasing variety of applications as well as an expanding range of hardware. It is also essential that an operating system provide a superior programming environment for application developers.

That is why I am very pleased to have this opportunity to introduce this first book about OS/2 Warp Connect (PowerPC Edition). This book showcases a powerful set of computing technologies that are the building blocks for enhancing your computing world today and that provide a solid foundation with which to propel your business into the twenty-first century.

OS/2 Warp Connect (PowerPC Edition) provides built-in connectivity services and is a true 32-bit operating system with a host of other features, such as Presentation Services and the newly designed File Services, which provide enhanced file management. In the tradition of its predecessors on the Intel platform, OS/2 Warp Connect (PowerPC Edition) still provides an award-winning interface—the Workplace Shell—as well as crash protection and superior multitasking capabilities. And, it provides all of these operating system services *and more* built on a single, small microkernel. This architecture helps provide an application development environment that is greatly simplified.

I am very excited about the possibilities that OS/2 Warp Connect (PowerPC Edition) brings to the world of computing. I am equally excited about this book, as it introduces these possibilities to the world. The authors, Ken, Scott, and Mary, have been involved with the development of this product and this book for some time. They have watched the operating system grow from just an idea to almost a product. They have insider knowledge of the development of the product, and they have done an excellent job of explaining the architecture and many of the features of the operating system.

I recommend this book to anyone who is interested in new and fascinating technologies. Computer users, MIS professionals, adminstrators, application developers, and corporate decision makers will find this book provides a comprehensive and understandable first look at a great new operating system.

John M. Thompson
IBM Senior Vice President and
Group Executive – Software

Introduction

Welcome to the first edition of *OS/2 Warp Connect (PowerPC Edition): Operating in the New Frontier*. If you are a business professional, a programmer, a user, or you are currently using a version of OS/2 on an Intel-based system, you will find that this book helps answer many of the questions you might have about this upcoming edition of OS/2 Warp Connect. Although the architecture for this product is different from the versions of OS/2 for Intel-based systems, if you have previously used OS/2, you still will find many of your favorite features described in this book.

This preview book provides a first look at the architecture and describes, in-depth and up-close, the technical details of this product. If you are planning to move your computing operations to PowerPC systems or you are planning to switch to a real 32-bit operating system, then you must read this book. It fully describes the benefits of this new architecture and is loaded with technical details and a number of *insider* tips. If you are planning to develop programs for OS/2 Warp Connect (PowerPC Edition), this book gives you the head start you need to develop those programs. It also provides a generous amount of tips designed exclusively for application developers.

This book also explains some of the features that are planned for OS/2 Warp Connect (PowerPC Edition). Almost all readers will be interested in finding out how to use these leading-edge technologies to their best advantage.

How This Book Is Organized

This book is organized so that an overview of the architecture and concise descriptions of the major features (and the benefits those features might provide to your computing environment) appear in the first two chapters, as follows:

- Chapter 1: *Introducing OS/2 Warp Connect (PowerPC Edition)!*

  This chapter discusses the major highlights and benefits of the operating system.

- Chapter 2: *A New Design for OS/2*

  This chapter discusses the architectural changes in OS/2 and provides an in-depth overview of the new architecture.

Preceding these two chapters is the preface, *The Road from Boca to You*, which provides a brief description of some of the highlights that occurred during the development of this operating system.

Subsequent chapters provide architectural, technical, and technological information as follows:

- Chapter 3: *The IBM Microkernel*

  This chapter introduces the IBM Microkernel and discusses how the IBM Microkernel interacts with operating system services.

- Chapter 4: *Name Services*

  This chapter introduces the Name Services and discusses how they are used by the operating system.

- Chapter 5: *Shared Services*

  This chapter introduces Shared Services and discusses how they are used in OS/2 Warp Connect (PowerPC Edition).

- Chapter 6: *OS/2 Operating System Services*

  This chapter describes the OS/2 Operating System Services such as the OS/2 Server and the Pipe Server.

- Chapter 7: *File Services*

  This chapter describes the File Services such as support for Physical File Systems.

- Chapter 8: *Presentation Services*

  This chapter describes the Presentation Services such as support for event and session management.

- Chapter 9: *Device Driver Services*

  This chapter describes the Device Driver Services such as the ADD and GRADD architectures.

- Chapter 10: *DOS/Windows Services*

  This chapter describes the DOS/Windows Services that provide support for running DOS and Microsoft Windows programs.

- Chapter 11: *Workplace Shell*

  This chapter describes the Workplace Shell, a graphical user interface that provides users with a consistent and easy-to-use interface.

- Chapter 12: *Networks*

  This chapter describes how networks can be supported using OS/2 Warp Connect (PowerPC Edition).

- Chapter 13: *OpenDoc*

  This chapter describes OpenDoc, an advanced technology for creating compound documents.

- Chapter 14: *Human-Centered Computing*

  This chapter describes the new technologies that make computing more natural and intuitive.

- Chapter 15: *Information and Help*

  This chapter describes the information and help system for OS/2 Warp Connect (PowerPC Edition).

- Chapter 16: *Application Development*

  This chapter provides information about developing new applications and migrating existing applications.

- Appendix A: *Frequently Asked Questions*

  This appendix answers commonly asked questions about the benefits of the operating system.

- Appendix B: *Creating Applications for the World*

  This appendix describes National Language Support and considerations for writing applications for a worldwide audience.

- Appendix C: *Examples of Workplace Shell Objects*

  This appendix contains code examples of Workplace Shell objects.

- Additionally, a glossary of terms used in this book is provided.

Conventions

In this book, italics are used to indicate a new term or concept. A description of the term or concept is usually provided immediately afterward for your convenience. You might also want to supplement the definitions provided in the text by consulting the Glossary, located in the back of the book.

The following graphics are used to denote a project milestone, a tip for application developers, or an insider's view:

Project Milestone Indicates a project milestone that was achieved during the development of the product.

Developer's Tip Provides information of special interest to programmers who are planning to develop applications for OS/2 Warp Connect (PowerPC Edition).

Insider's View Provides an insider's account of the development of the project.

This book also includes numerous conceptual illustrations. We hope that you will find the conceptual art helpful.

The Road from Boca to You

A new operating system doesn't just happen overnight. It begins with new ideas that take years of work (prototype, design, development, and test) to transform into reality. During those formative years, most software development companies attach one name to those ideas.

And so it has been with OS/2 Warp Connect (PowerPC Edition). You might be familiar with the term "Workplace" or "Workplace OS," as the ideas behind OS/2 Warp Connect (PowerPC Edition) have been called. The terms collectively referred to our new operating system, as well as its new architecture.

Well, there comes a time during software development to give the ideas a real name and to introduce them to the marketplace. That happened in the fall of 1994. The "Workplace" operating system was maturing (the first beta was almost ready). We started calling the product "OS/2 for the PowerPC."

Insider's View: When we stopped using the name "Workplace" and started calling the product "OS/2 for the PowerPC," you might have thought that the "Workplace" was dead. But the "Workplace" is far from dead. It has simply been renamed for prime time.

2

The new operating system you've heard about, based on the new architecture, is almost here. Its name has been changed once again to OS/2 Warp Connect (PowerPC Edition), but only to reflect the addition of connectivity features to the product.

The "Workplace" has evolved into a product that complements your business strategies by providing long-term benefits for your users and for the applications you will develop. Your users will move from older and slower-running software to newer and faster-running software. They will also move into a computing environment that more closely resembles the real world and that provides them with a much more realistic and simpler way to accomplish their work. OS/2 Warp Connect (PowerPC Edition) provides a robust application development platform that will help you develop new applications in record time. And you will be able to move those applications—nearly effortlessly—to other platforms.

The "Workplace" provides an opportunity for multiple operating system services, no matter how many are implemented initially, to run on the same microkernel, so that someday you might not have to worry about whether or not an application can run on your system.

The "Workplace" is really just OS/2 Warp, put together a bit differently for PowerPC machines. But that difference means that OS/2 Warp can move more quickly to new hardware platforms in the future, so that OS/2 Warp will be there when you want and need it.

Before we tell you what it's all about, let's take a look at the road from Boca to you.

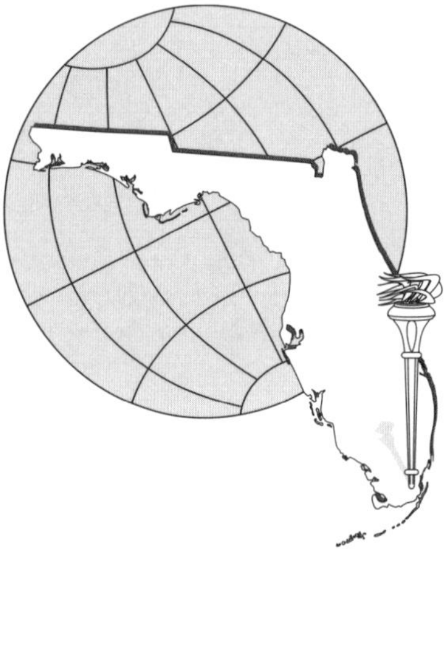

Over four years ago, a group of people at IBM started talking about a strategy for operating systems based on microkernels. Back then, the things that ran on microkernels were referred to as operating systems, API servers, or something like that.

The new strategy was based on a very procedural view of the world; the object-oriented piece evolved along with the strategy. The consensus was that we (IBM, as well as the rest of the computer industry) wanted to get to a new way of doing things. But most of all, we needed to get to a world where we could stop building things like DataBase for OS/2, DataBase for XYZ, and so forth. We needed to find a way to do a lot of common work and, at the same time, continue to support today's world of *heritage* applications. (Some people call these applications the *legacy*, but it is *heritage* that you carry with you and *legacy* that you leave behind. So it's the *heritage* that you want to deal with and support.)

Microkernel-based operating systems give you the perfect environment for doing that. Operating system services that run heritage applications are not layers on new operating systems. Each operating system service has the same unlayered access to the kernel and shared services as other operating system services, which means that their applications run as they do in their native environments.

The first presentation of the new idea for operating systems occurred in January of 1991. That presentation to the IBM Management Committee contained a chart that is still somewhat affectionately referred to as the Grand Unification Theory of Operating Systems (or GUTS, for short). GUTS outlined how one microkernel would unify operating systems with common subsystems.

Later that year, a small team of IBMers went to Taligent to look at their technology. Taligent had proven that an operating system or operating environment, in their case an object-oriented environment, could, in fact, be built on a microkernel. Taligent had broken their operating system into a set of parts. At the center was a microkernel. This microkernel then exported C++ interfaces, providing an object-oriented "wrapper." On top of that wrapper, they implemented a layer that was called Operating Environment Services (OES) or Taligent Object Services. All the code that traditionally had resided in a kernel was implemented in *system frameworks*. This was not a monolithic kernel, but a collection of object-oriented servers performing specific kernel-type tasks. There were frameworks for file systems, for device drivers, for databases, for networking, and so on. But they all resided outside the kernel. And in the Taligent world, these things were objects.

GUTS defined operating system components similar to Taligent's operating environment, only the components were defined procedurally and were called personalities (now called *operating system services*) and personality-neutral servers (now called *shared services*). From the concept of shared services and Taligent's concept of object-oriented system frameworks, an object model evolved that represents *the* new, faster, and more reliable way of building operating systems. What's more, because procedural and object-oriented components can coexist in a microkernel-based operating system, the evolution to a completely object-oriented world could be staged.

At the end of 1991, a small team from Boca Raton, Florida, and Austin, Texas, started working on an OS/2 version of the Mach Microkernel. This team was given the mission to prove that OS/2 could be implemented on a microkernel. Their goal was to do a prototype that would lead to a demo.

In the summer of 1992, the prototype was underway and going well. The IBM team liked the microkernel technology. It was a newer, more robust, more long-term technology than alternative technologies. It also had several significant advantages, including the ability to achieve "64-bitness" via a simple implementation tweak. (For other technologies, it was a major restructure or major redo of everything that was in a monolithic kernel, executive-type system.)

While the prototype was being completed, it was time to design an architecture on which to build a product. At that time, OS/2 2.1 was in heavy-duty development. So, in order to get the right people involved (and it wasn't easy because the right people were working on the current product), the entire design effort was disguised as a task force. The Joint Design Task Force brought together a significant number of people from across IBM: from Boca, from Austin (with LANs and performance), from Raleigh (with SNA and other transport services), from IBM Research (with operating systems and performance), and from Rochester (with the 64-bit, object-oriented view of the world from what they'd done on the AS/400). The task force completed the architecture early in 1993.

In the interim, at Fall Comdex 92, IBM demoed, for the first time publicly, OS/2, DOS, DOS/Windows, and UNIX running on a microkernel. It was supposed to be a private demo. An IBM Senior Technical Staff Member provides us with an eyewitness account.

Insider's View: As is typical in software development, millions of things were happening at once. We went off to set things up in Las Vegas for Comdex, while debugging was still going on in Boca. The room was set up. Lee Reiswig, President of IBM's Personal Software Programming Division, had a private audience of folks to which he was going to demo. The computers were set up, the room was completely ready, and the disks were still in Boca. The folks that finished the demo got on the plane Tuesday night in Boca about the same time the Micrografx cook-off was going on in Las Vegas. They rolled in about eleven that night. We returned from the cook-off about the same time. A few minor things were still being ironed out back in Boca. We installed the disks, and one of them crashed. We managed to download, or transmit, the last fixes from Boca and get things running, with two hours to spare. At 8 a.m., we had running demos, running machines, running presentations. We had enough time to go back to the hotel, shower, and get an hour's sleep. At 10 a.m., Lee stood up in front of a very small audience of selected folks and talked about the Workplace OS for the first time outside IBM. It went so well that the demo was on the floor of Comdex on Thursday. We were able to demo OS/2, DOS, DOS/Windows, and UNIX concurrently running in the same machine on a microkernel and the ability to switch between them with applications running in each of the personalities.

Since then, a lot more work has been done. The GUTSy vision of operating systems sharing common subsystems has remained the same. Some of the implementation details have changed (for example, getting to an object-oriented world versus a procedural one). Some of the terms applied to the components of the operating system have changed to match what they do (for example, personalities are now called *operating system services* and personality-neutral services are now called *shared services*). And, a significant thing has happened for IBM: we are educating people about what IBM is doing and talking publicly, and in great detail, about products under development.

So now, let's look closer at:

- Where we (IBM and OS/2 Warp) came from, where we are, and where we are going.

- What IBM's new microkernel-based operating system offers you: why it means more choices and new possibilities, and how it maintains and extends your current software and hardware investment.

- How we are taking OS/2 Warp to new hardware platforms (PowerPC and beyond) with this new microkernel-based software architecture.

- What the new system components are: how they work, how they fit together, and how they relate to OS/2 Warp for Intel-based systems.

- What's new inside OS/2: the version of OS/2 Warp Connect for Intel-based systems and the PowerPC version of OS/2 Warp Connect look and feel the same but are very different under the covers (frameworks, new device driver models, and so on).

- How OS/2 Warp Connect (PowerPC Edition) supports the heritage (your current DOS, Windows, and OS/2 applications) and helps you (with the assistance of a new set of migration tools) get there from wherever you are.

- New technologies and future directions.

When we're done, you will know what's so good about OS/2 Warp Connect (PowerPC Edition) and why it should be your operating system of choice.

Introducing OS/2 Warp Connect (PowerPC Edition)!

IBM now has a bold, new way to take computer technology into the twenty-first century: a new software architecture that blurs the boundaries between traditional operating systems, their applications, and the hardware they run on. It brings together a set of leading open standards and technologies that revolutionize the way software is designed and used, giving you:

- *Portable and scalable software*, which means that applications written for different hardware (such as Intel and PowerPC processors) and software environments (such as DOS, Windows, and OS/2) can run on the same computer, regardless of size (supercomputer, personal computer, personal digital assistant, or embedded system).

- *Consistent and natural user interfaces*, which means that you can focus on getting your job done instead of figuring out how to communicate with your computer, because it is a natural extension of yourself (that is, it is *human-centered*).

- *High-quality reusable software*, which means that less resource is required to build new applications upon existing, proven code, giving you a more competitive time-to-market.

- *Open and distributed computing*, which means that data and functions, across a client/server, networked environment, can be shared by anyone, anytime, anywhere.

- *Investment protection*, which means that today's and tomorrow's diverse hardware and software meet under one umbrella, where you can mix and match whatever you have and whatever you need to get your job done.

IBM delivers the promise of the future with OS/2 Warp Connect (PowerPC Edition). It's really just OS/2 Warp, with the same look and feel on the outside, but with a new and different look and feel on the inside.

What Comes with OS/2 Warp Connect (PowerPC Edition)?

OS/2 Warp Connect (PowerPC Edition) is a microkernel-based operating system that has the same features as OS/2 Warp Connect for Intel-based systems but runs on PowerPC RISC-based personal computers. OS/2 Warp Connect (PowerPC Edition) runs on the IBM Microkernel (PowerPC version) and includes an OS/2 Operating System Service and a DOS/Windows Operating System Service with a Workplace Shell user interface.

This means that users can run OS/2, Windows, and DOS applications in the same way that they run these applications today on Intel x86-based systems. All 32-bit OS/2 applications are source-code compatible and can exploit the native power of the RISC processor simply by being recompiled. Development of PowerPC-based OS/2 parallels enhancements and optimizations of OS/2 for Intel-based systems.

IBM Microkernel Product Description

The IBM Microkernel includes the microkernel and microkernel services and provides a base on which complete operating systems can be built (with the addition of operating system services and shared services). Device driver frameworks that are packaged with this product provide a base set of device drivers.

The IBM Microkernel is available for both Intel x86-based systems and PowerPC RISC-based systems, and, over time, other processors. It is packaged with microkernel-based operating systems that allow applications to run on those hardware platforms. It is available as object code for system developers who are building operating system services (operating systems) or shared services (subsystems). It is also available as source code for OEMs to port to new hardware processors, devices, and configurations (such as embedded systems).

OS/2 Warp Connect (PowerPC Edition) includes OpenGL 3-D graphics support. OpenGL is an industry-standard, 3-D graphics engine and application programming interface (API) that gives users and programmers access to graphics capabilities (such as CAD, industrial design and modeling, and scientific visualization) previously available only on more expensive workstations.

OS/2 Warp Connect (PowerPC Edition) contains XPG/4 — a library of functions, commands, and locales defined by the X/Open Portability Guide, Version 4. XPG/4 gives programmers the ability to create internationalized applications — that is, applications that are independent of natural language.

The multimedia application development support of OS/2 Warp Version 3 is carried over to OS/2 Warp Connect (PowerPC Edition). This includes CD Audio, MIDI playback, image support, animation, video support, Kodak PhotoCD, and support for the Yamaha OPL3 FM Synthesizer. Using the advanced architecture and floating-point capability of the IBM PowerPC processors, the IBM SoftMIDI Synthesizer responds to General MIDI files to produce high-quality music for multimedia presentations, games, and educational software without additional audio hardware. OS/2 Warp Connect (PowerPC Edition) audio drivers also support the Crystal 4231 Audio System, which is included on the ThinkPad Power Series, and the Crystal 4232 Audio System, which is included on the IBM Personal Computer Power Series.

The audio driver provides standard support of WAVE, AUX, and MIDI functions, as well as full-duplex mode of operation (playback and recording can be performed simultaneously), enhanced full-duplex mode (playback and recording can be performed simultaneously at different sample rates), and volume control of sound to be recorded.

OS/2 Warp Connect (PowerPC Edition) includes a new object-oriented scripting language, Object REXX. Object REXX is an extension to the REXX language and supports existing REXX programs.

OS/2 Warp Connect (PowerPC Edition) also provides a set of networking and communications software. Network Services provide a framework for multiple networking protocols including NetBIOS, IEEE 802.2, TCP/IP, and SNA APPC and APPN. Communications API, based on Berkeley sockets, support TCP/IP, NetBIOS, and local interprocess communication (IPC), as well. TCP/IP Version 3.0 for OS/2 Warp Connect (PowerPC Edition) offers TCP/IP LAN transports and LAN access to the Internet, including IBM WebExplorer. OS/2 Warp Connect (PowerPC Edition) LAN Requester, a subset of OS/2 LAN Server 4.0 LAN Requester, supports attachment to:

- OS/2 LAN Server Version 3.x or 4.0
- IBM LAN Server for AIX
- LAN Manager
- Windows for Workgroups 3.11
- Windows NT Advanced Server

The LAN Requester Redirector provides access to shared resources (files, CD-ROM, printers, modems).

The OS/2 Warp Connect (PowerPC Edition) BonusPak is similar to the OS/2 Warp Version 3 BonusPak, including:

- IBM Works and Personal Information Manager
- HyperACCESS Lite

- FaxWorks
- CompuServe Information Manager
- WebExplorer Client and UltiMail Lite from the Internet Access Kit

OS/2 Warp Connect (PowerPC Edition) means you have *more choices* from which you can make *simpler business decisions* that focus not on the hassles about what hardware and software work with what hardware and software, but rather on the hardware and software that are best suited to do the job.

The User Perspective

To users who are creating and processing data on their computers, IBM's OS/2 Warp Connect (PowerPC Edition) provides the features described in the following sections.

Support for a Variety of Applications

OS/2 Warp Connect (PowerPC Edition) gives you more software options. You can choose software based on preference (what you like) as well as needs (what it takes to get the job done). You no longer have to wait for software to be ported to the environment you work with. OS/2 Warp Connect (PowerPC Edition) supports:

- Native 32-bit procedural applications, such as OS/2 applications.

- A new generation of object-oriented applications built on IBM's System Object Model (SOM) and OpenDoc compound document technology, and other object-oriented frameworks.

- *Heritage* applications, with performance comparable to the native environment. Heritage applications are older applications, such as DOS and Windows applications, that you want to continue to use.

It supports these applications with:

- Multiple threads that allow applications to be more responsive to users
- Multitasking and crash-protection among applications, which keep multiple applications running even though one has failed
- Windowed presentation of all applications on the same Desktop, which makes navigation between different types of applications effortless
- Interoperability between applications, through IPC, a clipboard, dynamic data exchange, compound documents, and more, which allows applications to work together

A Natural and Intuitive User Interface

OS/2 Warp Connect (PowerPC Edition) provides an advanced graphical interface that is both intuitive for new users and productive for experienced users so that you can be more productive, faster. It offers:

- An object-oriented Desktop (the Workplace Shell)
- Integrated *human-centered* capabilities, including multimedia and speech recognition
- Full support for internationalization
- A document-centered approach to information

A Fast, Reliable, and Manageable System

Because of the new design for OS/2 Warp Connect (PowerPC Edition), you can make changes, such as upgrading the latest version of your favorite software service or installing the newest piece of hardware, without disrupting your system. Local and remote systems are transparent to the users (that is, the users do not necessarily know that they are working with a resource that is not located on their systems) and are easily managed by a set of system management tools.

Investment Protection

OS/2 Warp Connect (PowerPC Edition) supports the hardware and software you use today. Because of its new design, you can upgrade to leading-edge hardware and software technology at your own pace, when you are ready.

The Programmer Perspective

Your software can always be in the right place at the right time at the right price. To programmers who are writing applications and system software, IBM's OS/2 Warp Connect (PowerPC Edition) provides the features described in the following sections.

A Highly Portable Environment

You can use the same source code for your software for different hardware. Instead of rewriting your code for the new hardware, you simply recompile it. This means that you have a broad market for your software because it can, for example, run on PowerPC machines, as well as Intel-based machines.

Coexistence of Multiple Environments

Your software can work alongside and with a variety of other software written for other operating systems. This means that you have a broader market for your software because it can be used with any number of other applications to provide many more solutions for many more problems.

A Scalable Environment

You can tailor your software for a variety of hardware configurations. Services (operating system services, as well as shared services) that you create to run on the Microkernel can be broken down into smaller service modules that each perform very elementary functions. These very small services can then be mixed and matched to perform functions required for a specific system. For example, a small set of very small services running on the Microkernel can provide the software to control an appliance. This kind of system is called an *embedded* system. Embedded systems don't require the same services that a larger system, such as a workstation, requires. Yet the very small services used to build an embedded system can also be used to build the larger system. This means that you have an even broader market for your software because it can be part of software solutions for very small, embedded and mobile systems, as well as for very large immobile systems.

A Modular and Dynamic Environment

Your software upgrades can be staged so that you can start accommodating new technologies as they become available. This means that you can stay ahead of the game by always delivering leading-edge software to customers.

Better Development Tools and Reusable Software

You can deliver your software to your customers faster and at a more effective cost than ever before. OS/2 Warp Connect (PowerPC Edition) gives programmers the ability to produce new software and enhance existing software at a rate that keeps up with customers' demands by providing:

- A standard 32-bit procedural API for the OS/2 application environment.
- Classes of objects and object-oriented API for specific tasks, called *frameworks*, that make reusability of code practical. They are easy for programmers to understand and use and, therefore, simplify application development; and they can be shared between applications and across application environments.
- Compound document technology that allows programmers to build sophisticated applications from reusable software *parts*.
- The capability to define high-level system functions, such as device drivers, file systems, and networks, as shared services that can be used by different operating system services.
- A set of standard development tools for migrating old and building new applications.

A Base for Distributed, Client/Server Applications

The distributed capabilities of SOM technology, as well as the distributed compound document support of OpenDoc technology, give you the ability to easily develop distributed, object-oriented applications and systems. Network frameworks and Communications API give you the ability to easily develop your own network applications.

A New Design for OS/2

This chapter describes the new design for OS/2 Warp Connect (PowerPC Edition). It tells you what the new design is and why it is so important. This chapter also describes the most basic components of the operating system and how they work together.

What Are We Trying to Do and Why?

The following is based on a June 30, 1993, presentation to the Boca Programming Center by Larry Loucks, IBM Fellow and Vice President of Software Architecture, Personal Software Products Division (PSP).

What is the goal of the PSP strategy?

We are trying to achieve a balance between responding to existing customer requirements and exploiting new technology. Customers work in a variety of computing environments. The traditional commercial multiuser and numerically-intensive scientific computing environments consist of workstations connected to mainframes or supercomputers that do all the work. The new, open, and collaborative mobile and consumer computing environments consist of everything from mainframes to workstations to PCs to laptops, notebooks, and palmtops to embedded processors that put computing power in nontraditional places such as cars and appliances. These environments encompass a wide range of hardware technology. On the high end is hardware with infinite capability to do anything you can dream about (RISC 6000s connected by high-speed fiber, with infinite memory, passing messages at the rate of one every nanosecond). On the low end is hardware with zero computing power, comparatively speaking, with very little memory, little hard disk space, and very little or no glass. It is our goal to provide the software technology to exploit the emerging hardware technology for all these environments, while protecting our customers' investments in their application heritage.

How do we produce operating systems that span this hardware range?

We'll do this through a new software architecture: a collection of technologies that spans a variety of operating system environments and makes them work together. It is a technology base that is portable across hardware platforms, while supporting the software heritage very well.

What are these software technologies?

The new software technologies provide a common user interface (that is, a single object-oriented desktop across DOS, Windows, and OS/2), interoperability across environments, and common object-oriented programming interfaces for applications that run across these environments. They include microkernel technologies: a microkernel, operating system services, and shared services.

The microkernel is a very small kernel. It provides low-level virtual memory management, IPC, task, thread, processor, and I/O support. It is the only thing that runs at supervisor level; everything else you would find in a traditional operating system is defined as application tasks broken up into client/server structures.

An operating system service is a component that defines an operating system environment and runs applications written for that environment.

A shared service is a component that provides support to all other components in a microkernel-based operating system. A shared service provides high-level system things that should be done once (for example, file systems and networks).

What advantages does this concept offer?

The microkernel-based architecture provides us with a modular, flexible, expandable, and scalable way of building operating systems that can fit in everything from a PDA or embedded system to a system with relatively limitless space. Operating system components will become smaller and smaller, more modular for better software engineering. This means that our customers, as well as ourselves, can quickly take advantage of interesting, emerging hardware and software. We can break the cycle of monolithic software development—alphas, betas, test, and more test on the entire operating system—where it takes forever to develop and introduce new functions gracefully. Maybe we can get to a 64-bit operating system in our lifetime. An operating system that is modular can be converted piece by piece. As an example, we can have 64-bit client libraries and 32-bit client libraries. Because these are cross-address-space client/server distributed calls, things that are done in the clients and servers are encapsulated from each other. This gives us great flexibility in deciding which pieces we convert to 64-bit.

The new architecture in itself means a faster way of doing all of these things. And object technology, such as IBM's System Object Model (SOM) and object frameworks, already being applied to native OS/2, will get us there even faster. Object technology provides a new programming paradigm that can result in 10x, 100x productivity improvements in application development, as well as system development.

How does the new software architecture affect the heritage of traditional operating system environments?

The microkernel-based architecture means that operating systems are no longer tied to a particular processor and applications are no longer isolated by a particular operating system. Applications written for different operating system environments can share data and services and even run on the same platform. This becomes more significant as the lines blur between the traditional notions of PCs, workstations, and mainframes. There are people who want to use Intel x86 machines, instead of RISCs (reduced instruction-set computers), as workstations. RISC processors have historically been used in workstations for the technical and scientific marketplace. As the industry downsizes from its mainframe and midrange-type systems to PCs and workstations, there is a growing need to have more and more processing power on PCs, which have been dominated by CISC (complex instruction-set computer) processors (that is, the Intel x86 and Motorola 68K chips). RISC chips, such as IBM's PowerPC, can provide this power for the PCs.

The microkernel-based architecture rounds out the platform coverage of our operating systems by making today's OS/2 (for Intel-based systems) available on RISCs. The first microkernel-based product on the PowerPC is centered on OS/2 Operating System Services running on a PowerPC microkernel. This product will deliver the same functionality available with OS/2 on Intel-based machines today.

The new architecture provides for small operating system components. This means that the traditional operating system environments can reduce their footprints (for example, memory requirements) over time. This also means that the traditional operating system environments and their applications may someday run on something that we can carry in our hands.

While object-oriented applications are being written for OS/2, the new software architecture will continue to evolve. The components of microkernel-based operating systems will become object-oriented themselves, which, by the way, will still support the heritage of applications that are being written today!

A New Way to Build Operating Systems

IBM's software architecture is a new approach to building system software, where operating systems, such as OS/2, are modularized and built on a *microkernel* foundation. Microkernel-based operating systems consist of:

- A small *microkernel* that provides the most fundamental operating system functions and contains most of the hardware-dependent code
- One or more *operating system services* that provide functions specific to an operating system, such as the application programming interface (API), the user interface, and system policies and semantics
- *Shared services* that run outside the kernel and provide functions, such as device drivers, file systems, network services, and so forth, that are available to operating system services and other shared services running on the microkernel

The microkernel, operating system services, and shared services have a *client/server* task relationship. Code executing on the microkernel is structured into tasks, where a task is a multithreaded process inside its own address space. Every service typically consists of a client library (which requests services) and a server task (which performs the services). The client library is linked into an application's address space, which means that code within the client library executes as part of an application's task. Each server task has one or more microkernel *ports* that allow other tasks to request services. When a task requests a service by calling a function in a client library, the calls are translated into messages sent to a port of the server task.

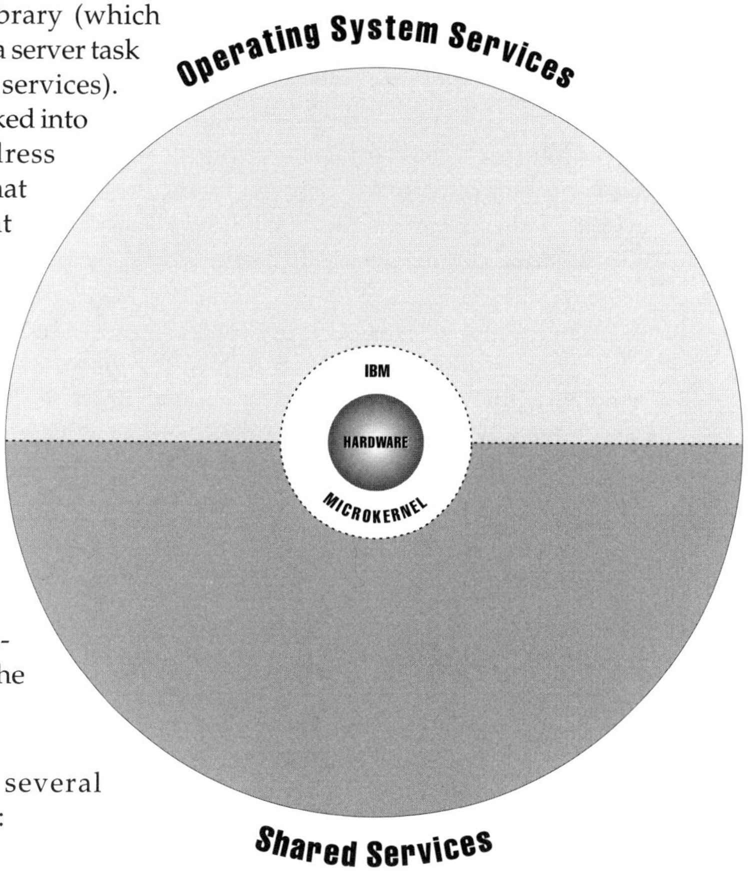

Figure 2-1. Elements of a Microkernel-Based Operating System

This approach has several significant advantages:

- The ability to support a variety of processors

  Microkernel-based operating systems are quickly and easily adaptable to new hardware architectures and configurations because they are highly modularized and scalable, with hardware-dependent code confined to a few modules.

- The ability to support a variety of hardware configurations

  The microkernel has built-in support for multiple processors, and the microkernel-based architecture is highly modularized (functions are implemented once and used where appropriate), which means that operating systems are scalable on hardware ranging in size from personal digital assistants (PDAs) to symmetric multiprocessors (SMP) to cluster processors to massively parallel processors.

In the long term, the portability of applications goes beyond the existing RISC and Intel architectures. Portability means the ability to support the new 64-bit world, as well as the 32-bit Intel x86 and non-Intel x86 world. The IBM Microkernel can just as easily be ported to these new technologies.

Portability also means support for different byte-orderings of the bytes in integers and word data stored in registers of machines. There are two basic ways to build data representation in machines: *Big Endian* and *Little Endian*. The Intel x86 world is the Little Endian world. PowerPC microprocessors actually support both worlds. The IBM Microkernel is built on Mach technology, which has already been ported to both worlds.

- The ability to support a variety of applications

  Multiple operating system services can run on the same microkernel sharing the same services, which means that you can run multiple applications written for different environments to get a job done while using a single system.

- The ability to deliver all of the above with a faster time-to-market

  System software can be shared and is highly modularized, with dependent code confined to a relatively small number of specific modules, which means that system software cannot only be reused for different processors, hardware configurations, and operating environments but also enhanced in a modular way.

This approach also increases the reliability of operating systems because they are now split into independent client/server tasks protected from each other. The reduced complexity and a modular structure allow new modules to be easily added or existing ones to be removed and allow the system to grow *horizontally* (rather than in vertical layers). Software development productivity is also increased because services are shared (reused), instead of functions being duplicated.

The bottom line is that new and emerging software technologies can be assimilated into microkernel-based operating systems much faster than in traditional operating systems.

A Good Foundation with the IBM Microkernel

Traditional operating environments are written for specific hardware platforms. OS/2 applications run on Intel x86 PCs. AIX applications run on RISC System/6000s. In order for developers to remain competitive, their applications need to run on a broad range of hardware platforms. But traditional operating systems consist of monolithic kernels, which means that porting these environments is a huge task.

Insider's View: Previous releases of the OS/2 operating system developed for the Intel x86 platforms were monolithic. Over the years, each new option or subsystem has been statically linked into the monolith. That is, the system can be viewed as a stack of subsystems, and each subsystem interacts with the others and with the nucleus kernel. This structure lends itself to a high-performance environment but makes portability to other platforms difficult.

The IBM Microkernel offers a solution to porting operating systems to new hardware platforms. The IBM Microkernel, the foundation for OS/2 Warp Connect (PowerPC Edition), is based on the Carnegie Mellon University Mach microkernel technology, incorporating technology developed by the Open Software Foundation and technology developed by IBM.

Functions of the Microkernel

The IBM Microkernel includes a microkernel that runs at the most privileged or kernel level of the machine. The IBM Microkernel provides a small but powerful set of low-level system functions that support the other parts of an operating system as a set of server applications. These functions fall into five groups:

- Tasks and Threads
- Virtual Memory
- Interprocess Communication

- I/O Support and Interrupts
- Multiprocessor Support

The IBM Microkernel shields most of the rest of the system from the processor and hardware architecture. The Microkernel itself contains hardware-dependent code and must be rewritten for new processors, but this is a relatively small job.

Keeping the microkernel small has two major benefits:

- Less code runs at the protected (kernel) level, thus increasing the reliability of the system

- Less code is processor-specific, thus increasing the hardware portability of the system

Microkernel Services

The IBM Microkernel also includes *Microkernel services* and device drivers that are fundamental to the running of the operating system and that are used by the operating system services, as well as by other shared services. They run at user level rather than at kernel level but are essential to the operation of the Microkernel. Microkernel services are written in an Endian-neutral fashion, so they can be used on both Big-Endian systems (such as RS/6000) and Little-Endian systems (such as Intel-based PCs).

The IBM Microkernel for OS/2 Warp Connect (PowerPC Edition) includes all of the physical device drivers for the keyboard, mouse, disks, CD-ROMs, and video and network adapters. It also includes the following Microkernel services:

- The Master Server loads and manages task resources for operating system services and shared services.

- The Default Pager provides the virtual memory paging for standard virtual memory objects running outside the kernel. Other pagers can be implemented (for example, for memory-mapped files).

- The Name Server provides a mechanism for objects and servers to identify and access each other and coordinates this information in a *name space*.

- The Device Driver Configuration Services and the Hardware Resource Manager work in conjunction with the Device Driver Frameworks to manage and control access to the physical hardware (apart from the processor) such as the buses and devices.

In addition, a Security Server is planned but might not be included in the first release. The Security Server will provide a mechanism for objects and servers to authenticate access to them by other objects and servers, thus providing global security at a fundamental level in the system.

For more information on the IBM Microkernel, see Chapter 3, "The IBM Microkernel" on page 33. For more information on the Name Server, see Chapter 4, "Name Services" on page 51. For more information on device drivers, the Device Driver Configuration Services, and the Hardware Resource Manager, see Chapter 9, "Device Driver Services" on page 165.

Operating System Services

Most traditional operating systems were not designed to run applications written for different operating environments. Each operating system has supported only applications written specifically for that environment. For example, DOS supports only applications written specifically for DOS; hence, OS/2 applications cannot run on DOS. OS/2, on the other hand, supports applications written for other operating system environments. DOS applications have run under OS/2 since its early versions. Windows applications run under 32-bit OS/2. But OS/2 achieved this through major design changes, such as the Multiple Virtual DOS Machines (MVDM) environment for DOS and WIN-OS/2 environment for Windows.

For microkernel-based operating systems, an operating system service provides the operating environment for an application. Because multiple operating system services can run on the same microkernel, applications written for multiple operating environments can run concurrently on the same system. For example, OS/2 Operating System Services can run concurrently on the same microkernel as DOS/Windows Services, with applications running concurrently in each environment. You can run your favorite application or whatever applications that you need to get a job done regardless of what operating system they were written for.

An operating system service provides the API as well as the policies that define the operating environment. Things such as the scheduler are part of an operating system service, so the operating system service schedules tasks and threads, just as the operating environment always did. The Microkernel dispatches tasks and threads, but it uses the policies dictated to it by the operating system service (for example, priority boosts) to determine how it dispatches those tasks and threads.

Operating system services are typically structured into:

- A client library, running in the same task and address space as an application.

  This library receives all calls to the API, handling them directly or routing them to the operating system server task or to the Microkernel or a shared service.

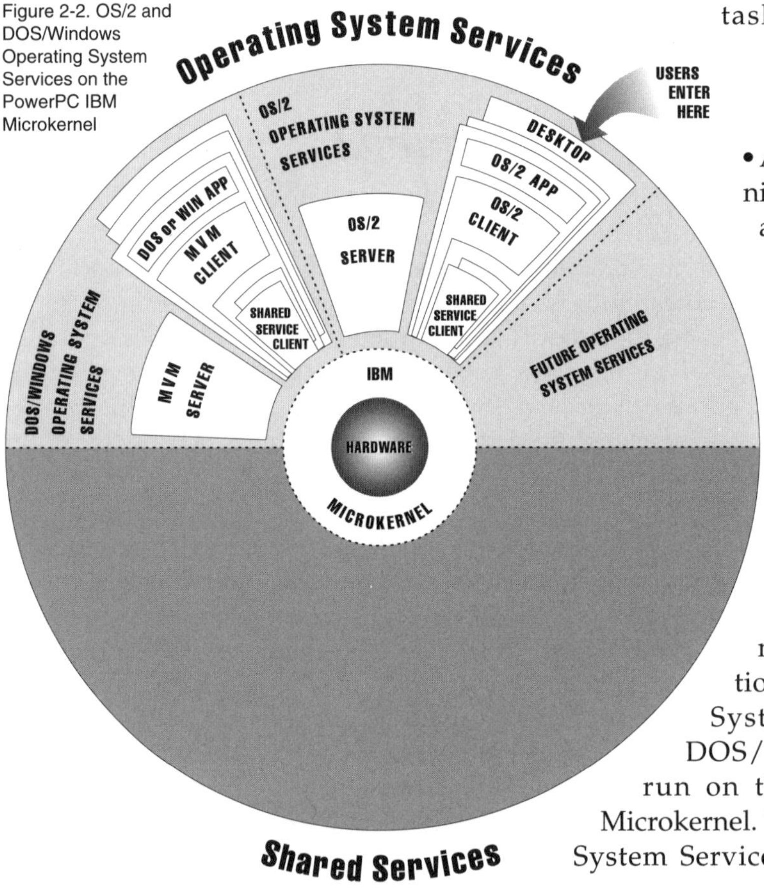

Figure 2-2. OS/2 and DOS/Windows Operating System Services on the PowerPC IBM Microkernel

- A server task, running in a separate task and address space, implements the operating system semantics and environment. The operating system server might also call Microkernel services or other shared services.

In OS/2 Warp Connect (PowerPC Edition), OS/2 Operating System Services and DOS/Windows Services run on the same PowerPC Microkernel. The OS/2 Operating System Services "own the glass."

They provide the Desktop (the Workplace Shell) and control overall system behavior (handling system startup, system shutdown, and session management). The OS/2 Operating System Services support the OS/2 API. The DOS/Windows Services support the DOS/Windows API.

As shown in Figure 2-2, the OS/2 Operating System Services consist of an OS/2 Server task and an OS/2 client library that runs as part of an OS/2 application task. Similarly, the DOS/Windows Services consist of an MVM Server task and an MVM client library that runs as part of a DOS/Windows application task. When, for example, an OS/2 application calls an OS/2 function, the OS/2 client library either performs the function or routes it to the appropriate server.

In a highly modularized microkernel-based operating system, only a small portion of operating system service code (in addition to microkernel code) deals with the hardware. (An exception handler that must deal with stacks and registers is one example of such code.) This means that a developer can easily port an operating system service from one hardware platform to another by rewriting a relatively small portion of software components and rebuilding them. In the future, the OS/2 Operating System Services can just as easily be ported to an Intel-based or other processor-based microkernel.

For more information on the OS/2 Operating System Services, see Chapter 6, "OS/2 Operating System Services" on page 83. For more information on the DOS/Windows Services, see Chapter 10, "DOS/Windows Services" on page 205.

Shared Services

Operating systems generally have some set of functions in common—file systems, graphics, windowing capabilities, networking, and so forth. For example, DOS includes the FAT file system, as does OS/2. If each operating system service running on a microkernel contained code to perform these functions—for example, if the DOS operating system service included the FAT file system and the OS/2 operating system service also included the FAT file system—there would be a duplication of code running on the same system. In a microkernel-based operating system, common functions can be abstracted from the operating system services into a set of services that are written once and used by one or more operating system services.

OS/2 Warp Connect (PowerPC Edition) includes the following shared services:

- File Services, which provide the FAT, HPFS, and CD-ROM (CDFS) file systems, all supported by a common File Server framework.

- Event and Window Services, which coordinate the sharing of the keyboard, mouse, and display between the various window and full-screen sessions across operating system services.

- Network and Communications Frameworks, which provide support for a range of pluggable network protocols (such as IPX and NETBIOS) across a range of pluggable data-link components (such as Token-Ring or Ethernet), all based around a common networking transport object framework.

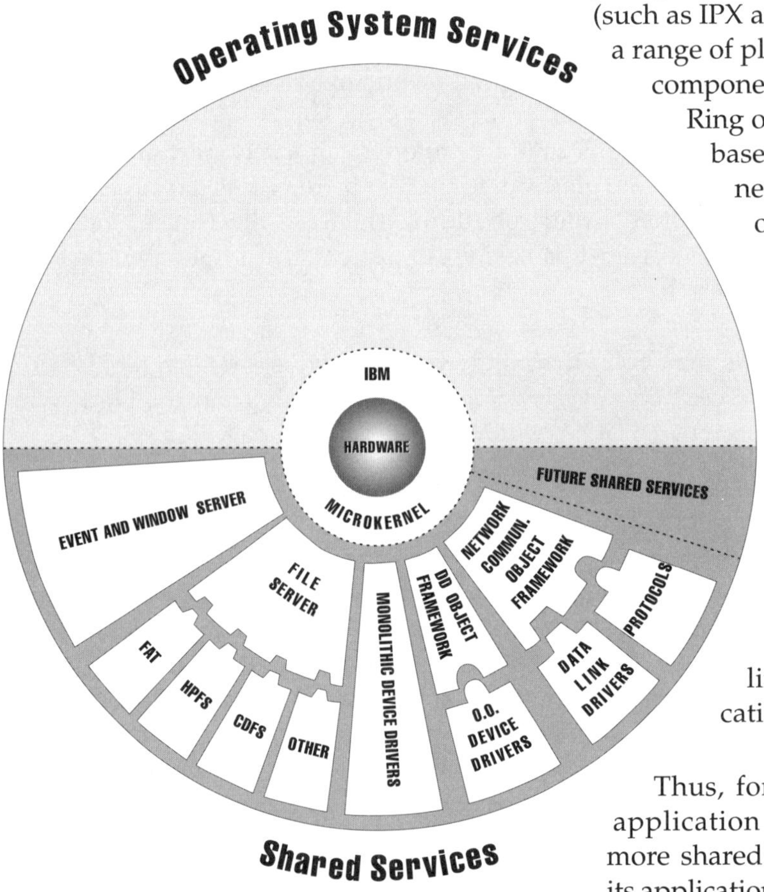

Figure 2-3. Shared Services for OS/2 Warp Connect (PowerPC Edition)

As shown in Figure 2-3, shared services, like operating system services, typically consist of a client or shared library and a server task. For each shared service, a shared library is linked into an application's address space.

Thus, for example, an OS/2 application might have one or more shared libraries linked into its application address space—one for File Services, one for Event and

Window Services, and so on. Shared libraries provide API to the shared services. When an OS/2 application calls a file system function, the shared library routes the call to the File Server via the microkernel.

Note: A shared library has no task of its own. It is a chunk of code (a dynamic link library, or DLL) that is linked into and executes within an application task. The first time a shared service is needed by a task, the system loads the shared library into memory, where it remains. When another task needs the shared library, it's already in memory. A shared library is *re-entrant*, which means that multiple tasks can enter it, execute their code, and then return. In contrast, if a shared library were not available, multiple copies of the same code would be loaded into memory each time a task called the shared library. This is decidedly inefficient, as loading the same code over and over takes up a lot (if not eventually all) of the memory.

When you build a shared service for a microkernel-based operating system, it is available to all services in the system, not imbedded under many layers of code. Because of the client/server structure of shared services, you can add new shared services to the system or replace existing shared services without shutting down the system and restarting. (You can, for example, add the latest version of your favorite database service without bringing your system to a halt.) Systems that can be dynamically modified are particularly important in situations where environments need to be preserved (such as patient monitoring in hospitals and flight scheduling in airports).

We all face a software development dilemma illustrated by the following spreadsheet example that Phillipe Kahn, former Borland executive, has used. Today's spreadsheets contain from 1 to 10 million lines of code, whereas the spreadsheets from 10 years ago contained approximately 100 thousand lines of code. In 10 years, to keep up with the connectivity and computing power trends, those spreadsheets will require 100 million lines of code if we keep writing them using the same programming models that we're using today. Apply that same analogy to the development of operating systems and the results are staggering. This means that in order to make our visions a reality, there has to be a fundamental change in how we write code. That fundamental change is object technology.

Initially, most shared services for OS/2 Warp Connect (PowerPC Edition) are procedural. In the future, object-oriented shared services will become more popular and will supplement or replace the existing procedural shared services. Many of these object-oriented shared services will be derived from object frameworks. The transition from the procedural to the object-oriented world is provided by a technique called *wrappers*, which allows procedural clients to access object-oriented servers and vice versa. For more information on shared services, see Chapter 5, "Shared Services" on page 69.

Device Drivers

Device drivers are shared services in a microkernel-based operating system. Shared device drivers make it easier to coordinate access to physical devices between operating system services. As shared services, device drivers also run in crash-resistant user mode (that is, outside the microkernel). You can load and unload device drivers dynamically, without taking the system down.

Figure 2-4. Device Driver Frameworks for OS/2 Warp Connect (PowerPC Edition)

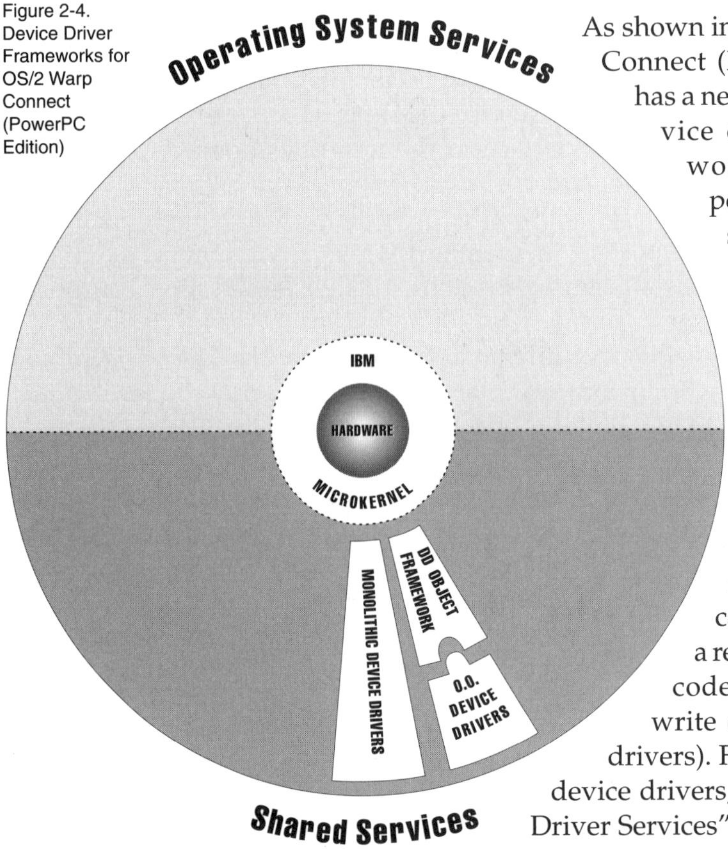

As shown in Figure 2-4, OS/2 Warp Connect (PowerPC Edition) also has a new framework-based device driver model. Frameworks provide common portions of the hardware-specific device drivers and the microkernel. Device drivers basically consist of only the code that is required to manipulate their specific devices. Independent hardware vendors (IHVs) can deliver support for new devices faster because they have to write a relatively small amount of code (instead of having to write completely new device drivers). For more information on device drivers, see Chapter 9, "Device Driver Services" on page 165.

Putting It All Together

The following diagram shows how all of the pieces that we have discussed fit together.

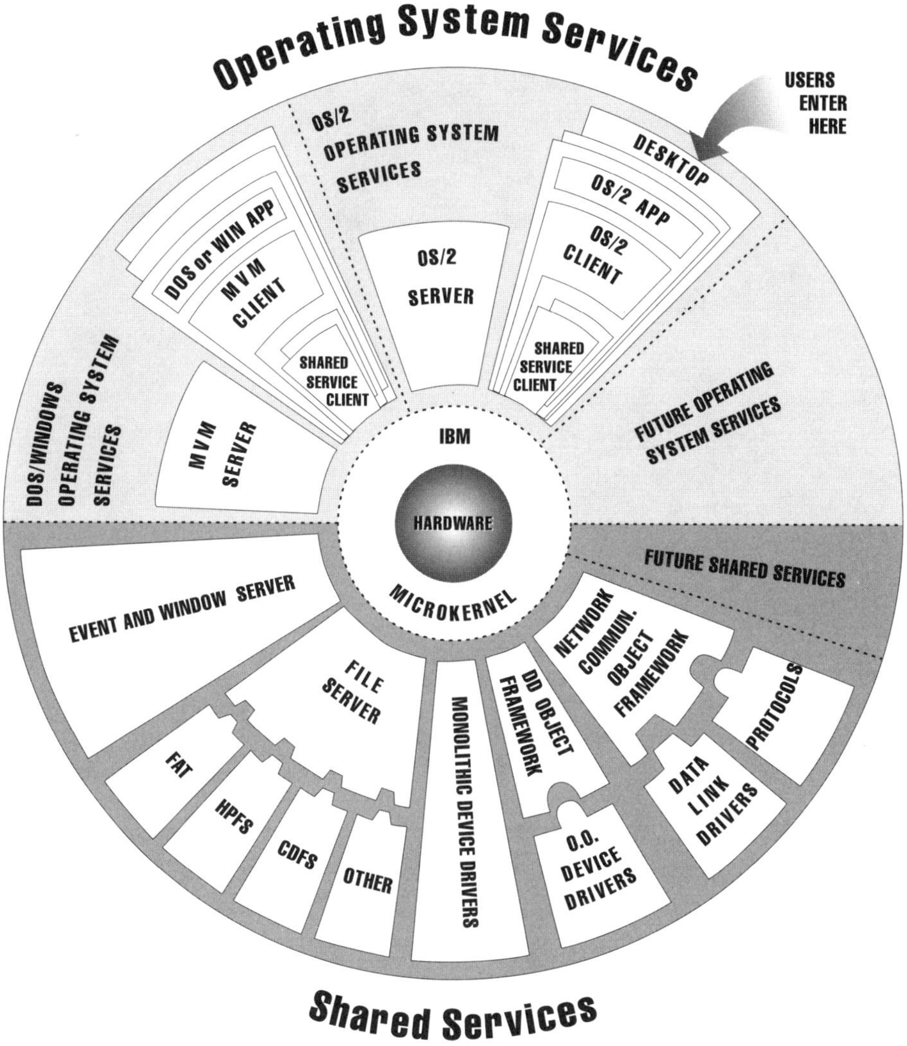

Figure 2- 5. Components of OS/2 Warp Connect (PowerPC Edition)

The IBM Microkernel

This chapter introduces and describes the IBM Microkernel. It provides information about how the Microkernel manages tasks and threads and how it manages virtual memory. This chapter also provides information about how the Microkernel communicates with operating system services and shared services.

Introducing the IBM Microkernel

The Microkernel handles the majority of the hardware interactions for the system. This means that neither OS/2 Operating System Services nor the DOS/Windows Services need to be particularly knowledgeable about the hardware on which they are running. This greatly simplifies the porting of those operating system services from one hardware platform to another. The Microkernel provides a set of standard, primitive operating system functions to all the tasks that run on top of it. The OS/2 Operating System Services and the DOS/Windows Services are composed of sets of tasks and libraries that run on top of the Microkernel. Being able to depend on a common set of primitive operating system functions not only simplifies the construction of each operating system service set, but it also makes it much simpler for the different operating system services to cooperate and communicate with each other.

The functions performed by the Microkernel are limited in order to reduce its size and to maximize the amount of code that runs outside the Microkernel. The

Microkernel includes only those functions required to provide a set of abstract processing environments for the operating system services and the shared services that run on top of it. The Microkernel provides the following five classes of functions:

- Task and Thread Management
- Virtual Memory Management
- Interprocess Communication (IPC) and Remote Procedure Call (RPC)
- Input and Output (I/O) Support and Interrupt Management
- Host and Processor Set Management

Task and Thread Management

Tasks and threads are the entities that execute on an OS/2 Warp Connect (PowerPC Edition) system. When an OS/2 program runs, it executes as a task. OS/2 programs can be written so that they run as one or more independent threads of execution. OS/2 Warp Connect (PowerPC Edition) builds its tasking and threading environment on top of the Microkernel's simple task and thread management facilities.

The Microkernel provides a basic execution environment for programs that allows multiple tasks to run concurrently. This is commonly referred to as *multitasking*. It also allows any single task to be subdivided into multiple concurrent paths of execution. This is commonly referred to as *multithreading*. OS/2 supports both multitasking and multithreading, so it is critical that the Microkernel provide a solid base for both of these capabilities.

From the Microkernel's perspective, a task is a collection of resources. There are many kinds of resources that are contained within a task. The virtual address space of a task is one of its resources. The threads contained within a task are another type of task resource. All of the resources that a task contains are identified by Microkernel *ports*. You can think of these ports as targets for messages.

In order to support multiple concurrent paths of execution within a program's address space, the Microkernel separates the execution environment from the execution of instruction streams. The separate instruction streams (including the processor resources needed to support them) are called *threads*. Threads are the entities that are scheduled for execution by the Microkernel. The OS/2 Operating System Services, however, provide the policy that manages the relative priorities of all threads running on the system.

All of the threads of a task share all of the task's resources (by sharing access to the task's ports). Task resources are shared between two tasks only if the two tasks take explicit actions to share those resources.

Tasks

The Microkernel maintains the following state for each task:

- The set of threads that are contained within the task
- The task's virtual address space
- The collection of ports that identify all the resources that are owned by the task. These ports include:
  - A port that identifies the task itself (its TASK_KERNEL_PORT)
  - A set of ports that identify the threads of the task
  - A set of ports that are used to perform exception handling on behalf of the task's threads
  - Special "bootstrap" ports that are provided so that a task can "find" key shared system services
- Default scheduling parameters for the task's threads
- Assorted task information such as task statistics and task special attributes

Figure 3-1. Task Management

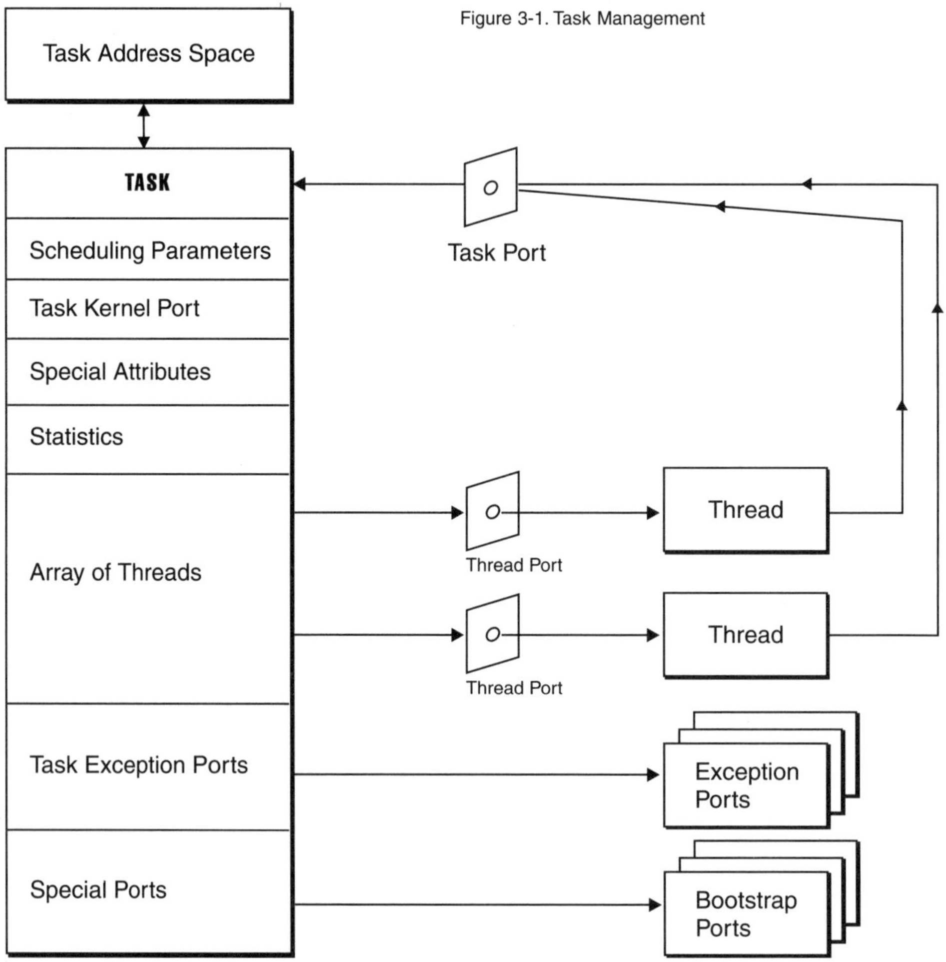

When you create a Microkernel task, you must specify the processor set on which the new task is to run. On a multiprocessor system, the processor set identifies the set of physical processors on which the task can be run. The parent of a new task can pass the child some or all of its own virtual address space by including those memory regions within the task.

The Microkernel provides system functions that can be used to perform the following task management operations:

- Creation and destruction
- Suspension and resumption
- Special port manipulation
- Manipulation of contained threads
- Manipulation of scheduling parameters

All of the Microkernel task management system functions require as an input parameter the TASK_KERNEL_PORT of a targeted task. The TASK_KERNEL_PORT identifies the target task to the Microkernel. Any task that holds a copy of another task's TASK_KERNEL_PORT can use these Microkernel task management system functions to manipulate the second task. This is an extremely powerful model for task manipulation. The OS/2 Operating System Services keep copies of all the TASK_KERNEL_PORTs that are created when an OS/2 task is created. This allows the OS/2 Operating System Services to maintain control over those tasks because they maintain the right to call any of the Microkernel task management system functions.

If the parent of a new task wishes to exercise even tighter control over a child task, it can reset the child task's TASK_KERNEL_PORT value to a new ("interposed") port value (which the parent task owns) before the child task begins execution. The parent task then uses one of its threads to "listen" for task management messages that are passed to the port whenever any other task calls a Microkernel task management system function using the interposed port. In this manner, the parent task can gain control whenever any task attempts to make changes to the child task's characteristics. If the parent task agrees to a subsequent request, it can then pass on the request to the Microkernel by repeating the task management system call using the "real" TASK_KERNEL_PORT for the child task.

Threads

The Microkernel maintains the following state on behalf of each thread:

- A small set of ports that are used by the thread:
  - A port that identifies the thread itself (its THREAD_KERNEL_PORT)
  - A port that is used to receive Microkernel system call results
  - A set of ports that are used to receive thread-specific exception messages
- The thread's machine state, which changes as the thread executes and which can also be changed by a holder of a copy of the thread's THREAD_KERNEL_PORT
- Resource scheduling parameters and thread statistics

The Microkernel provides system functions that can be used to perform the following thread management operations:

- Creation and destruction
- Suspension and resumption
- Thread machine state manipulation
- Special port (for example, exception port) manipulation
- Resource scheduling control

All of the Microkernel thread management system functions require as an input parameter the THREAD_KERNEL_PORT of a targeted thread. The THREAD_KERNEL_PORT identifies the target thread to the Microkernel. Any task that holds a copy of another thread's THREAD_KERNEL_PORT can use these Microkernel thread management system calls to manipulate the targeted thread.

Figure 3-2. Thread Management

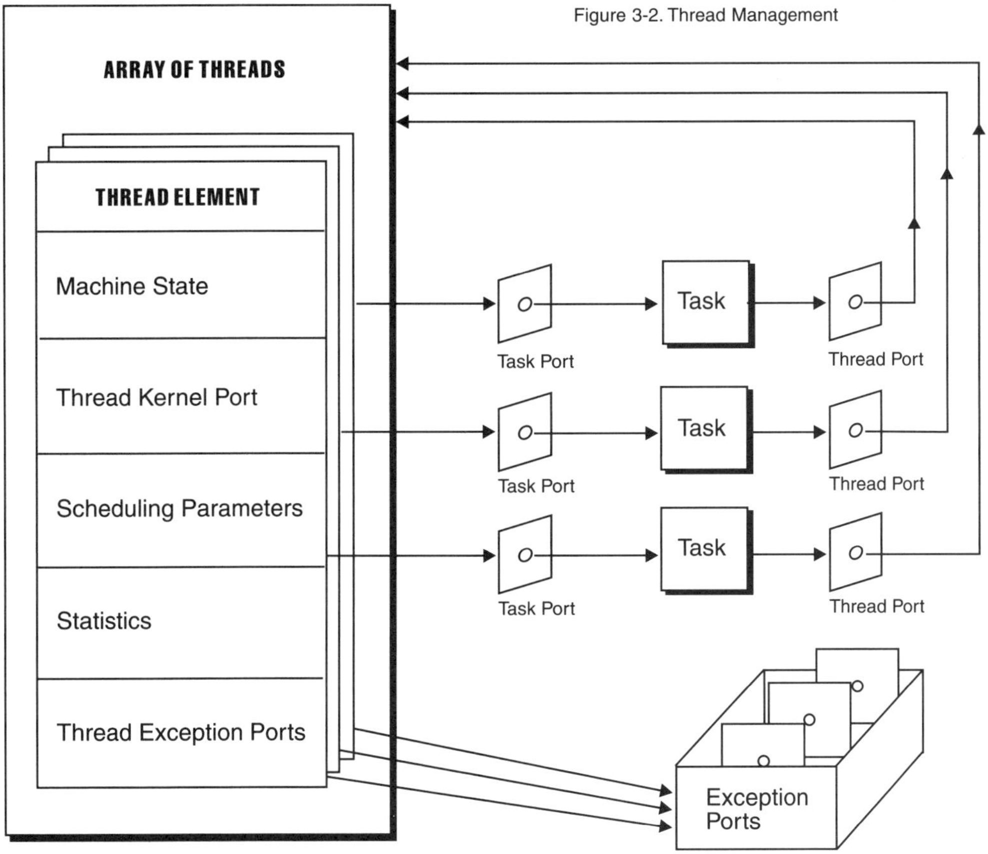

Exception Handling

Occasionally, unexpected things happen when a program is running. For example, sometimes a thread might trigger a program exception by performing an unacceptable operation, such as attempting to branch to an invalid address or attempting to divide by 0. These exceptions are raised by the system's processor. Other times, one task might send a signal to a thread within another task, perhaps to inform it of an unexpected external event or perhaps simply to get it to terminate. When a thread is unexpectedly interrupted in such a manner, it is said that the thread has "taken an exception."

The Microkernel provides basic exception management services that the OS/2 Operating System Services use as a basis for their exception management services. The OS/2 Operating System Services support a set of functions that are used to control the exception handling environment. This set of functions defines exception handling routines that are invoked when the operating system detects that an exception has been raised for the thread.

When an exception occurs in a thread, the Microkernel creates a message that describes the exception and then sends the message to an exception port that relates to the thread. For any given exception, there are two exception ports that can be used by the thread to receive exception messages:

- A thread-specific port for the specific type of exception

- A task-specific port for the specific type of exception

A thread can use a Microkernel system function to pass to the Microkernel the thread-specific exception port that it wishes to use. In that case, the exception message is sent to that thread-specific exception port. If no thread-specific exception port is set up, then the Microkernel sends the exception message to the task-specific exception port.

In order to receive exception messages, the task must set up threads that wait for those messages on the task-specific and possibly thread-specific exception ports. Once an exception-handling thread receives an exception message, it then performs logic that is intended to appropriately deal with the exception. In some cases, the thread can handle the exception and continue execution (for example, allocating additional stack space if a stack fault is detected). In other cases, the thread (and possibly the task) needs to clean itself up and then terminate.

When the thread is done with the exception message, it must respond back to the Microkernel as to whether it has successfully dealt with the exception. A successful reply causes the Microkernel to continue running the thread. An unsuccessful reply from the receiver connected to the thread-specific port causes the Microkernel to send the exception message to the receiver connected to the task port for the specific type of exception. An unsuccessful reply from the receiver connected to the task port causes the Microkernel to terminate the thread.

It is not necessary for the thread that handles an exception to reside within the same task as the target thread for the exception. In OS/2 Warp Connect (PowerPC Edition), the OS/2 Operating System Services actually receive all the Microkernel-generated messages on behalf of OS/2 threads. The OS/2 System Services then modify and relay those messages to the registered OS/2 exception handing routines (if any) within the targeted OS/2 task.

Virtual Memory Management

The Microkernel provides virtual memory management support for large, paged, sparse address spaces composed of *memory objects*. Each memory object is managed by a pager, which is a task outside the Microkernel that provides backing storage for the pages of the memory object. A task's virtual address space is built via the mapping of memory objects within it. The Microkernel manages memory protection and sharing on a memory object basis in an abstract way that is independent of any particular processor address translation hardware.

Each time an operating system or shared service calls the IBM Microkernel to allocate memory, a memory object is created. Simply put, a memory object is the "chunk" of memory allocated to the service. From the time it is allocated, the IBM Microkernel treats it as a single unique item. When the service is done with the memory object, the entire memory object is deallocated (or returned to the IBM Microkernel).

Memory objects are mapped into virtual address spaces. As part of the mapping, protection characteristics are set. These protection characteristics apply to all of the memory contained within the memory object. For example, suppose a part of a memory object is read-only; the entire memory object will also be read-only. (If any part of the memory object is read and write, then the entire memory object is read/write.) Additionally, if any part of the memory object is visible (addressable or accessible) to a program, then the entire memory object is visible to the program.

While each page of the memory object must have the same characteristics, each memory object does not have the same state. For example, a single memory object can be larger than the amount of physical memory available in your computer; some of the memory object pages can be in memory and others can be swapped out to the hard disk. If each page were required to have the same state, then the memory object would be limited in size to the amount of memory available in your computer.

The OS/2 Operating System Services provide a set of memory management functions for OS/2 programs. Tasks can share virtual memory regions with other tasks and can also manipulate memory regions that are known solely to themselves. The OS/2 Operating System Services support memory management by utilizing the virtual memory management services that are provided by the Microkernel.

There are two tasks in Figure 3-3 (Task One and Task Two) that map to the same memory object (Memory Object X) in different regions of their respective virtual address spaces. The memory object contains two pages of data (Page A and Page B) that have been mapped into different physical pages of system memory.

Figure 3-3. Example of How the Microkernel Manages Virtual Memory

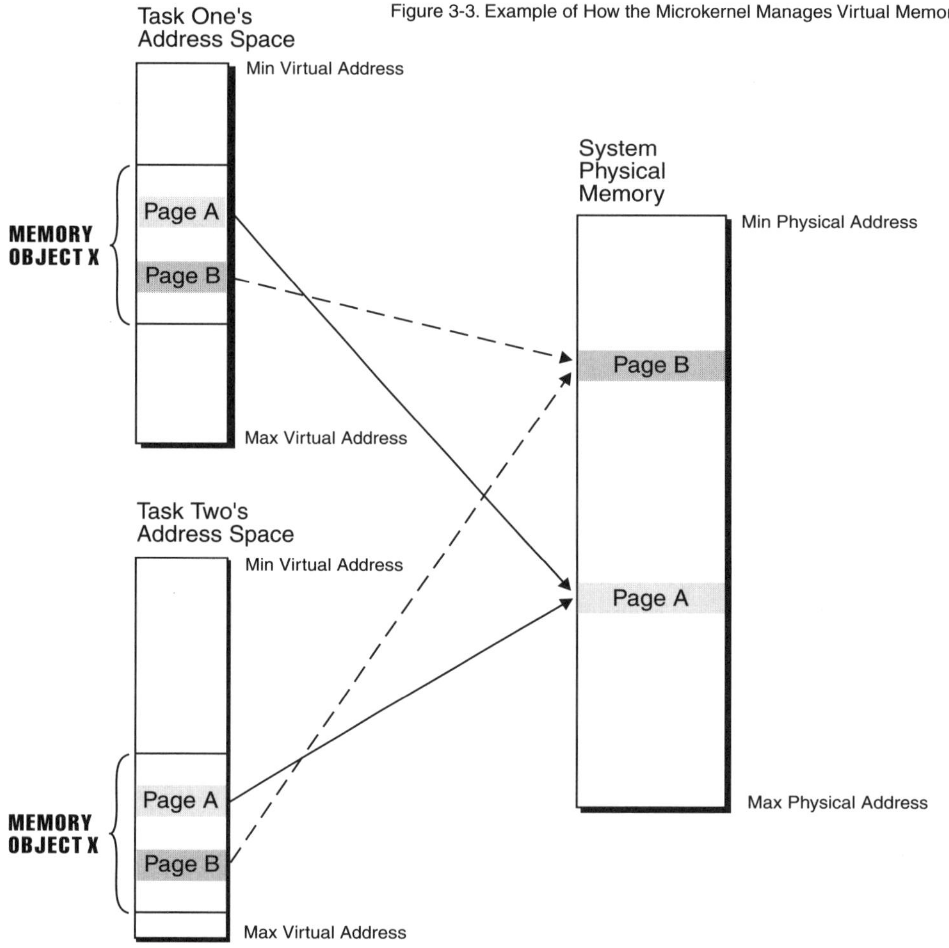

Virtual Memory Management System Functions

The Microkernel provides a set of virtual memory management system functions. Memory objects can be created, mapped into virtual address spaces, or destroyed. Regions of virtual memory can be copied, shared, or reserved. A copy of a virtual memory region is a snapshot of the source memory regions. Any modifications to the source after the point of copy are not seen in the copy, and any changes made to the copy are not seen in the source. For shared virtual memory regions, any changes made through any mapping of the memory object will be seen by all the mappings of the memory object. Reserved virtual memory regions are unavailable for memory object mapping until they are released.

The Microkernel allows memory regions to have associated protection levels. This is critical for actions such as making sure that code sections cannot be inadvertently written over. Each memory region has a maximum and current protection level. The current protection level must be a subset of the maximum allowed protection level. The maximum protection is specified when the memory object is mapped into the virtual address space. It cannot be changed to include more lenient protection. The current protection and the maximum protection levels are defined as a combination of read, write, and execute permissions.

Page Faults

OS/2 supports virtual memory management capabilities that allow programs to utilize more virtual memory than is physically present on a system. To support this, the Microkernel requires any memory object to be associated with a pager task. When a thread attempts to reference a page within a memory object and that page is not currently in physical memory, the processor generates a page fault that is fielded by the Microkernel. The Microkernel then suspends the faulting thread and constructs a page fault exception message that is sent to the pager task associated with the memory object.

Pagers are not part of the Microkernel; rather, they are part of the operating system shared services that run on top of the Microkernel. There are three different pager tasks:

- A Default Pager provides storage for read/write virtual memory pages. These pages are copied to the system page file when their physical memory pages are given to other virtual memory pages.
- A File Server Pager is used to page in (read-only) code pages. Code pages are not copied back to disk when they are discarded.
- An OS/2 Server Pager is used to uncompress special OS/2 resources when they are paged in.

When a pager task receives a page-fault exception message, it needs to go to whatever form of backing storage that it is using to hold an image of the missing page. For example, the Default Pager task uses the system's page file (the OS/2 SWAPPER.DAT file). After the missing page has been brought into memory, the pager task sends a message back to the Microkernel indicating that the page fault has been successfully resolved. At that point, the Microkernel permits the thread that caused the page fault to resume execution.

Developer's Tip: Very often, when one task sends a memory object to another task, the second task just reads the region without modifying it. It would be very expensive if the Microkernel actually made a real copy of each region when the region was sent. Instead, the Microkernel makes heavy use of a copy-on-write strategy to permit programs to inherit memory objects without copying large numbers of pages when the object is initially copied to the address space of another task.

Initially, both tasks share the same set of pages for the memory object. New copies of pages are created only when either task attempts to update a page within the memory object.

Messaging

On OS/2 Warp Connect (PowerPC Edition), much of what we think of as the operating system is actually implemented as a set of independent server tasks. This means that OS/2 system functions typically turn into messages that are passed between the operating system server tasks.

To support this, the Microkernel provides an Interprocess Communication (IPC) facility that allows system tasks to communicate with each other and also with the Microkernel itself. The communication is performed via the use of well-structured messages. This message-passing design is the key to the entire Microkernel system architecture.

The Microkernel supports two styles of message passing:

- Synchronous Remote Procedure Calls (RPCs)

- Asynchronous IPC message passing

When an asynchronous IPC is performed, the message sender does not wait until the message target sends back a response. When an RPC is performed, the message sender waits until the message target receives the message, performs some action based on the message, and then sends back a response. While both forms of message passing can be used to support a client/server model, the RPC message model permits more efficient message transmission. Therefore, most of the OS/2 Operating System Services use the RPC model.

Most of the Microkernel system functions are implemented as messages to the Microkernel.

Messaging Ports

At any given instant on an OS/2 Warp Connect (PowerPC Edition) system, there are typically a set of IPC and RPC messages flying around between different tasks. When a task wants to send a message, it needs some sort of target at which to aim the message. Within the Microkernel architecture, it is the port that serves as the message target. Ports are Microkernel resources. A port serves as a unidirectional communication channel between a client thread that sends a message to request a service and the server thread that provides the service after it receives the service request message. Each port is associated with a single receiving task, but it can have multiple senders.

In addition to serving as the target for messages, ports are also used by the Microkernel as *resource object identifiers*. The resource object identifier is simply an internal identifier, or nickname, for some resource that the Microkernel is managing for one or more of its services. This type of nickname is used throughout the computer industry; PC DOS, OS/2, AIX, and other operating systems utilize a nickname called a "handle" as a quick way for a program to identify a file that has been opened and is being processed.

When the Microkernel creates a resource, it passes back the port that acts as a handle to it. Subsequent calls to access or modify the resource use the port to identify the resource.

Port Rights

Earlier, in the discussion of Microkernel tasks and threads, it was mentioned that a task holds a collection of ports. Strictly speaking, a task really doesn't hold a collection of ports; it actually holds port rights.

There are two kinds of port rights:

- Receive rights
- Send rights

The task that holds the receive right to a port is allowed to receive messages that are sent to the port. Each port in the system has only a single receive right. When a task creates a new port it receives (owns) the receive right for that port. The task can hold and use the receive right, or it can pass the receive right on to another task. The destruction of a receive right causes the destruction of the associated port.

While a Microkernel port is associated with only one receive right, it can be associated with many send rights. A task that holds a send right to a port is allowed to send messages to that port. If a task holds a port send right, it can use that send right over and over again to send messages to the port.

The holder of a port receive right also holds the right to ask the Microkernel to create new send rights for the port. This allows a server task to generate as many send rights as it needs in order to support its client tasks (who send service request messages to the server via the port).

In Figure 3-4, there are three tasks (Task 1, Task 2, and Task 3). Tasks 1 and 2 hold send rights to a particular Microkernel port. Task 3 holds the single receive right to that port. This means that Tasks 1 and 2 can send Microkernel IPC messages to Task 3 by utilizing the Microkernel port send rights. Because of their fundamental role in the Microkernel architecture, ports are strongly protected. A task can make use of a port only if it holds a port right to that port. Microkernel IPC and RPC messages can pass port rights as well as other types of data.

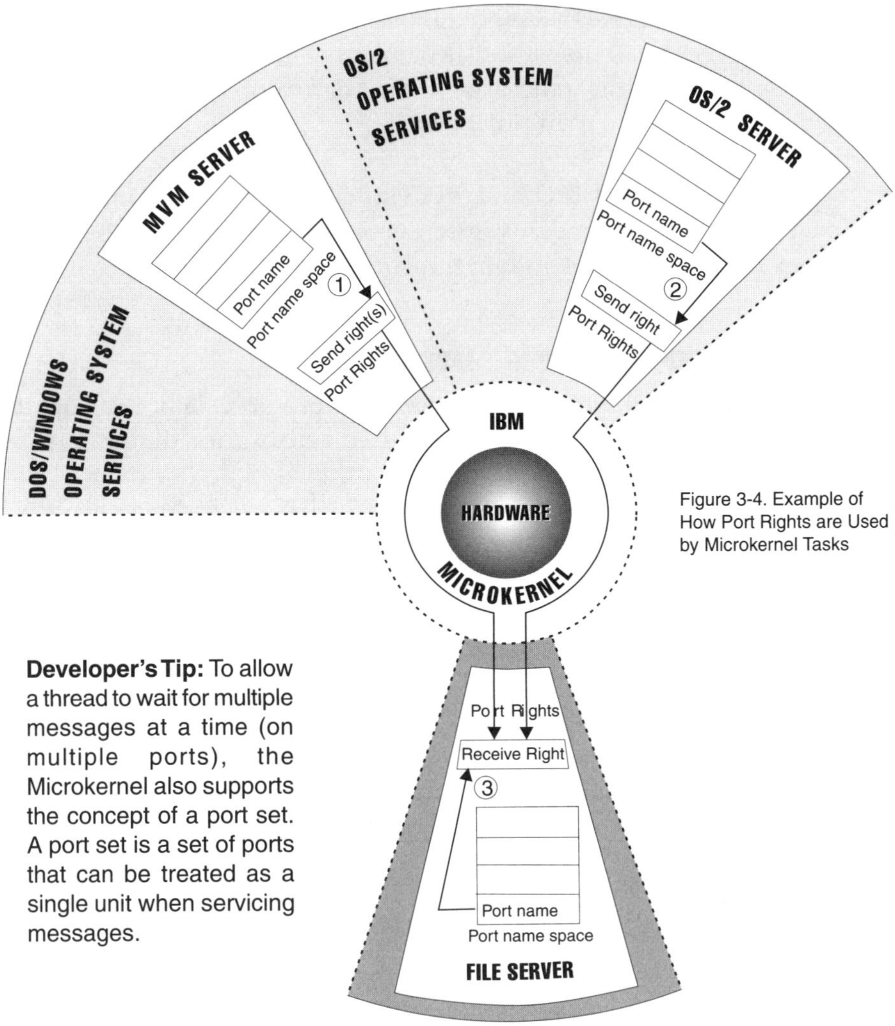

Figure 3-4. Example of How Port Rights are Used by Microkernel Tasks

Developer's Tip: To allow a thread to wait for multiple messages at a time (on multiple ports), the Microkernel also supports the concept of a port set. A port set is a set of ports that can be treated as a single unit when servicing messages.

System Traps vs. System Messages

The majority of the Microkernel system functions are implemented as messages to the Microkernel. There are two key classes of exceptions to this rule.

First, a thread needs a direct way to learn the identity of its own TASK_KERNEL_PORT and its own THREAD_KERNEL_PORT. The mach_task_self and mach_thread_self *system traps* provide these ports to the calling task. A system trap is a direct call into a portion of the Microkernel that is bound into each task. Once a thread has one or both of these ports, it can call the various Microkernel task and thread management system functions (by sending a message to the Microkernel that includes the appropriate identification port) to manipulate itself.

Second, the Microkernel IPC and RPC messaging system functions themselves (mk_msg_call, mk_msg_send, mk_msg_server, and mk_msg_receive) cannot be messages; they need to be direct system traps.

Port Classes and Structured Messages

Every Microkernel port is created as an instance of a port class. The port class defines the format of messages that can be transferred across ports of that class. Most ports have a well-defined set of messages that are passed across them. This approach allows these formats to be preregistered with the IPC system once, avoiding the overhead of verifying their correctness on each message transfer. If the format of all messages is not known at port-class creation time, a port class can be defined such that the message formats are presented at message transmission time. A single port can accept message formats from two or more otherwise unrelated port classes.

A message is a structured collection of direct data, indirect data, and port rights passed between two entities via transmission to a port. The signature information associated with the class of a port defines how the data is to be interpreted and passed by the IPC and RPC functions.

Because the message structure clearly defines which message parts are port rights, the Microkernel can translate transmitted port rights from the sending task's port to the receiving task's port.

Message Interface Generator

To simplify the generation of the specific send/receive message logic, a utility called the Message Interface Generator (MIG) is provided. For each message class that a server task is to handle, the server task programmer provides a client/server interface definition to MIG, and the utility generates source code for the client library and the server task dispatch logic. The automated generation of messaging protocol logic can greatly simplify the development of a client/server application.

IPC vs. RPC

As mentioned earlier, the Microkernel provides two different ways in which to pass messages between tasks:

- Asynchronous IPC message passing
- Synchronous RPCs (remote procedure calls)

Developer's Tip: A common operation in the Microkernel environment is the remote procedure call. Although it is possible to emulate this behavior at the user level through the use of two ports and the one-way message passing of IPC messages between the ports, this method could not approach the performance offered by a Microkernel-supplied primitive tuned for RPC.

The mk_msg_call system function is used by a client to invoke a remote procedure call. It will not return until a reply message is received or the RPC is ended. To service RPC requests, the server thread uses the mk_msg_server system function. The system function is used both to respond to a completed request and also to accept a new request.

The mk_msg_send system function is used to send a one-way message. Just as with RPC, the client thread is blocked until a server thread is found and the data transferred into the receiving task's address and port name spaces. But unlike RPC, as soon as the data transfer to the server is completed, the mk_msg_call is completed. If the sender (client) wishes to subsequently wait for a response from the server, it can call an mk_msg_receive system function. The server thread uses the mk_msg_receive system function to wait for client IPC requests. It uses the mk_msg_send system function to send back any responses to the requesting client thread.

Device I/O Support and Interrupt Management

In order to support device I/O, the Microkernel provides access to I/O resources, such as memory-mapped devices, I/O ports, and direct memory access (DMA) channels. The DMA interfaces are used in providing information and in programming certain hardware functions to transfer data between memory and a device.

The Microkernel also provides the ability to pass hardware interrupts to device drivers that execute as tasks (that do not run in a processor privileged mode). It has services that allow privileged tasks to acquire ownership of devices. The Microkernel must field all interrupts because interrupts are delivered to the privileged state of the processor. It has logic to determine whether it should process the interrupt or send it to a device driver task. Device drivers need to register with the Microkernel so that the Microkernel will know when and where to send a specific class of interrupt.

The Microkernel also has services that permit device drivers to add interrupt handlers and other low-level code to the Microkernel. Device drivers are discussed in more detail in Chapter 9, "Device Driver Services" on page 165.

Host and Processor Set Management

The Microkernel Host features return information about the processor running the system. They also provide a set of system management functions that:

- Manage the system clock (time/date)
- Start and stop the system
- Trace low-level events
- Take an image of the system (as either a hibernation image or a system dump)

The Microkernel Processor Set features are used on multiprocessor computers to group the processors into sets. Each task is bound to a single processor group. If a multithreaded task is bound to a processor set that contains multiple physical processors, then it is possible for some or all of the task's threads to run in parallel on the different physical processors within the processor set.

Name Services

This chapter introduces and describes the Name Services. It describes the fundamentals of Name Services and provides detailed information about how the Name Server and the system name space are used.

Introducing Name Services

Name Services provide a common abstraction for the identification and access of key resources on an OS/2 system, such as the devices in the computer or the network servers that the system is communicating with. The Name Services provide a set of interfaces that provide access to a system *name space* that is maintained in the form of a directed graph. The nodes within the graph hold data that identify named system entities. The Microkernel, the shared services, and the OS/2 Operating System Services use the name space to hold key configuration data and state data and to provide links to their server tasks.

The name space presents a powerful, general architecture for the organization of information on an OS/2 system. The name space is open and available for use by OS/2 programs.

While very complex in its internal structure and processing, the name space is actually a simple concept. It is just a place where information can be kept in a predefined and orderly way so that programs can easily process it. There are multiple subspaces within the name space, and each subspace can be managed by different programs. The name space contains a set of information that supports access to the entire system.

In some ways, it is used rather like your telephone book. The white pages contain an alphabetic listing of owners of phones and their phone numbers. The yellow pages contain groups of businesses, alphabetized by their business category; within the groups, they are alphabetized by business name. The yellow pages can contain advertisements as well as simple business listings. As a person can easily master the difference between the white and yellow pages, and the difference between the formats and contents of the advertisements within the yellow pages, a program can easily handle the various forms of information in the name space because it is kept in a well-understood format.

The name space is used for just about everything in OS/2 Warp Connect (PowerPC Edition). A listing of all of the available hardware is kept there, along with a list of all of the device drivers that are used to access the hardware. You will also find drive letters, file names, directory names, file system identifiers, network information, pipe names, semaphore names, printer information, as well as system management and performance monitoring information.

Because the name space is not specific to any operating system, it provides an excellent place for the Microkernel to record and exchange information about the multiple operating systems (such as OS/2 and DOS) that might be running on top of it.

The name space allows a system resource to be maintained in either a persistent manner (that is, maintained across multiple system boot-ups) or in a transient manner (that is, only kept until the system is turned off or rebooted). This allows OS/2 programs to view the entire set of OS/2 system resources as being organized into a single, global, directed name-space graph that is anchored by a single, well-known system root.

The name space is composed of nodes and links. Nodes are the primary containers of information; links are used to logically connect the nodes.

Name Space

The graph that represents the name space is divided into different, disjointed subgraphs that are administered by different servers. A server that underlies a portion of the name space is referred to as a name server. The set of name servers included with OS/2 Warp Connect (PowerPC Edition) are:

Root Name Server Administers the root portion of the name space. It manages a transient name-space region that is constructed each time OS/2 Warp Connect (PowerPC Edition) is started. This transient name-space region is discarded each time the system is turned off or rebooted. The root name space is used to anchor (in a well-known fashion) all the other name space regions.

The Root Name Server also is used to hold the names of the various OS/2 Shared Services and the port send rights that allow access to them. The service names are "well known" (that is, their names are publicly documented so that clients can know them). Once a shared service's node is accessed via its name, the client can obtain a port send right to the server from the node. The port right then allows the client to send requests to the shared service.

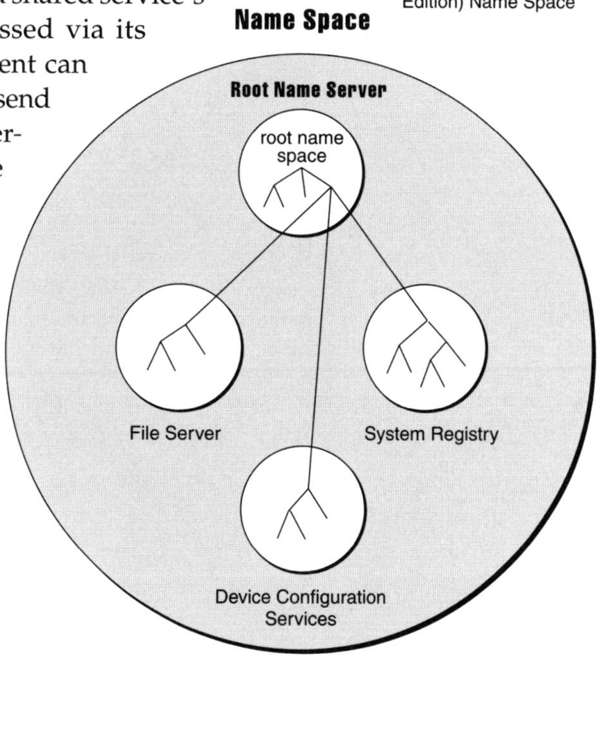

Figure 4-1. OS/2 Warp Connect (PowerPC Edition) Name Space

Device Configuration Serve — Presides over the transient portion of the name space that contains hardware configuration information that describes the physical system. The Device Configuration Services fill in this portion of the name space at boot time, often by walking the buses of the system. The information in this portion of the name space is used by device drivers.

System Registry Server — Provides persistent system and user configuration services. It supports a general-purpose name space that can be used by different shared services and applications to hold configuration and long-term data values. It also provides a framework that allows heritage OS/2 configuration mechanisms (for example, the CONFIG.SYS file and the various OS/2 INI files) to be viewed as being part of the name space.

File Server — Manages the directory and file name portions of the name space.

As various file systems are loaded (for example, FAT and HPFS), they are also loaded into the File Server portion of the name space. Each file system owns a portion of the name space that corresponds to the directory and file hierarchy that is administered by the file system.

Each file system is represented in the name space as a subgraph of the File Server. Note that OS/2 programs will use the OS/2 functions (for example, DosOpen) rather than the Name Services functions to navigate within the file system portions of the name space.

Name Space Architectural Elements

Before the Name Services and the name space are described any further, it is important to understand the elements of the name space, the rules for how they are connected and how they are allowed to interrelate with each other.

Nodes

Nodes are the data containers of the name-space graph. They are unnamed entities that typically contain user-defined or program-defined attributes that store arbitrary complex sets of information. All node attributes are named (by Unicode strings). An attribute can be *User Type* or *System Type*.

The User Type is provided so that a software developer can encode information that relates to the interpretation of the attribute. The OS/2 Operating System Services do not use the User-Type setting (name servers do not know how to interpret the contents of a User-Type attribute).

If the attribute is a System-Type attribute, then a name server knows how to interpret its value. The value of a System-Type node attribute can be:

- A simple value, which can be one of several types, including a Boolean, an ASCII Character, an unsigned or Unicode character, an unsigned or a signed integer (of either 8, 16, 32, or 64 bits), a single byte of unknown type, or a Microkernel port send right

- A homogeneous array of simple values, where each element in the array is of the same simple value type

- A heterogeneous array of simple values or nested homogeneous values or nested heterogeneous arrays

Links and Paths

Links are used to connect nodes. Links are named entities that do not contain any attribute data. More than one link can point to the same node (in other words, the name space is not strictly hierarchical).

Because nodes are unnamed, it is the sequence of links that establishes a named path to a node. More than one link can point to a node, so it is possible for multiple paths to point to the same target node.

Link names can contain any valid Unicode characters, including the null character. They are length specified.

There are two restrictions that are placed on links:

- A link cannot cross name-space boundaries. That is, the two nodes that are connected by a link must be managed by the same name server.
- The two nodes connected by a link must exist. If all the incoming links to a node are deleted, then the node is deleted.

Figure 4-2 illustrates how a set of unnamed nodes can be connected by named links. Some of the nodes in the figure are pointed to by more than one link. This illustrates the fact that in the name space, a given node can have more than one "parent." For example, the paths /A/E/J, /B/F/J, and /B/G/H/J all lead to the bottom left-most node in the diagram. In this example, the "/" character is used merely as a separator between path links.

Figure 4-2. Name Space: Nodes, Links, and Paths

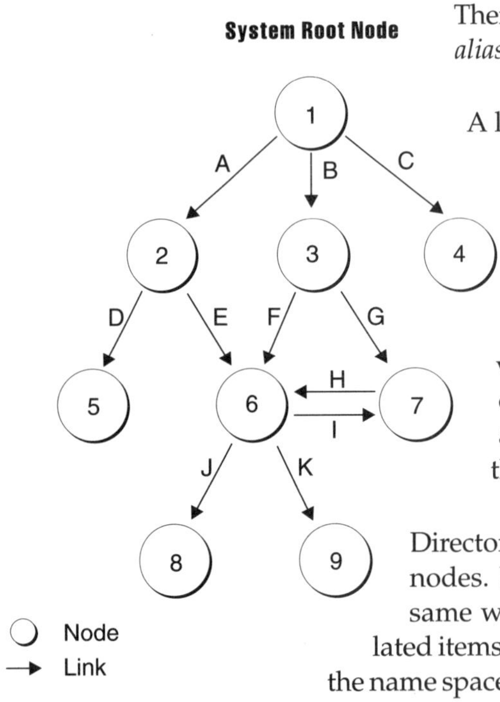

Types of Nodes

There are three types of nodes: *leaf*, *directory*, and *alias*.

A leaf node does not have any outgoing links (that is, it is the "end" of a name space path). A leaf node typically contains data that is used by a shared service or an application. Leaf nodes can contain a service port value (as a special attribute beyond its other data attributes). The service port attribute can be used by a client to communicate with a shared service. It can also be used to "jump" to other regions of the name space (as described later).

Directory nodes can contain outgoing links to other nodes. Directory nodes can be used in much the same way that they are used in a file system. Related items are grouped together and organized within the name space. Name-space directories can be empty, and directory nodes can contain different kinds of attributes.

Alias nodes are used to reshape the name space. They provide a way to "jump" from a portion of the name space to another portion of the name space. To accomplish this, an alias node contains a reference to a node and a path. When an alias is found during the name (path) resolution process, the resolution process jumps to the node referenced by the alias and resolves the path stored in the alias before continuing with the resolution of the rest of the original path.

Typically, an alias node jumps to another node in the same region of the name space. However, an alias node can also point to the root of the name space and provide a path that is within the root portion of the name space. This is the only case in which an alias node jumps from one name space region to another.

Figure 4-3 shows the name space redrawn. The leaf, directory, and alias nodes are clearly differentiated. A symbolic link, between the alias node in the figure and a directory node, is also added.

Borders

Links can be used to navigate within a portion of the name space that is administered by a single name server. As stated previously, alias nodes typically jump to other nodes within the same portion of the name space but can be used to jump to nodes in the root portion of the name space.

Leaf nodes in one name-space region can be used to "point" to nodes in another name-space region. Such leaf nodes contain a non-null value that identifies the send right of a service provider. This is a send right to a port within a name server that administers the next portion of the path.

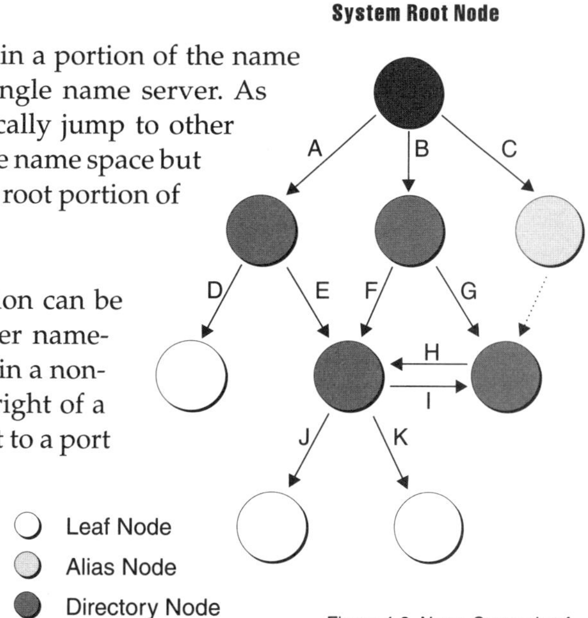

Figure 4-3. Name Space: Leaf, Directory, and Alias Nodes

Every path resolution call returns a pointer to a node (a port) and a path string. If the path string is NULL (for example, fully consumed), then the path resolution is complete. If it is non-NULL, then the path resolution can be continued using the port and the remaining path string.

Name Space Regions

Many different types of objects are created within the name space.

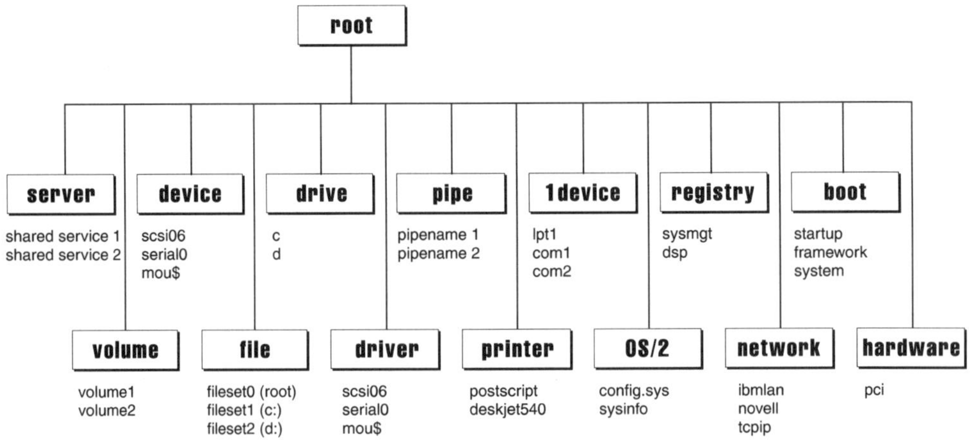

Figure 4-4. High-Level View of the Name Space

The following list provides a summary of the major related directories that are created off of the root of the name space:

/server Contains nodes that represent each of the shared services (for example, /server/file/FAT). Each shared service node contains a Microkernel port that enables access to the shared service provider. The /server directory is in a transient portion of the name space.

/volume Contains nodes that represent the available logical volumes upon which the various file systems can be mounted. The volume names are user selected at the time they are formatted or through the use of the heritage LABEL command. Refer to Chapter 7, "File Services" on page 125 for a description of logical volumes. The /volume directory is in a transient portion of the name space.

/file Contains nodes that represent the mounted file systems (for example, /file/fileset1/os2/appl/bin/lotus.exe). The directory levels below the /file directory represent the actual recorded directory levels of the various mounted file systems and are processed by the File Server. The /file directory is in a transient portion of the name space.

/drive Contains nodes that represent the drive letters that are currently defined for the system (for example, /drive/c is the name-space representation of C:). The file system is attached here as well as in the /file area (for example, /drive/c/os2/appl/bin/lotus.exe). The /drive directory is in a transient portion of the name space.

/device Contains nodes that represent physical devices (for example, /device/serial0). The /device directory is in a transient portion of the name space.

/driver Contains a node for each of the device drivers that have been loaded into the system to support the various physical devices attached to the system. The /driver directory is in a transient portion of the name space.

/pipe Contains nodes that represent named pipes (for example, /pipe/mypipe). The /pipe directory is in a transient portion of the name space.

/printer Contains nodes that represent the logical printers defined on the system (for example, /printer/postscript). The /printer directory is in a transient portion of the name space.

/ldevice Contains nodes that represent the OS/2 logical devices (for example, /ldevice/com1). A logical device can be different from the physical devices held in the /device directory. For example, both the AUX (/ldevice/aux) and the COM1 (/ldevice/com1) logical devices use the same physical device (/device/serial0). The /ldevice directory is in a transient portion of the name space.

/boot Is a persistent area of the name space that is available during system startup. It is the only directory for which there is guaranteed accessibility during the initial stages of the boot process. All data that is required before the loading of the File Server must be stored in the boot directory.

/registry Is the portion of name space that belongs to the System Registry Server and is where OS/2 maintains all persistent data that is not necessary during the boot process. It includes the names of service providers and the ports at which they can be located. The /registry and the /boot directory both point to some of the same directories.

/os2 Is a region of the name space used for data specific to the OS/2 operating system.

/network Is a region of the name space that contains subregions that represent the network connections that are supported on this system (for example, /network/novell/server1/appl/myapp.exe).

/hardware Contains nodes that represent hardware resources that were discovered by Microkernel "bus walker" logic. All hardware resources (including memory, buses, and adapter cards) found in the system during system startup are described here (for example, /hardware/pci/floppy0). Note that this data can only be read.

Name Services and Node Management Functions

The Name Services API functions include the ability to manage nodes (create, modify, destroy), manage links (create, modify, destroy), manage paths (create, modify, destroy), and to resolve or look up names in the name space. The node management functions allow for manipulation of nodes in the name space. Nodes can be added, modified, and deleted, and the contents of a node can also be read. All of the functions in this class require that a path to the target node be provided.

- Use the NameAddNode function to add a node to the name space. A completely formed node and an incoming link with which to connect the node into the name space must be provided. Additionally, the node to be added must have previously been constructed.

- Use the NameCloseNode function to close a node, which is how the storage that the node takes is freed up. The handle for the node is deleted, but the node itself is not deleted. Nodes are deleted only when all the incoming links to the node are deleted.

- Use the NameModifyNode function to modify the contents of a node. The handle of a target node (the node to be modified), an input node structure (that contains a set of attribute values), and a flags word (that guides how the modification is performed) must be provided. A flags word has the following update options:

  - The set of attributes in the input node can be interpreted as a delta over the existing attribute values in the targeted node. In this case, the attributes in the input node are added if they are not already present in the targeted node; the attributes in the input node are used as replacements if they are already present in the targeted node.

  - Specifically identified attributes in the input node can be set to indicate that the corresponding attributes in the targeted node are to be deleted. In this case, all attributes in the targeted node that are not present in the input node are left unchanged.

  - The set of attributes in the input node structure can completely replace the targeted node.

  - For targeted leaf nodes, the service provider's port send right, which causes the new service provider's port right to be included within the input node.

- Use the NameReadNode and NameReadLong functions to read the contents of targeted nodes. NameReadNode is typically used to read the contents of a node. You can choose to read all of the node's attributes or just a subset of them. You can also choose to read just the types and names of the attributes, or that information and the attribute's values.

  Because it is possible for the attribute values of a node to be very large, NameReadLong is provided as an adjunct to NameReadNode. NameReadNode can be used to read the first part of a large attribute value and one or more NameReadLong calls can subsequently be used to read the rest of the information within the attribute.

Link Management Functions

The link management API functions are used to manipulate links in the name space. Links can be added and deleted, or a pair of nodes can also be relinked.

- Use the NameAddLink function to create a new link between a source node and a target node.

- Use the NameDeleteLink function to delete a link between a source node and a target node. If the last link to a target node is deleted, then the node is also deleted. If the target node is a directory, this deletion can cause other nodes and links to be deleted.

- Use the NameReLink function to sever two old links and forge a new link between a source and target node. If the relinking operation causes another node to be isolated, that node is automatically deleted.

Path Resolution Function

You can use the NameResolve function to locate a node or a node's service provider. This function traverses paths within the name space.

You need to provide a set of parameters that include a starting node handle and a path to follow from that node. The name resolution process follows the specified path until it either reaches the end of the path or runs into a leaf node (which indicates a terminal point within the portion of the name space administered by the current name server).

If the end of the path is reached, the function returns the type of the node (directory, alias, or leaf) and the handle of the end node. The node handle can be used in subsequent calls, such as calls to the NameReadNode function.

If the NameResolve function runs up against a terminal leaf node, then the function returns the port send right that is contained within the leaf node (if any) and the remainder of the (unresolved) path. You can then continue the path resolution process by calling the NameResolve function again, passing in the port send right as the starting node handle and the unresolved path portion as the path to follow from the start of the name space region.

Search/Notify Functions

The search/notify API functions are used to search a subgraph of the name space for all nodes that comply with a condition. When a call is made to the function, it can return node handles or any node attribute values that are desired. The functions can also return other types of information such as Boolean values, numeric values, or the names of path links.

The functions can be used to either perform an immediate search or to set up a continuous background search (notification search). Immediate searches can be limited by timeout parameters. Notification searches must be explicitly terminated by a NameSearchClose function.

A search returns as soon as it completes its tour through the specified subgraph of the name space. A notification search waits for the specified modification events to occur within the name space subgraph.

The search subgraph must lie completely within a name-space region that is administered by a single name server.

The following provides information about the Search and Notify functions:

- Use the NameSearchAndNotify function to trigger a name-space search (or notification search). You need to supply a number of input parameters that include:
  - A Starting Node Handle that indicates the root of the search subgraph.
  - A Num_Levels value that can be used to limit the search to nodes that are within a specified number of links from the starting node. This establishes the bounds of the subgraph search.
  - A set of flags that tell the name server how to perform the search, including whether to perform an immediate or a notification search. For notification searches, other flags control which events within the search subgraph should trigger the notification search (for example, node addition, modification, or deletion within the search subgraph).
  - A Search Filter program. This program is evaluated on every node in the search subgraph. The filter starts executing on each node with an empty stack, and after the execution of the filter, the node is considered to be selected if and only if the stack is not empty.
  - A Timeout value that indicates how long the function should be blocked while waiting for a result to be returned on the stack.
  - A Num_Entries value that can be used to limit the number of stack results that are pushed on the stack by the call.
  - A pointer to a Stack Buffer that will receive the results of the search. When Null, this pointer indicates that you want to have the stack automatically allocated within the workspace that is being used by the function.
  - A pointer to an Events Buffer that, on output, will contain an array of flag entries that provide information about each of the entries that are returned within the Stack Buffer.

If NameSearchAndNotify returns successfully, the stack buffer and events buffer contain information relating to the nodes that were selected in the search. This is true for immediate searches. It is also true if NameSearchAndNotify starts a notification search and immediately finds some result.

In the event that NameSearchAndNotify finds more matches than you have provided space for, it returns only the portion of the information that it can handle. In that case, NameSearchNext can be used to continue the search that was started by NameSearchAndNotify. A series of calls to NameSearchNext can be used to return all the information found by the search.

- Use NameSearchNext to inquire about more results for a notification search. NameSearchNext supports a timeout limit value.

- Use NameSearchClose to terminate a notification search. It can also be used to terminate an immediate search that requires a series of calls to NameSearchNext in order to return all of its result data. NameSearchNext will cause an automatically allocated results stack to be deleted.

Workspace Management Functions

The Name Services workspaces have two purposes: to provide a region of working space into which Name Services transactions can be generated and to hold information that is returned by Name Services functions that return information (for example, NameReadNode and NameSearchAndNotify).

Not all name servers support workspaces. The System Registry is a name server that does support workspaces. There are three types of Name Services workspaces:

- The Default Workspace, which is allocated on behalf of each task that utilizes name-space functions. The node handle for the root node in the default workspace is assigned to a global program variable named "NameRoot." The NameRoot variable can be imported at link time. (Variables, like system service entry points, are imported from the dynamic link libraries that contain them).

- Private Workspaces, which are created by calls to the NameCreateWorkspace function. These are available only to the task that creates the private workspace.

- Shared Workspaces, which are created by calls to the NameCreateWorkspace function via the use of a special feature flag value. Other tasks gain access to the shared workspace by using NameAllocWorkspace, passing the node handle that is returned when the shared workspace is created.

  Tasks that share a shared workspace share any and all memory objects created within the workspace (nodes, links, stacks, and so on). They also share any uncommitted transactions that are in progress.

  Tasks that share a shared workspace do not share name-service object handles (for example, node handles). The values of handles are unique to each task (even though different tasks can share access to the same name-service object).

A task can create and use multiple workspaces (both private and shared). Whenever a workspace is created, a handle is returned to the root node of the workspace. The global NameRoot program variable is the root node for the default workspace.

The root node handle of a workspace is the workspace's logical connection to the root node of the entire name space. The root node handle for any workspace is different from the root node handle for any other workspace (even though they all logically point to the same root node of the name space).

Any nodes or paths that are resolved from a node handle that is in one workspace will also be in that workspace (even if the path resolution process crosses name-space boundaries). This implies that when a node is added, modified, or deleted, that action occurs in the workspace that is associated with the node handle or path.

You can use NameDeleteWorkspace to delete private workspaces. Note that shared workspaces are automatically deleted when the last task that created or allocated the shared workspace terminates. The default workspace for a task and any private workspaces for the task are deleted when the task terminates.

In general, any name-space objects (such as handles, links, and nodes) that are created by Name Services functions are created within the workspace that is associated with the call. This frees the writer of a shared service from having to worry about returning the memory that is associated with objects. When a nondefault workspace is deleted, all the memory objects associated with it are deleted. This will cause the deallocation of any port send rights that are associated with the workspace.

Some of the Name Services API functions do allow the option of explicitly supplying memory for certain name-space objects. For example, the NameSearchAndNotify and NameSearchNext functions can be used to choose to supply memory for the stack object that is returned when a call is made. If you do not choose to supply space for a stack object, then the functions will allocate storage for the stack object in the associated workspace.

Developer's Tip: In general, it is recommended (for reasons of both simplicity and performance) that you allow the Name Services functions to perform implicit memory management within your workspace.

Transaction Management Functions

A Name Services transaction allows multiple calls to the Name Services API functions (that can be used to modify information in one or more portions of the name space) to be treated as an all-or-nothing change. A transaction is defined over a name-space subgraph, which can cross name-space boundaries. Not all Name Services support transactions. At this time, only the System Registry supports transactions.

Only one task can be performing transaction management in a particular name-space subgraph at a time. During name-space transactions, other tasks have the right to look into that subgraph, but they do not have the right to change that subgraph while another task has a transaction in progress. The other tasks will see only the complete effect of a transaction on the subgraph.

Because a name space subgraph is bound to a single workspace, this implies that a transaction is also bound to that single workspace. However, there can be multiple separate transactions underway in a workspace at the same time. Similarly, there can be multiple separate transactions underway in different workspaces at the same time.

Name Services transactions can create nodes, modify nodes, create links, modify links, and delete links (which might, in turn, cause nodes to be deleted). All these changes are temporarily made in the transaction's workspace until the transaction is committed.

The Transaction Management functions are described in the following list:

- Use NameCreateWork to create a transaction handle for a name space subgraph. The subgraph is described in the same manner as is used in the Search/Notify functions. A starting node handle and the number of link levels is provided by NameCreateWork. A transaction handle is returned.

- Use NameStartWork to start a transaction. You must provide a transaction handle that identifies the name space subgraph that is affected.

- Use NameCheckPointWork to commit a set of changes from the workspace and to continue the transaction.

- Use NameCommitWork to commit a set of changes from the workspace and to complete a transaction.

- Use NameAbortWork to end a transaction. All region modifications that have not yet been committed are discarded from the workspace.

Shared Services

This chapter describes how shared services for Microkernel-based operating systems are structured. It tells you how shared services interact with the Microkernel to allocate memory, create threads, register themselves with the system name space, and communicate with each other.

Introducing Shared Services

Shared services for Microkernel-based operating systems can be mapped into the old notion of subsystems or resource managers. They perform a specific set of functions to manage or control a specific set of resources. Because they perform functions (such as File Services) useful to all operating systems, they can be shared by all operating system services. Because they perform functions (such as Name Services) useful to other subsystems, as well as to operating systems, they can be shared or used by other shared services.

Shared services for Microkernel-based operating systems are typically divided into two parts:

- A client library
- A services task (or server)

A shared service provides a client library (also known as a *shared library*) that consists of the programming interface for client tasks that want to use the service. Client libraries are typically written as sets of shared (DLL) code that are linked into the client task address space. The client library hides from the client task the details of how the client library and service task communicate.

The service task contains the code that actually performs the service that has been requested. The service task executes within its own address space, separated from the client task that requests the service.

The client library, on behalf of the client task, communicates with the server task through the IBM Microkernel Interprocess Communication (IPC) or Remote Procedure Call (RPC) facilities, as shown in the callouts in Figure 5-1:

Figure 5-1. Example of Shared Services Communication

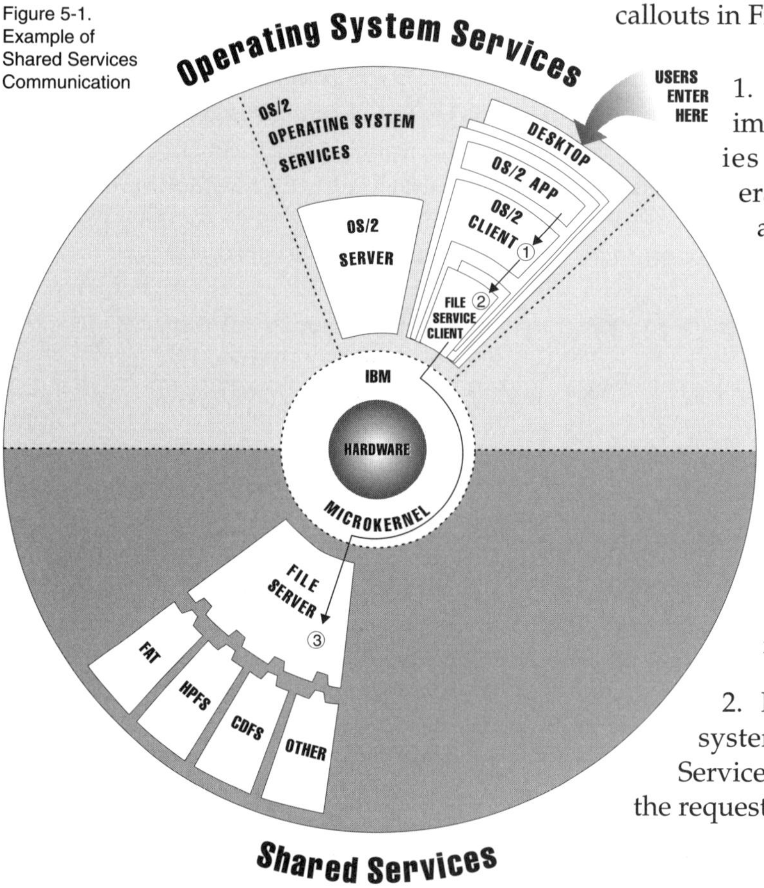

1. An OS/2 application imports the client libraries of the OS/2 Operating System Services, as well as the client libraries of shared services (such as File Services). This means that client libraries run in the address space of an application. When an OS/2 application calls an OS/2 function, the OS/2 client library fields the request.

2. If the function is a file system function, the File Services client library fields the request.

3. The File Services client library routes the file system function request to the File Server, via the IBM Microkernel, where the function is performed.

The code in the OS/2 application never really "sees" the File Server. It merely calls a function and gets a result.

Separating the client task from the service task has the following advantages:

- It protects the service task from program failures in a client task. This makes it less likely that a failure in one client task could negatively affect other clients of the shared service.

- It makes it simpler for the shared service to manage concurrent service requests from multiple clients. The IBM Microkernel IPC mechanism is used to queue incoming requests. The service task chooses to spawn multiple threads to perform concurrent service processing.

- It provides an architectural model that is easily extended. Because the details of the communication mechanism are hidden from the client task, the service task can reside on a separate computer system.

The client/service task separation has one important potential disadvantage—the reliance on the IBM Microkernel IPC facilities adds overhead to the shared service. This overhead includes both the expense of sending messages between the client task and the service task and also the cost of context switching between the client task and the service task.

Developer's Tip: If the cost of the intertask communication between the client library and the service task is unacceptable, the entire shared service can be designed to execute solely as a client library. That is, the code that performs the services is contained in the client library; there is no "server" associated with this kind of shared service.

When a shared service is completely contained within a client library, the client library must allocate the memory objects that it requires to service its clients. While some of these memory objects are unshared (unique to one client task that is using the client library), the client library typically needs to allocate shared-memory objects so that it can coordinate concurrent service requests from different client tasks.

While this use of shared code and shared memory offers less overhead on a single local system than the use of a separate service task, it is significantly less robust than the use of a separate service task. Software failures in a client task—either accidental or unexpected—that modify the client library shared memory have fatal consequences for other client tasks of the shared service.

The use of shared memory is not an efficient way to perform IPCs for distributed systems. For distributed shared services (for example, shared services that support distributed or nonlocal clients), shared memory should not be used for IPC. For this reason, it is generally suggested that shared services for Microkernel-based operating systems, such as OS/2 Warp Connect (PowerPC Edition), be designed to perform critical processing in separate service tasks.

Developer's Tip: Shared services should depend on, or use, only Microkernel services provided with the IBM Microkernel (such as Name Services) or other shared services (such as File Services) that are part of OS/2 Warp Connect (PowerPC Edition). Shared services should not use services provided by operating system services, such as the OS/2 Operating System Services for OS/2 Warp Connect (PowerPC Edition). Shared services that use services provided by a specific operating system service cannot be "shared" by other operating system services.

Memory Management

Shared services for Microkernel-based operating systems use memory management Microkernel services to request virtual memory regions. The service task typically requires only unshared memory regions. The service task uses these regions for private storage, which includes storage for the objects that it parcels out to the shared service clients. The client library uses both shared and unshared memory regions. If a shared service is implemented entirely as a client library, then shared memory regions are used to hold information that describes and coordinates the shared service clients.

A shared service allocates the following two types of shared memory regions:

Noncoerced shared memory A memory region that is shared in multiple address spaces but that is mapped to different virtual addresses in each participating address space.

Coerced shared memory An allocated memory region that is forced to be at the same virtual address in all tasks that share the region.

Both types of shared regions are used to share data between different tasks. However, coerced shared-memory regions are used in the following ways that noncoerced shared-memory regions cannot be used:

- They contain pointers that point within the region.
- Tasks that share the region pass pointers back and forth into the region.

Allocating Memory Regions

You allocate a page of memory from the address space of a shared service task by calling the IBM Microkernel's vm_allocate function. vm_allocate is used for all memory allocations—shared, private, coerced, or noncoerced. In general, you use the vm_ functions to allocate local heaps, which are then used in suballocation requests. These functions are similar to the OS/2 DosAllocMem function.

When you use vm_allocate to allocate pages of memory, the IBM Microkernel Default Pager task pages them in and out of real memory. Initially, there are no access restrictions on pages allocated with vm_allocate. Protections are set with vm_protect.

Access Protections

Each memory region has two access protection values: the current access protections and the maximum possible protections. The protection values are ORed combinations of VM_PROT_READ, VM_PROT_WRITE, and VM_PROT_EXECUTE. The current access protections define the current access permissions for the pages of the region. The maximum protections define the bounds for vm_protect. You can change the protection values using vm_protect. The new protections specified in vm_protect must be a subset of the protections specified by the maximum protections.

Allocating Noncoerced Shared Memory Regions

You use the IBM Microkernel vm_remap function to share a page of memory allocated in one address space with another address space. The IBM Microkernel maintains independent attributes and protections for the shared region for each address space. Initially, the attributes and protections for the shared region in the target address space are copied from the source address space. Afterward, you can independently reset them by using vm_protect.

The key characteristic of memory shared in this way is that the shared region can be located at a virtual address in the target address space that is different from its location in the source address space. Therefore, data structures placed in the shared region memory must be position-independent; the data must not contain pointer values.

You can also allocate a shared page of memory and set the access protections by calling a single IBM Microkernel function, vm_map, instead of by calling vm_remap and then vm_protect.

Noncoerced shared memory is useful for service tasks that maintain control blocks of information for each of their clients. The service task has read and write access to the block, and the clients have read-only access to their control block. For example, the OS/2 Server maintains handle tables and thread and process information for each OS/2 operating system client task. These data structures are updated when the OS/2 operating system client task requests a Dosxxx function from the OS/2 Server.

Reserving Pieces of the Address Space

When you allocate a new memory region, you can locate it ANYWHERE (that is, the IBM Microkernel will find any available hole in the address space large enough to fit the new memory region) or in a RESERVED area of the address space. Arbitrary memory allocations cannot take chunks of reserved memory areas. Reserved memory areas play a role in the support of coerced general memory. You reserve areas of the address space by calling the IBM Microkernel vm_reserve system function.

Allocating Coerced Shared Memory Regions

Global memory regions are memory regions used for global data, visible to all tasks in the system. They are directly addressable, with exactly the same access protections, in every task in the system. Users that require more restricted control over the addressability of a memory region (that is, the ability to set per-task access protections) should use the system's coerced general-memory area.

In this area, memory is allocated in blocks where each block can have different access attributes for each task that has addressability to the block. Unlike the global area, memory regions allocated in the general area need to be explicitly remapped to allow sharing. This area is used for blocks of memory that must be mapped at the same address in each client task, but the tasks do not share the contents of the blocks (such as library instance data).

You allocate coerced shared memory in the same way that you allocate noncoerced shared memory, with the exception that you control the location of the remapped memory region.

Thread Management

Client libraries for shared services are written to run in different environments, such as OS/2 Warp Connect (PowerPC Edition). Hence, they are also called shared libraries. Shared libraries are unique in that they must depend on function supplied by the environment for creating threads, exiting from a thread, obtaining the thread identification, and manipulating the stacks of threads.

The root of a task is that portion of a program that is aware of its run-time environment. For example, the root of an OS/2 task is aware of the OS/2 run-time environment, while the root of a shared service task is aware of the IBM Microkernel run-time environment function.

An operating system service needs to know when a thread is created and terminated, must allocate the stack for the thread, and needs to make available information about the thread. Therefore, a shared library must be able to invoke run-time dependent entry points that perform these and possibly other functions.

Thread Management Services

A shared library normally exports symbols that are available to the root of the program and to other shared libraries. The reverse is not true; shared libraries do not import symbols from the root of the program. Therefore, there is a need for a mechanism to allow a shared library to access common interfaces. This mechanism is referred to as Operating System Abstractions.

Specifically, in order to achieve a common set of threading functions that support different environments, a set of threading functions is abstracted into a set of functions that a shared library can use. This abstraction layer implements the right threading for the particular environment.

It is important for the developer of a shared library to know that, although there are Microkernel services available for these functions, the shared library writer must call the equivalent Operating System Abstraction instead.

In general, all threading packages are based on IBM Microkernel threads, and there is a direct correspondence between any threading package thread and an IBM Microkernel thread. However, not all IBM Microkernel threading interfaces are directly invoked by a shared library because those threading functions are run-time dependent. Following is a list of those run-time dependent functions along with their corresponding abstraction:

ThreadCreate	Create a thread.
ThreadExit	Exit from a thread.
ThreadStackUp	Obtain direction of stack growth.
ThreadGetId	Obtain the thread identification.
ThreadGetStack	Obtain the stack base of a thread.
ThreadGetStackSize	Obtain the stack size of the thread.
ThreadAtExit	Add a function to the per thread exit list.

Lock Services

A shared library needs locking primitives to synchronize between threads. These functions are memory-based locks—as opposed to port-based locks. They are used only when synchronizing user threads in a local node, whether from within the same task or between threads of different tasks. Memory-based locks are allocated either in task local memory or in shared memory. However, it is the user's responsibility to allocate shared locks. In either case, the lock data structures are part of the user-task address space.

Semaphore Services

Shared services use IBM Microkernel semaphores, which are simple counting semaphores, with or without timeout. Memory-based semaphores are intended for use between threads within a task and between threads from different tasks. Semaphores can reside in task local memory or in shared memory. The user must make the necessary arrangements to designate a semaphore as shared.

Thread Management Guidelines

The following are thread management guidelines for the shared libraries:

- If a shared library needs to manipulate threads in any way, such as creating a thread or exiting a current thread, the Operating System Abstraction must be used, if one exists. Otherwise, the IBM Microkernel service is used.
- A shared library does not call the following IBM Microkernel functions:
  - thread_create
  - thread_create_running
  - thread_terminate
  - task_create
  - task_terminate
- To use any of the abstracted thread services, a shared library must include the abstraction's header file.
- A shared library cannot depend on environment variables, because there are no abstractions for *getenv* and *putenv*. Instead, a shared library should export initialization functions that are called to provide environment variable information.
- A shared library cannot output strings directly to the user terminal. Another mechanism must be used instead.

- All shared libraries should be thread-safe and should use the provided memory-lock set library.

- Many shared libraries need to maintain per-thread data. It is the responsibility of the shared library to manage its own thread local data.

Intertask Communication

OS/2 Warp Connect (PowerPC Edition) shared services use IBM Microkernel IPC or Named Pipes through the IBM Microkernel Pipe Services to communicate between their client libraries and their service task. While this communication is hidden from the client tasks (that is, it is hidden within the encapsulation provided by the shared services function definitions), the shared services writer must decide the best way to perform the intertask communication.

IBM Microkernel Interprocess Communication (IPC)

The IBM Microkernel IPC facility allows threads to receive messages through ports. Multiple clients send messages to a single service port. Ports are multiplexed into port groups so that a single thread waits for messages to come in on any of a set of ports. Send rights to ports are passed from one task to another, a standard way that a server task gives access to a client task. Name Services provide a standard way in which port rights are associated with well-known names, so that a client task, or the client library linked into a client task, can find and acquire send rights to a service task.

IPC messages pass information in two general ways:

- The information is completely contained within the message and is queued up as part of the message.

- The information is passed as out-of-line data, as a memory region that is pointed to by the message.

The IBM Microkernel manipulates out-of-line data memory regions by using copy-on-write semantics whenever the sender or receiver modifies any of the pages that comprise the memory region. Out-of-line data is a useful enhancement to performance, but should be used only for relatively large amounts of information (for example, greater than 8KB).

IPC provides a standard low-level intertask communication abstraction that is used by shared libraries (that is, the client associated with a shared service).

IPC supports client/service task termination notification semantics. They are a strictly local communication abstraction. They offer no heritage support for DOS or Windows clients.

IBM Microkernel Named Pipes

The named-pipe Microkernel services provide named-pipe semantics through a named-pipe intertask communication abstraction. A named pipe supports either simplex or duplex communication. A service task supports multiple clients on a single named pipe. It controls the number of clients that have concurrent access to a named pipe. Messages within a pipe are either destructively read or nondestructively peeked. Data is read from a pipe in either a raw (byte-by-byte) fashion or in a message-oriented fashion.

Named pipes are typically more expensive to use than IPC. However, they provide a higher-level set of communication services than IPCs.

Named pipes support client/service termination notification semantics.

Given Network Redirection support on an OS/2 Warp Connect (PowerPC Edition) system, named pipes are used as a seamless local and remote communications abstraction.

Named pipes are used to communicate with DOS and Windows clients. The DOS and Windows clients are a named pipe, functioning as though they are merely reading and writing to a simple file.

IBM Microkernel Name Services

For shared services that utilize one or more service tasks, it is necessary to establish intertask communication between the shared services client libraries and the service tasks.

- If named pipes are used for intertask communication, then all the client libraries have to know is the name of the named pipe.

- If IBM Microkernel IPC functions are used for intertask communication, then each service task must register with the root of the system name space.

Registering a Shared Service

A service task registers itself during its initialization with the system name space by creating a leaf node that represents the service task. The link pointing to the service-task leaf node must have a name that is well known to its client libraries. This is because the client libraries follow a well-known path through the name space to the service-task leaf node.

The service-task leaf node is placed within the subgraph underneath the /service directory node. The name space subgraph under the /service directory node contains leaf nodes that represent registered system service tasks. Some portions of the /service subgraph might be several layers deep. This allows the /service subgraph to be capable of representing shared services and shared service classes that contain multiple service tasks.

The service-task leaf node has its service port value attribute set to contain a send right to the port that the service task uses to accept service requests. The service task must be preregistered in the name space each time it is created because its service request port changes each time it is allocated.

The service-task leaf node also contains any other attributes that the service task desires. Typically, these other attributes are read by the client library and used in establishing communication with the service task.

When the service task has registered itself within the system name space, it is ready to start accepting service requests.

The shared service deallocates all its service-task leaf nodes as part of its termination logic.

Shared Services Configuration Data

The persistent portion of the system's name space is a useful area to place configuration data for shared services. Because Name Services support transaction semantics within the name space, shared service configuration data is protected from being incompletely updated as a side effect of some other software or hardware failure.

The shared services installation procedure creates a configuration data subgraph in the system's name space and initializes the configuration leaf nodes appropriately. The root of this subgraph is at a well-known path location (that is, a path that is known to the components of the shared service).

A shared service can encapsulate name space updates within higher-level functions exported by the service or publish the topology and structure of the service's configuration leaf nodes. In general, it is recommended that shared services hide the format of their configuration data within their own configuration functions.

Temporary and Persistent Data

A shared service can use the system name space as a storage repository for temporary and permanent data that it creates and manipulates.

The name space is useful for holding structured data, but should not be used to store large amounts of nonstructured data. Nonstructured data is typically best stored within simple sequential files. There is more overhead associated with name space storage than with simple file I/O.

OS/2 Operating System Services

This chapter provides information about the OS/2 Operating System Services that come with OS/2 Warp Connect (PowerPC Edition). The OS/2 Operating System Services provide the same 32-bit application programming model that is offered in OS/2 Warp and OS/2 Warp Connect for the Intel family of processors.

This chapter describes how the OS/2 Operating System Services help manage processes and threads, scheduling, and exceptions. It also describes the OS/2 Loader and provides information about Debug support and memory management. This chapter provides information about semaphores, pipes, queues, and the System Management Services.

Introducing OS/2 Operating System Services

OS/2 Warp Connect (PowerPC Edition) provides operating system services through a set of client libraries that interface to multiple servers that run on top of the IBM Microkernel. This set of client libraries and multiple servers supports many of the same 32-bit OS/2 application interfaces (API functions) that were available in previous releases of OS/2 Warp. Additionally, there are many new 32-bit functions.

Developer's Tip: This support means that you do not need to wait for OS/2 Warp Connect (PowerPC Edition) Developer's Toolkit to begin developing applications. You can use your existing OS/2 Warp Developer's Toolkit (for Intel-based systems) now to develop applications that are enabled for the future.

Develop your applications in a reasonably high-level language, such as IBM C. Be sure to use the 32-bit OS/2 Warp interfaces. Then, develop and test your application.

In the future, simply recompile your application using an edition of IBM C Set/2 for the PowerPC and you will have most of the work behind you. A recompile, some testing, perhaps some performance tuning, and you will be ready for prime time.

For more information about developing applications, refer to Chapter 16, "Application Development" on page 339.

OS/2 Servers

The multiple servers contained in the OS/2 Operating System Services exist as separate tasks, running independently and asynchronously. This separation provides for improved performance and reliability. In addition, the servers are re-entrant and can provide their services to multiple clients without unnecessary interference and blocking.

The following OS/2 servers are described in this chapter:

OS/2 Server The OS/2 Server coordinates the startup and shutdown of your programs. It provides a broad variety of operating system services, such as thread management, exception handling, and virtual memory management.

Pipe Server The Pipe Server controls and provides access to all OS/2 named pipes, both local and remote.

System Management Server The System Management Server provides software and hardware service aids that help diagnose and solve problems.

The following OS/2 servers are described in separate chapters:

File Server The File Server provides file services by acting as both an access and support framework for the Physical File Systems (PFSs). The PFSs provide the actual support for the physical file system such as FAT and HPFS.

For more information on the File Server, refer to Chapter 7, "File Services" on page 125.

Event and Window Server The Event and Window Server is the single point of control providing for the sharing of the console devices among processes and programs. It coordinates the management of OS/2 sessions and windows, and it handles the delivery of keyboard, pointer, and timer events throughout the system.

For more information on the Event and Window Server, refer to Chapter 8, "Presentation Services" on page 139.

Multiple Virtual Machine (MVM) Server The MVM Server supervises the execution of DOS and Windows program sessions. The MVM Server can supervise Multiple Virtual DOS Machine (MVDM) tasks. Each Virtual DOS Machine provides an independent execution environment for one or more DOS/Windows programs.

For more information about the MVM Server, refer to Chapter 10, "DOS/Windows Services" on page 205.

OS/2 Client Libraries

When an OS/2 program is loaded into the computer, the system automatically links the program with the OS/2 Operating System Services. This process is called *dynamic linking*. Dynamic linking connects the program to the client libraries. Programs refer to client libraries to get access to the functions they call. Dynamic linking is a style of linking libraries at run time rather than at compile/link time.

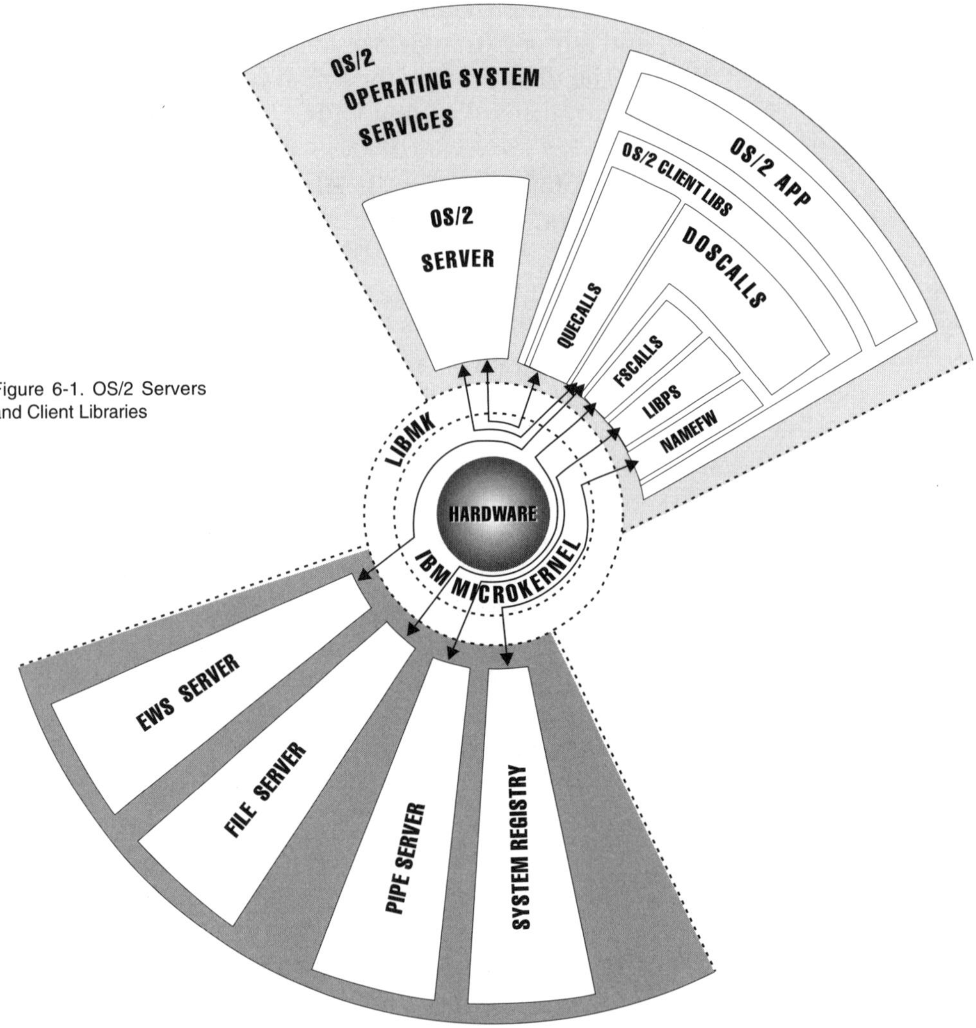

Figure 6-1. OS/2 Servers and Client Libraries

The following client libraries provide access to the 32-bit OS/2 API functions. They also provide compatibility with previous releases of OS/2:

DOSCALLS.DLL This library contains most of the heritage OS/2 control program type interfaces (for example, DosExecPgm and DosAllocMem). With a few exceptions, this DLL provides access to the OS/2 Server.

The most notable exceptions are the File Services (for example, DosOpen, DosRead, DosWrite, DosClose, and so on), which are provided by the File Server.

QUECALLS.DLL This library contains heritage OS/2 queue interfaces (for example, DosReadQueue, etc). Queue interface support is provided for local queues (those defined within your computer) and for remote queues (those defined in another computer).

LIBPS.DLL This library contains the heritage OS/2 pipe interfaces (for example, DosReadPipe). All of these services are implemented in the Pipe Server, both for local pipes (those defined within your computer) and for remote pipes (those defined in another computer).

Other heritage DLLs, such as PMGRE.DLL, PMGPI.DLL, and PMWIN.DLL, provide Presentation Manager functions to applications. These functions are described in Chapter 8, "Presentation Services " on page 139.

The following client libraries are new:

FSCALLS.DLL This library provides direct, low-level access to the File Server, which is part of File Services. This library is invoked from within DOSCALLS.DLL.

NAMEEFW.DLL This library provides access to the Name Services API functions.

LIBMK.DLL This library provides direct access to the Microkernel services. This library is referenced from within all other functions.

The OS/2 Server

The OS/2 Server is responsible for a number of operating system services. It manages processes and threads, handles scheduling, priority, and exceptions, loads the operating system tasks, provides debug-related exception handling, manages memory, and provides semaphore and queue support.

Process and Thread Management

An OS/2 *process* refers to any number of things that are happening when the operating system or an application is running. In simplified terms, when the user presses a key on the keyboard or an application requires more memory or an error occurs, a process is happening.

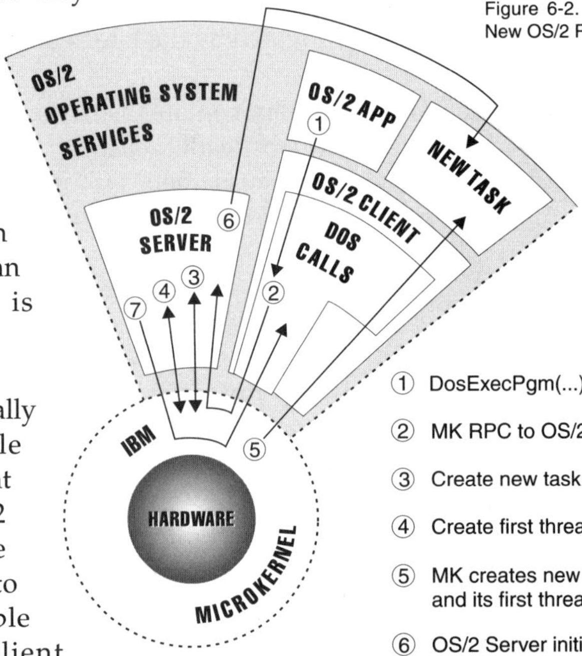

Figure 6-2. Creating a New OS/2 Process

① DosExecPgm(...)
② MK RPC to OS/2 Server
③ Create new task
④ Create first thread
⑤ MK creates new task and its first thread
⑥ OS/2 Server initializes new task as an OS/2 application
⑦ MK RPC return to OS/2 application

All OS/2 processes are logically connected to the multiple servers by the multiple client libraries. When an OS/2 program calls a function, the execution logic branches to code in one of the multiple client libraries. The client library will frequently then package and send a request to one of the multiple servers via a Microkernel message. For example, the DosExecPgm function (which is used to create a new OS/2 program) causes a branch to the DOSCALLS.DLL (client library). Inside DOSCALLS.DLL, a message is packaged and sent back to the OS/2 Server. The OS/2 Server then performs the activities necessary to start up the new OS/2 program. The OS/2 Server activities include calling the Microkernel to create a task, initializing the new task as an OS/2 process, and initializing the first thread of the task. When it completes these activities, the OS/2 Server sends back a response to the waiting thread in the

DOSCALLS.DLL. Then, the DosExecPgm function sends back a response to the calling program.

The OS/2 Server coordinates and handles process and thread management for all OS/2 processes. The OS/2 Server provides functions that can be used to perform the following process and thread management operations:

- Creation and termination
- Suspension and resumption
- Manipulation of thread priority
- Running exit-list routines upon process termination

OS/2 processes and threads map directly to Microkernel tasks and threads, however; the tasking component of the OS/2 Server keeps track of the OS/2-specific process and thread information. The process information is kept in the Per-Task-Data-Area (PTDA) control block and the thread information is kept in the Thread Information Block (TIB) control block. These control blocks are kept, for security reasons, within the private address space of the OS/2 Server (that is, the server side). Some OS/2 functions (for example, DosGetInfoBlocks) require access to these control blocks. Those portions of the control blocks are copied into the OS/2 process's address space (that is, the client side) so the process can directly read or modify them. This helps improve performance as it reduces the number of client/server transactions.

Process/Thread Creation and Termination

As previously mentioned, when an OS/2 process asks to create a new OS/2 process, it sends a process creation request message to the OS/2 Server via a Microkernel message. The OS/2 Server calls the Microkernel to create a new process and then again to create the first thread for the process. The OS/2 Server creates the PTDA for the new process and the TIB for its first thread. The OS/2 Server then calls the OS/2 Loader to initialize the address space for the new process. Once the address space is initialized, the OS/2 Server maps the appropriate portions of the PTDA and TIB in the new process's address space.

The OS/2 Server does not make Microkernel port rights directly available to the OS/2 process. It stores the TASK_KERNEL_PORT port right for the new process in the server-side version of the PTDA and the THREAD_KERNEL_PORT port right for the new thread in the server-side version of the TIB. The saved task and thread port rights are subsequently used by the OS/2 Server task when it needs to use Microkernel functions to manipulate the OS/2 process and thread state. A number of OS/2 functions (for example, DosSuspendThread) cause the OS/2 Server to issue Microkernel functions on behalf of the process.

The OS/2 Server also saves the new process and thread exception ports in the server-side versions of the PTDA and TIB. It maintains the *real* exception ports of the OS/2 process so that the OS/2 Server (instead of the Microkernel) is called when the process generates an exception. This allows the OS/2 Server to orchestrate OS/2 exception management in the same way that previous releases of OS/2 did.

During process creation, the OS/2 Server generates a new port that can be used to receive subsequent calls to functions from the OS/2 process. It passes back a send right to the port, and the send right is stored in the client-side version of the process's PTDA. The OS/2 Server maintains a pool of threads that waits for requests from the client processes. All the OS/2 Server request ports are bound into a single port set so that an OS/2 Server thread can wait for a request from any of its clients.

Whenever the client process uses the DosCreateThread function to create a new thread, the OS/2 Server calls the Microkernel to create a new thread and then appropriately sets up both the server and client versions of the TIB.

The OS/2 Server is also involved in the mapping of OS/2 handles to Microkernel ports. Although the definition of a handle was provided in Chapter 3, "The IBM Microkernel," it is repeated here, just to clarify how handles are used by the OS/2 Server. An OS/2 handle is an abstraction that allows OS/2 to rapidly identify a resource (such as a file, a named pipe, shared memory, and so on) that is being referenced by the calling program. Many OS/2 functions, such as DosOpen, require the calling program to identify the resource by name and then return a handle that the calling program uses in additional calls (for example, DosRead and DosWrite). This identification helps the program to later quickly locate the resource, as needed.

A Microkernel resource (when it underlies an OS/2 resource) is represented by a port send right. These port rights are typically stored within the OS/2 Server address space, which prevents an OS/2 process from inadvertently damaging port rights that it is unaware of.

When an OS/2 process is terminated, the OS/2 Server first runs any OS/2 exit-list routines that have been registered by the process. Then, the OS/2 Server *cleans* up the OS/2 resources that were being used by the process. When a thread within an OS/2 process is terminated, the OS/2 Server first calls the Microkernel to destroy the analogous Microkernel thread. The OS/2 Server then removes the server and client versions of the analogous TIB.

OS/2 Process and Thread Scheduling

OS/2 Warp Connect (PowerPC Edition) supports prioritized and preemptive scheduling of OS/2 processes and threads. Processes and threads that are created by the OS/2 Server are prioritized by the OS/2 Server and then passed to the Microkernel so that the Microkernel can properly schedule the OS/2 processes and threads. Processes and threads have priority classes, and, within the priority classes, there is a set of priority levels. OS/2 processes can modify their own or another process's priorities. The four classes of scheduling priorities that OS/2 Warp Connect (PowerPC Edition) provides are:

Time-Critical The highest-priority class. It ensures that the OS/2 process always receives time slices before any other priority class. Time-critical threads have a static priority that is not varied by the OS/2 Server. Within the Time-Critical class, threads are scheduled among themselves in priority-level order, with round-robin scheduling of threads that have equal priority.

Fixed-High This next class (obviously) executes before the remaining two classes and executes only if there are no time-critical threads ready to run. Based on the activity of the system and that of the individual fixed-high priority threads, the OS/2 Server will vary the priority of the fixed-high threads around a base value. The base value can be set by the thread itself or other threads in the system.

Regular This class holds the majority of the threads in the system. As with the Fixed-High class, the OS/2 Server will vary the priority of a Regular-class thread around its base value.

Idle-Time This last class can execute only after all other classes. As with the Time-Critical class, Idle-Time threads have a static priority that is not varied by the OS/2 Server.

Within each of these priority classes, the OS/2 Server maintains a priority level for each thread. Each of the four priority classes has 32 priority-levels (0 to 31). A thread with priority-level 31 always receives a time slice before a thread with priority-level 30, and so on. The priority class and priority level of a thread can be set using the DosSetPriority function.

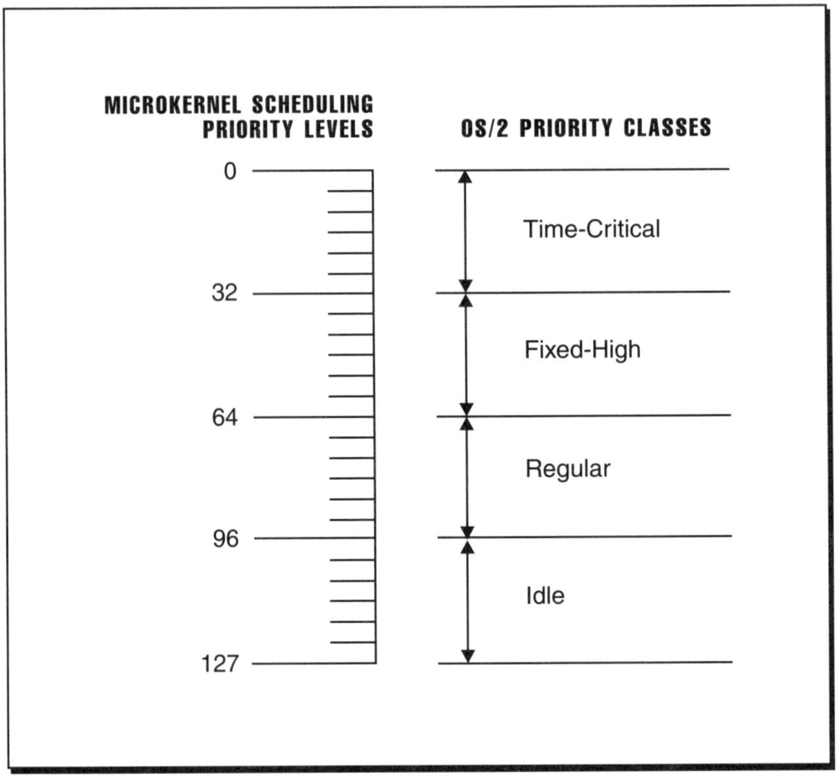

Figure 6-3. Mapping OS/2 Scheduling Priorities to Microkernel Scheduling Priorities

You can dynamically configure the OS/2 operating system to alter the priority of a process. The PRIORITY statement in the CONFIG.SYS file can be set to either ABSOLUTE or DYNAMIC (the default). If PRIORITY is set to the ABSOLUTE option, all processes receive processor time based on the priority that was established on the DosSetPriority function. If PRIORITY is set to the DYNAMIC option, OS/2 adjusts priorities based on system load and process activity and on whether the process is in the foreground (that is, whether it owns the window focus).

You can use the TIMESLICE statement in CONFIG.SYS to set the minimum and maximum amount of processor time allocated to processes and programs for both OS/2 and DOS sessions. The default is dynamic time slicing, which varies the size of the time slice based on system load and paging activity.

The Microkernel provides system calls that can be used to specify its scheduling policy and the priorities that are assigned to different threads. These system calls are protected; some are limited to holders of send rights to the PROCESSOR_SET_CONTROL port. Others (the ones that vary the priority of a specific thread) require the TASK_KERNEL_PORT of the containing task or the THREAD_KERNEL_PORT of the thread itself.

The OS/2 Server holds send rights to all of those ports and will pass them only to specially privileged tasks. The OS/2 Server uses the Microkernel scheduling functions to have the Microkernel enforce scheduling policies.

The Microkernel provides 128 scheduling priority levels. The OS/2 Server maps its four priority classes onto these 128 levels. It then tells the Microkernel to follow a round-robin scheduling policy.

While the Microkernel defaults to using 10ms time slices, the OS/2 Server uses the protected Microkernel system functions to dynamically change the time slice value as needed.

Exception Handling

An exception is an abnormal condition that can occur during program execution. There are two general classes of exceptions:

Synchronous Exceptions A Synchronous Exception is caused by the direct action of the executing thread (for example, divide by zero or invalid instruction). When the exception occurs, the thread's normal execution is interrupted and is redirected to the thread's registered exception handler. Once the exception is handled, normal processing is resumed.

Asynchronous Exceptions An Asynchronous Exception is caused by an event external to the executing thread (for example, signal exceptions or asynchronous process termination exceptions such as when a user presses Ctrl+Break). When this occurs, thread 1 of the OS/2 process is always used to handle the asynchronous exception.

In OS/2 Warp Connect (PowerPC Edition), exceptions can have two distinct origins:

Microkernel-Raised Exceptions These are synchronous exceptions that are typically hardware generated exceptions (for example, memory access violations, bad instruction encountered, divide by zero, and so on).

OS/2 Client-Side-Raised Exceptions These are asynchronous exceptions that are not considered exceptions by the Microkernel but are considered exceptions by OS/2. These exceptions are generated as a result of an OS/2 exception API (such as DosRaiseException, DosKillProcess, or DosSendSignalException).

The OS/2 Server supports an exception management architecture that allows multiple exception handlers to be registered and chained together. OS/2 processes can define exception handling routines that deal with different classes of exceptions. Exception handling routines can be specialized for different executing threads, and they can be nested as appropriate as an OS/2 application enters and exits from different levels of functions. When an exception handling routine in your application returns to the OS/2 Server, it informs the OS/2 Server whether the exception handler has appropriately handled the exception. When an exception handling routine returns an indication that it did not resolve the exception, OS/2 invokes the next exception handling routine in the chain. When no exception handling routine in the chain indicates that it successfully resolved the exception, then OS/2 terminates the process that received the exception.

The exception handling component of the OS/2 Server is responsible for handling exception messages received by the OS/2 Server. As described earlier, the OS/2 Server saves the OS/2 process's Microkernel task and thread exception ports. The OS/2 Server combines all of its exception ports into a single port set so that it can use one of its threads to wait for exception messages on behalf of any of its client processes. All exceptions raised by the Microkernel (for this task) arrive as messages to this OS/2 Server exception port set. The same exception port set is also used to receive signals and exceptions that are raised via OS/2 API functions. To raise an exception, the OS/2 client library sends a Microkernel message to the port set, which arrives at the OS/2 Server and is processed similarly to the Microkernel-raised exception.

When OS/2 functions are used to raise exceptions (such as DosRaiseException or DosSendSignalException), these functions cause the OS/2 client library to send a Microkernel RPC message to the OS/2 Server indicating what sort of exception the function wishes to raise. The exception to be raised can specify a different OS/2 process as its target. In this case, the OS/2 Server needs to dispatch the appropriate exception-handling routine to the process that was targeted by the OS/2 function.

Once the OS/2 Server receives an exception message on behalf of one of its client threads, it needs to dispatch the appropriate exception-handling routine within the process that was targeted by the exception message.

To dispatch an exception-handling routine, the OS/2 Server builds an exception record and places it on the targeted thread's stack. The OS/2 Server targets thread 1 of the client OS/2 process for asynchronous exceptions; it targets the thread that caused the exception for synchronous exceptions. The OS/2 Server triggers the dispatcher by using Microkernel functions to change the machine state of the targeted thread so that it will resume execution at the exception-handling routine dispatch logic within the OS/2 client library (DOSCALLS.DLL). When the targeted thread resumes execution, it starts dispatching exception handling routines in the client process. The exception handling routines run within the context of the targeted thread.

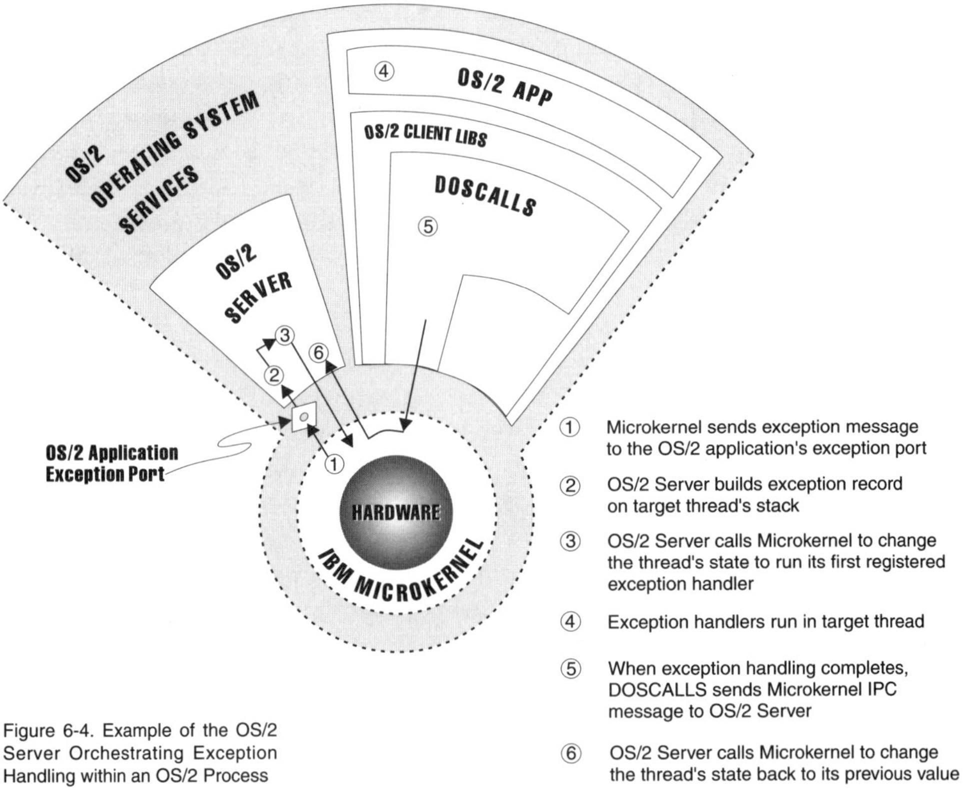

Figure 6-4. Example of the OS/2 Server Orchestrating Exception Handling within an OS/2 Process

When exception handling is completed, the targeted thread exits by returning to the OS/2 client library, which in turn continues by sending a Microkernel message to the OS/2 Server indicating the result of the exception handling exercise. If the exception was successfully resolved, the OS/2 Server resets the machine state of the client's targeted thread to continue from where it was earlier interrupted. If the exception was not successfully resolved, the OS/2 Server terminates the client OS/2 process.

The OS/2 Loader

The loader component of the OS/2 Server (often referred to as the OS/2 Loader) is responsible for loading executable files and also for managing the run-time loading and linkage of library modules. On OS/2 Warp Connect (PowerPC Edition), once the OS/2 Server is initiated, the OS/2 Loader takes over and becomes the single loader for all tasks on the system.

The OS/2 Loader automatically resolves all library module dependency chains when it initializes an OS/2 program for execution. The OS/2 Loader also provides support for execution time library module loading (using the DosLoadModule function).

The OS/2 Loader provides support for the loading of the resource files that are linked to an OS/2 program. It also contains support for querying module information.

The OS/2 Loader supports 32-bit Little-Endian modules that adhere to the ELF (Executable and Linking Format) load module format. The ELF format is new for OS/2 Warp Connect (PowerPC Edition). (OS/2 Warp on Intel-based systems uses the LX load module format for 32-bit OS/2 programs.)

Developer's Tip: When you recompile and relink a 32-bit OS/2 program so that it can be run on OS/2 Warp Connect (PowerPC Edition), the compile and link steps create an executable file in ELF format.

The OS/2 Loader uses the services of the Microkernel to acquire the virtual memory resources that it needs to set up a process's address space. It also provides support to the debug component of the OS/2 Server, thereby allowing breakpoints to be appropriately inserted and removed.

The OS/2 Loader is responsible for performing *fix-ups* on pages of code whenever they are brought into memory. The ELF format reduces the need for dynamic relocation of pages of code. This is because the LX format is based on the use of position-dependent code. In position-dependent code, the offsets contained within individual machine instructions typically point to locations that are not known until run time. Whenever position-dependent code pages are brought into memory, the OS/2 Loader must fill in the appropriate displacements into the instruction offsets. ELF format, on the other hand, supports the use of position-independent code. In position-independent code, the relocation records of a library are applied to the data areas of the library rather than the code areas. The small exception to this policy is that code pages do contain a pair of tables (the Program Linkage Table, PLT, and Global Offset Table, GOT) that do need to be *fixed up* by the OS/2 Loader.

Debug Support

The OS/2 Server supports the well-known DosDebug function and manages debug-related exceptions (such as single step and breakpoint). DosDebug enables one OS/2 application to control the execution of another OS/2 application for debugging purposes. DosDebug is the heart of the various OS/2 assembler and high-level language debugger tools. The function permits the debugging application to perform a variety of operations on the debugged application that include:

- Setting breakpoints
- Reading and modifying the machine state of selected threads
- Reading and modifying program memory
- Single-stepping selected threads

The client libraries for DosDebug send Microkernel RPC messages to the OS/2 Server. The Microkernel sends exception messages to the OS/2 Server when debug exceptions occur.

The Debug component of the OS/2 Server controls the execution of threads being debugged. This includes suspending the threads when a breakpoint is encountered, resuming the threads, and changing the thread state according to parameters in the DosDebug calls.

The OS/2 Server uses Microkernel functions to accomplish these actions. Because the OS/2 Server holds the TASK_KERNEL_PORT right and all the THREAD_KERNEL_PORT rights for the process being debugged, the Debug component of the OS/2 Server has the right to ask the Microkernel to perform the appropriate control operations on the process and its threads.

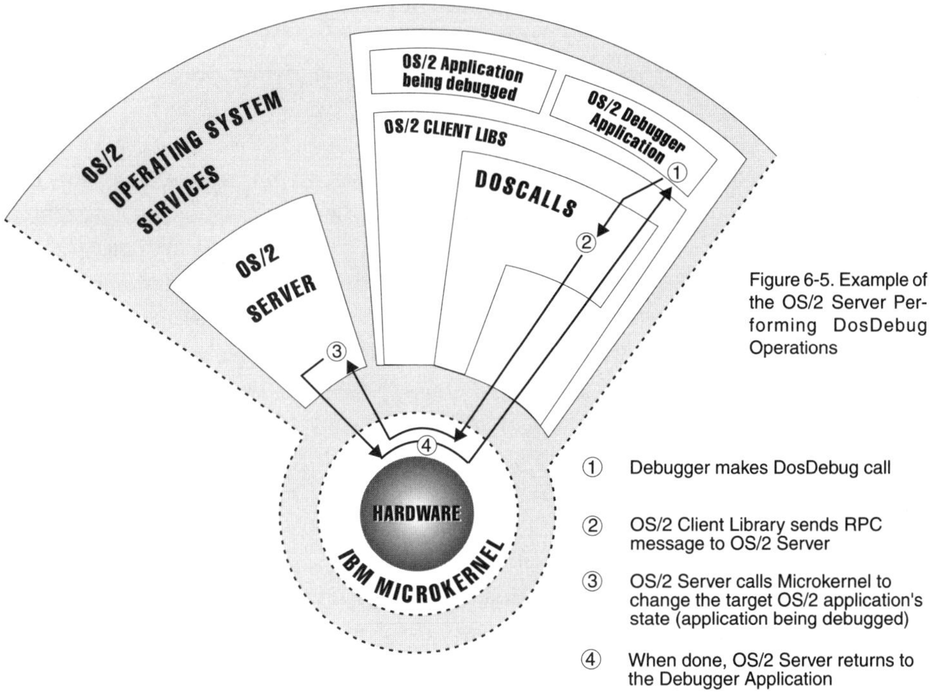

Figure 6-5. Example of the OS/2 Server Performing DosDebug Operations

Memory Management

The OS/2 memory management features support the manipulation of both private and shared memory objects within the virtual address space of an OS/2 process. OS/2 memory management support concentrates on three general classes of capabilities:

Private Memory Management Private Memory Management handles the allocation and deallocation of memory regions that are accessible to a single OS/2 process. These memory regions can be passed to OS/2 services such as DosRead even though they might ultimately call another server such as the OS/2 Server or the File Server.

Shared Memory Management

Shared Memory Management handles the allocation, control, access and deallocation of memory regions that are accessible by multiple OS/2 processes. These memory regions can either be named or unnamed, depending on how the program wants to handle the sharing of access to the memory regions.

Named shared memory regions can be accessed by another OS/2 process when that process requests the region by name. Unnamed shared memory regions must either be allocated to another OS/2 process, or some other form of communication must be used to pass their internal identifiers so that another OS/2 process can request access to them.

The creating process of a memory region controls how other processes can acquire the region and what access rights they will have to the region.

The use of shared memory as a basis for interprocess communication is frequently paired with other OS/2 IPC facilities such as Queues or Named Pipes.

Memory Heap Suballocation

After allocating a private memory region, an OS/2 process can *carve it up* by using the Memory Heap Suballocation services. OS/2 provides a set of suballocation functions that makes it easy for an OS/2 process to subdivide the heap into smaller portions for the process's use.

Suballocation is an inexpensive operation because it does not require OS/2 to invoke its memory allocation facility; it merely divides up virtual memory that has already been allocated. Because the OS/2 Server's memory allocation facility is not accessed (and the OS/2 Server is not called), the entire memory heap suballocation service is implemented in the DOSCALLS.DLL client library.

The OS/2 Server's memory management component extends the Microkernel memory management semantics in order to emulate OS/2 behavior with regard to shared memory and compressed data objects. Heritage OS/2 Warp programs expect specific behavior with regard to memory allocation and shared memory. (For example, they expect that all shared memory regions will be loaded at the same virtual address in all OS/2 processes that load the region.)

On a 32-bit PowerPC system such as the 601 or 604 processors, the 4GB of virtual memory is divided into 16 separate 256MB segments. OS/2 Warp Connect (PowerPC Edition) uses these 16 segments to organize the virtual address space of each OS/2 process.

Developer's Tip: The 16 segments described here are not the same construct as a segment on an Intel-based computer. To start with, an Intel segment is limited to just 64KB, which is not even close to these megabyte sizes.

On OS/2 Warp Connect (PowerPC Edition), the virtual address space of an OS/2 process is divided into the following four areas:

Microkernel Area The Microkernel Area starts at the 3.75GB virtual address. Segment 15 (as it is referred to) contains the IBM Microkernel, and all of its corresponding code and data.

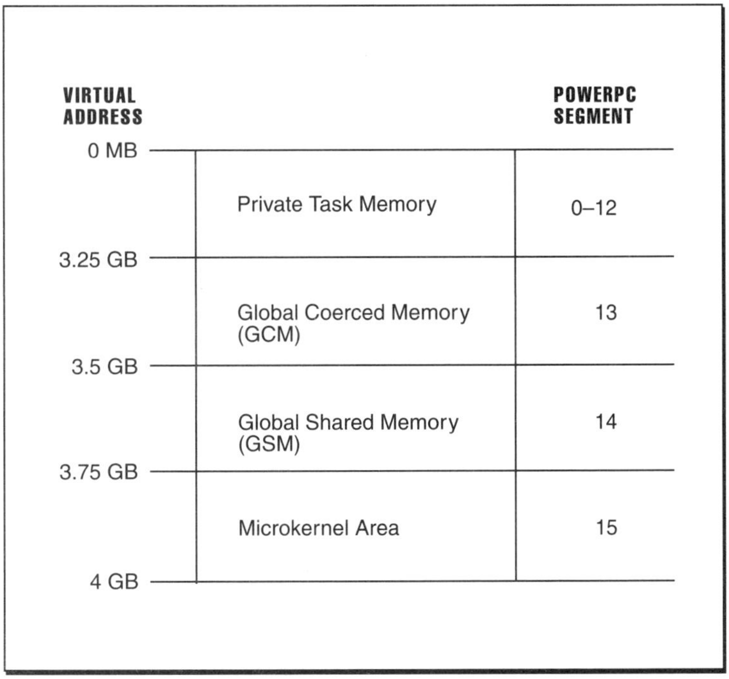

Figure 6-6. Virtual Space Layout for an OS/2 Process

Global Shared Memory Area

The Global Shared Memory (GSM) area contains only memory objects that are visible or accessible to all tasks in the system. No special action is required to gain access to these memory objects; they are there for the accessing! Typically, only the servers that make up the operating system (the OS/2 Server, the File Server, and so on) will have read/write access to regions in this area. Application programs will usually be restricted to read-only access to these objects.

The GSM area is used for the shared code and data of the client libraries, shared SOM meta-data, and any system services requiring global data (for example, the system's Major Event Trace Code bit map). The GSM area is implemented in PowerPC segment 14 and can contain 256 megabytes of code and data. As all the page tables for this area are shared across all tasks, when a context switch from one task to another occurs, the page entries for the GSM area are constant and do not need to be flushed.

Global Coerced Memory Area

The Global Coerced Memory (GCM) area contains memory objects that are shareable only if they are allocated in a manner that allows the same virtual address to be used in each task that is accessing the memory object (that is, the memory object is *coerced* to reside at the same virtual address in each task). In the GCM area, memory is allocated in blocks, where each block can have different access attributes for each task with addressability to the block.

Functions such as DosAllocSharedMem and DosGetNamed SharedMem use this area to get or give named shared memory. The memory objects then exist in each process at the same virtual address, and they are shared across multiple processes. This area can also be used for situations in which memory blocks must be mapped at the same address in all processes but the processes do not, in fact, share the block. This area can also be used for OS/2 unnamed shared memory (DosAllocSharedMem, DosGetSharedMem, and DosGive SharedMem).

Unlike in the GSM area, all tasks do not automatically have access to memory objects in the GCM area; they must explicitly request addressability to a GCM virtual address region to gain addressability to the shared region. The GCM area is implemented in PowerPC segment 13 and, like the GSM, is limited to 256MB in size.

Private Task Memory Area

The Private Task Memory area, as its name implies, contains virtual memory regions used for private purposes by an OS/2 process. Memory objects in this area are created through the DosAllocMem service and do not interfere with other processes' private memory objects.

This area is typically reserved for use by application programs and has been given the largest region of virtual memory. This area is made up of PowerPC segments 0 through 12.

The distinctions between these four areas is an OS/2 construct. With the exception of the Microkernel itself being mapped into the highest PowerPC segment (for universal addressability by all tasks), the Microkernel does not recognize these areas; it merely deals in the allocation and deallocation of memory objects. The OS/2 Server defines and implements the policy of how the memory objects are mapped in the virtual address spaces of individual OS/2 processes.

The OS/2 client library transmits OS/2 private and shared memory API requests to the OS/2 Server via Microkernel messages. The OS/2 Server memory management component handles memory allocation and deallocation by calling various Microkernel virtual memory management functions. In order to change the virtual address space of a client OS/2 process, the OS/2 Server must supply the TASK_KERNEL_PORT of the task (which the OS/2 Server maintains in the server-side copy of the process's PTDA).

Semaphore Support

OS/2 Warp Connect (PowerPC Edition) provides two classes of OS/2 semaphores, 32-bit *System Semaphores* and 32-bit *RAM Semaphores*.

System Semaphores

System semaphores are fully protected in the sense that they are maintained by OS/2 in protected memory. Also, OS/2 will automatically clean up the semaphore state in the event that an OS/2 process dies while holding ownership of one or more system semaphores. There are three types of system semaphores:

Event Semaphores Event Semaphores provide a signaling mechanism between threads, possibly in different processes, allowing the system and your applications to ensure that events occur and are processed in the desired sequence. Event semaphores are used by one thread to signal other threads that an event has occurred.

An event semaphore has two states, reset and posted. When an event semaphore is in the reset state, OS/2 blocks any thread that is waiting on the semaphore; when an event semaphore is in the posted state, all threads waiting on the semaphore resume operation.

Mutual Exclusion (Mutex) Semaphores A Mutex Semaphore is used to protect resources (such as files and data in memory) from simultaneous access by multiple threads (again, possibly in different processes). Mutex semaphores enable threads to serialize their access to resources.

When a thread requests ownership of a mutex semaphore that is already owned by another thread, OS/2 blocks the requesting thread; when more than one thread requests ownership of the same mutex semaphore, OS/2 queues the requests and grants ownership based on the thread's priority and the order in which the requests were received. When the owner of a mutex semaphore relinquishes its ownership, OS/2 passes ownership to the first waiting thread in its queue and allows that thread to resume execution.

Multiple Wait (Muxwait) Semaphores

Muxwait Semaphores enable threads to wait on several event or mutex semaphores simultaneously. They are compound semaphores that consist of a list of up to 64 event or 64 mutex semaphores (the two types cannot be mixed).

There is a two-by-two selectability in how a thread can wait on the muxwait semaphores: all in the list versus any in the list and released versus posted. Threads can choose to wait for all of the mutex semaphores to be released or for all of the event semaphores to be posted. Likewise, they can choose to wait for any of the mutex semaphores in the list to be released or for any of the event semaphores in the list to be posted.

System semaphores can either be named or anonymous. A named semaphore is always shared (that is, it is always available to any process that knows its name). An anonymous system semaphore can either be private to the threads of one process, or it can be shared among the threads of different processes. A shared muxwait semaphore must contain either all shared event semaphores or all shared mutex semaphores. However, a private muxwait semaphore can contain a combination of shared and private event or mutex semaphores.

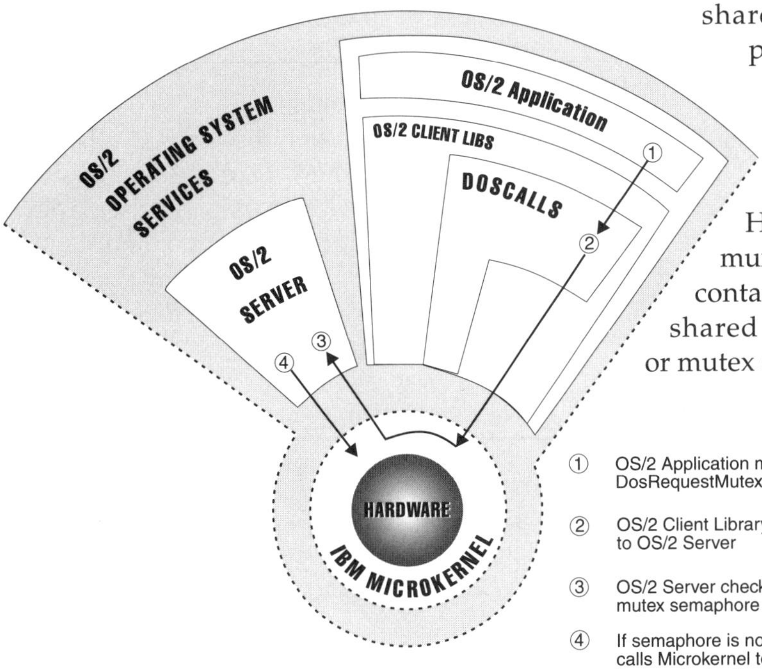

① OS/2 Application makes DosRequestMutexSem() call

② OS/2 Client Library sends RPC message to OS/2 Server

③ OS/2 Server checks to see if system mutex semaphore is available

④ If semaphore is not available, OS/2 Server calls Microkernel to suspend the thread that made the DosRequestMutexSem() call, until OS/2 Server gets confirmation that the semaphore has been released

Figure 6-7. OS/2 Semaphore Support

OS/2 permits a system-wide limit of 65536 (64KB) shared semaphores. In addition, each OS/2 process can use up to 64KB private semaphores.

The OS/2 Server handles the semantics of OS/2 system semaphores. The OS/2 client library causes all system semaphore functions to be translated into Microkernel messages to the OS/2 Server. The OS/2 Server maintains control information for every OS/2 system semaphore that is in existence. This means that all calls to query a system semaphore result in Microkernel messages, even in the case of requesting ownership of a mutex semaphore that is available for immediate ownership.

The OS/2 Server maintains all the queues of threads that are *pended* (waiting) on any system semaphore. It makes calls to Microkernel threads to suspend threads and to subsequently wake them up. It uses the THREAD_KERNEL_PORTs that are stored in the server-side TIBs to identify the threads to the Microkernel.

Whenever the OS/2 Server handles the death of an OS/2 process or one of its threads, it checks to see if any of the dying threads either owns any mutex semaphores or is waiting for a mutex semaphore or waiting for an event semaphore. If so, the OS/2 Server will clean up the system semaphore control state appropriately.

RAM Semaphores

The 32-bit RAM semaphores are new OS/2 synchronization resources available for the first time in OS/2 Warp Connect (PowerPC Edition). Like the OS/2 system semaphores, the 32-bit RAM semaphores provide a multiprocessor-safe semaphore mechanism. They should be used to protect small sections of code or memory where the expectation is that no wait will be necessary. The time for the no-wait case is very small, but the wait times might be longer than the wait times when using system semaphores.

There are four new OS/2 API functions associated with 32-bit RAM semaphores:

DosOpenRamSem Opens or creates a RAM semaphore structure. The first call to DosOpenRamSem for a given semaphore causes the OS/2 client library to allocate memory for the RAM semaphore. Once a RAM semaphore is opened by a process, it can be accessed by any thread within the process.

DosRequestRamSem Attempts to gain ownership of a RAM semaphore. If the semaphore is available, the OS/2 client library logic will place the identifier of the owning thread in the RAM semaphore structure. If the semaphore is not available, then the OS/2 client library must send a Microkernel message to the OS/2 Server so that the OS/2 Server can pend the calling thread until the RAM semaphore is made available. The OS/2 Server makes calls to the Microkernel threads to suspend the calling thread. In this case, the client library must also make an indication in the RAM semaphore structure that there are threads waiting for the RAM semaphore.

DosReleaseRamSem Releases ownership of a RAM semaphore. If there are other threads waiting for the RAM semaphore, the OS/2 client library must send a Microkernel message to the OS/2 Server so that the OS/2 Server can wake up any pended threads.

DosCloseRamSem Closes access to a RAM semaphore. Because a process must explicitly open and close RAM semaphores, the OS/2 client library and OS/2 Server will typically be able to clean up when the process is terminated.

However, because some of the RAM semaphore control state is maintained in the RAM semaphore structure (in client memory), it is possible that the control state can be overwritten by an errant RAM-semaphore using the process (for example, a bug in your program). This implies that RAM semaphores are not as safe as system semaphores. In the case where semaphore performance in the no-wait case is of paramount importance, this risk in semaphore integrity might be an acceptable design trade-off.

RAM semaphores are maintained as RAM semaphore structures in client virtual address space. They can be placed in shared memory regions so that multiple OS/2 processes can share them. For performance reasons, as much of the processing of RAM semaphores as possible is performed in the OS/2 client library (rather than in the OS/2 Server task).

Queue Support

An OS/2 queue is a named, ordered list of elements that is used to pass information between threads of the same process (related threads) or between different processes (unrelated threads).

Processes pass information to a queue in the form of elements. An element is a 32-bit unit of information. Queue elements can be values, flags, or pointers to shared (or private) memory regions. The format of a queue element is determined by the owner of the queue (the process that creates the queue). Only the queue owner can read elements from the queue. Other processes can write only to the queue. When an element is read, it is automatically removed from the queue. Queue owners have the option of peeking at entries on a queue, which does not remove the entries from the queue. Queue owners can also write to the queue. The owner of a queue determines the order in which elements are read from a queue. This allows OS/2 queues to be utilized in First-In-First-Out (FIFO), Last-In-First-Out (LIFO), or priority-based order.

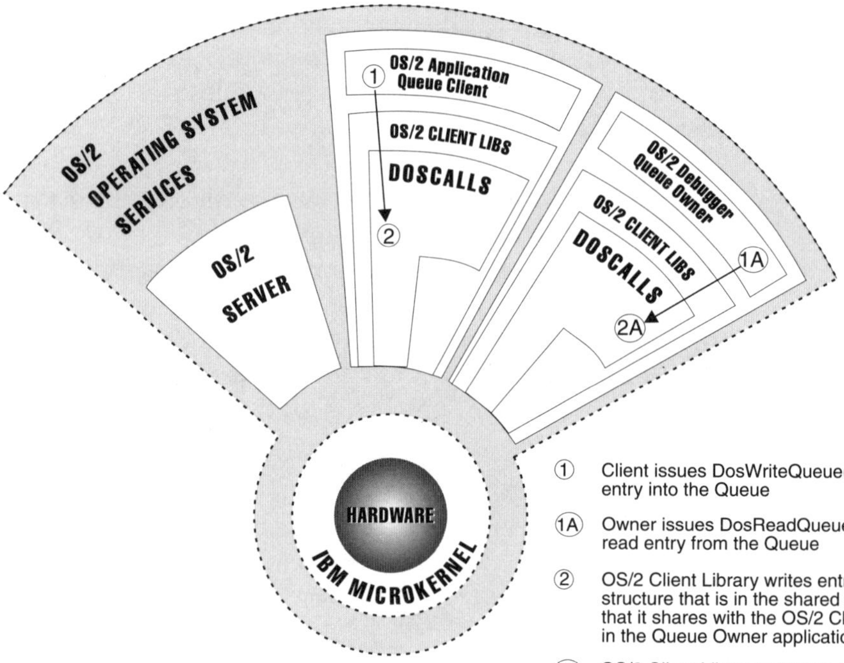

① Client issues DosWriteQueue() call to write entry into the Queue

(1A) Owner issues DosReadQueue() call to read entry from the Queue

② OS/2 Client Library writes entry into queue structure that is in the shared memory region that it shares with the OS/2 Client Library in the Queue Owner application

(2A) OS/2 Client Library attempts to read entry from the shared queue structure; if queue is empty and caller requested to wait until an entry is available, then the thread is put to sleep, waiting on an semaphore event

Figure 6-8. OS/2 Queue Support

A queue owner might want to wait until an element has been written to a queue before reading the queue. If so, the owner must explicitly provide an event system semaphore that OS/2 can use to suspend the owner until a write event places an element on the queue.

The owner of a queue is an OS/2 process, and, therefore, any of the owning process's threads can perform all ownership operations on the queue. The owner of the queue is referred to as the server process of the queue. Client processes open queues in order to pass information (via the queue) to the server process. All the threads within a client process (for a queue) gain the ability to write elements to the queue.

In OS/2 Warp Connect (PowerPC Edition), all of the queue-oriented system logic is contained on the client side (and is contained within QUECALLS.DLL). When an OS/2 process calls the DosCreateQueue function to create a queue, the OS/2 client library creates a queue data structure in the coerced shared memory area. The new queue is accessible to any OS/2 process that chooses to open the queue. As additional memory is needed for new queue elements, the OS/2 client library allocates that memory in the coerced shared memory area at appropriate times.

Pipe Support

An OS/2 pipe is a logical buffer used to pass data between processes. A process writes to or reads from a pipe as if the pipe were standard input or standard output.

There are two types of pipes:

Unnamed Pipes Unnamed Pipes can be used only to transfer information between related processes (for example, a process's parent or child). A child process started by a parent process (via a call to the DosExecPgm function) inherits the read and write handles to any unnamed pipes created by its parent. This inheritance enables the parent process and the child process to communicate with each other in a duplex manner (that is, there is a separate line of communication in both directions). Unnamed pipes can be used to redirect the standard input and standard output files of the child process.

An unnamed pipe is closed when both the parent and the child close the handles that allow their access to it. No controls or permission mechanisms or checks are performed on operations to unnamed pipes.

Named Pipes

Named Pipes enable related and unrelated processes on either the same computer or different computers connected by a network to communicate with each other. Any process that knows the name of a named pipe can open and use the pipe.

The local name of a pipe always follows the \PIPE\pipename naming convention, which requires all local pipe names to start with the characters \PIPE\. You can access a remote named pipe by following the similar \\servername\PIPE\pipename naming convention. A single named pipe can be both a local pipe for processes in the server computer that it is defined in and a remote pipe for processes in the client computers accessing the server.

One process, the server process, creates the named pipe and connects to one end of it. The server process then creates one or more instances of the pipe. Other processes, the client processes, connect to an instance of the pipe by opening it using a call to the DosOpen function that is also used to access files through the File Server. The server and the clients can then pass data back and forth through the named pipe by calling the DosWrite and DosRead functions. The server process controls the access that client processes will have to the named pipe. The server process:

- Specifies whether the named pipe will be an inbound pipe (client to server), an outbound pipe (server to client), or a duplex pipe (communication in both directions).

- Controls how many instances of the named pipe will be open at a time (each client is connected to a separate instance of the pipe).

- Specifies whether data will pass through the pipe as bytes or as complete messages or records.

- Specifies whether child processes will inherit the named pipe and whether subsequent calls to the DosRead and DosWrite functions will suspend the caller or immediately return with error indications, such as when a pipe is empty (for DosRead) or full (for DosWrite).

As with an unnamed pipe, the server process can peek into an instance of a named pipe, as well as read from it.

Support for remote procedure calls over named pipes is provided by the DosCallNPipe function.

On OS/2 systems, OS/2 programs and DOS programs can intercommunicate via named pipes. The DOS program deals with named pipes as if they were sequential files.

On OS/2 Warp Connect (PowerPC Edition), the Pipe Server supports both unnamed and named OS/2 pipe processing. It handles the semantics of both local and remote pipe communication. The Pipe Server uses the Network Redirector tasks as communications vectors to remote pipes (such as named pipes that were created on remote systems).

Figure 6-9. OS/2 Pipe Support

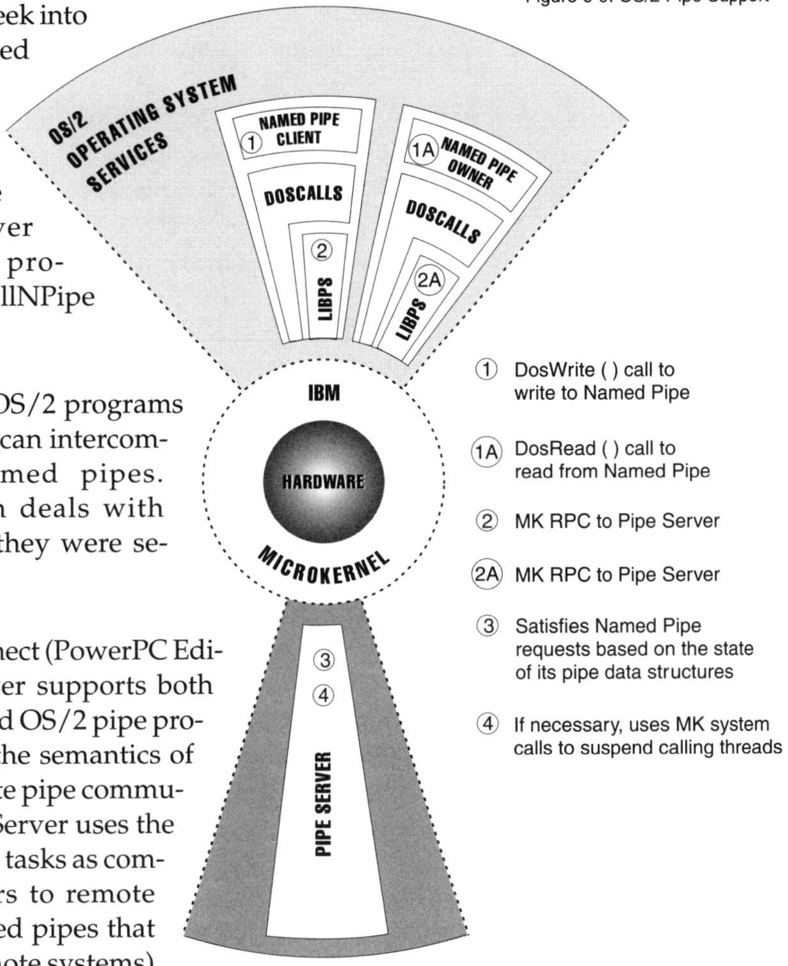

The Pipe Server and the Network Redirector tasks use the system name space for coordination purposes. When the Pipe Server task is initialized, it creates a directory node named /pipe under the root of the system name space. Every time a named pipe is created, the Pipe Server registers the named pipe in the system name space by creating a node for that named pipe under the /pipe directory node. The name of the node is the local name of the named pipe.

The Pipe Server task also creates a node under the /server directory node so that it can advertise the availability of its services. It places a Microkernel port send right to its service port within the node that it creates (the /server/pipe system name space node). The OS/2 client libraries can read that node in order to get a copy of the send right, which they can subsequently use to send Microkernel messages to the Pipe Server.

Network Redirector tasks also register themselves in the system name space. As part of its initialization, each Network Redirector task adds a name space node under the /network directory node.

Each time a pipe is created, the Pipe Server creates internal data structures that model the pipe and Microkernel ports that identify the pipe. In response to both pipe creation and open requests, the Pipe Server passes appropriate Microkernel ports back to the OS/2 client library. The OS/2 client library then stores the ports, creates local OS/2 handles that represent the pipe, and passes the handles back to the calling process.

When the OS/2 client library receives subsequent pipe requests, it converts local pipe handles into Microkernel port send rights and uses the send rights to send Microkernel messages to the Pipe Server. The Pipe Server combines its pipe ports into a port set so that it can employ a single thread to wait for requests concerning any of its pipes.

When a call is made to the DosOpen function and the call specifies the name in the form *servername**PIPE**pipename,* the request is passed along from the OS/2 client library to the Pipe Server. The Pipe Server uses its knowledge of the registered Network Redirectors (gained from the */network* portion of the system name space) to determine which of the redirectors (if any) provide access to the *servername* specified in the call. Once the connection is established, the Pipe Server passes remote writes directly to the appropriate Network Redirector task for transmission to the remote system.

When a Network Redirector receives a named-pipe open request message from a remote system, the Network Redirector calls the Pipe Server to open a local connection to the named pipe. When the Network Redirector receives named-pipe write messages from the remote system, it calls the Pipe Server to perform the write operation. Named-pipe read operations are always local because the Pipe Server internally buffers any data that has been written into the pipe.

System Management Services

The System Management Services provide an extensive set of capabilities that can be used to manage hardware, system software, and application software. The System Management Services provided are:

- First Failure Data Capture (FFDC)
- Software and Hardware Vital Product Data Logging (based on the Desktop Management Interface (DMI) standard)
- Event Trace Monitoring
- Performance Monitoring
- Resource Monitoring

First Failure Data Capture

First Failure Data Capture (FFDC) reduces the need for you to reproduce the failures and problems in your applications and OS/2 by capturing the data associated with a failure as soon as it is detected. Once a failure condition is detected, key internal state information can be logged for subsequent analysis. The primary FFDC tool is the First Failure Support Technology (FFST). FFST provides the FFSTProbe API functions that can be used to create failure data sets, which are collections of state information associated with the service being performed when a failure occurs.

FFSTProbe is used within all the OS/2 system code. It is also available for use by all OS/2 programs. Calls to FFSTProbe normally result in the addition of an error log entry to the System Error Log file. Calls to FFSTProbe can also result in the creation of custom dump files and event trace snapshot files.

FFSTProbe Placement

FFSTProbe deals with what to do when an error is detected. In particular, it is concerned with capturing sufficient failure-related data so that the error can be subsequently diagnosed and corrected. Some rules of thumb that you ought to be aware of:

- Make sure that your code contains appropriate defensive logic, such as verifying that the values passed in to you are correct.
- Use calls to the FFSTProbe function within each piece of defensive logic to capture important failure-related data in a uniform fashion.

The following is a short list of potential classes of errors that can occur within any software module and the associated data that are likely to be relevant for FFDC:

- A function you call returns an error. The relevant failure-related data might include:
  - The return code itself
  - Input parameters to the function
  - Output parameters from the function
  - Any internal variables that determined/affected the input parameters to the function
- Detection of corrupted component data structures. To catch this class of error during normal processing, your component must have designed some scheme for periodically *sanity-checking* important internal data structures. Such logic is an important step toward improving the reliability and availability of the component.

Relevant failure-related data might include:

- The component data structures themselves
- Any historical information that indicates when the component data structure was most recently found to be correct
- Any general system historical data that indicates what else has been executing on the system

- Unexpected timeouts and detected hangs. To detect timeouts and hangs, a component must be designed so that it has a sense of how long a given request should take and must set up and honor *watch-dog* timeouts around time-consuming algorithms.

  Relevant failure-related data might include:

  - Current timeout values
  - Any state information that describes what the timed-out function is currently doing
  - IPC-related state information that might explain the approximate cause of the timeout or hang (for example, the owners of relevant semaphores or the states of relevant pipes, queues, and IPC messages)
  - States of resources that might relate to the timeout or hang
  - Any historical information that describes what the timed-out function had been doing in the recent past

- Unexpectedly slow performance of a software module. Again, to be able to detect unexpectedly slow performance, a component must be designed so that it has a sense of how long a given service should take and how long it is taking.

Relevant failure-related data might include:

- States of internal resources that might relate to the slow performance of the service
- Any historical information that indicates who has been using that service and what requests the user made of the service

- Unexpected traps. It is usually awkward to detect a failure within an exception-management routine because it is much more difficult to deduce exactly what was being attempted at the time of the exception. Exception-management routines should catch only the few (we hope) failures that fall through an otherwise well-thought-out defensive programming design.

  Relevant failure-related data might include:

  - Exception blocks that contain the hardware state at the time the trap occurred
  - Any context data that helps indicate what was being executed at the time the trap occurred (for example, call stacks or internal state variables)

FFSTProbe Operation

A call to FFSTProbe is uniquely identified as a single location within a single software module. This gives you the ability to collect a variety of failure information, including process memory blocks, register values, and process and system control blocks.

Historical data is typically made available through the use of Event Trace entries. FFSTProbe can capture any system tracepoint data that is being collected at the time an error is detected. Alternatively, you can maintain a local *trace buffer* that continually maintains a small historical record. FFSTProbe would then just capture your local trace buffer as another region of local memory.

Each time a call is made to FFSTProbe, an Error Log record is created. The system automatically logs any software Vital Product Information that is registered for the software component that logged the error. You can also specify which failure-related informational and diagnostic messages you want to be associated with the Error Log entry.

A system Error Logging framework is used to log errors in the system Error Log file. The Error Logging framework also allows OS/2 programs to be notified whenever failures of different specified types are logged. The Error Logging framework can be used to trigger user or network failure notifications.

FFSTProbe is also dynamically controllable by the user. Each FFSTProbe can be controlled by a Probe Control Table (PCT) entry. PCT entries can be used to suppress FFSTProbe execution or to modify the action of an FFSTProbe. Among other things, the user can use PCT entries to cause the execution of a particular FFSTProbe to trigger a full system dump, instead of just perform its normal data capture. OS/2 Warp Connect (PowerPC Edition) provides a variety of integrated serviceability tools that can be used to examine and analyze the FFDC data:

- Error Log Formatter utility (SYSLOG)
- Event Trace Formatter utility (TRACEFMT)
- FFST Dump Formatter (FFSTDF)
- FFST Probe Control utility (FFSTPCT)

The tools are integrated in the sense that the user can choose a specific failure occurrence from the Error Log Formatter and then jump back and forth between the Error Entry itself and any Dump or Event Trace files (that have also been created by the FFSTProbe which caused the Error Log entry to be created).

System Dump

OS/2 Warp Connect (PowerPC Edition) provides a full system dump capability. System Dumps can be logged to preallocated hard-disk regions and can capture a full image of system memory at the time the dump was triggered.

The System Dump facility is configurable. The user can choose to have System Dumps triggered in a variety of manners:

- When a specified FFSTProbe is executed
- When a serious system failure is detected
- When the user types a specific hot-key sequence

After a System Dump is taken, the system will automatically reboot itself. When the system reboots and discovers that a new System Dump is logged, OS/2 will automatically call FFSTProbe. This call causes an Error Log record to be created that records the fact that a System Dump was taken.

A special tool, the Presentation Manager Dump Formatter (PMDF), is provided so that you can analyze System Dumps.

Software and Hardware Vital Product Data Logging

The Software and Hardware Vital Product Data (VPD) facility provides a framework within which to characterize the software and hardware components that reside on the system.

The VPD facility is based upon the use of the Desktop Management Interface (DMI) industry standard. The DMI standard is an open system management standard that was designed by the Desktop Management Task Force, a consortium of software and hardware companies that includes such members as IBM, Microsoft, Intel, Digital Equipment Corporation, Hewlett-Packard, Compaq, and Dell. The DMI standard was created to provide a local operating system framework that links network-management protocol agents to the hardware and software components running on the system. The DMI standard was specifically designed so that agents for the major existing network management protocols, for example, SNMP (Simple Network Management Protocol) and CMIP (Common Management Information Protocol), could be easily written to run on top of the DMI API set. The DMI standard was also designed so that a component needed to be extended only once so that it could be managed by any of the DMI-compliant network-management agents.

The DMI Service Layer provided with OS/2 Warp Connect (PowerPC Edition) can be accessed from the OS/2, DOS, and Windows environments. The DMI Service Layer exports a standard API layer (the DMI Management Interface, MI, layer) that management applications and network-management protocol agents can program to. It also exports a standard SPI (Service Provider Interface) layer (the DMI Component Interface, CI, layer) that hardware and software component vendors can write to. Each component is described in a special data description file, the DMI Management Interface Format (MIF) file.

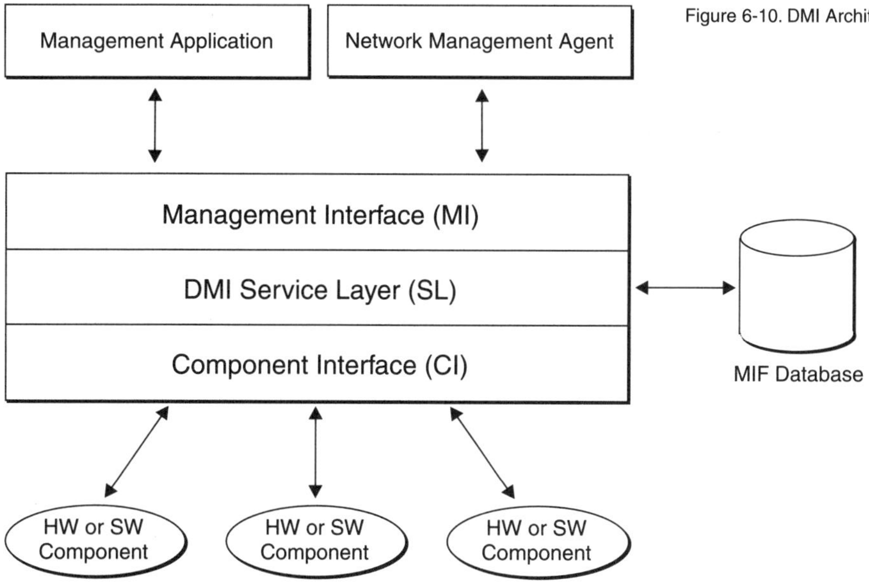

Figure 6-10. DMI Architecture

In addition to providing DMI support for generalized network management of OS/2 systems, the DMI framework also serves as the heart of the OS/2 Software VPD facility.

Every software product that is installed with the Software Installer facility provides a set of vital product information that includes:

- Product Name
- Manufacturer Name

- Product Revision Level
- Product ID
- Modification Level
- Fix Level

This software VPD information is stored within the software-inventory object that is created when the software product is installed. The Software Installer facility provides a dynamic DMI component that allows this software VPD information to be made available to other components that use the DMI Management Interface functions. These components include the Error Logging facility and the OS/2 SYSLEVEL utility (an OS/2 tool that can be used to report about the various software products that are installed).

Because the software VPD facility is based on the DMI framework, it is also possible for software products that are not installed with the Software Installer to register themselves with the software VPD facility. All such software products need only create a DMI component that contains the same DMI-standard component groups as the DMI components registered by the Software Installer on behalf of the software products that it installs.

While OS/2 Warp Connect (PowerPC Edition) does not contain an explicit hardware VPD facility, many hardware component vendors can use the DMI Component Interface to register both VPD and dynamic monitoring/control information for their components.

Event Trace Monitoring

Event Tracing allows a user to query and sample running systems in order to better understand the operation of those systems. Event Trace functions and an enhanced version of the OS/2 Trace formatter are provided for this purpose. OS/2 Warp Connect (PowerPC Edition) system components are designed with trace points so that they can be effectively serviced. The Event Trace functions are also available to OS/2 application developers.

You can use the OS/2 TRACE utility to turn tracepoints on and off. When a tracepoint is turned on, it is considered to be active. Whenever an active tracepoint is executed, a tracepoint entry is created within the system trace buffer.

There are two ways in which the tracepoint entries can be logged to Event Trace files:

- The OS/2 TRACELOG utility allows you to specify that all tracepoint entries are to be automatically logged to Event Trace Log files.

- If the TRACE utility is used to turn on tracepoint activity, but you do not use the TRACELOG utility to specify continuous Event Trace Logging, then the tracepoint activity is assumed to be intended as an adjunct to FFST and FFDC processing. In this case, whenever FFSTProbe executes, a snapshot of the system event trace buffer will be captured and then saved as an Event Trace Log file (which is pointed to by the Error Log record generated by FFSTProbe).

The OS/2 TRACEFMT utility is used to view logged Event Trace entries. TRACEFMT can be used directly to view an Event Trace Log file. It can also be invoked from the OS/2 SYSLOG Error Log Formatter utility to view the Event Trace snapshot that was captured as part of an FFSTProbe.

Tracepoint Operation

Tracepoints are identified by a pair of numeric values as follows:

- Major Code (12-bit integer value)
- Minor Code (16-bit integer value)

Different software components will have different tracepoint Major Codes. Minor Codes identify the location where the trace entry is located within the component. Tracepoints are coded as function calls within the software component. Static tracepoints can be placed anywhere within a software component.

The TraceCreateEntry function is used to create static tracepoint entries. Alternatively, the Microkernel exports a set of primitive tracepoint creation functions.

Performance Monitoring

A software Performance Monitoring facility based on the Data Capture Interface (DCI) performance monitoring framework is provided. DCI is a proposed X/Open standard.

The DCI framework provides a set of SPIs that allow software developers to design their software tasks so that key performance statistic counters can be made externally visible to software monitoring tasks. These counters can be made available on an individual basis or as instances of a class of performance statistic counters. The DCI provides a hierarchical-naming architecture for such classes of counters.

The key DCI SPIs include:

- dciRegister and dciUnregister, which are used to register or remove a list of performance metrics

- dciAddInstance and dciRemoveInstance, which are used to add or remove an instance or a list of instances to or from a list of performance metrics

Figure 6-11. DCI Architechture

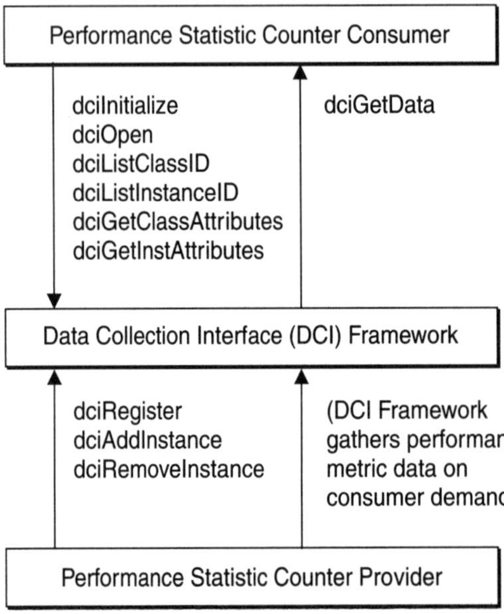

The DCI framework also provides a set of functions so that monitoring tasks can learn what performance statistic counters are available on a system and then gain monitoring access to those counters.

The key DCI functions include:

- dciInitialize and dciTerminate, which are used to initialize and terminate a connection to the DCI

- dciOpen and dciClose, which are used to open and close a list of performance metrics

- dciGetData, which is used to get data from an open list of performance metrics

- dciListClassId and dciListInstanceId, which are used when looking up a list of performance metric class identifiers and instance identifiers in the DCI metrics name space

- dciGetClassAttributes and dciGetInstAttributes, which are used to acquire performance metric class and metric instance attributes

The DCI framework is available to both system developers and to OS/2 application developers. Key OS/2 system components are designed to export performance statistic counters. A general-purpose, performance-monitoring utility, System Performance Display (SPD), is provided so that you can log performance monitoring data and graph it for display.

Resource Monitoring

There are two 32-bit OS/2 resource monitoring functions:

- DosQueryProcessInfo
- DosQueryThreadInfo

DosQueryProcessInfo returns information about the processes that are running on the system.

This information can include the identities of all processes running on the system, the identities of their parent processes, the sessions that they are connected to, and the library modules that they are using.

DosQueryThread returns information about the threads that make up the specified processes. This information can include the identity of each thread, the address of its client side TIB, its scheduling priority, and its state.

Both functions use the PSTAT utility provided with OS/2 Warp Connect (PowerPC Edition) to acquire reports about the process, thread, and library module resources that are currently being used.

File Services

This chapter provides information about the File Services for OS/2 Warp Connect (PowerPC Edition). It introduces File Services, describes File Services, and provides information about the file systems that are supported by the OS/2 operating system.

Introducing File Services

The file system is a key part of an operating system. It is responsible for all of the file input and output (I/O) operations, the formats that files use, and the physical location of the file data on the storage device (for example, a hard disk). OS/2 Warp Connect (PowerPC Edition) provides file management for files and disks through *File Services*. File Services, like other shared services provided by the OS/2 Warp Connect (PowerPC Edition), collectively refers to the logical grouping together of all functions and features related to file systems. The placement of like functions and features, as previously mentioned, makes isolating operating system problems related to the file system a much easier task.

File Services consist of a File Server and File Services clients. The File Server is made up of a *Logical File System* (LFS), *helper routines*, and one or more Physical File Systems (PFSs). (The LFS manages requests from the File Services server. Helper routines are a set of common functions generally required by a PFS. A PFS manages the storage media such as a CD-ROM or hard disk.) File Services clients request services and help resolve File Services system functions. The File Services system functions are designed so that multiple operating systems such as OS/2, DOS, and UNIX are supported.

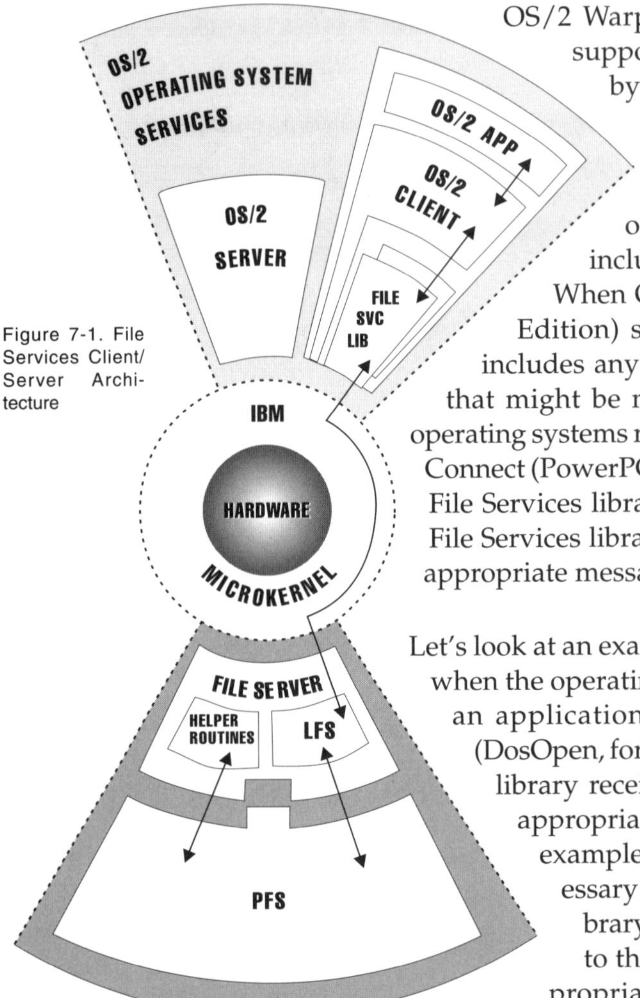

Figure 7-1. File Services Client/Server Architecture

OS/2 Warp Connect (PowerPC Edition) supports multiple operating systems by starting a task that includes the client library for each operating system. The operating system client library then resolves the operating system functions, including the file system functions. When OS/2 Warp Connect (PowerPC Edition) starts this task, it additionally includes any other shared services libraries that might be needed by the client. As most operating systems require a file system, OS/2 Warp Connect (PowerPC Edition) typically includes the File Services library when it starts the task. The File Services library then handles the sending of appropriate messages to the File Server.

Let's look at an example of how File Services work when the operating system client is OS/2. When an application calls a file system function (DosOpen, for example), the operating system library receives the call and then calls the appropriate File Services function (in this example, FS_Open), providing the necessary parameters. The File Services library responds by sending a message to the File Server requesting the appropriate action (in this example, an open file request).

Logical File System

The LFS provides a single entry point to the File Server. It receives all file system requests and provides one consistent view to the multiple PFSs it supports. When the LFS receives a file system request, it acts as a router and sends the request to the appropriate PFS.

There are some instances where the LFS routes multiple calls to the PFS to satisfy a single call from a client. A good example of this is when, for example, the PFS's single call is to open a file or directory. The LFS must resolve the path to the file or directory before it can open the file or directory. The LFS makes multiple calls to the PFS to resolve the parts of the path name, one by one, until the file or directory is located. When the LFS locates the file or directory, it then issues the open request.

The LFS also provides PFSs with a notification mechanism that allows the client to request a message any time that a particular change has been made to a file or directory. For example, if a file or directory is created or deleted, the LFS handles getting that information to the PFS so that it can update the information that is displayed on the screen.

In addition, the LFS provides a way for a client to claim the data in an open file so that the data can be memory mapped into the client's address space. This function is provided by the LFS using a feature called the Token Manager. When a client claims data, it must specify what type of token it is requesting (for example, Read or Write) and what type of tokens to deny to others (in the event that another client tries to claim the same data).

Helper Routines

The helper routines, provided as part of File Services, are a set of common functions generally required by a PFS. This set of common functions includes much of the common code normally found in a file system.

One of these helper routines is the File Services Pager. The File Services Pager handles all file I/O activity on behalf of the File Services. This includes receiving page requests and returns from the IBM Microkernel, and handling I/O to device drivers. By providing I/O for the File Services, the File Services Pager helps shield the PFS from having to deal directly with the device interfaces and the thread and port interfaces.

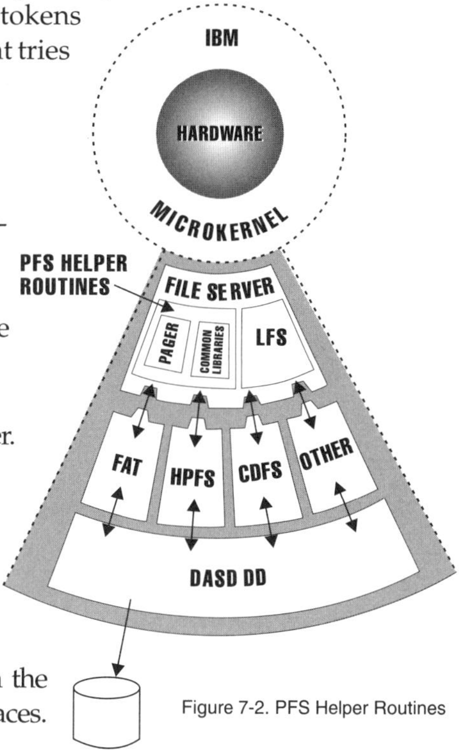

Figure 7-2. PFS Helper Routines

In addition, when the File Services Pager interacts with the IBM Microkernel, it uses a global cache approach that puts all pages (for example, virtual memory, file, and database pages) into a single cache. This prevents the pages from being pinned into memory and it also allows the IBM Microkernel to run a single LRU on all pages of memory. This approach can improve overall performance as the thread that needs the most physical memory gets it.

The File Services Pager also provides a memory object manager abstraction that is much simpler than the IBM Microkernel's external memory pager manager interface (EMMI). This simpler memory management interface is used by the PFSs to manage file data.

The helper routines also include other routines such as a Lock Manager that is used to support byte-ranging locking and other routines commonly found in file system code. The File Services Pager benefits include providing common file system code, shielding the file system from device, thread, and port interfaces, and global caching. Additionally, it also lays the foundation for support of memory-mapped files.

Physical File System

A PFS manages the storage, indexing, and recovery of data. In addition, it defines the set of system functions that the file set supports, including naming conventions, user-defined attributes, long file names, hard-linked files, symbolic-linked files, and Access Control List (ACL) support.

OS/2 Warp Connect (PowerPC Edition) provides support for the following PFSs: File Allocation Table (FAT), High Performance File System (HPFS), and CD-ROM. In addition, a Journaled File System (JFS) is planned for subsequent releases.

The design of the File Services provides support for other PFSs as long as they adhere to the Service Provider Interface (SPI) or the Virtual File System++ (VFS++) interface (developed for OS/2 Warp Connect (PowerPC Edition)).

Note: Sun Microsystems originally designed the VFS interface to enable different file systems to use one UNIX kernel. The original VFS interface was updated (to meet networking requirements) and that version of the interface is called VFS+. The VFS+ interface is defined in the Open Software Foundation (OSF) document available from Transarc Corporation.

VFS++ expands on the VFS and VFS+ interface as it supports Unicode and Code Page, user-defined attributes, and the File Services Pager (described earlier). The interface helps provide a consistent view to the PFSs. As an abstraction, it specifies a set of file system operations that file systems must include in order to carry out an LFS request.

Additionally, PFSs must use the buffer management provided by the File Services Pager.

Additional File Services

File Services also include support for local and remote drives, file-naming, extended attributes, and utilities that are used to support PFSs. This section describes these other File Services.

Local and Remote Drives

The File Services support local and remote drives by establishing a connection to the local or remote drive. Once this initial connection is made, however, the File Services handle the local and remote drive a little differently.

When a connection is established with a local drive (the OS/2 Operating System Services always automatically connect to all local drives), the File Services Pager accesses the drive hardware by calling a device driver to handle the I/O for that device. When OS/2 is the operating system service, the drive name is placed into the IBM Microkernel name space so that the drive is visible to the File Services system functions. Correspondingly, the OS/2 Operating System Services also place the drive name into its name space so that the PFS can access system functions provided by the OS/2 Operating System Services.

When a connection is established with a remote drive, the PFS gets access to the drive through a communications or network device. The actual device, remember, is remote (or located on another computer). The computers that make up a network communicate requests and data through the network connection. Once the PFS makes the connection, the operating system or an application can access files and directories on that remote device by simply using the assigned drive name.

Volume Management

Local and remote drives can be divided into one or more logical partitions. These partitions can be either primary or extended. The total number of partitions supported is four, and only one of these partitions can be extended. The extended partition can be further divided into multiple logical drives. The primary partitions and the multiple logical drives on the extended partition are called *volumes*.

A volume is typically formatted for a particular operating system and is assigned a drive letter. For example, let's suppose there are two logical drives on the extended partition. One logical drive can be formatted using FAT and the other can be formatted using HPFS. The logical drive formatted for FAT might be assigned drive letter "E," while the logical drive formatted for HPFS might be assigned drive letter "F."

File Services provide a Volume Manager that helps manage the volumes. The Volume Manager interacts with the File Server and the device driver. It monitors changes in device status such as when a diskette is placed into a drive. It also makes changes to the volumes such as extending and replacing partitions independently of the File Server and the device driver.

The Volume Manager also provides the File Server with information about where the physical devices are located and how they are divided. It does this by searching the name space and finding all leaf nodes under the /device subtree with an attribute that identifies the device type as DASD. The Volume Manager then reads and interprets the partitioning information for each device type and places an entry for every volume it finds into the name space under the /volume subtree. Using the example provided earlier, if an extended partition is formatted with one logical drive that is FAT and another that is HPFS, when the Volume Manager reads the drive, it will make two entries in the /volume subtree—one for the FAT volume and one for the HPFS volume.

Every volume the Volume Manager finds is considered to be an object. The PFS views each object as a device it can talk to. The PFS "adopts" the object, and the object is placed in the name space in the /file subtree. As all this happens, the Volume Manager remains transparent to the PFS.

Insider's View: For future releases, there are plans to include support for logical volumes. This will provide a simple way to combine multiple volumes and will allow the Volume Manager to support spanning, striping, and mirroring.

File Names

File names are the identifiers used by the PFS to uniquely identify files. Every PFS has specific rules for constructing names for files and directories. The rules differ from one PFS to another, and each PFS defines and enforces its own naming rules. For example, the FAT file system uses the DOS naming conventions. HPFS also uses the DOS naming convention and provides support for long file names and additional characters.

In addition to the specific rules the PFS might impose on file naming, an operating system (for example, DOS) can impose file-naming restrictions on all other file systems. This means that another operating system (for example, OS/2) has to filter out invalid names or convert names. File Services, however, provide a way for any operating system to request the PFS's naming rules and limits. This service uses an extension of the name space. When a drive is accessed, its name is placed into the File Services name space under the /file directory located in the name space and, along with the name, the entry includes a service port that is used to access the drive.

The File Services portion of the name space consists of a hierarchy of directories. A directory is a flat set of names that reference other File Services such as another directory or file. The elements that are contained in a single directory are called components and each element has a component name. A path is simply a sequence of component names. File Services resolve paths by traversing through the name space.

Even though a PFS might have restrictive file naming, the File Services use a generic path structure designed to add a minimum of additional restrictions on path names. This generic path structure uses Unicode characters. When a File Services system function is called, the path name is represented as a full path name, starting from the file set mount point. This requires that operating system dependent paths (such as OS/2 path names) be converted to File Services path names.

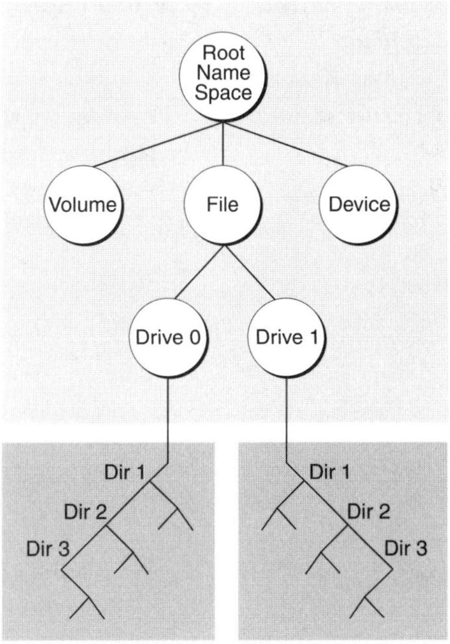

Figure 7-3. File Name Derivation from the Name Space

Developer's Tip: If a file is migrated to a different physical file system with a different set of naming rules, and the naming rules are incompatible, the migration is not automated. The application must handle this situation by converting names to a format that is compatible with the target PFS.

There are many PFSs that support case-sensitive names; however, for some operating systems, this can produce unacceptable results. For instance, many DOS and OS/2 applications expect the file system to be case-insensitive, and, therefore, they convert the file name to all uppercase or lowercase before issuing a call to the file system. Case-sensitivity makes it impossible for the application to access a file whose name is mixed case, and if an application converts the file name to uppercase and the file system accepts only lowercase (or vice versa), it is also impossible for the application to access the file.

File Services solve this problem by including flags on all functions that contain a file or directory name as an input parameter. This allows the operating system to define how case-sensitivity will be handled. The flags provided are:

Case-Insensitive Matching If the PFS supports case-sensitive searches, this flag instructs it to perform a case-insensitive search.

Fail-On-Collision This flag instructs the PFS to fail when the Case-Insensitive Matching flag is set, and, as a result, the directory contains two or more names that match the search name.

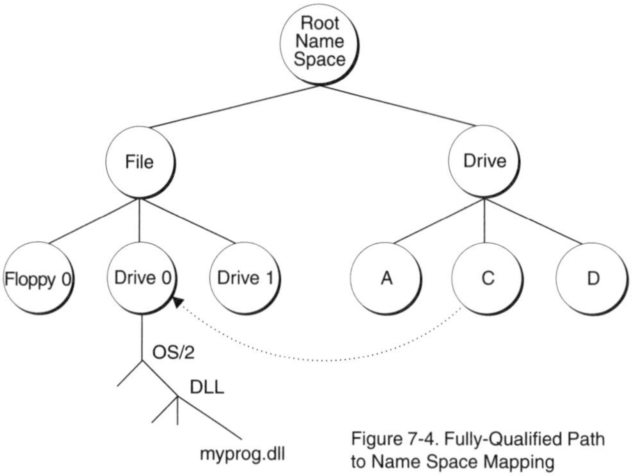

Figure 7-4. Fully-Qualified Path to Name Space Mapping

The name space also supports aliases. Aliases allow one node in the name space to point to another node. This feature is useful when OS/2 and DOS drive names are translated into File Services names.

Both OS/2 and DOS refer to a drive by using drive letters (for example, A:, C:, D:, and so on). Because OS/2 drive names are placed into the name space and those drive letters are mapped to File Services names, all operating systems can translate an operating system name into a File Services name. For example: C:\os2\dll\myprog.dll would map to /file/drive0/os2/dll/myprog.dll.

Extended Attributes

File Services maintain a standard set of information about files referred to as attributes. The standard set supplies information about the name and size of the file, the date and time the file was created, last accessed, and last written to. The attributes are retrieved with FS_GetAttr and are set with FS_SetAttr.

Support for extended attributes (EAs) is provided as well, so that applications can attach additional information about the file that can be used by another application or by the OS/2 Operating System Services. EAs can be used to store notes about the file (for example, the name of the person who created the file), or to categorize the file (for example, as a source, icon, bit map, or sample file). Additionally, the format of the file can be an extended attribute (for example, data record), and additional data (as needed) can be appended to the file.

When an application uses EAs, the application does not place them in the file or directory. Instead, they are stored separately from the data in the file or directory. The PFS manages the location of the EA file and provides a link to the corresponding data file.

Applications can look at, add, and replace EAs. An application reads the EA by using FS_GetAttr. It adds or replaces EAs using FS_SetExtAttr. A file can have any number of EAs. If, for example, a file called My File was created that contained information about the text file that contains information found in this chapter, its EAs might look like Figure 7-5.

Attribute	Value
History	Created by myself, 1994
Version	1.00
Keyphrases	This is my key phrase
Subject	My Subject

Figure 7-5. EA Example

Physical File System Utility Support

For each physical file system there is a set of file system utilities. These utilities include FORMAT, CHKDSK, DEFRAG, RECOVER, and SYS. To support these utilities, the File Services provides a Logical Utility File System (LUFS), which serves as a router, and a Physical Utility File System (PUFS), which understands the physical layout of the data and performs any requested functions. This allows for maximum flexibility for the PUFS. See Figure 7-6.

Support for Physical File Systems

OS/2 Warp Connect (PowerPC Edition) provides support for FAT, HPFS, and CD-ROM. In the future, support for a JFS is planned. As mentioned earlier, file systems generally manage the storage, indexing, and recovery of data.

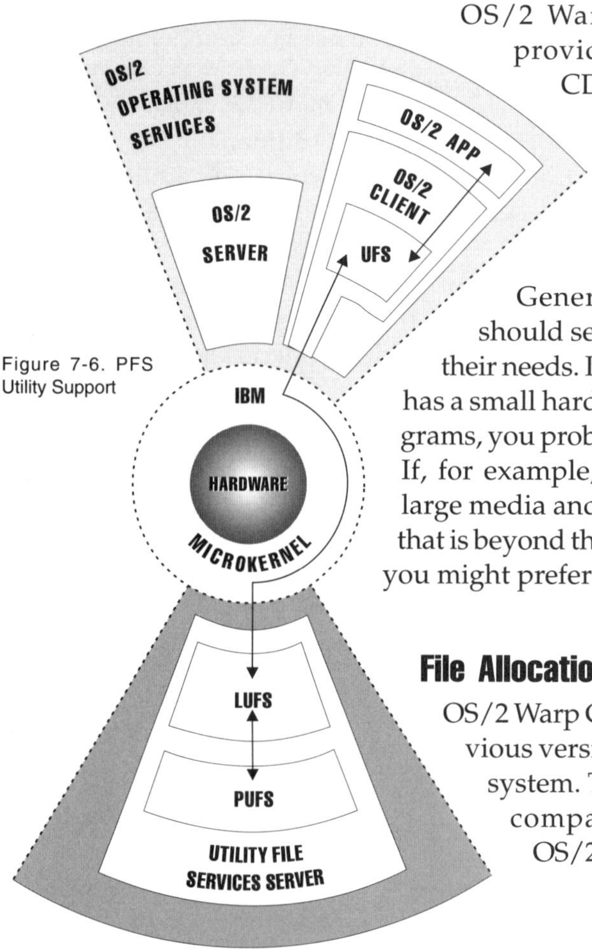

Figure 7-6. PFS Utility Support

Generally, businesses and users alike should select a physical file system based on their needs. If, for example, your home computer has a small hard drive and you run many DOS programs, you probably can use FAT quite comfortably. If, for example, your business needs support for large media and requires a file-naming convention that is beyond the limited one provided by FAT (8.3), you might prefer HPFS.

File Allocation Table File System

OS/2 Warp Connect (PowerPC Edition) and previous versions of OS/2 supported the FAT file system. This file system provides backward compatibility for previous versions of OS/2 and for DOS.

The FAT file system uses a file allocation table to organize data. The table links from one *cluster* to another. A cluster is an allocation unit made up of one or more sectors.

Bios Parameter Block	FAT1	FAT2	Root Directory	File Data Area

Figure 7-7. Physical Layout of FAT File System

Originally, FAT was designed to support smalls disks with simple directory structures. Through the years, its design has changed so that it can support larger disks, a hierarchical directory structure, and OS/2 extended attributes. However, FAT still does not efficiently support large media. To support large media, the cluster size must be large; this wastes space. For example, the cluster size for a 540MB hard disk is 16KB. This means the disk space must be allocated in 16MB increments. As a result, even a small file of 1MB will occupy 16MB of disk space. Or another way to look at it is that, on an average, there is a file waste of approximately half a cluster, or 8MB.

FAT continues to limit file names to "8.3" (an 8-character name with a 3-character extension). Additionally, the FAT file system has no recoverability or security features.

High Performance File System

The HPFS file system was created for OS/2. HPFS was designed to efficiently support large disk volumes. In addition, HPFS supports long file names (up to 254 characters) so that users can give files a more descriptive name. File names are preserved in either uppercase or lowercase, or a mix of both. Searches, however, remain case-insensitive.

HPFS places the boot block at the beginning of the partition. This is followed by the super block, which is used to maintain primary information and the spare block, which is used replace bad sectors. Then, HPFS places a pair of 2KB bit maps every 16MB throughout the entire partition. Each of these bit maps uses one bit for each sector in the 8MB band to indicate that the sector is in use. The bit maps are located at the beginning and end of each band so that the maximum amount of contiguous space is provided to the data. To minimize disk fragmentation, HPFS plans each new file write so that each file has room to grow into a contiguous space on the partition.

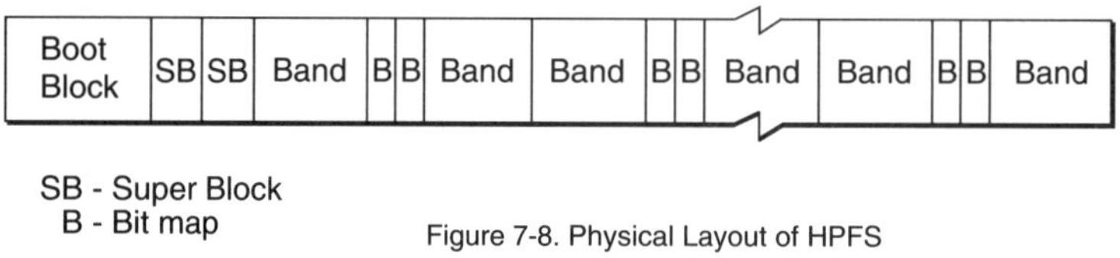

Figure 7-8. Physical Layout of HPFS

HPFS uses B-Tree structures for its directories, which provide fast access to files and directories. A B-Tree structure sorts the data into a tree structure that can be traversed very quickly. Partitions that contain a large number of directories perform much better using this method than the method that is used by FAT. Each directory entry points to an Fnode. The Fnode is one sector in size. The Fnode contains information about the file or directory, including the length, the time and date created, last written, last accessed, and the location of the file's data. The Fnode also contains information about the file's EAs and the ACL. If the EA or ACL is small enough (approximately 200 bytes), the data is placed in the Fnode; otherwise, the Fnode points to the sectors containing the data.

Figure 7-9. HPFS Directory/Fnode Relationship

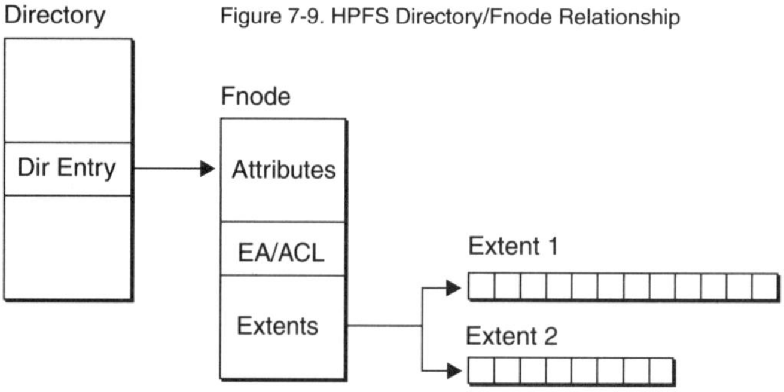

To point to the file's data, the Fnode contains a series of extents that point to a contiguous range of sectors. Because that maximum contiguous space on the disk is a little less than 16MB, large files require multiple extents. The Fnode contains up to eight extents. If the file requires more than eight extents, the Fnode can be used to point to other sectors that are used for more extents.

HPFS also supports disk caching and lazy writing to help improve performance. When data is read from the partition, the data is placed in the disk cache. This minimizes the number of disk reads when multiple reads are made to the same area on the disk. When data is written, it is also placed in the disk cache, and later, when the disk is idle, HPFS actually writes the information to the disk. This technique is called lazy writing. Because it is possible that a write error could occur after an application has completed the write, HPFS provides a method of handling these errors called "hot-fixing." When a write error occurs, HPFS takes a free sector out of the spare block and writes the data there.

Note: As mentioned earlier, HPFS does not need to maintain its own cache. The File Services Pager, which participates in the global caching provided by the IBM Microkernel, takes care of the caching.

CD-ROM File System

The CD-ROM File System (CDFS) supports the ISO 9660, Level 1 format that is used by DOS and the OS/2 operating system. It also provides support for EAs. (Most CD-ROM programming software does not support the OS/2 EAs and writing to the ISO 9660 extended attribute space.) OS/2 Warp Connect (PowerPC Edition) does, however, provide a solution that will allow you to create a CD-ROM with existing software and hardware.

CDFS provides a utility (EAUTIL), which you can use to split the EA data from the file. When you use the utility, the EAs are placed into a standard file (called a hold file), as data. Because the file is a standard file, you can use the EA hold file with existing CD-ROM programming software. EAUTIL also allows you to join EAs contained in the hold file to the data file.

In order for the CD-ROM physical file system to find the EA hold file, the EA hold file must be placed in a file of the same name in a directory named "EAS" with the same parent directory as the data file. This is the default method that EAUTIL uses to create the EA hold file name.

Figure 7-10. Example of CD-ROM Creation Using EAUTIL

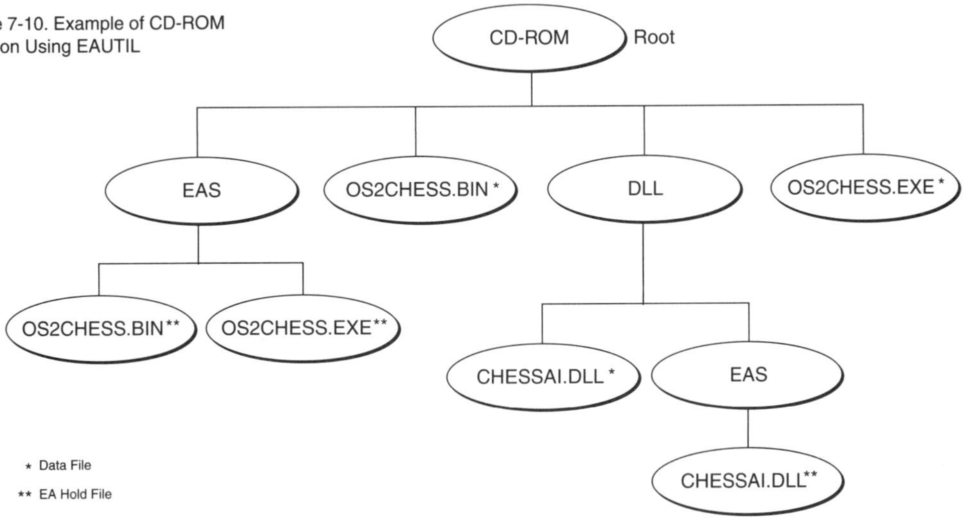

Note: This solution does have one minor restriction. Because ISO 9660 restricts the number of directory levels to eight, files that are eight levels deep cannot have EAs.

Journaling File System

In the near future, OS/2 Warp Connect (PowerPC Edition) will include support for a Journaling File System (JFS). A JFS provides improved structural consistency and recoverability when compared to non-journaling file systems such as FAT and HPFS.

Non-journaled file systems are susceptible to corruption in the event the system fails (for example, during a power outage) because a file system operation often takes multiple I/O operations. To illustrate this, a non-journaled file system might, for example, be performing a write operation that increases the file size. In addition to the data being written to the disk, the meta data that identifies the location of this new file data must be updated. Updating this meta data requires additional writes to the disk. If there is a power outage between the time the file data is written and the meta data is written, then file data can be lost as the file system has no record of the file data ever having been written.

To prevent this from happening, a JFS writes information about the file system operation to a log as atomic transactions. In the event of a system failure, this log is replayed when the system is restarted, and the appropriate transactions are completed or backed out. This leaves the file system in a consistent state and protects the file system from most corruption resulting from system failures such as power outages. However, it does not guarantee that the user's data is preserved in a consistent state.

A JFS also supports very large drives, long file names, extended attributes, security ACLs, hard links, and symbolic links. Hard links let a user attach multiple file or directory names to the same file or directory. They provide a simple way for users to share a file or the contents of a directory. Symbolic links let a user create a file name or directory that is an alias into another file or directory. They provide a simple way for users to indirectly share a file or the contents of a directory.

Presentation Services

This chapter tells you how the Presentation Manager for versions of OS/2 for Intel-based systems is evolving into a set of Presentation Services for microkernel-based versions of OS/2, starting with OS/2 Warp Connect (PowerPC Edition). It describes the five major functions of the Presentation Manager, one of which is supported by a new shared service, the Event and Window Server.

Introducing Presentation Services

Presentation Services is the name applied to the components of the OS/2 Presentation Manager (which provides the OS/2 graphical user interface). Presentation Services include:

- PMWIN, the component name for the PM *window manager*, which provides the WINxxx API for creating and managing windows, provides window controls (such as sliders, scroll bars, menus, entry fields, and so on), and handles system input events from the *single input queue*.

- PMGPI, the component name for the PM graphical programming interface. It manages presentation spaces and provides the 32-bit 2-D graphics API.

- PMGRE, the component name for the graphics engine, which supports hardware devices, such as displays, printers, and plotters. It is sometimes referred to as the *graphical kernel* of the OS/2 GUI because it provides 32-bit GRExxx API that support both the GPI as well as the presentation drivers for the output devices.

- PMSHAPI, the component name for the PM Shell API, which supports the Workplace Shell. It includes the PM session management API (such as WinAddSwitchEntry, WinStartApp, and so on).

For previous releases of OS/2, Presentation Services were constructed as shown in the following figure.

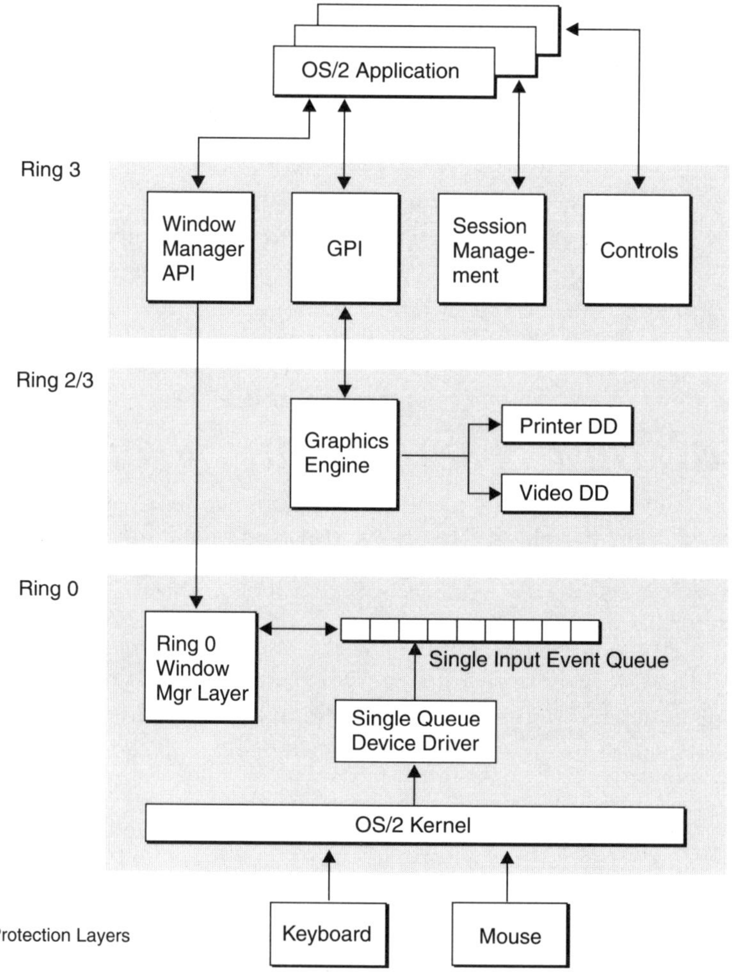

Figure 8-1. Protection Layers

Versions of OS/2 Warp for Intel-based systems have three protection layers:

- Ring 0, in which kernel code and device drivers run
- Ring 2, in which privileged-I/O PM display drivers often run
- Ring 3, in which user programs and nonprivileged system code run

Ring 1 is not used by OS/2. Because of this, parts of the Presentation Manager (PM), most notably the single-input-queue (SINGLEQ$) device driver, which processes mouse and keyboard events at the lowest level, have to run at Ring 0. Some presentation drivers and parts of the Graphics Engine run at Ring 2. With the new microkernel-based design for OS/2 Warp Connect (PowerPC Edition), the concept of code running at different ring levels goes away.

In the version of OS/2 Warp for Intel-based systems, Presentation Services are fully integrated into the OS/2 kernel. In addition, seamless WIN-OS/2 requires a duplicate window manager, graphics engine, and presentation drivers. With the new microkernel-based design of OS/2, however, the pieces of the old Presentation Manager can be abstracted (over time) into Presentation Services that can be shared by all operating system services.

The version of OS/2 Warp for Intel-based systems processed mouse and keyboard events differently (and used different parts of the system) depending upon what class of application was running (OS/2 Full Screen, DOS Full Screen, or Presentation Manager). OS/2 Warp Connect (PowerPC Edition) processes common event and window services in a shared service—the Event and Window Server (EWS).

OS/2 Warp Connect (PowerPC Edition) also provides a major enhancement to the existing Graphics Engine–full software rasterizer capability. This means that the task of writing video and printer presentation drivers is now much easier.

Developer's Tip: Every function that was previously available for versions of OS/2 Warp for Intel-based systems is also available on OS/2 Warp Connect (PowerPC Edition). In addition, functions whose documentation was previously available only upon special request are included with the Developer's Toolkit for OS/2 Warp Connect (PowerPC Edition).

Presentation Manager Window Manager

The PM Window Manager provides the basic framework needed to write a PM application. It provides an API for the creation, manipulation and destruction of windows. Like most of today's GUI environments, PM provides an event-driven programming model. Applications create their windows using PM Window Manager API functions and then respond to messages that get sent to them by the PM Window Manager when significant events take place. Examples of such events would be the user clicking the mouse on an application window, a window changing its size or position, or a window needing to be repainted.

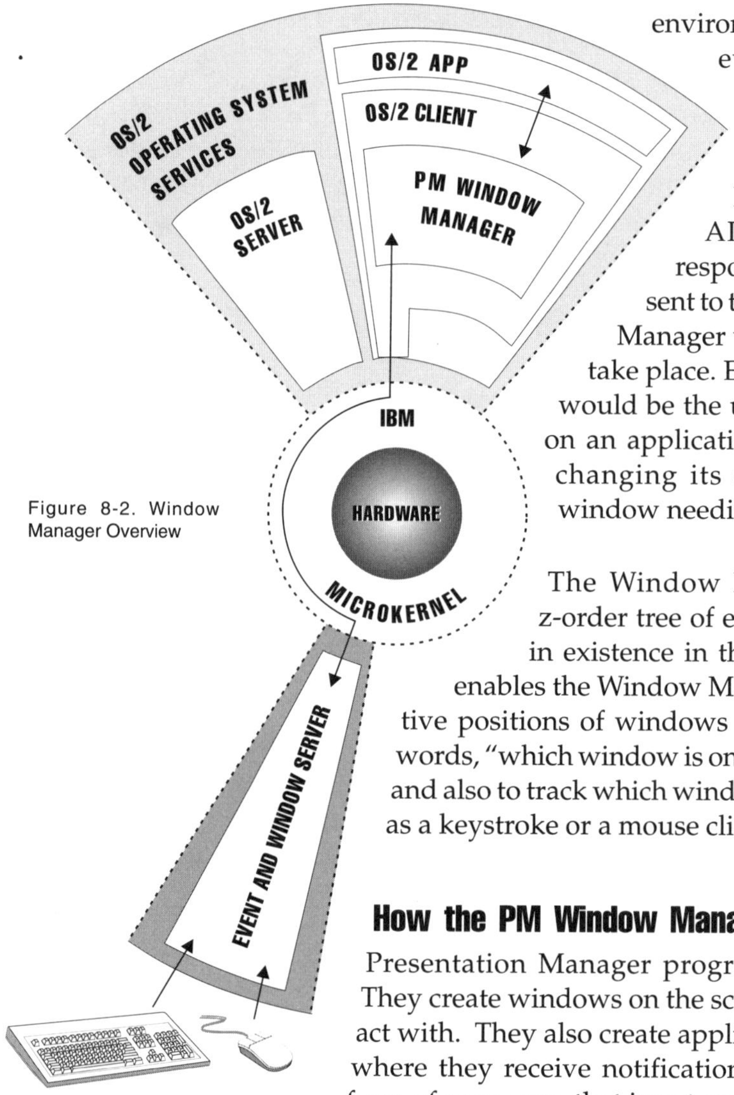

Figure 8-2. Window Manager Overview

The Window Manager maintains a z-order tree of every window currently in existence in the system. This z-order enables the Window Manager to track the relative positions of windows to each other (in other words, "which window is on top of which window") and also to track which window an input event, such as a keystroke or a mouse click, should be routed to.

How the PM Window Manager Works

Presentation Manager programs are event-driven. They create windows on the screen, which users interact with. They also create application message queues where they receive notification from PMWIN, in the form of messages, that input events have occurred. An input event is a keystroke or a mouse click that a user makes in response to something in the window on the screen (such as a push button, a slider control, or an entry field).

PM programs also create window procedures for each window they create. When a PM program receives an input event message in its message queue, it dispatches the message to the window procedure associated with the window in which the user interaction occurred. The window procedure handles the message according to the type of message that was sent.

PM programs, then, all have the same basic format:

```
WinInitialize (…)
WinCreateMsgQueue(…)          /* create the application's message queue    */
WinCreateStdWindow(…)         /* create a window on the screen             */
while WinGetMsg(...)          /* get a message from the message queue      */
        {WinDispatchMsg(…)}   /* if it's not an 'exit program' message,    */
                              /* dispatch it to the window's procedure     */
WinDestroyMsgQueue(…)
WinTerminate(…)
```

And window procedures contain code that has a large set of case statements:

```
switch(msg)   {
       case WM_xxx:{…}        break;
       case WM_yyy:{…}        break;
       and so on.   }
```

How Input Events are Processed

When an application calls WinGetMsg or WinPeekMsg, PMWIN looks for messages to process in the following order:

1. Sent messages (WinSendMsg)
2. WM_SEM1 (the highest-priority posted message)
3. All other posted messages (WinPostMsg), except for WM_SEMn, WM_PAINT, and WM_TIMER
4. Mouse and keyboard (input) events
5. WM_SEM2 messages
6. WM_PAINT

7. WM_SEM3
8. WM_TIMER
9. WM_SEM4

Notice that input events are number four in the priority order. This might surprise some people who might expect these events to be the highest-priority event in the system. An application looking for an event to process will see an input event only if nothing of a higher priority is pending. If an input event is found for the application that called WinGetMsg or WinPeekMsg, then the system event queue gets locked out on behalf of that application as the message is dequeued. The system only unlocks the queue again when the message that caused the lock to occur has been processed by the application.

Because of this, applications must read their messages regularly to keep the system responsive. Thus, in the application message dispatch loop, as shown below, the system event queue is locked from the point when the application calls WinGetMsg until it calls WinGetMsg again after returning from the WinDispatchMsg call.

```
while WinGetMsg(...)          /* get a message from the message queue     */
 {WinDispatchMsg(...)}        /* if it's not an 'exit program' message,   */
                              /* dispatch it to the window's procedure    */
```

Developer's Tip: So that your application does not hang the system, it should not only look at its message queue frequently (at least once every 50 milliseconds is recommended), but it should also have responsive window procedures. Things window procedures might do to cause the system to hang include: wait on system semaphores; call DosSleep; open files out on the network; open and read a 50MB file; calculate Pi to 1000 decimal places; start writing to a serial device; and wait for a device to become free. If you must do these things, do them on another thread of execution.

Input Event Processing Discussion

In previous releases of OS/2, one of the most discussed and, in most cases, misunderstood components of the Presentation Manager was the single, system-wide input event queue. Several articles have been written about the power and flexibility of the Presentation Manager. However, it has become "fashionable" to cite the single input event queue as the Presentation Manager's "Achilles' heel."

It is possible for a PM application that does not read its message queue frequently (in less than approximately 100 milliseconds) to cause parts or all of the GUI desktop to appear to be hung. This apparent hang has always been attributed solely to the single input event queue. However, the single event queue is not the sole cause of the hang. Two facts are true: The system should not allow itself to be so badly damaged by a rogue application program, and if programmers followed good programming practices and always used at least two threads in their programs (one dedicated to reading the input queue in a timely manner), then this would be a moot discussion.

When the Presentation Manager was first introduced in OS/2 Version 1.1 back in 1988, the Intel 286-based computers of the day were not nearly as powerful as 486, Pentium, and PowerPC computers. The single input queue came into being so that application programs such as the IBM Communications Manager could allow users to type ahead and not lose input. At that time, any form of asynchronous queuing algorithm was made impossible by the speed in which the computer could process keyboard events. Also, at the time the Presentation Manager was introduced, there were very few GUI desktop systems available to application programmers and even fewer (if any) that were based upon multithreaded operating systems.

Almost all of the early PM programs were written in a single-threaded fashion. Even programs that were ported from other single-threaded environments, such as Microsoft Windows running on top of DOS (a single-threaded environment), were left single-threaded during the port.

For similar historical reasons, the Window Manager handles focus change notifications between windows in a very synchronous fashion. Consider two applications, each one having a frame window but only one having the input focus. When the user clicks on the nonfocus frame window to give it the focus, several messages are exchanged between the two windows before the focus change is completed. If one or the other of the two windows is heavily single-threaded or does not read its message queue in a timely fashion, both applications will hang, blocked by each other.

This hang condition occurs because the messages are sent rather than posted between the windows. Sent messages are fully synchronous and so the sending application is blocked until the receiving application responds to the message. In this example, the single input event queue is not the fundamental cause of the problem. The problem is the synchronous nature of the focus exchange. The messages are sent rather than posted primarily because they have to be processed in a particular order and, again, for historical reasons, to provide a responsive desktop on the slower processors of the late 1980s on which timing was essential. This architecture remains in current releases of OS/2 for Intel-based systems.

It also should be noted that not all system hangs are caused by the input queue. Many things, such as hardware malfunctions, can also cause the computer to hang. However, users equate a desktop lockup with an input queue problem.

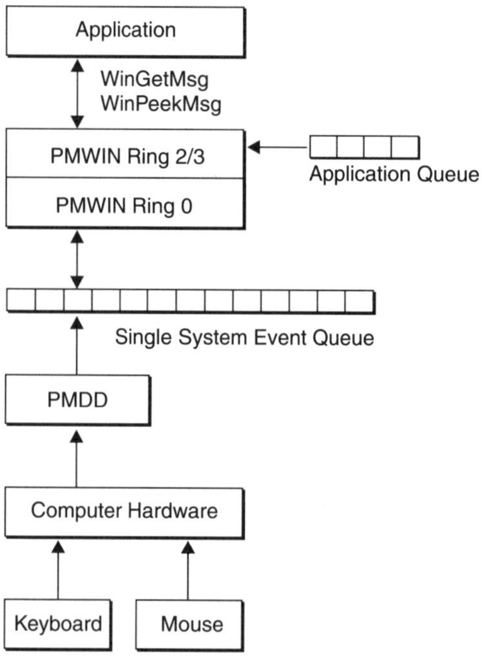

Figure 8-3. OS/2 Warp on Intel Event Processing

In the existing releases of OS/2 on Intel-based systems, most badly behaved applications can be terminated when the tasklist realizes that an application has gone bad and offers the user a chance to end it. However, in some hang cases, a reboot is required, and that is never a good thing. At the risk of sounding repetitive, if all applications were written to be responsive, then we could focus on other issues. It is important to realize that the existing Presentation Manager event-processing model does provide a very responsive system if programmed with a little care. Users have been trained to ask for the "single input queue fix" or to demand "asynchronous event delivery" without being told what they are really asking for. Imagine for a minute every PM application in the world, having been coded to expect (in many cases require) synchronous event delivery and interfacing with other applications, suddenly receiving their events in a nonguaranteed order and in a fully asynchronous fashion. The end result would be little short of desktop anarchy. Pieces of windows would be painted incorrectly. Frame windows would lose track of who had the focus, and a number of other problems would occur. Now, clearly, things can and should be done to avoid the application (perceived as desktop) hangups we have all come to dread. However, these few words of caution should be remembered when demanding a fix to a problem that has not always received the accurate explanation it requires.

In any event, no pun intended, and not necessarily just for the reasons listed, it was necessary to review and re-architect the system-wide input event processing and delivery model for this release of the operating system, and this is one of the major reasons that the Event and Window Services were created.

The Event and Window Services

As mentioned at the start of this chapter, one of the most significant changes made to the Presentation Services for this release is the way that input events are handled and distributed. Event and Window Services (EWS) provide a server that runs as a Microkernel task with a client/server interface to the various operating system services that might be running (such as OS/2 and DOS). The EWS performs two major tasks. It handles and distributes input events, and it controls the system-wide creation and deletion of sessions and provides, again on a system-wide basis, a number of session management services.

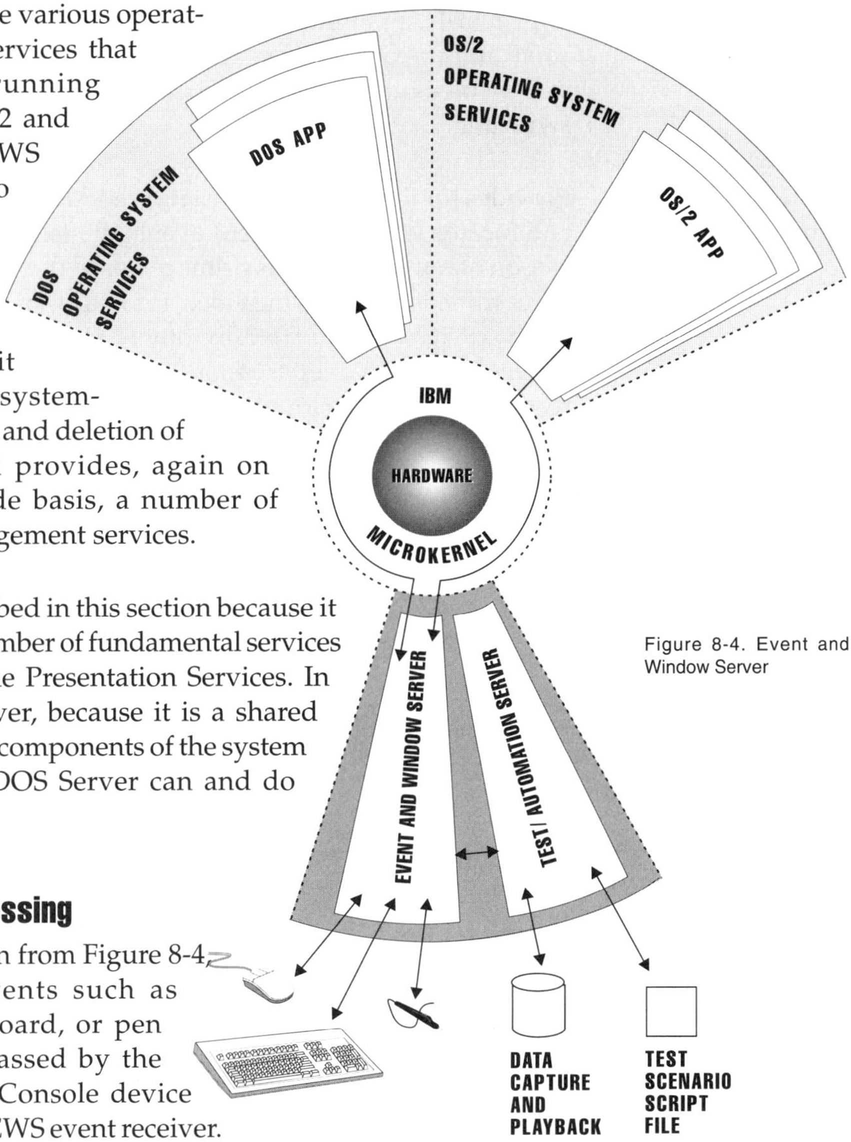

Figure 8-4. Event and Window Server

EWS is described in this section because it provides a number of fundamental services utilized by the Presentation Services. In reality, however, because it is a shared service, other components of the system such as the DOS Server can and do utilize EWS.

Event Processing

As can be seen from Figure 8-4, all input events such as mouse, keyboard, or pen events get passed by the Microkernel Console device driver to the EWS event receiver.

The Event and Window Services provide a mechanism for sharing the console among applications. The events handled by the Event and Window Services are low-level events and include keyboard and locator (mouse) events.

The Event and Window Services consist of two primary pieces:

Session Manager Is primarily a communications mechanism. It maintains a small amount of session state and provides a means of notification of events such as session creation and session switching.

Event and Window Server Provides for the common translation and routing of keyboard and locator (mouse and pen) events. It also handles the detection of hot keys. EWS is primarily used by the OS/2 Server to coordinate the use of the video, keyboard, and locator. Some of its services can be used by others to gain notification of session events, to query session status, to set hot keys, and to record and simulate input events.

Session Management

A session is a group of tasks that share a console state. A screen group is a session that controls the state of a physical video device, keyboard, and locator. A session might itself be sharing the physical resources with another session's physical resources.

As an example, an OS/2 *command window* is a session, and an OS/2 *full screen* is a screen group. It is possible to change a session to be itself a screen group or to be part of another screen group. Thus it is possible to change an OS/2 command window into an OS/2 full screen, and back again.

The Session Manager has the following main responsibilities:

- Creates and destroys sessions and screen groups
- Maintains session states and interrelationships
- Provides a means of communicating to exclusive sessions (for example, the Hard Error Pop-up session)

- Facilitates the switching of screen groups by notifying the screen groups being switched in and out of the foreground

- Notifies screen group owners, session owners, and session watchers of session management events

Note: A session can create child sessions. In most cases, the child/parent relationship of sessions is not important, but this knowledge can be used on termination of the session.

A session can have several states, starting with *inactive* when the session is first created. After a task has been started within the session, it becomes both *active* and *selectable.*

OS/2 Warp Connect (PowerPC Edition) provides a task that implements a *task list* (Window List). Users can view this list (through the Workplace Shell) by simply pressing the Ctrl and Esc keys at the same time. The task list is notified when the state of a session is modified. The task list knows about active sessions and allows the selection of certain sessions. Any active session can be explicitly switched or selected. Other tasks can register interest, and the Session Manager will notify them of session events. These tasks are called *session watchers* and are used by programs that need to keep track of the current session state (for example, the Asian language Input Method Editors or Screen Reader).

Event Services

The Event and Window Server provides a common point for all low-level events (such as keystrokes and mouse movements) to enter the system. It provides for the synchronization of keyboard, locator, and simulated events. The Event and Window Server provides a mechanism for common translation of keyboard events to all servers and programs in the system. This is accomplished through a series of translations for each event.

The Event and Window Server takes input from the Microkernel input event port, receiving messages from the interrupt logic for the keyboard and mouse devices. Event messages can also be sent by others to the event input port, thereby giving other subsystems (for example, Pen Support) the ability to create a virtual keyboard and to send results to the event port.

The Event and Window Server normally routes translated events to the input queue of the current session. It is possible to register key sequences that are then sent to other tasks. These events are called hot keys. A hot key is specified by a shift state, a PM (Presentation Manager) scan code (representing the physical key pressed), and a set of option bits.

The Event and Window Server allows five types of messages on its input event port. These messages can come from the console device driver, another device driver simulating a console driver, or from a program simulating keystrokes and mouse input. The following list describes the five types of messages:

Keyboard scan code Sent from the console device driver about a keyboard primitive event. This message type consists of a packet containing a timestamp and a single byte of AT-enhanced scan code.

Locator record Sent from the console device driver about a primitive mouse event. This message type consists of a packet containing a timestamp, any mouse-button action, and two position coordinates.

Control Sent by a device driver when it needs to send a status change request to the Event and Window Server. This message type indicates a state change in a physical device and requests that the Event and Window Server update the device's state.

Multi-event Sent by any of the events previously described. This message type provides a programmable interface that allows the input of Unicode characters, virtual keys, and PM scan codes. It consists of a packet containing a header that includes a length, a logical device ID, a timestamp, a set of control values, and a set of data values that indicate events.

Notification Sent to the Event and Window Server from other threads within EWS. This message type is used to tell the Event and Window Server that such things as session termination have occurred.

Regardless of how an event is specified, it is translated into a complete keyboard or locator event. These events are processed automatically by the Event and Window Server and placed on the input queue of the current session.

Events from real keyboard and locator devices tend to consist of a single action. The simulated multi-events are often more complicated and consist of a series of events that must be synchronized. For example, a multi-event might consist of a mouse move, a button down, and the simulated typing of several characters. Some control values (such as the scan code input) represent a single event. Other control values (such as Unicode characters) contain a length followed by a series of data values. Different kinds of control values can be interspersed within a multi-event.

When event data comes from a simulated device, it is necessary to understand how the state of the real device affects the simulated event. It is also possible for there to be a long-term state within the simulated device. The Event and Window Server defines three separate classes of logical console devices as a means of describing these states. They can be used to maintain separate settings (such as shift state) for the various logical devices. This can be useful for programs that wish to simulate keyboard and mouse events without changing the state of the real shift and button states.

The three classes of logical console devices are:

Real Device Any changes made to this class of device are affected by and affect the state of the real device (such as the keyboard).

Long-Term Logical Device Users of this device should be careful to complete a set of actions (for example, any keys that are pressed should be released).

Transient Logical Device Users of this device need to include an EV_RESET (reset event) control event at the start of each record, which sets the state to match the physical device and a known shift-state.

The Graphics Subsystem

The Graphics Subsystem can be thought of as having two major components—the Graphical Programming Interface (GPI) that application programs use to display graphics on the screen or other output device and the Graphics Engine. The Graphics

Engine is the graphical kernel of the system. It is at the heart of all graphical operations and contains all of the algorithms needed to render the many primitive and complex shapes that are provided to applications by the GPI.

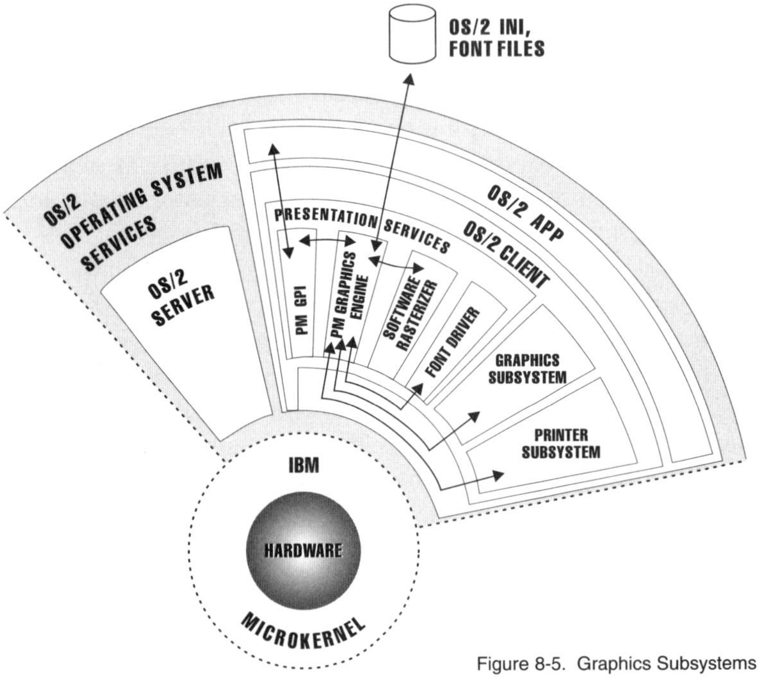

Figure 8-5. Graphics Subsystems

The Graphical Programming Interface

The Graphical Programming Interface (GPI) is a 32-bit application programming environment that provides a comprehensive two-dimensional imaging model.

It provides extensive support for the following classes of drawing operations such as:

- Creating and managing presentation spaces
- Setting and querying attributes of:
  - Colors
  - Line styles
  - Fill patterns

- Drawing basic graphical primitives:
  - Simple lines and polylines
  - Arcs and curves
  - Bezier splines
  - Boxes
  - Markers
  - Polygons
  - Bit maps
- Functions to build complex shapes:
  - Regions
  - Areas
  - Paths
  - Clipping
  - Geometric wide lines
- Functions to transform data:
  - Translate
  - Scale
  - Rotate
  - Shear
- Functions to create and manipulate graphical text:
  - Bit map fonts
  - Outline fonts
  - Includes support for ATM and Truetype fonts

- Functions to save and move data to:
  - Metafiles
  - Retained graphical segments
  - Correlation (hit testing)
  - Bounds accumulation
- Functions to print to hardcopy devices

The Graphics Subsystem supports several coordinate spaces to enable complex picture construction and modeling as well as various types of page units that allow the programmer to work in pels, fractions of millimeters, fractions of inches, or arbitrary units when constructing pictures. The following drawing coordinate spaces are provided:

- World Space
- Model Space
- Page Space
- Device Space (matches the device resolution)

In World Space, the coordinates allowed by the system range from 0x800000000 to x7FFFFFFF (that is, from -134717728 to +134217727). These coordinates allow large pictures to be created "off screen" in World Space in pieces and then assembled (or subpictured) in Model Space before being displayed in Device Space. The system provides many different transformations that can be applied to the World Space picture to scale it down so that it can be displayed on the output device. Support is also provided for panning, zooming, rotating, and shearing.

The following page units are provided:

- Pels (1 unit = 1 pel)
- LoMetric (0.1 mm)
- HiMetric (0.01 mm)

- LoEnglish (0.01 inches)
- HiEnglish (0.001 inches)
- Twips (1/1440 inches)
- Arbitrary (specified by programmer)

The origin of the picture on a device such as a screen (that is, coordinate 0,0) is always to be considered at the bottom left of the screen when you are working with the GPI. This is true for both graphical primitives and text. In some other GUI environments, 0,0 is at the top left of the screen.

Developer's Tip: Graphical metafiles, created by Presentation Manager applications, will be compatible between previous releases (for Intel-based systems) and this release. A picture that is created on a previous release can be ported to this release and vice versa.

Likewise, bit-map formats are compatible between releases. A bit map that is created under a previous release will be readable by this release and vice versa. The native bit-map format will continue to be the OS/2 2.0 bit-map format. (This format is the same as used by OS/2 Warp on Intel-based systems.) The earlier OS/2 1.3 bit-map format will also continue to be supported.

The Icon format is also unchanged. Icon (.ICO) files from previous releases can be read quite easily in this release.

The Graphics Engine

As mentioned previously, the Graphics Engine is the part of the Graphics Subsystem that does the "real work." It contains the algorithms needed to support the interface that the GPI provides to application programmers.

This version of the Graphics Engine, for the first time, allows both video and printer driver vendors to create OS/2 drivers that are completely independent of the Presentation Driver graphics model.

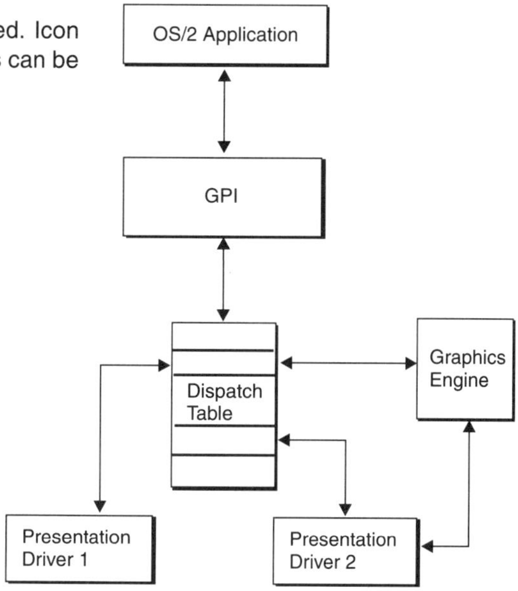

Figure 8-6. Old Graphics Engine Dispatch Model

Developer's Tip: Previous versions of the Graphics Engine for OS/2 did not provide some basic functions or algorithms. It was expected that these would be provided by the presentation driver for the specific device being drawn to. This expectation meant that every single display presentation driver written had to provide support for (effectively "hook out") 75 basic drawing functions, and printer presentation drivers had to support about 59 functions. Writing these functions was clearly a major burden for presentation driver writers, who were effectively having to duplicate algorithms in every driver they created.

This version addresses this expectation by providing a full software rasterizer.

SOFTDRAW

SOFTDRAW, the full software rasterizer, provides support for many functions that, previously, presentation driver writers had to provide themselves. Creating a presentation driver, in the past, might have taken several months. SOFTDRAW helps make the task easier, as several months' work can now be done in only a few days and with very little effort.

All you need to do is to give the Graphics Engine the address of the video frame buffer and ask it to take care of all drawing and clipping calculations. When the presentation driver is up and running, then selected functions can be "hooked out" and implemented in the driver. These functions would typically be the functions for which some degree of acceleration is provided by the hardware.

The Graphics Dispatching Model

To understand this better, it is useful to look at the Graphics Engine work dispatching model.

It is interesting to note that the GPI is really, for the most part, a wrapper library that abstracts the lower-level functionality of the Graphics Engine to a higher, more friendly level for application programmers. The GPI provides the programming model of logical presentation spaces for applications to draw into. In most cases, the layer between the GPI and the Graphics Engine is quite thin (that is, not much work is performed by the GPI before calling the Graphics Engine). When a PM application makes a call to a graphics GPI function, such as GpiLine, control is passed almost immediately by the GPI layer to the Graphics Engine layer to do the "real" work. Sometimes, however, it is not always the Graphics Engine that handles the call.

There are certain cases, two in particular, where the GPI layer itself has some substantial work to do. If a program is creating a metafile of drawing orders, then all of the work of creating the metafile is performed at the GPI level. Likewise, support for retained drawing (that is, drawing to one or more retained graphical segments) is provided by the GPI.

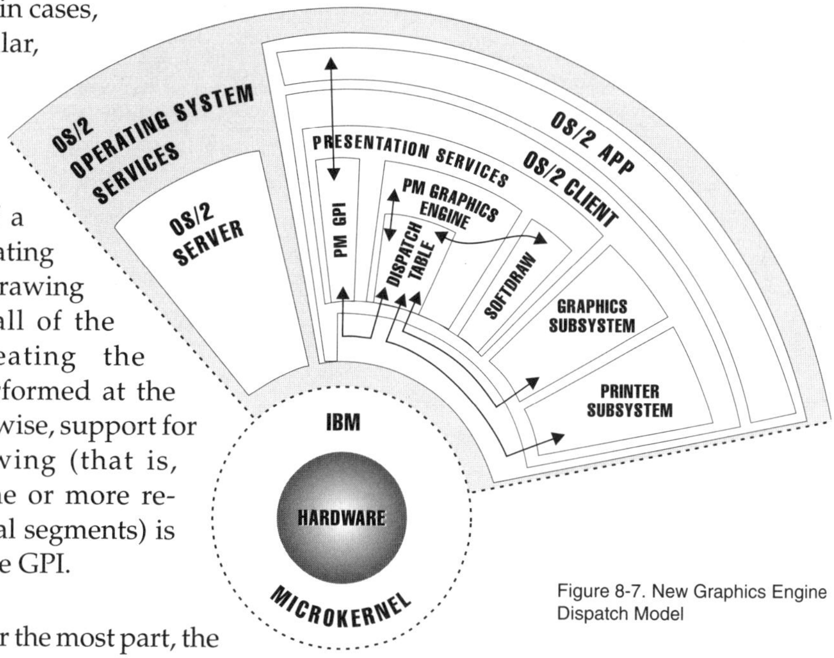

Figure 8-7. New Graphics Engine Dispatch Model

Nonetheless, for the most part, the actual work of rendering graphics primitives to an output device is performed by the Graphics Engine. As can be seen from the diagram, unless an application is creating a metafile or retained segment, when an application makes a call to a GPI function, the GPI passes the parameters (modified as necessary) to the Graphics Engine. There is a close mapping between the notion of a presentation space maintained by the GPI and the equivalent logical device context maintained by the Graphics Engine. In fact, in many cases, the mapping is one-to-one. Each time an application requests a presentation space to draw into (using a call such as GpiCreatePS or WinGetPS), an equivalent device context is created by the Graphics Engine. For each device context, the Graphics Engine sets up a function dispatch table (or "jump table") for each of the graphics functions it exports. In other words, when the GPI makes a call to the Graphics Engine, it does not call the required function directly; rather it calls the function whose address is stored in the specified entry of the dispatch table.

The addresses in the dispatch table are initialized at the time the device context is created. When a new device context is being set up, the Graphics Engine initializes each entry in the table with the addresses of its own functions and then asks the presentation driver supporting the logical device context (for example, a video display or printer driver) if it wishes to handle or "hook out" any of the functions. The presentation driver then replaces the addresses in the table with its own addresses for those functions that it wishes to handle. So, for the GpiLine example, when the GPI calls, via the jump table, the Graphics Engine line function, the call will either be handled by the presentation driver, if it has chosen to hook it out, or by the Graphics Engine. Even if a presentation driver has hooked out a function, it might still decide, upon getting called, to call back to the Graphics Engine for help. A reason for this call back would be if the driver decided that the current state of clipping was too complex for it to handle. In this case, it can call back to the Graphics Engine, which will handle the clipping and send back preclipped lines to the driver.

As mentioned in an earlier Developer's Tip, in previous versions of OS/2, presentation drivers had no choice but to hook out a large number of functions because no support was provided in the Graphics Engine. Again, now that the Graphics Engine does not require this mandatory hooking out of functions by presentation drivers, they have become much easier to write. However, it should also be noted that "old style" presentation drivers (those that do choose to hook out large numbers of functions) will still work under OS/2 Warp Connect (PowerPC Edition).

At a minimum, using the new presentation driver model, the Graphics Engine requires only the presentation driver to export (that is provide) five functions. These are:

- The device initialization interface
- The hardware capabilities query function
- The DevEscape (device escape) interface
- The interface to set and query the hardware palette
- The interface to move the cursor (video devices only)

Developer's Tip: There is another new improvement that has been made to the presentation driver model. The Video Manager (VMAN) and Graphics Adapter Device Driver (GRADD) models have been added. There is a detailed discussion of VMAN and GRADD in Chapter 9, "Device Driver Services" on page 165.

Font Support

OS/2 Warp Connect (PowerPC Edition) provides support for outline and bit map (raster) fonts and Adobe Type Manager outline fonts and includes (for the first time) native support for Truetype fonts, making them available to PM applications as well as Microsoft Windows applications. The ATM font support is compatible with (at least) ATM, Version 2.6 for Microsoft Windows. This level of ATM includes support for DBCS (composite) fonts and for Unicode fonts. The Unicode support uses a special combined font technology such that one (virtual) Unicode font can be generated by selectively combining multiple fonts together.

The Intelligent Font Interface

Font drivers for the various font technologies that OS/2 supports are loaded via the Intelligent Font Interface (IFI), sometimes referred to as the Installable Font Interface. The Graphics Engine using this IFI support is able to communicate with whichever font drivers are available in the system. A font driver is really a dynamic link library (DLL) that understands one or more font file formats. Font drivers are effectively font file processors. Take, for example, an application that wants to draw a text string using a 24-point Helvetica outline ATM font. For each character in the text string, the Graphics Engine makes a call to the appropriate font driver (in this case, the ATM one). The font driver reads the appropriate font file for the metrics that describe the particular character and returns to the Graphics Engine a bit map representing that character. The Graphics Engine is then able to go ahead and render (draw) the character to the output device.

To facilitate fast drawing of text, the Graphics Engine places the character bit maps into a local cache as they are returned from the font driver. This way, the next time that character is needed, the Graphics Engine will look first into the cache before making a call to the font driver. This activity is sometimes visible to an observant user in that the first time a page of text is drawn (in a new font), it appears slower than in all subsequent refreshes of the pages. This slowness is caused because the Graphics Engine is reading from its cache after the first draw. It should be stated that the size of the cache is not infinite and that an algorithm is employed to selectively delete characters used least frequently from the cache to make room for new ones, if and when the cache becomes full. Also, for very large point sizes, typically those in excess of 300 points, the font driver will not return a bit map to the Graphics Engine for individual characters but will return a path structure made up of lines and Bezier splines to represent that character.

At system boot time, the Graphics Engine looks into the system .INI files and looks for the PM_Font_Drivers entry. There will be one entry for each font driver giving the path to where the font driver DLL file is located. All font drivers present in the .INI file are then loaded by the Graphics Engine.

For the first time in this release, three font drivers are included as part of the operating system. The supplied font drivers will support:

- The Adobe Type Manager (ATM) fonts
- Truetype fonts
- Raster (bit-map) fonts for DBCS

Historically, double-byte character-set (DBCS) raster fonts have been handled by the Graphics Engine directly. That work will now be done by a dedicated raster font driver.

As with other releases of OS/2, a basic set of bit-map and outline fonts will be included with the operating system, as follows:

- Outline fonts
  - Courier
  - Helvetica
  - Times New Roman
  - Marksym (the outline font version of the marker symbols)
  - Symbol Set
- Bit-map fonts
  - System Monospaced
  - System Proportional
  - System AVIO fonts (typically used in OS/2 character windows)
  - Times Roman

  - Helvetica
  - Courier
- ISO 9241, Part 3 compliant versions of selected bit-map fonts

  Certain countries have strict standards that affect such issues as the clarity and readability of text on visual displays. For that reason, OS/2 continues to include certain fonts that comply with these standards. Two of the major standards in existence today are:

  - International Standards Organization (ISO) standard 9241 Part 3
  - German DIN 66234

  ISO-compliant versions of the Times Roman, Helvetica, Courier, and System Proportional bit-map fonts are also provided.

Users can add other fonts to the system by using the Font Palette object, located on the Desktop. The locations of the font files that contain the definitions of the various font typefaces are stored in the .INI file under the PM_Fonts category.

OpenGL – Industrial-Strength 3-D Graphics

OS/2 Warp Connect (PowerPC Edition) supports OpenGL. OpenGL is fast becoming recognized throughout the computer graphics world as the standard for industrial-strength (CAD) 3-D graphics rendering. OpenGL has an architecture review board (ARB) made up of leading industry players, including Silicon Graphics Inc. (SGI), who originally created OpenGL, IBM, and Microsoft. Traditionally, OpenGL has been thought of as a high-end workstation graphics tool. Because the PowerPC has excellent floating-point support, the power of OpenGL is becoming available for affordable prices and is now within the grasp of a much wider group of users and application programmers.

Fundamentally, OpenGL is a programming API that facilitates the generation of rendered images of 3-D objects. It exploits floating point, therefore providing very accurate rendering of objects and texture mapping. OpenGL is not designed as a low-end game-builder's API. There are several other 3-D programming interfaces that are designed to provide those types of services. Typically, the lower-end 3-D engines use integer mathematics rather than floating point, which sacrifices accuracy but makes them faster for "real time" gaming. Also, the 3-D engines that are game-oriented tend not to be so precise or provide the graphics resolutions that OpenGL does.

OpenGL excels when accuracy, precision, and quality of image are really important. It has become widely adopted in areas such as CAD/CAM design, natural gas and chemical exploration, scientific visualization, and medical research, not to mention the movie industry, where the chances are that your favorite dinosaur or other monster was created using sophisticated OpenGL-based tools.

OpenGL 3-D Services

In technical terms, what OpenGL provides is a set of "vendor-neutral" 3-D services. The term vendor-neutral is used because the core OpenGL algorithms don't care what hardware or software platform they are running on. The types of services provided include:

- Modeling
- Lighting
- Smooth shading
- Good texture mapping
- NURBS (Non-Uniform Rational B-Splines)
- Fogging of images
- Transparency (Alpha blending)
- Motion blur

The OpenGL implementation included with OS/2 Warp Connect (PowerPC Edition) is considered a "soft" implementation (that is to say, no hardware support is needed beyond a standard video adapter card). All of the creation of the 3-D image is done by the software and then sent directly to the frame buffer as one or more bit maps. This type of creation is, of course, not going to generate images as quickly as if there were some degree of hardware acceleration being used, but it allows everyone to experiment with OpenGL without the need for special hardware. In fact, OpenGL uses the same Direct Interface Video Engine (DIVE) or EnDIVE (Enhanced DIVE) technology that the multimedia subsystem uses to get data out to the video hardware as quickly as possible. Using the DIVE interfaces on PowerPC computers and faster Pentium-class computers, the performance of OpenGL is quite reasonable even without hardware acceleration.

The OpenGL implementation included with OS/2 Warp Connect (PowerPC Edition) is derived from IBM's AIX implementation. As such, it is already highly optimized to exploit the features of RISC processors. Now, the software pipeline has been enhanced even more, to fully exploit the best features of the PowerPC microprocessor.

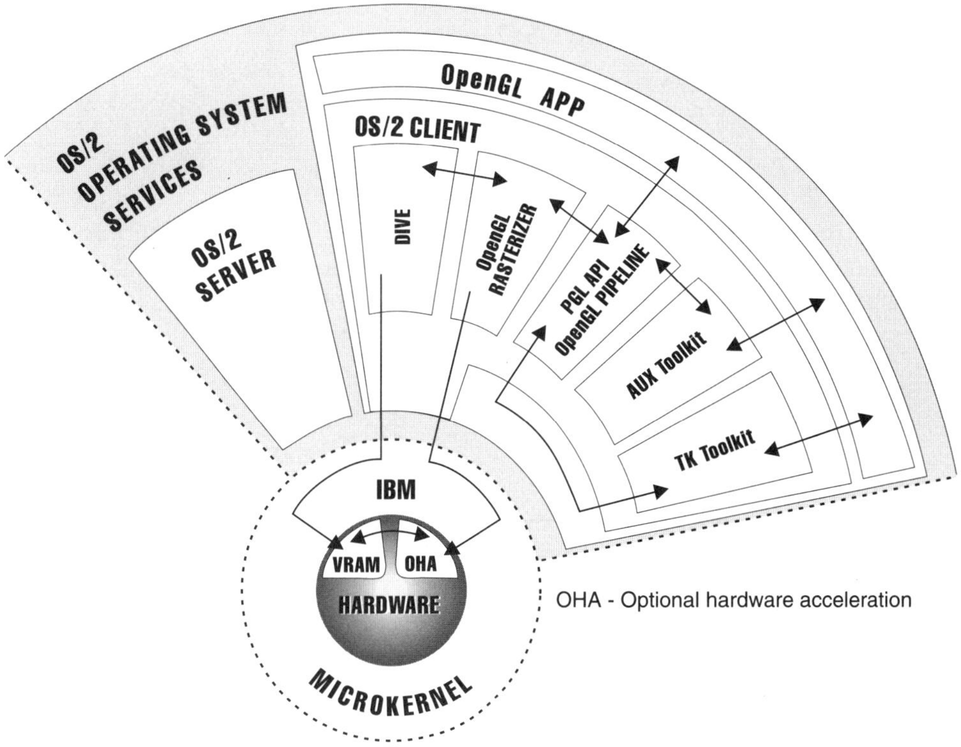

Figure 8-8. OpenGL Overview

The Presentation Manager OpenGL Interface

In order for application programmers to be able to combine OpenGL 3-D objects with their PM applications, a small set of interface functions is provided. This interface is known as the Presentation Manager OpenGL interface (PGL), pronounced "piggle." This is similar in nature to the WGL interface to OpenGL, which is provided in the Microsoft Windows environment on Windows NT today.

PGL provides the following capabilities:

- Specification of visual configurations
- Context creation
- Binding an OpenGL context to a PM client window
- Swapping a window's buffers
- Integration of OpenGL and OS/2 drawing
- Utilization of OS/2 fonts with OpenGL

OpenGL is implemented through a set of DLLs. The interface library provides the PGL support, the OpenGL software pipeline, and the OpenGL rasterizer. OpenGL also has two toolkit helper DLLs known as AUX and TK. These toolkit libraries facilitate the creation of certain 3-D objects so that the programmer doesn't have to write quite as much OpenGL code. However, it should be noted that it does not take more than a few hundred lines of C code to create a very useful OpenGL program.

Device Driver Services

This chapter provides a brief overview of the Device Driver Services for OS/2 Warp Connect (PowerPC Edition). It also provides detailed information for developers of device drivers.

Introducing the Device Driver Services

Device drivers provide the low-level I/O support for a device. They provide standard device access to the operating system and to applications running on the operating system. OS/2 Warp Connect (PowerPC Edition) provides a wide set of standard device drivers that support a broad range of devices.

Device Driver Services in OS/2 Warp Connect (PowerPC Edition) are shared services.

User-Level Device Driver Architecture

User-Level Device Drivers (ULDDs) are the critical link between OS/2 Warp Connect (PowerPC Edition) and the I/O hardware devices. ULDDs remove from the application the responsibility to be knowledgeable about the devices it interacts with. Also, ULDDs are responsible for serializing access to the device to prevent corruption of data.

The ULDDs provided with OS/2 Warp Connect (PowerPC Edition) are highly portable because the programmed I/O abstraction layer isolates ULDDs from the architectural differences between I/O devices.

One of the major improvements in this release is the dynamic loading of device drivers. Run-time loading provides great flexibility in system configuration and lowers memory requirements during boot time.

The ULDDs interact with other operating system components in order to perform their duties. The following illustration represents the relationship between the operating system infrastructure and the device drivers.

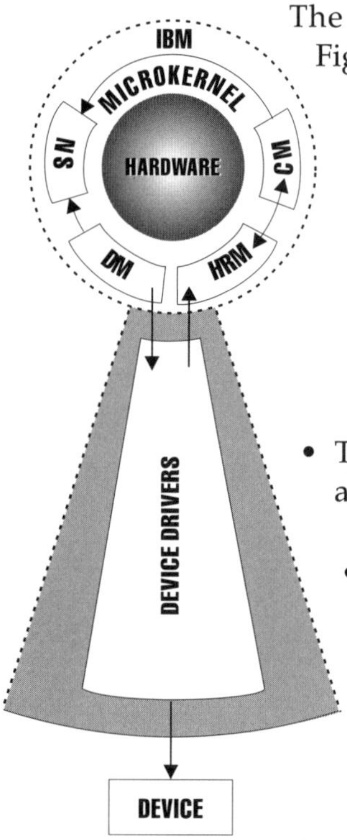

Figure 9-1. Device Driver Infrastructure

The ULDD architecture has five major components (see Figure 9-1):

- The Hardware Resource Manager is responsible for naming, initializing, and allocating I/O resources.

NS - Name Server
DM - Device Manager
HRM - Hardware Resource Manager
CM - Configuration Manager

- The Device Manager is responsible for starting the ULDDs and associating physical devices with logical devices.
- The Configuration Manager walks through the hardware to identify the devices installed on the system and creates the Hardware Resource Manager object tree that represents the system configuration.
- The Name Server is the database or repository of the system information.
- The Device Driver searches for the object representation of the device on the name space and sends a request to the Hardware Resource Manager to create an instance of the object.

The first step toward configuring the system hardware is to identify the device drivers that need to be loaded. The Configuration Manager uses several bus walkers and information files (stanza files that have an extension of *.STZ) to determine the hardware that is installed on the system.

During the system initialization, the Configuration Manager reads, from nonvolatile random access memory (NVRAM), the Global Environment Area (GEA) to obtain basic information such as IP addresses and the boot-device, and the POS registers to identify the type of PowerPC that the operating system is running on. However, this information says nothing about the devices installed on the system.

The Configuration Manager uses the Resource Description stanza files to obtain memory address ranges, I/O ports, and interrupt levels, and to manage the resource arbitration for Micro Channel and ISA devices. The Configuration Manager calls the Hardware Resource Manager (HRM) for each of the devices found in the stanza files. The Hardware Resource Manager makes the necessary node entries in the name space to represent the system hardware configuration in a hierarchical structure.

After the Configuration Manager is up and running, the Device Manager is started. The Device Manager searches for the logical devices and starts the necessary device drivers. After the device driver is loaded, it creates an entry for itself in the name space directory "driver." This entry must contain at least one attribute called "primary_port," which is the port utilized by the DD_Init and DD_Terminate functions. The logical device entries contain the information necessary to load the devices. The Hardware Resource Manager grants access to the hardware and initializes the hardware entry.

The Hardware Resource hierarchical structure in the Name Server that describes the system hardware configuration has two names per object device—the port right (port_t) used by clients on service requests and the textual name utilized in human-interaction operations such as error logging.

In the name space, the hardware resources tree contains objects representing the I/O memory, I/O ports, and IRQs for each device. In this hierarchical structure, each object represents a device managed by a device driver. Active uses of a device are represented by device instances. A device driver can have zero to several instances open at any given time. For example, if a system has four SCSI devices but only two of these are currently in use, the name space contains only two instances for that device. See Figure 9-2.

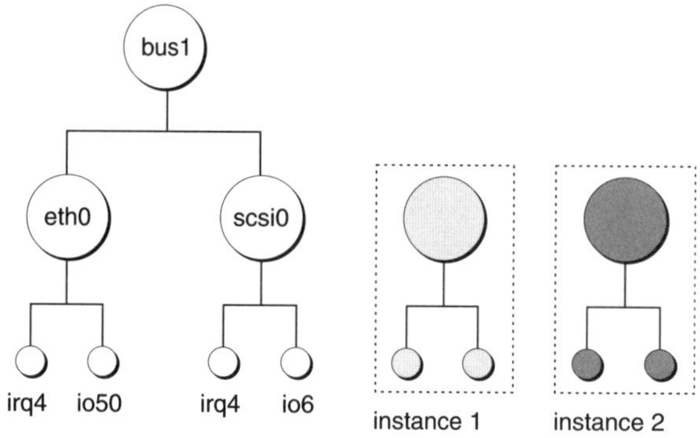

Figure 9-2. Instance Data Representation

Character-oriented devices, such as printers, keyboards, and serial communication ports, process one character at a time. Device drivers communicate with the character device using either a synchronous or asynchronous approach. The synchronous approach blocks other incoming data until the transaction (a read or write operation) is performed. This approach can be used when there is no need to perform concurrent I/O operations on the device.

The asynchronous approach is more complex because it uses a transaction-based operation to communicate between the client and the device driver. A transaction operation is divided in two parts—the client request to the device driver and the client reply from the device driver. The asynchronous approach does provide more flexibility to handle concurrent I/O operations; however, this approach requires more handshaking between the device and the device driver.

Block devices, such as diskettes, virtual disks, and CD-ROMs, typically hold large volumes of data that are accessed in a random fashion. Some block devices, such as SCSI disks, have a well-defined block size, while others, such as tape drives, have different block sizes.

Most character and block device drivers (depending on the function of the device itself) use a common set of interfaces (see Figure 9-3) that includes:

- An initialization call to initialize the device.

- An open call that sets the mode of operation and initializes an instance of the device on the Hardware Resource Manager.

- Some I/O operation to transfer data. Block devices would use some record-oriented set of instructions, and character devices would use simple read and write operations.

- Information management functions that are used to request the current device status as well as to set up a new device state.
- A close call that is used to remove the instance data placed in the Hardware Resource Manager by the open call.
- A termination routine to inform the device driver that the object device needs to be disconnected (made inaccessible to the client).

Other devices, such as serial ports, require additional function to configure the various transmission formats and signaling behavior of the device.

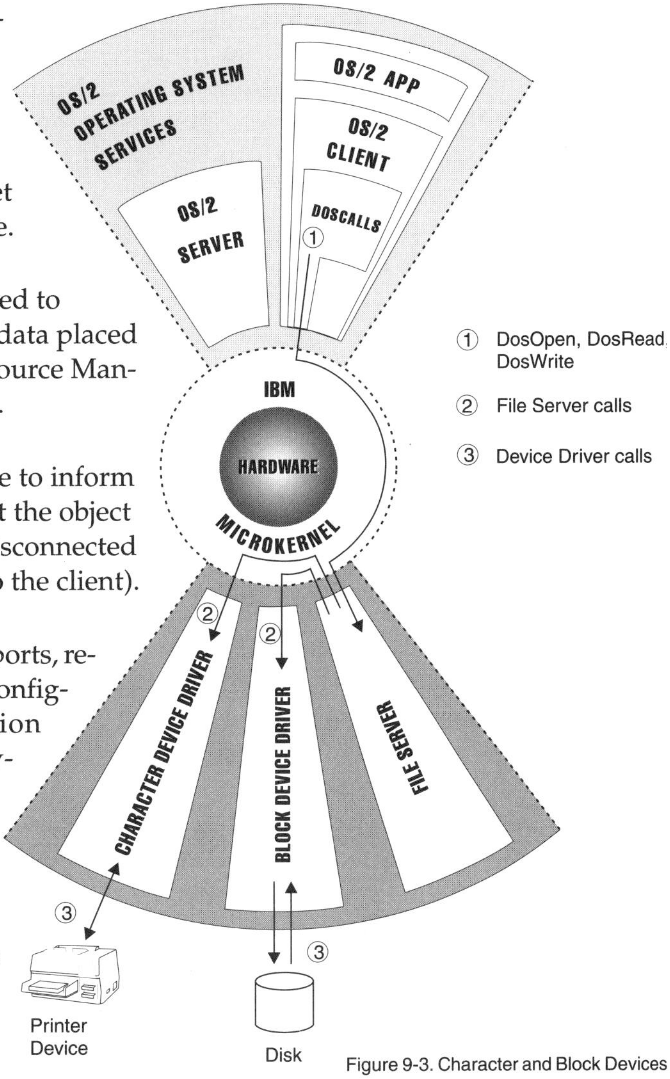

Figure 9-3. Character and Block Devices

The Hardware Resource Manager

The Hardware Resource Manager (HRM) controls the access to hardware resources by issuing Microkernel system calls on behalf of the HRM clients. The hardware information stored for each object includes the I/O address range, IRQ levels, buses, and interrupt handlers. The Configuration Manager and the user-level device drivers are HRM clients that utilize the HRM server and API services. The HRM functions manipulate the hardware resource tree on the name space. They create and modify objects, add device instances, provide a locking mechanism, search or query the tree, and delete objects. The HRM client creating a device object must call the add object function with the specific information necessary about the hardware device. The HRM client must include the I/O address range, the bus type, and the attributes associated with the device. It must also provide a server port to the device driver NotifyClient interface of the HRM server component. The HRM will issue a device instance whenever the Resource Manager issues a request for hardware access.

There are two modes that are available when a device instance is requested—OBJECT_MODE_SHARED and OBJECT_MODE_EXCLUSIVE. The exclusive mode should be used only when an HRM client wants to prevent other HRM clients from using a device. HRM clients can share only those devices that were created with the shared attribute.

Sometimes, operations on devices depend on the hardware platform they are executed on; however, these hardware dependencies are transparent to the HRM clients using the HRM interfaces.

Programmed I/O Abstraction Layer

The programmed I/O (PIO) abstraction layer isolates the user from hardware architecture differences. The PIO accomplishes this isolation through a series of macros and data structures. Because of this hardware abstraction layer, the ULDDs can be used on different platforms. This architecture provides the user with a common set of interfaces to transfer data.

The PIO abstraction layer hides the platform-specific instruction from the user and handles data transfers of various widths (from 8- to 64-bits) automatically. Other hardware architecture discrepancies, such as I/O address differences between a processor and devices, are also handled by the PIO layer. For example, if you have an ISA I/O memory of 64KB (0x00CF000), it would be translated to 0x00 CF000 in the PowerPC 601 by the PIO layer.

The PIO abstraction layer helps with other hardware annoyances, such as the differences in the addressing mode on the PowerPC. The PowerPC architecture, as mentioned previously, has two addressing modes: Little Endian and Big Endian. The Big Endian architecture has byte 0 as the most significant byte and the Little Endian design has byte 0 as the least significant byte.

The PIO layer makes the byte swapping necessary between Big Endian and Little Endian transparent to the user. This transparency means that a user of a PowerPC 601 that runs on Big Endian mode can transfer data to a Little Endian device without worrying about the differences in mode.

The PIO abstraction layer has several performance implications. The PIO operations perform on the local task address space and have very low system overhead. The PIO abstraction layer information is located in the data structure pio_info_t, which is allocated in the client's space. The Microkernel interrupt-handler interface uses this structure to pass the I/O addresses to the ULDDs. This structure contains basic I/O information such as the type of byte ordering expected by the hardware, the physical start and end addresses, address alignment, and virtual start and end addresses. The PIO interfaces can be compiled with the ULDD module as macros or as function calls. The ULDD links by default with the function calls, but the interrupt-handler routines must be compiled with the macros. The ULDD interrupt-handler routines can't execute function calls; thus they need to use the PIO macro interfaces to access the processor's I/O addresses.

The basic PIO setup interfaces include the pioAccess, pioInit, and pioRevokeAccess (see Figure 9-4). The call to pioAccess initializes the PIO structure and accesses the I/O address it represents. A call to pioAccess must be made before any data transfer interfaces can be called. The call to pioInit restricts the access to a given I/O address range. A client that wants to initialize a region and transfer some data must call pioInit followed by pioAccess. The call to pioRevokeAccess removes any resources associated with the PIO structure in the client space.

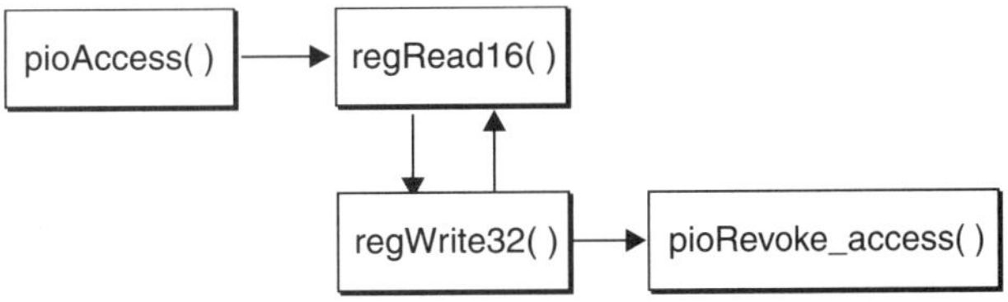

Figure 9-4. Programmed I/O Sequence

Configuration and Stanza Files

Stanza files are a collection of attributes that define a piece of hardware. Utilizing bus walkers and stanza files, the Configuration Manager can identify the hardware resources on the system. The hardware identification on the Micro Channel bus is obtainable by scanning the device ID register for each slot on the bus.

On an ISA bus, the Configuration Manager relies heavily on the stanza files because bus walking doesn't provide the necessary information. The stanza files have the following format:

- Comment lines start with #
- Stanza names must be left-justified and end with a colon
- Attribute lines must use the following format:

  <attr_name> = <attr_value>

The following provides an example of a stanza file for DASD devices:

```
# Definition of SCSI controller disk unit 0, attached to a
# Micro Channel adapter on slot 1

scsi06:

        dev_class =           dasd
        dev_subcasse          =          ""
        driver_name           =          scsi
        driver_per_instance   =          false
        hrm_resource          =          mca0/4CFF:1
        driver_path           =          "/os2/devices/dd_scsi"
        driver_args           =          ""
        unit                  =          0
        lun                   =          0
        primary_port          =          0

# Definition of SCSI controller disk unit 1, attached to a
# Micro Channel adapter on slot 2

scsi05:
        dev_class             =          dasd
        dev_subclass          =          ""
        driver_name           =          scsi
        driver_per_instance   =          false
        hrm_resource          =          mca0/8EFF:2
        driver_path           =          "/os2/devices/dd_scsi"
        driver_args           =          ""
        unit                  =          1
        lun                   =          1
        primary_port          =          1 <:f>
```

Each entry in this stanza file generates a device object in the name space, which is to the correct leaf entry under the "devices" tree. The user can change the system configuration by updating the stanza files. The stanza files can be manually edited because they are flat ASCII documents.

If a server needs to read the stanza files, the Microkernel provides functions to read these files into the ns_object_desc_t structure. After the stanza information is on this structure, the Name Server functions can be used to read this information.

Boot Sequence

When a PowerPC computer is turned on, the first thing that it runs is the firmware. The firmware searches for a special partition (called the x41 partition) on the boot device and does an image blast (to RAM) of the partition. The boot loader uses the BOOT.CFG file to identify the files and servers that need to be loaded into RAM. In the sample BOOT.CFG file that follows (see Figure 9-5), notice that the Name Server is the first server loaded on the system. The Resource Manager is next, followed by the default stanza file (BOOT_P1.STZ), which contains the basic device drivers required during boot time. The Device Manager and the device drivers are the last pieces of the infrastructure to be loaded. The device drivers that are not part of the basic set described in BOOT_P1.STZ are loaded later by the OS/2 server and are specified under the BOOT_P2.STZ. The boot sequence shown here must be preserved to maintain and support the current architecture. Loading all the devices on the BOOT_P1.STZ is possible but it should be avoided because of the higher memory requirement at boot time that this can cause.

When additional devices are added to a system, the stanza files need to be updated to incorporate the hardware definition, device I/O address, and IRQ information. Also, the CONFIG.SYS file needs to be updated to add a DEVICE statement. The OS/2 Warp Connect (PowerPC Edition) installation program will update the stanza file and CONFIG.SYS automatically.

```
PN_MK_NAME="\micro\machkern"
PN_BS_NAME="\pns\bstask"
PN_GSM_SIZE="256"
PN_GCM_SIZE="256"
PN_FILE_NAME="\pns\libmk.so"
PN_FILE_NAME="\pns\libpn.so"
PN_FILE_NAME="\pns\libc.so"
PN_FILE_NAME="\pns\libdd.so"
PN_SERVER_TYPE="NS"
PN_PROG_NAME="\pns\rs"
PN_SERVER_TYPE="DP"
PN_PROG_NAME="\pns\defpager"
PN_FILE_NAME="\hrm\resmgr"
PN_FILE_ARGV=""
# Stanza file with minimum boot configuration
PN_FILE_NAME="\hrm\boot_p1.stz"
PN_FILE_NAME="\hrm\cfgmgr"
PN_FILE_ARGV=""
PN_FILE_NAME="\hrm\devmgr"
PN_FILE_ARGV=""
PN_FILE_NAME="\dev\dd_scsi"
PN_FILE_NAME="\cps\vm"
PN_FILE_ARGV=""
PN_FILE_NAME="\os2\bvm"
PN_FILE_ARGV=""
PN_FILE_NAME="\cps\fsserv"
PN_FILE_NAME="\cps\fatpfs"
PN_FILE_ARGV="-t"
PN_FILE_ARGV="-l 3"
PN_FILE_ARGV="-f FAT"
PN_FILE_NAME="\os2\pagrinit"
PN_FILE_ARGV="-c config.sys"
PN_FILE_ARGV="-o os2serve"
PN_FILE_ARGV="-i pinstall"
PN_FILE_ARGV="-d resmgr boot_p2.stz"
PN_FILE_ARGV="-r nameserv reg"
PN_FILE_ARGV="-p pager_file"
PN_FILE_ARGV="-s 10"
PN_FILE_ARGV="-k locklist"
PN_FILE_ARGV="-l lock.lis"
PN_FILE_ARGV="-a \os2\bin\arcrecov"
```

Figure 9-5. BOOT.CFG File

ADD Architecture

The ADD, or ADapter Driver architecture, comprises the new device driver model for OS/2 Warp Connect (PowerPC Edition). The main goal of the ADD model is to ensure that there is a platform for robust device support that is extensible and flexible. Supporting goals build on this extensibility and solidify the central principles necessary to achieve this robust support.

The benefits of this architecture are as follows:

- Simplicity

  Because the model is simple, Independent Hardware Vendors (IHVs) will be able to reduce the amount of time necessary to learn, write code for, and maintain new drivers. ADD interfaces are defined for different device classes, so IHVs learn only the ADD definition for their hardware.

- Portability

  ADDs are easily portable to other hardware and operating system platforms. The ADD definition does not assume any particular hardware, processor, or operating system.

  ADDs are shared services and, therefore, independent of the hosting environment. ADDs work with all operating system services.

- Consistency

  The ADD architecture presents a consistent interface for common functions across a diversity of adapter class implementations. For system-level functions (such as interrupt services and resource management), all ADDs will be treated in a common manner.

- Flexibility

  The ADD architecture together with the ADD class implementations allow the developer to solve the specific problems of each adapter class. The ADD architecture is a layered design that provides a flexible method for providing adapter device support. Figure 9-6 illustrates the main layers of the ADD device driver model in the I/O subsystem. With the exception of the video-related subsystems (which are discussed later in this chapter), the ADD is responsible for directly supporting hardware devices.

The ADD establishes an interface to the framework that abstracts the physical hardware. The interface is common to all adapters within a particular adapter class. Because the framework is able to support any adapter within a class of adapters (through the use of an ADD abstraction layer), the effort of supporting similar hardware devices has been dramatically reduced.

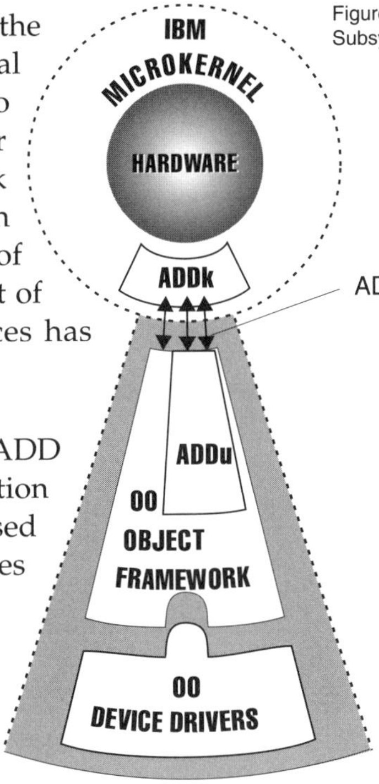

Figure 9-6. I/O Subsystem Overview

The external view of an ADD is the set of ADD interfaces. These interfaces form an abstraction of the adapter hardware. The ADD is composed of two main interfaces. The first set of interfaces is referred to as the *common set.*

Interfaces in the common set are defined for all ADDs and form the foundation of the ADD architecture. The second set of interfaces is related to the adapter class. Adapter hardware can be classified by its functionality, such as SCSI or serial. This unique functionality forms a set of adapter classes. Because adapter functions are separated by class, a shared set of functions can be defined for supporting any adapter in a particular class. This shared set of functions forms the ADD class definition for that adapter class. Each adapter class will have a unique ADD class definition.

The component responsible for interfacing to the ADD is the framework. Because there will be multiple ADD class definitions, there will be multiple framework definitions. Together the framework and ADD form an ADD class/framework pair. Because the framework represents an abstraction from the ADD and adapter-specific hardware interface layers, it will not be discussed in detail.

Functional Split

The ADD model is implemented in the IBM Microkernel environment. The Microkernel environment imposes certain safeguards and restrictions based on its programming model. One of these restrictions is the separation of user and kernel space code.

One goal of the ADD architecture is to place as much code as possible in user space. Because the ADD is the lowest layer in the device driver, the boundary crossing from user to kernel space will be in the ADD. This boundary is illustrated in Figure 9-6. With the transition from user to kernel space falling within the domain of the ADD, it is possible to implement support entirely in user space, entirely in kernel space, or in a hybrid of both user space and kernel space. For performance-critical operations, some kernel support will most likely be required.

In addition to the split of function between user space and kernel space, certain kernel-level services have been relocated from the ADD to a library of ADD services. This library implements a set of functions that gives the ADD access to kernel-level services and primitives. There will be an ADD services implementation for each part of an ADD driver. Each implementation will define the services that are available to that portion of the driver.

The freedom and decision of where to place the function is left to the ADD writer.

ADDu/ADDk Communication

Because the ADD is split between user and kernel spaces, there must be a mechanism for the two environments to communicate.

There are two communication paths between the user and kernel level parts of the ADD. These two parts are referred to as user-to-kernel (ADDu) and kernel-to-user (ADDk). Each of these paths has different semantics. Figure 9-6 illustrates the user/kernel space transition path by double arrows. This path can also be referred to as the intra-ADD interface.

This interface is not defined by the architecture, although for each ADD class definition, IBM will supply a minimal user-level ADDu and RPC (remote procedure call) handling layer that defines the ADDk interface. In most cases, this will allow the

ADDk interface to be consistent with the ADD class interface. ADD writers who want to implement the entire ADD in the kernel can use this minimal ADDu so that only an ADDk needs to be written.

The primitives described in the following sections form a logical connection between ADDu and ADDk. A single connection is used for each adapter that the ADD is controlling.

User-to-Kernel Interface

The kernel-level component of the ADD (ADDk) is loaded by the framework. After it is loaded, the framework will use interrupt services to create an I/O extension. The I/O extension is referred to as the kernel extension.

The kernel extension is represented by a port, which is called the Kernel Extension Handle. The Kernel Extension Handle is used for operations against the extension, not for communicating between both parts of the ADD. Once the kernel extension has been created, the framework will create the Command Handler port.

The Command Handler port is the primitive that is used by the ADD to communicate with ADDk. It is used by ADDu to send messages to ADDk. Interrupt services that own the receive right for the Command Handler port will route all messages to ADDk. Both the Kernel Extension Handle and the Command Handler port are made available to ADDu during adapter initialization.

All ADDu-to-ADDk calls are RPCs. An RPC is a synchronous call into the kernel. Although this call is synchronous, the programming model for executing I/O requests is an asynchronous model. Typically an RPC would be used to call ADDk to start I/O. On return from the RPC, the I/O would have been started. When the I/O is completed, the user-level portion of the ADD would be notified asynchronously. This notification uses the mechanism described in the next section ("Kernel-to-User Interface").

The reason for using a port to communicate with ADDk is that an address boundary must be crossed. ADDu passes ADDk parameters that must be mapped into the kernel to be valid. A specific example is a user buffer. The buffer address will have to be translated into the kernel's context. All parameters that are address-space-sensitive must be passed as a parameter in the RPC call.

Kernel-to-User Interface

While the user-to-kernel interface uses a call/return model, the kernel-to-user interface is an asynchronous notification model. The Microkernel environment does not allow kernel code to call into user space at interrupt time. Therefore, the ADDk environment cannot call ADDu or the framework. The ADD architecture provides a mechanism for the communication from ADDk to ADDu. Furthermore, this mechanism must be able to handle the "queuing" of requests. This allows ADDk to send multiple events to the framework/ADDu at a time. The mechanism used is called the *reply pipe*.

The reply pipe is the upward connection between the framework and ADDk. The reply pipe is a unidirectional, fixed-size, circular queue that requires no synchronization between user and kernel space. ADDk will "enqueue" elements into the pipe while the framework asynchronously removes them.

The framework has a dedicated thread for removing elements from the pipe. This thread, called the *dequeue* thread, is automatically created when the pipe is created. The reply pipe is created by the framework prior to adapter initialization. Each adapter requires a separate reply pipe.

The ADDu must specify, during adapter initialization, the address of a routine to process the reply elements. This routine will be called to process elements as they are removed from the pipe. If the request is completed, then the ADD must initiate the completion callback. Because this processing is asynchronously triggered, a "sleep/wakeup" mechanism is needed. Interrupt services provide a mechanism via a *client connection*. Figure 9-7 illustrates the reply pipe in detail.

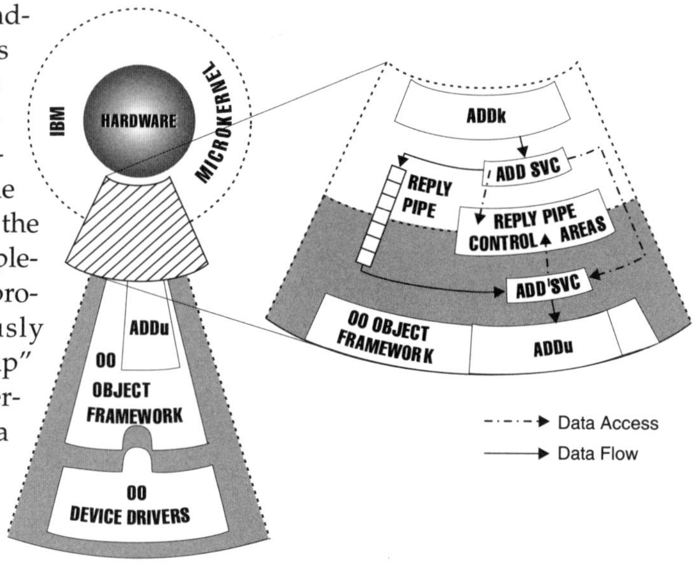

Figure 9-7. Reply Pipe

ADDk Signaling

The ADD driver writer does not have to explicitly issue a signal whenever an element is placed in the reply pipe. This signaling mechanism is hidden or abstracted by the ADD services, which allows the ADD to be independent of the mechanisms used. It also allows the reply-pipe handling mechanisms to be changed as more efficient mechanisms are found.

In summary, the ADD model provides a flexible and extensible architecture. This function-rich architecture allows for a freedom of implementation with an emphasis on commonality among adapter classes.

GRADD Architecture

While the OS/2 Warp Connect (PowerPC Edition) video architecture is evolved from the OS/2 Warp video architecture, it has been significantly modified so that the writing of video device drivers is greatly simplified.

In OS/2 Warp, the video device driver writer needed to write two or three separate video drivers:

- A base video driver that handled such tasks as video device initialization and mode switching
- A PM video display driver that handled some or all of the PM GPI API graphics calls
- An optional WIN-OS/2 video display driver that handled the Windows GDI API graphics calls

Both the PM and WIN-OS/2 presentation drivers made use of the base video driver to set the video modes to appropriate values. The OS/2 VIO functions directly called the base video driver. The OS/2 session manager also used the base video driver when it switched between full-screen sessions. All three of these drivers were relatively large and complex to construct.

The OS/2 Warp Connect (PowerPC Edition) video architecture (GRADD) maintains the distinction between base video support and higher-level presentation drivers but provides a much richer system infrastructure that allows both classes of video drivers to be produced in a much simpler manner. GRADDs (Graphics Adapter Device Drivers) are the video display device drivers that provide the video graphics device support to the graphics subsystems.

The GRADD Model

The GRADD model comprises several different components that provide video-related services for OS/2 Warp Connect (PowerPC Edition). The following components are contained in the GRADD model:

- Video Manager (VMAN)
- Video Manager Interface (VMI) programming interface
- A translation layer for each operating system service
- SOFTDRAW, a software graphics operation simulator
- Graphics Adapter Device Drivers with the Graphics Hardware Interface (GHI) programming interface

The GRADD model uses a layered approach, which provides that only device-dependent code (code that is specific to a particular graphics device) is contained in the GRADD. The code contained in the GRADD is common among the other graphics subsystems that comprise the operating system.

Translation layers exist between the graphics subsystems and the GRADD. These translation layers are responsible for the conversion of complex graphics subsystem calls into the GHI or Graphics Hardware Interface protocol for the GRADD.

The GRADD Model effectively replaces the PM display driver model that is prevalent in previous versions of OS/2. The list of mandatory functions has been layered in such a way as to provide a fast and efficient coding cycle for developers. As you will discover, the list of mandatory functions is very small, allowing a GRADD writer to implement single functions at a time while regression testing in parallel.

Provided the graphics adapter supports direct (nonbanked) access to video memory, all GHI functions other than initialization, returning capabilities, returning mode information, setting the mode, and setting the palette (256-color modes only) are considered optional.

A software component called SOFTDRAW provides software simulation of drawing functions. The GRADD writer can return RC_SIMULATE from any optional GHI call to have SOFTDRAW handle the rendering. In this way, after a developer has completed coding the mandatory functions, the developer is free to incrementally implement the code that is needed to take advantage of the hardware acceleration features, returning RC_SIMULATE for those GHI functions not yet coded.

The following provides a brief description of the components that comprise the GRADD model with a description of their function or purpose.

- Video Manager

  VMAN synchronizes the communication between translation layers and a GRADD. VMAN also manages the graphics pointer. When an operating system service requests a graphics operation, the associated translation layer sends one of the defined Video Manager Interface (VMI) commands to VMAN. Upon receiving a VMI command, VMAN will either handle the request or send it down to the appropriate GRADD.

- Translation Layers

  The translation layers convert function calls, made by the graphics engines of the various operating system services, to the VMI protocol required by VMAN.

- SOFTDRAW

  When a GRADD requests that a drawing operation be simulated in software, VMAN can default to SOFTDRAW for the operation.

- Graphics Adapter Device Driver

  The GRADD executes the requested operation or returns it for simulation.

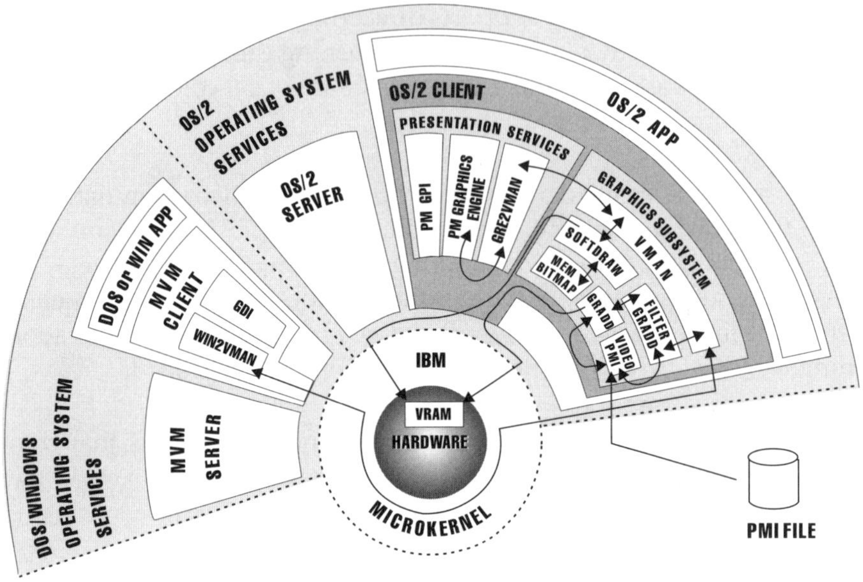

Figure 9-8. Components of the GRADD Model.

When a GRADD receives a GHI function call that is not mandatory from VMAN, the GRADD has the option of performing the requested operation or returning the request to VMAN with a return code of RC_SIMULATE. The RC_SIMULATE return code informs VMAN that the operation needs to be simulated in software.

The highest layers in the Figure 9-8 are the OS/2 and WIN-OS/2 presentation layers. The OS/2 presentation layer (which is also known as the PM Graphics Engine, or PMGRE) supports the OS/2 Graphics Programming Interface (GPI) API set. The WIN-OS/2 presentation layer supports the Windows Graphics Device Interface (GDI) API set.

The Video Manager

The Video Manager component receives requests from the various translation layers. VMAN relies on a special protocol to receive these requests. The protocol or Video Manager Interface represents a small number of operations, each identified by a unique function number. Because VMAN exports a single entry (essentially a router), these function numbers are required to qualify the operation.

The exported function from VMAN is called VMIEntry. VMIEntry requires four parameters from each function call that it receives from a translation layer.

The declaration for VMIEntry is as follows:

```
ULONG VMIENTRY(GID gid, ULONG ulFunction, PVOID pIn, PVOID pOut);
```

During the initialization of VMAN, several components are loaded and initialized. Among these components are SOFTDRAW and any GRADDs that are needed for the available graphics adapters. Each graphics adapter is not limited to a single GRADD.

Multiple GRADDs are supported in this model. It is possible to both filter and extend the GRADD operations by implementing a filter GRADD that can be placed between VMAN and the main GRADD. This chaining provides a means of modifying the GRADD's behavior without rewriting the code. Extending the GRADD architecture is discussed in more detail in the section "GRADD Programming and Extensions."

The GID or GRADD identification parameter of the VMIEntry function is used to discriminate the requests from the different translation layers. The GID parameter corresponds to the ID number of the GRADD receiving the operation.

The next parameter is ulFunction, which is the GHI function number identifying the requested operation.

Parameters 3 and 4 are pointers to input and output data structures (pIn, pOut) that are specific to each of the VMI functions.

Differences between the VMAN protocol (VMI) and the GRADD's (GHI) protocol include the following:

- The Video Manager Interface (VMI) is a superset of the Graphics Hardware Interface (GHI).
- The ulFunction parameter for GHI changes to the appropriate VMI_CMD function name. VMAN is responsible for managing the pointer or cursor.

When a pointer movement occurs, VMAN receives notification through the VMI_CMD_MOVEPTR function. VMAN calls down the GRADD chain for the pointer update. The GRADD can either return RC_SIMULATE to VMAN, allowing VMAN to update the pointer simulate, or handle the update directly. If RC_SIMULATE is returned, VMAN simulates the pointer movement via the bitblt command.

The state of the pointer is tracked by VMAN. When VMAN receives a drawing operation, a check is made to determine if the pointer needs to be removed or disabled around the call. This situation is common when a software pointer is in use. VMI commands that affect the display must include the areas of the screen being updated. VMAN will use this information to determine if the pointer needs to be removed before passing the drawing command down the GRADD chain. When the drawing command returns, VMAN will restore the pointer if it was previously removed.

Translation Layers

Translation layers gain access to the hardware capabilities and available modes through the CHAININFO structure. The CHAININFO structure is returned from the VMI_CMD_QUERYCHAININFO function call. Translation layers communicate to VMAN through the VMIEntry function. After checking the function number passed to VMIEntry, VMAN either processes the call or passes the call along to the GRADD chain. If the GRADD returns RC_SIMULATE, VMAN will process the call.

The OS/2 Graphics Engine (GRE) has associated with it a translation layer call GRE2VMAN. GRE2VMAN is the first component loaded for the GRADD model. It calls VMIEntry with the VMI_CMD_INIT command. The first time VMAN encounters this call, it loads additional GRADD components.

The translation layer for the DOS or Multiple Virtual Machine (MVM) environment is called GDI2VMAN. GDI2VMAN maps the graphics primitives of the WIN-OS/2 Graphics Device Interface (GDI) to the VMAN protocol. A virtual device driver called VVMI allows GDI2VMAN to call VMAN. First, GDI2VMAN calls VVMI using the VMI calling convention. Then, VVMI calls VMAN.

The extensibility of the GRADD architecture allows the adaptation of other graphics subsystems. For each new or different graphics subsystem, a translation layer must be written that maps its graphics primitives to the VMAN protocol. To further extend the GRADD model, the VMI extension protocol can be used. For more on this, please refer to the section "GRADD Programming and Extensions."

The Software Simulation of SOFTDRAW

The SOFTDRAW component simulates graphics functions for nonaccelerated graphics operations.

When a GRADD returns RC_SIMULATE, VMAN uses the SDBITBLT and SDLINE functions exported by SOFTDRAW to "software simulate" the drawing operation. This simulation is a powerful concept that allows many functions in the GRADD to be scaled down from mandatory to optional. It also makes possible the concept of the generic GRADD or GENGRADD. GENGRADD allows for the non-chip-specific support of drawing functions.

The VMAN/GRADD Interface

Each GRADD exports a function called HWEntry, which is the same function type as VMIEntry in VMAN.

```
ULONG  HWENTRY(GID gid, ULONG ulFunction, PVOID pIn, PVOID pOut);
```

VMAN calls the GRADD through the HWENTRY function.

A GRADD contains the code that exploits the accelerated features of a graphics adapter. If a GRADD elects not to handle a particular operation, it can return RC_SIMULATE. Returning RC_SIMULATE allows the SOFTDRAW component to draw directly to the video memory of the hardware. VMAN manages video memory serialization through the GHI_CMD_REQUESTHW function.

Each GRADD must process the following GHI_CMD functions:

- GHI_CMD_INIT
- GHI_CMD_QUERYCAPS
- GHI_CMD_QUERYMODES
- GHI_CMD_SETMODE
- GHI_CMD_PALETTE (This function is mandatory only when a 256-color mode has been chosen.)

The following GHI functions can return RC_SIMULATE and let VMAN handle the operations:

- GHI_CMD_BITBLT
- GHI_CMD_LINE
- GHI_CMD_SETPTR
- GHI_CMD_MOVEPTR
- GHI_CMD_SHOWPTR

GRADD Programming and Extensions

The extensibility of the GRADD model is key, because graphics hardware is always changing. Using the VMI_CMD_EXTENSION command, the GRADD writer can create an extension that passes its own commands to the GRADD. Because the GRADD model allows chaining, extensions can be made to existing GRADDs or to a new GRADD.

```
SET GRADD_CHAINS=CHAIN1,CHAIN2,CHAIN3
SET CHAIN1=GRADD1,FILTER1A,FILTER1B,FILTER1C
SET CHAIN2=GRADD2
SET CHAIN3=GRADD3,FILTER3A
```

Figure 9-9. Configuration Statements That Specify GRADD Chains

Figure 9-9 shows an example of configuration statements that specify three GRADD chains. The first GRADD chain contains three filter GRADDs. The second GRADD chain contains no filter GRADDs. The third GRADD chain contains a single filter GRADD. The names of the GRADDs and filter GRADDs are completely arbitrary for this example. In the example, for instance, the names GRADD1 and FILTER1A correspond to the library files GRADD1.DLL and FILTER1A.DLL.

Adding Extensions to an Existing GRADD

When VMAN initializes a GRADD by calling the GHI_CMD_INIT function, it passes the GRADD a unique ID, the GID. The GRADD then returns the number of function classes that it supports.

The GRADD is responsible for assigning a unique GID to each of its function-class instances. VMAN increments the GID, which it passes to the GRADD for each function-class instance.

Developer's Tip: For Presentation Manager and seamless Windows functions, a GRADD must support the Base Function class of services. The GRE2VMAN component looks specifically for a GRADD that supports this class of function.

VMAN allocates a GRADDINFO structure for every class of function that a GRADD supports. VMAN calls GHI_CMD_QUERYCAPS once for every function-class instance. In this way, an extension layer can associate a GID with a set of function classes.

The VMI_CMD_EXTENSION function is used by the extension to communicate with a GRADD. The extension layer defines its own unique extension functions. The extensions must utilize VMAN to communicate with the GRADD. The input packet to the VMI_CMD_EXTENSION function includes information about screen change areas and hardware serialization. With this information, VMAN is able to maintain hardware pointer support and serialization to the hardware.

The extension GRADD uses the pszFunctionClassID field, located in the CAPSINFO data structure, to identify itself to the system. VMAN uses the GHI_CMD_QUERYCAPS command to get this information. An example of an extension is the EnDive extension, which is discussed in the following section.

The Graphics Adapter Device Driver Interface (GHI) functions are listed on pages 185 and 186. Each of these functions has an identical corresponding VMAN VMI_CMD function. Remember that the VMI functions use VMIEntry, while the GHI functions use HWEntry.

Providing EnDIVE Support as an Extension GRADD

EnDIVE (Enhanced Direct Interface Video Extension) is a software extension that provides a multimedia mechanism for the accelerated display of video images (see Figure 9-10). Today's video accelerator cards are capable of performing stretch blts, or scaling, in hardware.

In addition to stretch blt capabilities, features such as color conversion, compression, and decompression are found in the more powerful video accelerators. Multimedia acceleration software can take direct advantage of these capabilities when implemented as a GRADD extension.

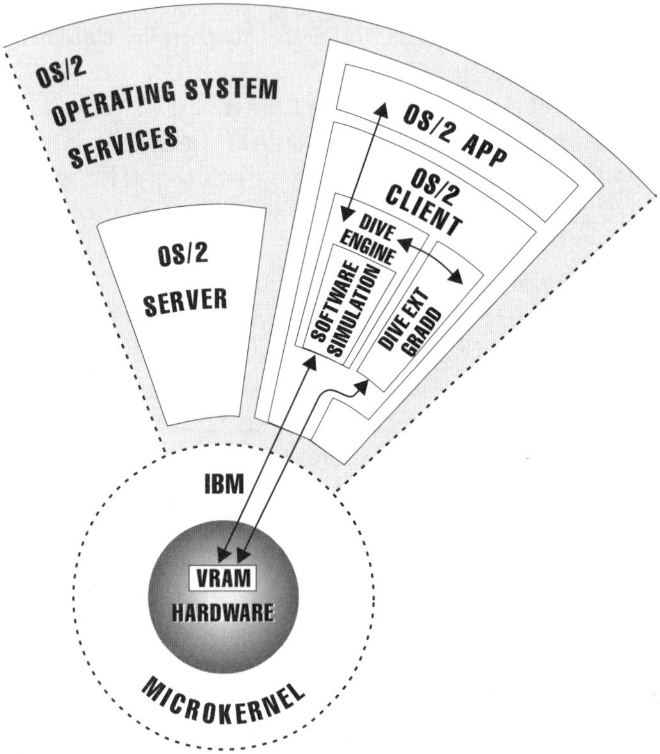

Figure 9-10. EnDIVE Display Engine

Note: Because the OS/2 Warp EnDIVE drivers are implemented as GRADD extensions, they can be easily ported to OS/2 Warp Connect (PowerPC Edition).

Four functions make up the EnDIVE multimedia extension GRADD. These functions are contained in the ulXSubFunction field of the HWEXTENSION packet. For each extension function, the pXP1 field of the HWEXTENSION packet points to the input packet.

The following table provides a list of the EXT_CMD functions that are specific to the EnDIVE. These EnDIVE functions have no corresponding VMI_CMD functions.

Function	Type
EXT_CMD_ENDIVE_GET	Optional
EXT_CMD_ENDIVE_INIT	Mandatory
EXT_CMD_ENDIVE_PUT	Mandatory
EXT_CMD_ENDIVE_QUERY	Mandatory

So far, we have seen how acceleration or exploitation of a graphic chip is accomplished. In the next section, we will explore how the video chip is programmed for various text and graphic modes in a manner that is independent of any particular operating system service.

VIDEOPMI

The VIDEOPMI layer supports video device control operations. It is a standard OS/2 Warp Connect (PowerPC Edition) system component that implements an extension of the VESA Super VGA Protect Mode Interface (SVPMI) standard.

The SVPMI standard was developed so that Intel 80x86 protect-mode applications would have a standard way of accessing and controlling the proliferating versions of modern graphics adapters (as an alternative to the Intel 80x86 real-mode BIOS interfaces). SVPMI describes a graphics adapter in terms of its ports and memory space. It provides a means to query, set, save, and restore supported video modes.

In addition to being called from the GRADD layer, the VIDEOPMI layer is also called from other portions of the OS/2 Warp Connect (PowerPC Edition) system (for example, the OS/2 VIO functions and the DOS Virtual SVGA (VVIDEO) device drivers).

The VIDEOPMI layer is a generalized piece of code that contains no specialized knowledge of particular video cards. It gains its specialized knowledge from a configuration file, the Protect Mode Interface (PMI) file.

The PMI file tells the VIDEOPMI component what video capabilities a given video device supports. It also tells VIDEOPMI how to transform generic video device control operations (such as the setting of a specific video mode) into the appropriate video card-specific operations.

The PMI file can be generated manually. OS/2 Warp Connect (PowerPC Edition) also provides utilities for the automated creation of a PMI file. If the video device driver developer wishes to subsequently modify the generated PMI file, the developer edits the PMI in order to optimize the video control logic contained within the configuration file.

The VIDEOPMI layer provides a standard simplified framework into which to code base video support. Typically, the video device driver developer produces a PMI file rather than writing an entire base video driver. In OS/2 Warp Connect (PowerPC Edition), a relatively simple GRADD library and a PMI file provide complete video device driver support for a new video display device.

VIDEOPMI Functions

The following are the video control functions supported by the VIDEOPMI layer:

PMIREQUEST_LOADPMIFILE	Load the specified PMI file.
PMIREQUEST_SETMODE	Set the specified video mode.
PMIREQUEST_LOCKREGISTERS	Lock extended registers.
PMIREQUEST_UNLOCKREGISTERS	Unlock extended registers.
PMIREQUEST_CLEANUP	Clean up extended registers.
PMIREQUEST_SAVESTATE	Save video adapter state.
PMIREQUEST_RESTORESTATE	Restore video adapter state.
PMIREQUEST_GETBANK	Get currently addressed video memory bank.
PMIREQUEST_SETBANK	Set currently addressed video memory bank.
PMIREQUEST_GETCLUT	Get Color Lookup Table.
PMIREQUEST_SETCLUT	Set Color Lookup Table.
PMIREQUEST_GETPALETTE	Get copy of palette registers.
PMIREQUEST_SETPALETTE	Set palette registers.
PMIREQUEST_GETFONT	Get currently loaded font.
PMIREQUEST_SETFONT	Load given font.
PMIREQUEST_TUNEDISPLAY	Tune the display.
PMIREQUEST_IDENTIFYADAPTER	Identify the installed graphics adapter.

PMIREQUEST_QUERYMAXMODEENTRIES	Return the number of available video modes.
PMIREQUEST_QUERYMAXMODELISTSIZE	Return maximum size required to store video mode data.
PMIREQUEST_QUERYMAXMODEINFODATA	Return table of video mode information.
PMIREQUEST_QUERYMAXTRAPENTRIES	Return number of trap entries.
PMIREQUEST_QUERYTRAPLISTDATA	Return table of data for trapped ports.
PMIREQUEST_QUERYMODEHRDWRLIST	Return the set mode command list.
PMIREQUEST_WPOSVIDEOACCESS	Map the video resource to the address space of the calling process.
PMIREQUEST_WPOSGETPIOINFO	Get the virtual address of the passed physical address.

PMI File Language Elements

A PMI file is divided into a series of sections. Each section is identified by a keyword identifier. The front of the file contains a set of header sections that describe the graphics adapter and the PMI file itself. The header sections are followed by a series of sections that contain lists of commands that are used to perform global adapter operations such as hardware locking and unlocking. There are sections that describe the writeable I/O and memory space registers. The remainder of the PMI file is a series of sections that describe the various modes supported by the graphics adapter and contains sections of commands that are required in order to manipulate these video modes.

Figure 9-11 illustrates two portions of a PMI file.

```
[PMIVersion]
        1.0

[Hardware]
        BusType         = PCI
        OEMString       = "S386C864 SDAC, S3 Incorporated"
        Version         = "Diamond Stealth 64 DRAM"
        DACString       = "S3SDAC_RGB S3 Incorporated"
        TotalMemory     = 0x200000        /* 2MB */
        MemoryIOAddress = 0x00000000
        Endian          = LITTLE

[ProgramDAC]
        inb(r5, 0x3c8);
        rmwbi(0x3d4,0x3d5,0x55,0xfe,0x01);
        outb(0x3c6,r0);
        outb(0x3c8,0x02);
        outb(0x3c9,r1);
        outb(0x3c9,r2);
        outb(0x3c8,0x0a);
        outb(0x3c9,r3);
        outb(0x3c9,r4);
        rmwbi(0x3d4,0x3d5,0x55,0xfe,0x00);
        outb(0x3c6, 0xff);
        inb(r5, 0x3c8);

[UnLock]

        outw(0x3d4, 0x4838);
        outw(0x3d4, 0xa539);
        rmwb(0x3d4, 0x3d5, 0x40, 0xfe, 0x01);
                .
                .
                .
[comment]
       Graphics Mode: 640 x 480 x 256 colors.

[ModeInfo]
       ModeAttributes   = 0x18
       BytesPerScanLine = 640
       XResolution      = 640
       YResolution      = 480
       TextRows         = 30
       BitsPerPixel     = 8
       NumberOfPlanes   = 1
       PageLength       = 307200
```

Figure 9-11. Portions of a PMI File

In the example, the PMIVersion, Hardware, ProgramDAC, UnLock, comment, and ModeInfo sections make up the header sections of the PMI file. They provide descriptions of the PMI file version and type of hardware contained within the graphics adapter.

The UnLock section contains a set of I/O commands that are to be used in order to make the hardware available for the execution of the mode setting commands, as well as for the saving and restoring of the controller and video buffer. The UnLock section is truncated in the example.

The example then continues at the start of one of the video mode sets of sections. The ModeInfo section lists the various attributes that characterize the video mode. The ModeInfo section is followed by other sections that contain commands that are involved in the setting and resetting of the video mode described in the ModeInfo section.

The Character Mode Subsystem

OS/2 Warp Connect (PowerPC Edition) preserves the text mode environment available in previous versions of OS/2. These text mode environments include the DOS Full Screen, DOS Window, OS/2 Full Screen, and OS/2 Window session types.

Most DOS programs access the video hardware either through direct port I/O, video memory access, or through calls to the video BIOS. Calls to the video BIOS (through software interrupt 10H) will either be passed to the hardware or emulated by the Virtual Video Subsystem. Video-hardware-related operations in a DOS window will always be abstracted from the hardware and emulated.

From a functional point of view, users should see very few differences between OS/2 Warp Connect (PowerPC Edition) and previous versions of OS/2 in terms of the operation and behavior of DOS applications.

To protect the investment for OS/2 Full Screen and OS/2 Window applications, the VIO, KBD, and MOU functions are preserved. In order to present a consistent programming model for such things as input queue hooking, the OS/2 base and Presentation Manager subsystem have been integrated. All user interaction in OS/2 goes through the Presentation Manager Subsystem. Because VIDEOPMI is capable of setting text modes, PM is free to use these text modes when appropriate to facilitate performance. Full-screen sessions are simply VIO windows with no border. The Presentation Manager Subsystem and character-mode OS2CHAR dynamic link library decide whether to use a graphical mode or a hardware text mode to display output to the monitor. Both DOS and OS/2 sessions are dynamically switchable between window and full-screen states. An ALT-HOME hot key initiates this dynamic session switch transition in either environment.

The OS2CHAR (OS/2 Character Subsystem) implements support for full-screen or windowed VIO as a common code base. OS2CHAR maintains a logical video buffer for each session.

Keyboard and Mouse Support

Text mode consists not only of the video support but also of support for the keyboard and mouse (see Figure 9-12). The OS/2 text-mode support is handled by a set of functions implemented in OS2CHAR, which in turn uses Event and Window Services to implement most of the function. The video support for the DOS environment is implemented in the Virtual Video device driver. For further detail on the Event and Window Services, see Chapter 8, "Presentation Services" on page 139.

OS2CHAR Kbd Implementation

The keyboard support is functionally equivalent to the VIO window support in previous versions of OS/2. An additional function is added to get either keyboard or mouse information from the console. This simplifies the synchronization of the mouse and keyboard. Some functions that were hardware dependent have been eliminated. Functions to set the keyboard type have been added.

Getting input from the console device (STDIN) is implemented by the KbdGetConsole function for keyboard and mouse buttons only. Each character is placed in the input buffer. With the exception of terminal mode, an extended character (such as a function key) is indicated by a leading zero character.

Kbd implements support for several keyboard modes:

Binary Returns characters one at a time.

ASCII Buffers returned data until a line end or extended key is pressed. This is incompatible with Binary mode.

Term Converts extended codes to escape sequences.

Echo Translates to a DosWrtTty of the character. This is incompatible with Binary Mode.

Shift Reports shift-key transitions and key-up events. This is incompatible with ASCII and Term modes.

Developer's Tip: The Keyboard IOCtl calls of previous versions of OS/2 are emulated in OS/2 Warp Connect (PowerPC Edition) when you call the Kbd functions.

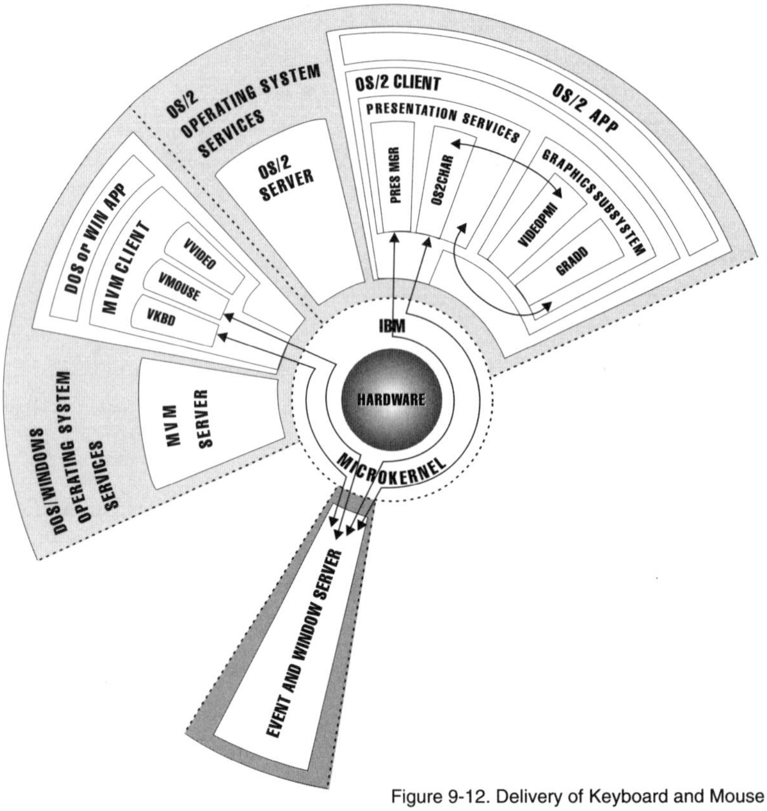

Figure 9-12. Delivery of Keyboard and Mouse Events

OS2CHAR MOU (Mouse) Implementation

The mouse support is functionally similar to that of previous versions of OS/2. The open and close operations are no longer necessary.

Developer's Tip: The Mouse IOCtl calls of previous versions of OS/2 are emulated in OS/2 Warp Connect (PowerPC Edition) when you call the MOU functions.

Keyboard and mouse support in the DOS environment is implemented as the virtual device drivers VKBD and VMOUSE. Both are coupled to the Event and Window server for the delivery of keyboard and mouse events.

This section has covered the low-level management of the video hardware. Let's now move on to the Print subsystem, focusing on the overall architecture and protection of your investment in existing code.

Printing

The Print Server (spooler) provides printing functions largely equivalent to those in OS/2 Warp. The spooler:

- Provides printing from multiple operating system services. Among those services are OS/2 and MVM (DOS).
- Uses interfaces consistent between printing and display, such as GPI, GDI, and X.
- Handles the printing of print data streams.
- Manages the serialization and prioritization of print jobs.
- Allows attributes to be specified for print jobs through an Application Programming Interface (API).
- Provides compatibility for existing OS/2 and Windows applications.
- Extends the 32-bit OS/2 print-driver code using the new Omni driver support.

The spooler normally controls all devices specified as printers. The print queue is the target for printing. Operating system services can provide an interface that redirects output from such a device to the spooler. Previous versions of OS/2 do this when a file is copied to LPT1. The current Spl, Prt, and Dev calls can be used from OS/2.

OS/2 applications can direct the spooler into either raw or std mode. In raw mode, the presentation driver converts the data stream in the user process and then calls the spooler to spool the data. In std mode, the presentation driver journals the GRE calls and converts them to a data stream as the job is removed from the queue. The MVM operating system service always uses std mode.

The spooler is multithreaded, with a thread for each printer device and one or more for control functions.

The 32-bit user level (ring 3) presentation drivers used in OS/2 2.1 and later versions can be used as the base for creating spooler print drivers. It might be desirable to recode parts of these devices to make use of the new graphics engine.

Spooler Objects

The spooler objects are described in this section.

- Logical printer

  The logical printer matches the selected OS/2 print queue. Users can have as many of these as they want. Logical printers are put into the name space in the PRINTER directory.

  The persistent state of the logical printer is kept as a set of attributes in the registry. Normally, this data is accessed only by the spooler. The attributes include the print drivers and port drivers associated with the logical printer.

  There can be multiple print drivers and port drivers associated with a logical printer. However, at the time a spool job is opened, one of them must be selected. Normally, the default print driver and port driver are used.

  Many of the attributes of the logical printer can be overridden as job attributes. The printer attributes can be thought of as the job default attributes in this case.

- Print drivers

  The print driver matches the selected OS/2 print driver object. The print driver determines the Printer Description Language used (for example, PostScript, PCL5, or Dot Matrix).

  The print driver has a set of attributes. These attributes are specified on a per-printer or per-job basis (printer properties or job properties). Many attributes can be specified in either place.

- Port drivers

  The port driver is a high-level controller for data going across a port. It provides a high-level interface to the physical device. The port driver handles the bidirectional interface with the printer and maintains the current state of the printer.

  The persistent state of the port is kept as a set of attributes to the port driver in the registry. Normally, this data is accessed only by the spooler.

- Spool job

  The spool job is created when a logical printer is opened. The spool job inherits the attributes from the logical printer, print driver, and port driver. Many of these attributes can be specified on an individual job basis. The job also has a set of attributes that are unique to the job.

Printing from OS/2

There are several methods of printing in OS/2:

- Use the Presentation Manager interfaces that print using the GPI functions.
- Drag a file to the Printer desktop object.
- Copy a file to a logical printer using the COPY or PRINT commands.
- Use an application that opens the file using the Spl functions.
- Copy a file to a port (such as LPT1) or use an application that opens the port as a file. OS/2 selects a logical printer associated with that port.

Printing from DOS and Windows

There are several methods of printing from DOS and Windows:

- Use the Windows Print interfaces that print using the GDI functions.
- From DOS, copy a file to a port using the COPY or PRINT command or use an application that opens the port as a file. DOS selects a logical printer associated with that port.

DOS printing is done by having the OS/2 spooler do a DosFSAttach in place of the parallel port for the logical devices supported by the spooler (LPTx).

The MVM server provides a virtual device driver (VLPT) that handles the DOS side of these communications. VLPT must be modified to know that there is a spooler at the other end rather than a printer. VDH Services detect that the logical device is attached to the spooler and make the appropriate spooler calls.

LAN-Based Printing

The spooler must be able to run as a complete system without a LAN attachment. However, many users will be in a LAN-based environment. Printers that are connected to other nodes in the network should behave the same as local printers whenever possible.

Redirection of the spool job is done at a single point in the port driver. The LAN server will not need to redirect the port as is done in previous versions of OS/2.

Normally, redirection is done without the data being spooled to disk. However, the placement of the redirection is such that all processing for local printers can be done for LAN-attached printers.

Homogeneous Networks

For homogeneous networks, it is possible to run the common print client library on one computer and run the spooler on another computer. This setup requires that resources that are normally passed by reference be sent across the network.

Heterogeneous Networks

For heterogeneous networks, all conversion must be done before the spool job leaves the originating computer. The attributes of the spool job must be in an external form.

OS/2 Printer Objects

Printer objects are based on the spooler interface used in previous versions of OS/2. Most of this code can be taken unmodified from the earlier 32-bit code.

The OS/2 Warp Port Driver user interface will be used as the basis of the OS/2 Warp Connect (PowerPC Edition) port objects. There is one port object instance for each port that can support a printer. Setup of the port is supported by the port object.

There can be as many printer objects in the system as the user desires. Each printer object defines a set of attributes including the current print driver and port.

The LAN-aware interfaces of previous versions of OS/2 are maintained.

Reuse of Current Print Drivers

It is highly desirable that current investment in print drivers be maintained. The source for existing printer drivers can be used if the following restrictions are followed:

- All code must be 32-bit C code.
- All code must execute in user mode (ring 3 on Intel-based systems).

Port Drivers

The function of Port drivers will be implemented for OS/2 Warp Connect (PowerPC Edition), but bidirectional printer communications will not work because the required device driver support is not available. Port drivers can be used to implement functions that were previously implemented with device monitors.

Print Presentation Drivers

Print presentation drivers are supplied for the following printers.

All of these are 32-bit C presentation drivers that are source-compatible between OS/2 2.0 (and later versions) and OS/2 Warp Connect (PowerPC Edition). Most non-IBM print drivers will not be easily recompiled because they are 16-bit assembler. However, this list includes almost all PC-attached printers.

- IBMNULL (passthrough)
- PostScript (level 1, level 2)
- HP LaserJet (III, 4)
- PPDS (4019/4029)
- Omni driver (HP DeskJet, HP PaintJet, Epson)

Omni Printer Support

The Omni driver will support Epson, DeskJet and PaintJet devices. The Omni driver will also provide a means of quickly supporting other raster printer devices.

The objective of the Omni driver is to provide a portable printer presentation driver. The driver should be able to generically print to a large set of raster printer devices.

This driver replaces several existing printer drivers and provides support for many printers that are not currently supported.

The Omni driver supports as many functions as are needed by existing raster printer devices without becoming specific to any one device. (Examples of these functions are generic tray, form, and font handling.)

Device-specific data and functions should be removed from the Omni driver itself in a binary data format and functions too specific to one device should be provided in a library when necessary.

The components of Omni printer support are as follows:

- Omni Printer Driver

  A generic raster printer driver that interfaces with the OS/2 graphics engine. The Omni driver is able to send raw or standard data to the spooler and provide generic job and printer Property dialogs for user configuration and setup. This raster driver supports monochrome and color raster devices at any defined resolution. Support of devices is based on information provided in binary data files that describe each device.

- Generic Print Library

  A library of printer-centric functions used by the Omni Printer Driver to aid in banding, compression, journaling, memory management, device font management, and more. This library's functions can be used by other printer drivers as well.

- Device Description Files

  Binary data files that generically describe to the Omni driver an individual device or group of similar devices. The data includes physical characteristics of each device to be supported, such as resolutions, color information, tray information, form information, font information, and language commands. This data is used by the Omni driver to display dialogs and set up its internal rendering parameters and functions.

- Device Function Libraries

  An optional function library that allows devices with special characteristics to supply their own functions to perform certain tasks in the driver (such as compressing data). The presence of the library and its functions can be indicated in the Device Description File.

- Device File PM Application

  An application used to create and modify binary Device Description Files that describe devices to the Omni driver. This application provides the operator with the ability to input all the device capabilities including forms, trays, and fonts.

- Application interface to the Omni driver

  Applications print to the Omni driver as they do to any other OS/2 printer driver, by using the OS/2 functions (Gpi, Spl, and Dev functions). There are no special entry points for applications into the Omni driver.

- GPI interface to the Omni driver

  The Gpi interface to the Omni driver is unchanged from the interface used in previous versions of OS/2. All Gpi calls are screened by PM GPI and passed to the OS/2 Graphics Engine. There are no special entry points for the PM GPI into the Omni driver.

  Note: The PM GPI is still responsible for recording Gpi graphics commands when an application prints PM_Q_STD.

- Graphics Engine interface to the Omni driver

  The Omni driver uses the new GRE generic rasterization support (SOFTDRAW). This support allows the Omni driver to call the graphics engine to perform graphic rendering to a raster space owned by the printer driver. The graphics engine when rendering will provide some basic functions that are expected from printed raster output, such as dithering and grayscaling. The GRE supports all OS/2 bit-map formats.

- PM Spooler interface to the Omni driver

  The Omni driver provides for additional entry points that the spooler requires for bidirectional printing.

The Omni driver allows for the proper termination code for printer driver unloading.

- PM Print Object interface to the Omni driver

  The Omni driver provides entry points for installing device description files.

Shared Services Interface

The following shared service functions are available for DOS to communicate with a printer. Currently, these functions do an IPC to an OS/2 process that can run the equivalent Spl function. These functions are designed to provide minimal functionality.

- typedef unsigned long prt_hand_t;
- ulong prt_openldev(char * name, prt_hand_t * hprt);
- ulong prt_close(hprt);
- ulong prt_write(hprt, char * buffer, unsigned long len);

The prt_openldev function takes an ASCII name of a logical device. The logical device must be in the LDEVICE directory. This is normally a name such as "lpt1." The function returns a handle that is used when the prt_write and prt_close functions are called.

Common Code

Almost all of the printing logic will be common between OS/2 Warp and this release. A small amount of code that is unique to OS/2 Warp Connect (PowerPC Edition) is necessary to allow MVM printing. The major device drivers were recoded in 32-bit C for OS/2 Warp and will be usable in OS/2 Warp Connect (PowerPC Edition), largely by recompilation.

Internationalization

Internal font lookup is done with Unicode instead of the UGL used in previous versions of OS/2. Fonts that represent the additional character sets for all supported countries will be included.

The Omni driver design will allow for support of DBCS-enabled printers, including allowing LTR, RTL, HOR, VER printing. Most of the consideration is in the support of device (printer H/W) fonts such as handling their character width information, negative character indexing, Unicode, and large character sets/code pages.

User Interfaces

The device driver user interface is a set of Workplace Shell objects. These are the same as the objects used in previous versions of OS/2.

Installation

The spooler is a required part of OS/2 Warp Connect (PowerPC Edition). The user is given the opportunity to install one or more printers during installation.

Registry

The persistent state of the spooler object's logical printer, print driver, and port driver are kept in the registry. The persistent state of the spool job and its attributes are kept in the file system.

Performance

The key measurements of a printer driver from the user's point of view are:

- The time it takes to create the spool file in standard mode via the graphical interfaces in OS/2 and Windows.

- The speed of the transfer via the physical device driver. Note that the physical device driver is not actually a part of the spooler, but the user will see this as a major component of print speed.

DOS/Windows Services

This chapter provides information about DOS/Windows Services. It describes services that have been available in previous releases of OS/2 as well as services that are new for this release. This chapter also provides information about emulation support, WIN-OS/2 support, and about installing and migrating DOS and Microsoft Windows programs.

Introducing DOS/Windows Services

Since the introduction of OS/2 Version 2.0, OS/2 users have had the ability to run multiple DOS and Microsoft Windows applications concurrently, exploiting the preemptive multitasking abilities and memory protection capabilities of OS/2 to accomplish this. With OS/2 Version 2.1, improved support for Microsoft Windows applications was provided with the incorporation of Microsoft Windows 3.1 features. The *DOS/Windows Services* provide these same capabilities on the microkernel-based architecture.

WIN-OS/2, the component specifically responsible for running Microsoft Windows applications, remains architecturally unchanged on the new platform. The result is that OS/2 users will continue to have the ability to run their Microsoft Windows 3.0 or 3.1 applications in concurrent sessions, even on the PowerPC edition.

The interface to DOS and WIN-OS/2 sessions appears exactly as it did in OS/2 Warp Version 3.0. Users have the option of initiating DOS or WIN-OS/2 sessions that run full screen or in a window by selecting the appropriate icon, as shown in Figure 10-1.

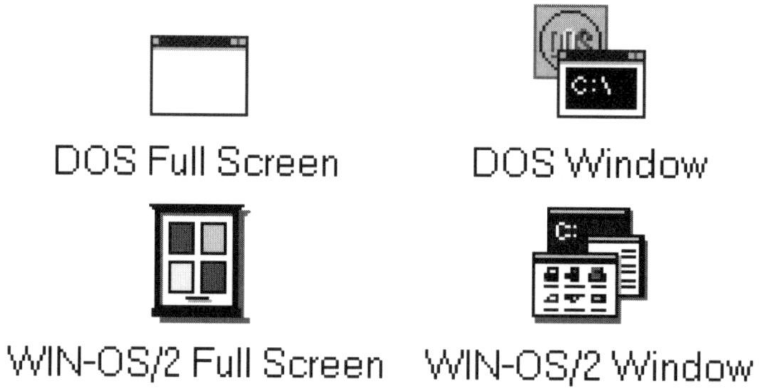

Figure 10-1. DOS and WIN-OS/2 Icons

One possible scenario might include an OS/2 window, a DOS program window, and a Microsoft Windows application, all running on an OS/2 Desktop at the same time.

The flexibility of this platform becomes immediately obvious from this example—users have the ability to exploit a more powerful hardware platform while maintaining the ability to utilize a familiar operating environment (OS/2 Warp Connect) and run their heritage DOS and Microsoft Windows applications, unchanged, in a window on the Desktop with other OS/2 applications.

Summary of MVDM Architecture

Beginning with OS/2 Version 2.0, support for multiple concurrent DOS applications has been provided. Each application has run as a single-threaded, protect-mode OS/2 program. This capability was provided via the introduction of a set of components known as *Multiple Virtual DOS Machines (MVDMs)*. MVDM exploits the Virtual 86 (V86) mode of Intel 80386 and later processors to establish separate instances of independent *Virtual DOS Machines (VDMs)*. Each VDM is a separate 80386 task, running as a protect-mode process, just as any OS/2 application might.

The result is that multiple DOS or Microsoft Windows applications can run simultaneously in an environment in which every application (DOS or OS/2 application) and other system resources are protected from any applications that are not well behaved. If one DOS session terminates abnormally, it does not affect the rest of the system. This feature is referred to as "crash protection."

OS/2 Version 2.0 also provided the ability to run DPMI applications. *DOS Protect Mode Interface (DPMI)* is a programming interface for DOS applications that use real-mode operations (such as direct hardware access or interrupts) that are not permitted in a protect-mode task. DPMI functions allow an application to enter protect mode and perform real-mode functions (such as allocating real-mode memory or simulating real-mode interrupts) by doing appropriate address translations, switching the processor to real mode, and making the appropriate DOS service requests. Results of the request are translated back to protect-mode format, the processor is returned to protect mode, and control is returned to the application.

What Remains the Same?

DOS/Windows Services in OS/2 Warp Connect (PowerPC Edition) provide the following functions that are compatible with those in previous releases of OS/2:

- Boot a DOS emulation kernel in a VDM
- Boot true DOS in a VDM
- Run (multiple) DOS applications full-screen or in windows
- Provide DOS and Microsoft Windows applications access to a common set of file systems
- Provide virtual device support to allow sharing of devices between DOS and Microsoft Windows applications and OS/2 applications
- Provide EMS 4.0, XMS 2.0, and DPMI 0.9+ host support
- Provide support for Microsoft Windows applications (Versions 3.0 and 3.1)
- Provide support for user configuration of the DOS/Windows environment on a per-VDM basis through user-modifiable DOS properties

What Is Different?

While the DOS and WIN-OS/2 functionality provided with OS/2 Warp Connect (PowerPC Edition) is equivalent to previous releases of OS/2, there are a few key differences in the architecture of the DOS/Windows Services. The *Multiple Virtual Machine (MVM) Server* is responsible for providing the DOS/Microsoft Windows/DPMI program compatibility. MVM manages and supports execution of multiple x86 programs, both real mode and protect mode, each in its own Virtual DOS (x86) Machine. The set of VDMs and the MVM Server that manages them collectively make up the DOS/Windows environment.

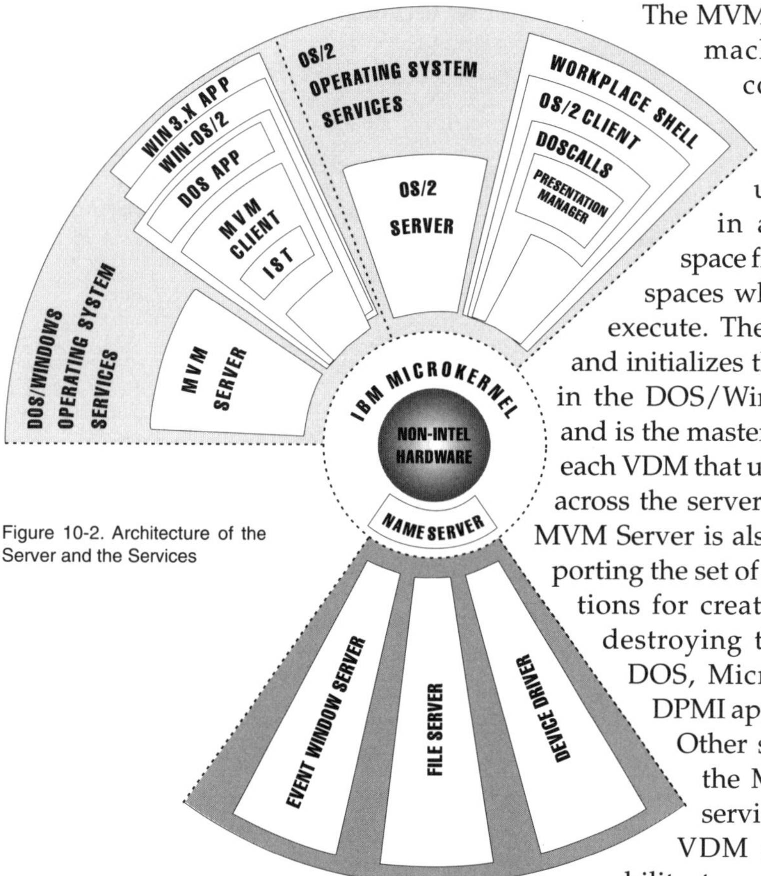

Figure 10-2. Architecture of the Server and the Services

The MVM Server is the virtual machine management component of the DOS/Windows environment (see figure 10-2). It executes in a separate address space from the VDM address spaces where the applications execute. The MVM Server loads and initializes the other components in the DOS/Windows environment and is the master copy for portions of each VDM that utilize shared memory across the server and the VDMs. The MVM Server is also responsible for exporting the set of message-based functions for creating, managing, and destroying the VDMs in which DOS, Microsoft Windows, or DPMI applications can be run. Other services provided by the MVM Server include services that facilitate per-VDM configuration (the ability to query or modify DOS Settings, also called DOS Properties). These functions or services are available to other servers in the system (specifically, the OS/2 Server).

The MVM Server runs as a Microkernel task. Although it depends on other Microkernel tasks (for example, shared services) for items such as file system management and mouse and keyboard events, the MVM Server is architecturally capable of running stand-alone, without the OS/2 Server present. However, for the first release of OS/2 Warp Connect (PowerPC Edition), the MVM Server utilizes many of the services provided by the OS/2 Server for booting and shutting down. It utilizes the user interface for modifying DOS Settings and the window management services for window sessions on the OS/2 Desktop.

The DOS/Windows Services use a sophisticated emulation technology for executing Intel binaries on the PowerPC. This technology means that users can install DOS or Microsoft Windows applications (purchased off the shelf) in their current Intel binary format and be able to run these unchanged on OS/2 Warp Connect (PowerPC Edition).

The Instruction Set Translator (IST) provides the emulation engine. The IST emulates Intel instructions on non-Intel hardware. It supports 386, Ring 3 protect-mode and real-mode applications. DOS and Microsoft Windows applications running on the IST believe that they are executing on a 386DX processor.

Developer's Tip: What is an application's view of the kind of processor it is running on (under the emulation provided by IST on OS/2 Warp Connect (PowerPC Edition))?

Try running the MSD application (Microsoft Diagnostics) from the DOS prompt and query the computer information. The result of the query will show that applications believe they are running on an 80386 processor with an 80387 coprocessor, even though this DOS application is running on a PowerPC!

The IST examines a block of instructions at a time and utilizes a translation buffer in virtual memory to enable re-execution of the translated instructions as long as they remain in the buffer. The buffer acts as a cache in that, as soon as the buffer is filled, the least-recently-used translations are purged from the buffer, and that space is reused for newer translations.

The user can modify the size of the translation buffer (via a DOS property) using a Settings notebook. The size of the buffer will have an effect on the efficiency and performance of the application emulation. If the buffer is too small, excessive buffer purging and retranslation will occur, resulting in much slower performance. If the buffer is larger than necessary, the IST will be utilizing more virtual memory than required, causing unnecessary paging in the system. The default size for the translation buffer is 5MB. This value was determined from a performance analysis on a set of common DOS and Microsoft Windows applications running with varying buffer sizes.

The IST Interface consists of a set of IST helpers that are part of the EM86 component of the MVM Server. The interface maps existing Virtual Device Helpers (VDH services) to the IST's "Black Box Translator." One of the goals of this component is to keep the interface between the MVM Server's Virtual Device Drivers (VDDs) and the IST as small as possible to minimize the area in the MVM Server that cares about whether it is executing on non-Intel hardware. The VDDs continue to utilize VDH services independent of whether the hardware platform requires emulation of Intel instructions.

Emulation Support

DOS/Windows Services provide emulation support using Virtual Device Drivers (VDDs), an 8086 Emulation component (EM86), and a component for DOS emulation. The following sections describe how this support is provided.

Virtual Device Drivers

VDDs are part of the DOS/Windows environment, just as they were in previous releases of OS/2. They exist to allow DOS or Microsoft Windows applications to believe that they are the only applications running in a DOS environment. While in the OS/2 environment, they are actually running in an environment that emulates DOS and must share resources. The VDDs are provided to:

- Arbitrate for ownership of a device or resource
- Virtualize a device or emulate a service by communicating with other servers such as physical device drivers or the Event and Window Server
- Emulate DOS memory extensions
- Virtualize other hardware aspects of a PC environment

A number of VDDs known as *base VDDs* are packaged with DOS/Windows Services. Examples include Virtual Keyboard, Virtual Mouse, Virtual CDROM, Virtual BIOS. There are about 20 in all.

Other VDDs can be added to the DOS/Windows environment to provide support for additional functionality, such as the TCPIP VDD for TCP/IP support. This type of VDD is called an *installable VDD* because you can load it into an address space simply by specifying its name in the CONFIG.SYS file.

VDDs, both base VDDs and installable VDDs, are loaded into shared memory that is utilized across the MVM Server and each VDM.

The MVM Shield provides the interfaces between the OS/2 Server and several VDDs (specifically, VMOUSE, VKBD and VVIDEO). It is a key component of the ability to run DOS or Microsoft Windows applications in a window on the OS/2 Desktop. The MVM Shield captures console input and routes it to the corresponding VDDs. The MVM Shield is also responsible for capturing the output from the video component, translating it, and routing it to the corresponding window.

8086 Emulation

The 8086 Emulation component, commonly referred to as EM86, provides 8086 emulation support in the DOS/Windows environment. EM86 is a shared emulation library that is mapped across all VDMs. It is first loaded into the MVM Server address space and then cloned into each VDM that is created. EM86 provides a set of services that support software interrupt handling and I/O port trap routing. These services are used to switch execution mode (between real mode and protect mode), manage interrupt and exception handlers of protect-mode applications, and control execution flow in the VDMs.

In addition, as explained earlier, EM86 is the component that encapsulates the interfaces to the IST on a non-Intel hardware platform, via IST helper routines.

DOS Emulation

The MVM Server with 8086 emulation (EM86) and VDDs work together to provide an environment that supports hardware and ROM BIOS compatibility for DOS and Microsoft Windows applications. The software aspects of DOS and Microsoft Windows compatibility are provided by the component called DOS Emulation (otherwise known as DEM). The DOS Emulation kernel emulates the DOS environment (such as DOS data structures and interrupt 21s) for each DOS session.

DOS Emulation has two major parts:

- Intel binary form. There is a portion of DOS Emulation that runs in the Intel address space, utilizing the IST for translation.

- Native PowerPC form.

The portion of DOS emulation that runs in the Intel binary space receives application requests in the Intel space, updates the appropriate data structures, and passes the request to the native portions of DEM.

The native PowerPC code acts as a router and ensures that the requests are routed to the appropriate "worker" routine, such as a File Server "worker." The return codes from these worker routines are returned to the Intel portion of DEM, which ensures that the proper response is returned to the application.

The DOS Emulation provided with OS/2 Warp Connect (PowerPC Edition) provides DOS services that are compatible with IBM DOS, Version 6.3. It supports all documented DOS interrupts and features of that version.

WIN-OS/2 Support

The Microsoft Windows environment provided by DOS/Windows Services utilizes the same WIN-OS/2 support provided in OS/2 Warp, Version 3.0. WIN-OS/2 provides very good compatibility for Microsoft Windows applications and supports the running of Microsoft Windows applications in a window on the OS/2 Desktop.

For the first release of OS/2 Warp Connect (PowerPC Edition), WIN-OS/2 is primarily a set of Intel binaries that run in emulation space on the PowerPC. Several functions within WIN-OS/2 have been ported to run natively on the PowerPC to provide better performance of key Microsoft Windows functions. Future releases are expected to provide additional native code to continue to improve the performance of key Microsoft Windows functions.

Win32s, as developed by Microsoft, is a set of 32-bit DLLs and one VxD that are included with Microsoft Windows applications, allowing Microsoft Windows NT executables (EXEs) to load into Microsoft Windows 3.1.

Users might be completely unaware that they are running a Win32s application. Because the Win32s DLLs and VxD are included with the applications that exploit them, users need not care.

Win32s support is provided in OS/2 Warp Connect (PowerPC Edition) in the form of a VDD that provides the same function as the Win32s VxD but that is written utilizing OS/2 services. Win32s DLLs are loaded as if they were any other application. These DLLs, together with the VDD supplied by OS/2, provide all necessary support for Win32s applications.

The VDD included with OS/2 Warp Connect (PowerPC Edition) supports Win32s Version 1.2.

Installing and Migrating DOS and Microsoft Windows Applications

In general, installing and migrating DOS and Microsoft Windows applications can be done along with the installation of the operating system, or applications can be installed later (or updated later). As part of the Feature Installation process, users need only to drag and drop the installation object onto the target folder or Desktop, which will initiate the installation process.

The installation objects for DOS and Microsoft Windows include:

- DOS and WIN-OS/2 Installer, which contains all of the base components required to run DOS
- WIN-OS/2 Installer, which contains all of the WIN-OS/2 base components

These installation objects are set up in a hierarchy, with dependencies defined where appropriate. For instance, WIN-OS/2 cannot be installed without DOS, nor can the WIN-OS/2 Screen Savers Installation object be installed without WIN-OS/2.

To install a new or different printer driver after the WIN-OS/2 installation has completed (if no comparable PM printer driver is available), the user can install the printer driver via the WIN-OS/2 Control Panel or through the program provided with the printer driver. If there is a PM printer driver that matches the Microsoft Windows printer driver, the Microsoft Windows driver is installed automatically when the PM driver is installed.

To change the language support after WIN-OS/2 Installation, the user can select the International icon from the Control Panel. Again, the exception to this process is when matching PM language support exists.

Workplace Shell

This chapter describes the Workplace Shell. The Workplace Shell is the primary user interface for OS/2 Warp Connect (PowerPC Edition). This chapter provides information about the user interface elements that are common throughout the Workplace Shell. This commonality provides users with a consistent, predictable, and easy-to-use interface.

This chapter also provides information about the rich and powerful programming interface that is available to programmers when creating applications for OS/2 Warp Connect (PowerPC Edition). It explores the architecture of the Workplace Shell, examines the System Object Model and the Workplace Shell as an object-oriented class hierarchy, and discusses the classes that make up the Workplace Shell and how application programmers can create their own Workplace Shell objects.

In addition, this chapter provides information about common sequences of methods invoked against an object or a set of objects and shows the collaboration among the various window procedures and object classes that make up the Workplace Shell. It also describes the Workplace Shell from the file system perspective and discusses how the Workplace Shell stores its information, both in INI files and as extended attributes on files and directories.

Two examples of object creation are provided in Appendix C, "Examples of Workplace Shell Objects" on page 389. The objects created are a ledger folder and a ledger entry that resides in the folder.

The User's View

The user model is based upon a metaphor of the everyday office. The intent of this common metaphor is to provide familiarity to the user. Some amount of recognition of the purposes and capabilities of objects should be immediately apparent to the user, simply because the objects mimic the real world, and the user's real world knowledge transfers to the virtual world presented by the system.

For example, in the real, physical office, a shredder is a device used to destroy things. Likewise, the Workplace Shell provides a Shredder object whose purpose is indeed to destroy things. The OS/2 Desktop is intended to mimic the office itself, providing a frame of reference for the user and providing a place for objects that are often used to be kept handy.

Because most offices present many ways of organizing things, the Workplace Shell presents multiple organizational paradigms. The primary organization constructs available to the user are the OS/2 Desktop, folders, the toolbar, and drawers located on the toolbar. Obviously, additional organizational constructs might be desirable. Maybe not so obviously, these additional constructs can easily be treated as folders with a unique kind of icon, to represent things such as cabinets, drawers, or bookshelves. Within these various organizational constructs, users are allowed to place other objects, including nesting of the organizational constructs.

In a real office, people tend to work with documents and forms of many different types, such as ledgers, notes, memos, letters, reports, books, business cards, and insurance forms. People tend to focus on the paper trail, on the documents themselves, and not on the tools that are used to work with those documents.

It is believed that a computer system organized around these same kinds of documents and forms is more intuitive to most people. The Workplace Shell interface is document-centric. By using a document-centric design, it is intended that users focus on the documents, not on the programs that are used to manipulate those documents.

The user is allowed to go to the virtual forms drawer or the virtual office supply store and get new things. In the Workplace Shell, this is the intended purpose of the Templates folder. Users are given the ability to create their own templates. Indeed, much of the common customization performed by organizations and users is to create templates for their most frequently used types of documents.

Many operating systems, such as DOS or Microsoft Windows, have a program-centric view of the virtual world. It is believed that users, particularly those with little or no previous computer experience, are better served by the document-centric approach. In particular, as computing moves toward compound documents, which are actually created by the coordinated work of many different applications, the program-centric model continues to break down.

This office metaphor is extended to encompass the computer system itself. The devices that make up the computer system, such as disk drives, CD-ROM drives, printers, displays, a mouse, and a keyboard, are likewise represented as objects on the system.

For example, a printer is often attached to a computer system and is represented as an object on the Desktop as well. If users wish to print something, they should be able to simply drag the object to be printed to the icon representing the printer they want to print on.

Finally, the software available on the computer is presented to the user as a set of objects: namely, program files and program objects. That is, even though a document-centric view of the computer system is desirable, and more usable, it is understood that the program-centic model is very familiar to many, many people, and hence important to support as well. In addition, not all programs are designed to work with documents; for example, games are just games. If users want to play a game, they need only open the game and begin playing.

This metaphor can be extended by programmers wishing to create their own objects. Indeed, several available applications extend this metaphor by adding additional familiar objects to the system.

Some of the common additional office objects that one might expect to see are:

- Telephones
- Fax machines
- In-Baskets
- Out-Baskets
- Calendars

- Trash Cans
- Card files
- Phone books

OK, so the Workplace Shell is document-centric and uses a desktop and folder paradigm for containment of these documents and devices. What next?

Well, folders can be presented to the user in many different forms. The user selects the format desired by opening the settings for the folder. The settings are presented in a series of pages that enable users to customize their view of the folder.

The available views are:

- Icon view

  Within the Icon view, there are three choices for arranging icons.

  - Flowed

    Icons are arranged in columns, with the icon on the left and the text on the right. It is called flowed because icons flow from top to bottom and into new columns based on the height of the containing window. If the window height changes, the icons rearrange themselves automatically.

    - Large, small, or no icons
    - Visible or invisible text

  - Nonflowed

    Icons are arranged in a single-column, with the icon on the left and the text on the right. It is called nonflowed because the icons do not flow in the window; they are just presented as a single column.

    - Large, small, or no icons
    - Visible or invisible text

  - Nongrid

The icons are arranged initially from right to left, and top to bottom, but the users can place them anywhere they want, and the placement will be preserved.

- Large or small icons
- Visible or invisible text

- Tree view

  The containment hierarchy is displayed as a tree. That is, folders, drives, and shadows of folders or drives are displayed.

  – With or without lines

  – Large, small, or no icons

- Details view

  A columnar presentation of the objects. Each different class of object might provide a unique set of columns. The user can select which class of objects and columns of data are presented and, further, can select which of the available columns for that class are actually displayed.

Different objects might have different actions that can be performed on them.

Each and every object in the system might provide a myriad of options for setting everything from the icon used for the object to the name of the object to the color of the background to the fonts used, and so on.

Each object normally has a settings view, which enables users to tailor the system to their specific desires and needs. This settings view is presented to the user as a notebook containing many different pages. Each page presents to the user a set of options for the object (see Figure 11-1).

For example, the pages in a folder's Settings notebook are:

- Three View pages, which allow the user to specify the setting of options for each of the available views for a folder. One is for the icon view, one for the tree view, and one for the details view.

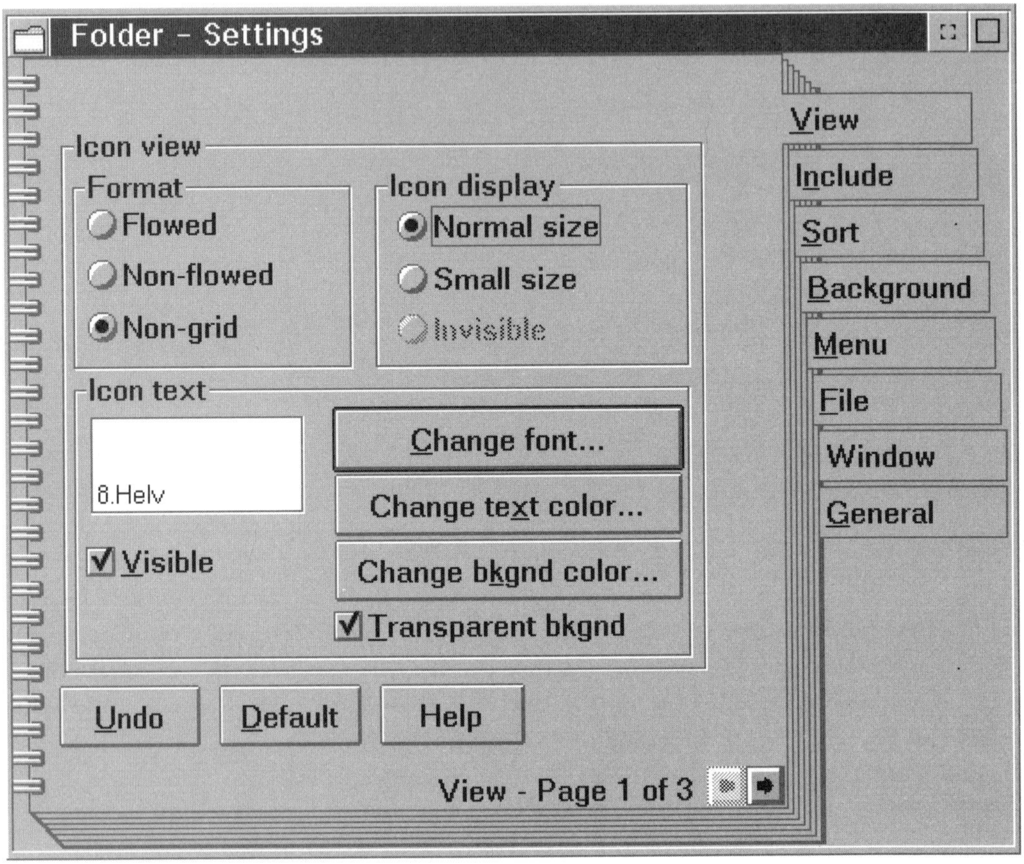

Figure 11-1. Settings Notebook Page

- An Include page, which allows the user to modify the objects that are visible in a folder. For example, objects that have the hidden file system attribute are normally excluded from the user's view of the folder.

- A Sort page, which allows the user to specify the default sort field for a folder, and if the folder should always maintain that sorted order.

- A Background page, which allows the user to specify how the surface of the folder should appear. This page allows the user to specify both a color and a bit map, that should appear behind the icons in the folder. In addition, on the view pages, the user can specify if the background for the icon text is to be transparent, allowing the background to show directly beneath the text, or if the text should be drawn with a background color of its own.

- A Menu page, which allows a user to customize the pop-up or context menu for the folder and to specify the default view for the folder.

- Three File pages, which display information about the file attributes. Information such as the subject, the physical file system name, whether the folder is a work area, the date and time the file was created, changed, and last accessed, the number of objects in the folder, and the file system attributes, such as hidden and read-only, can be displayed. The third page displays comments, key phrases, and history information for the file.

- A Window page, which specifies where the folder's minimized view should be displayed and whether or not a new view of the folder should be opened or if an existing open view should be surfaced.

- Two General pages, the first of which allows the user to modify the title for the object, as well as the icon for the object, and to specify that the object is a template object. The second general page allows the user to specify a different icon to be used for the folder whenever the folder is open.

So, you can see that a variety of customization options are available. In fact, there are so many options that some users find it daunting.

Each object has a pop-up, or context menu, which displays the set of actions that can be performed on that object. This menu is displayed when the user points to the object's icon, or on the white space in a folder, or on the icon on the left side of the title bar, and then presses mouse button 2 (see Figure 11-2).

Figure 11-2. Pop-Up Menu

Note that if multiple objects are selected and the menu is requested, the pop-up menu applies to the entire set of objects.

The following describes the menu items that might be found on a pop-up menu for a folder:

Open Displays the default view.

This menu choice displays as a conditional cascade, where you select the view to be opened by following the cascade. If the cascade is not expanded, the default view will be opened. The default view can be customized on the Menu page of the Settings notebook.

Settings Displays the Settings notebook for the object.

Open parent Opens the folder containing this folder.

Refresh now Updates the folder contents.

This menu choice is usually not of much use on folders that reside directly on the computer, because the Workplace Shell is able to monitor local drives, but it is really useful on diskettes and on remote drives.

Help Displays the default help view.

This is a conditional cascade that allows the user to select the level of help desired.

Create another Creates a new folder with exactly the same characteristics as the folder from which the menu choice is invoked.

Copy Creates a duplicate of the folder.

Move Moves the folder to a new location.

Create shadow	Creates a duplicate of the folder (that is, it *shadows* the original folder). Changes made in the original are also made in the shadow.
Delete	Deletes the folder and all its contents.
Pickup	Picks up the folder and holds it until the user is ready to drop it or perform some other action on it.
Window	Provides additional menu choices that enable the user to perform other operations, such as moving the window or displaying the Window List.
Find	Searches for objects according to many different attributes.
Select	Selects or deselects all objects in the folder.
Sort	Provides additional menu choices that allow the user to sort the objects in the folder.
Arrange	Rearranges the icons in a regular pattern.
Close	Closes the open folder.

Finally, just like in the physical world, objects in the virtual world can be moved, or copied, or thrown away. That is, users can directly manipulate objects in their virtual world. Users normally do this by holding down mouse button 2 and dragging the object.

In addition, the user can also pick up an object from the pop-up menu for the object and then drop the object using the pop-up menu at the target location. This lazy drag has the added benefit of allowing users to move windows around or open new windows while the drag operation is pending.

The Programmer's View

The Workplace Shell uses the OS/2 Presentation Manager and the controls provided by the Presentation Manager to implement the on-screen representations of all objects. In other words, the Workplace Shell is a Presentation Manager program.

The Workplace Shell, like other programs, uses many threads so that long-running tasks are not performed while a system input message is processing or is available for processing. This allows it to remain responsive to mouse and keyboard input.

Developer's Tip:
Programming Rule One: In order to create good OS/2 applications, make sure that any thread that has visible windows processes user input messages within 1/10th of a second.

User input messages, and any other processing that is done on a thread with visible windows, must get back to a dispatch loop within 1/10th of a second. Otherwise, the user will be unable to do such simple things as changing the focus to another application.

One consequence of this rule is that ALL good Presentation Manager programs are multithreaded.

Developer's Tip:
Programming Rule Two: All threads that are created in the Workplace Shell process, and that have methods called on them, MUST create a message queue.

In OS/2 2.0, message queues were created on these additional threads only when the implementation of the methods that would be invoked on that thread required a message queue. This creation was a serious architectural oversight, because application programmers can certainly add Presentation Manager calls that require a message queue to their implementation of method overrides. For example, during code development, it is often useful to call WinMessageBox in the middle of a method to let the developer know that the code has reached this point in processing. Calling WinMessageBox on a thread that does not have a message queue could produce undesirable results. So beginning with OS/2 Warp, Version 3, any methods invoked by the Workplace Shell are done on a thread that has a message queue.

Developer's Tip:
Programming Rule Three: All threads, other than the primary user interface thread in a process, that create a message queue should call WinCancelShutdown in order to keep the system from posting a WM_QUIT message to them.

This third rule is necessary because the system posts only *one* WM_QUIT message per process, regardless of how many message queues that process has, and expects the recipient message queue to either cancel the shutdown or to terminate the process. Almost all instances of systems that do not shut down properly can be traced to some application that breaks this rule.

Because there is currently no thread-level exit list support in OS/2, there is no way for Presentation Manager to clean up after a thread that exits while still having a message queue. So, later on, another thread might get created and already have a message queue from the last time a thread had that ordinal number.

Developer's Tip:
Programming Rules Four and Five: All threads should destroy their message queue before they terminate, including abnormal termination.

All threads should use DosSetExceptionHandler to catch abnormal terminations and clean up after themselves as well.

In order to display the context menu for an object, the Workplace Shell responds to a WM_CONTEXTMENU message by creating the menu for the object and calling WinPopupMenu. In order to allow the programmer to modify the pop-up menu displayed for an object, the Workplace Shell invokes the _wpModifyPopupMenu and the _wpFilterPopupMenu methods against the object.

Container Controls

Most of the interaction with the Workplace Shell is actually provided via the container control. Indeed, the client window area of the Desktop, as well as the client window area of any open folders, is implemented as a container control. The Workplace Shell implements much of its functionality in response to messages from a container control.

This implementation means that to understand much of what happens on the Workplace Shell, a programmer needs a solid understanding of the container control. For example, a full understanding of implementing custom details for an object requires that the programmer understand the multicolumn support provided by the container control.

When a window is registered with the Workplace Shell, via the _wpRegisterView method, or when an object is added to a container window with the _wpCnrInsertObject method, the Workplace Shell inserts a window procedure into the window hierarchy. This subclass window procedure responds to container control messages to provide much of the Workplace Shell's function. In the case of _wpRegisterView, the frame window passed in is subclassed. In the case of _wpCnrInsertObject, the owner of the container control window passed in is subclassed.

Further, for performance reasons, the Workplace Shell simply assumes that a one-to-one relationship between a container control and its owner exists and that the container window's ID is FID_CLIENT.

The mini-record core structures provided by the Workplace Shell to represent objects are NOT allocated using WM_ALLOCRECORD, but are instead directly allocated by the Workplace Shell. Indeed, the Workplace Shell allocates an additional eight bytes preceding the mini-record core structure and stores the SOMANY pointer for the object at that location. This allocation and storage is how the OBJECT_FROM_PREC macro is implemented.

Because the Workplace Shell uses the OBJECT_FROM_PREC macro to translate from a container record back to an object, and because the Workplace Shell does this often in its implementation of the subclass window procedure used by the Workplace Shell, only containers using CCS_MINIRECORDCORE can be used as containers for inserting objects into, and further, only objects should be placed in such a container. That is, if an application programmer tries to intermingle application records with the Workplace Shell records, the Workplace Shell will be unable to sort out which is which and will not work correctly.

Drag and Drop Protocol

The Workplace Shell implements direct manipulation of objects using the standard drag and drop functions and protocols provided by the Drg* functions. For example, when the user places the mouse cursor over an object, holds down the mouse button, and drags the object, the Workplace Shell responds by calling DrgDrag.

As the object is moved around the OS/2 Desktop, the Workplace Shell responds to the WM_DRAGOVER messages generated by DrgDrag. When the user releases the mouse button, DrgDrag sends a final WM_DRAGOVER message, and if this final WM_DRAGOVER message returns that the drop can be performed, then a WM_DROP message is sent to the Workplace Shell window that the mouse pointer is over. The Workplace Shell then performs the appropriate transfer of data according to the rendering mechanism specified.

When a Workplace Shell object is being picked up for the purpose of direct manipulation, the _wpFormatDragItem method is invoked on the object. This method is expected to fill out the dragitem structure, indicating things such as the rendering mechanism and formats the object can be provided in.

When a Workplace Shell object is dropped, the Workplace Shell decides which object the objects being directly manipulated were dropped on and invokes the _wpDrop method against that object.

Workplace Shell Classes

The Workplace Shell is written in C and uses the System Object Model (SOM) to implement the classes that make up the Workplace Shell. Bindings for creating objects in either the C or C++ languages are available.

Some of the key characteristics of SOM are:

- Language independence.
- Ability to evolve a class hierarchy.
- Binary compatibility. It is possible for objects written on release M to still function on release N.
- Ability to add methods to a class.

- Support for distribution.
- Ability to add, remove, and modify instance data for a class.

On OS/2, with the ability for a class to be contained in a DLL, this combination of SOM and class libraries, such as the one provided by the Workplace Shell, supports an extremely powerful programming metaphor.

SOM provides serious, industrial-strength plumbing for the definition and reuse of classes. Reusable classes continue to work across releases, so that each program that desires to use the classes already provided does not need a special version just for it. This also means that applications integrate well with one another. My objects, your objects, and their objects can all communicate and interact with one another, even though they were all developed separately in time and space. Additionally, multiple copies of the DLL containing the code being reused, each with its own special name and each a part of the working set for the system, are not necessary.

Several C++ compilers now provide support for implementing SOM classes directly. This support promises to continue to improve.

SOMObject

All objects utilized by the Workplace Shell are descended from SOMObject. SOMObject provides a set of methods that allow an object to be instantiated in memory, and it provides a whole slew of *plumbing*.

WPObject

The ancestor class of all objects that are visible to the user in the Workplace Shell is WPObject. Some of the methods provided by WPObject are really just virtual methods, intended to be overridden by one of its descendant classes. Some of the methods provide base structure for a user interface object and are not intended to be overridden. Some of the methods are provided such that a lot of the functionality is provided directly by WPObject, but it is expected that the method will normally be overridden.

WPObject implements an icon, a title, styles, and some details for an object and provides methods for specifying these.

The concept of locking an object is implemented here.

WPObject implements the settings view of an object and provides the General page and the Window page of a Settings notebook.

Each object can be given a handle that can be used to retrieve the object at a later date. The actual implementation of the handle is done by one of the storage subclasses.

Each object can be given an object ID. An object ID is a character string enclosed in angle brackets, such as <WP_DESKTOP>. Objects can be located using the object ID.

Developer's Tip: It is not expected that application programmers use classes that descend directly from the WPObject class, but instead, it is expected that the classes an application uses are inherited from one of the classes farther down in the class hierarchy.

Base Classes

The next three classes provided by the Workplace Shell are referred to as base classes or storage classes. These classes have a special role in the Workplace Shell because they are involved in the implementation of persistence. Today, it is not possible for a programmer to create additional base classes.

WPTransient

This class is intended to represent objects for which the Workplace Shell does not implement persistence. However, if you wanted to implement your own kind of persistence, such as by storing the data for your objects in a database file, this would be a good class to descend from.

This class is used to represent objects that are temporary in nature and are not expected to live across boots or to represent objects that are stored by some other mechanism.

WPTransient objects can have _wpSaveDeferred invoked upon them, and in OS/2 Warp Connect (PowerPC Edition), as well as in OS/2 Warp Version 3, this indeed results in invocation of the _wpSaveImmediate method on a background thread. In OS/2 2.1, however, _wpSaveDeferred for a transient object is ignored. This procedure was changed in OS/2 Warp Version 3 in order to make it easier for programmers to implement transient classes that implement persistence. Objects descended from _wpTransient can be placed into a folder but are not required to live in a folder.

WPAbstract

This class is used for objects that are associated with a particular computer.

Printer objects, the Shredder object, program objects, shadow objects, and most of the objects in the Setup folder are descended from this class.

All abstract objects have an object handle. This handle is allocated when the object is created and is used as the key to uniquely identify this object in the OS2.INI file.

This class of objects is stored persistently in the OS2.INI file. That is, the _wpSaveImmediate implementation in WPAbstract writes the block of data collected by _wpStoreState to the OS2.INI file.

Note: The following information on the actual application names, key names, and formats of data in the OS2.INI file is subject to change, and is being presented only to further understanding of the Workplace Shell. It does not constitute a programming interface.

The persistent data of the object is stored using the application name PM_Abstract:Objects. The key name is the object handle for the object, and the key value is the persistent data for that object. The icon for abstract objects, if they have been given a custom icon, is stored in the OS2.INI file using the application name PM_Abstract:Icons. The key name is again the object handle for the object, and the key value is the icon data.

Each object of this class is created in a folder. The association of which abstract objects exist in which folders is maintained in the OS2.INI file. The set of abstract objects contained in a folder is kept in the PM_Abstract:FldrContent application name, with the object handle of each folder that contains abstract objects as the key name. The value is the set of object handles of the abstracts contained in that folder.

Because abstract objects persist in the OS2.INI file, they cannot be placed onto removable media or onto network drives. This means that I cannot do tasks such as copy an abstract object to disk and give a copy of it to you.

Further, if the OS2.INI file is rebuilt, or damaged in some way, the abstract objects are also damaged or lost.

Classes Descended from WPAbstract

The following classes are either descended directly from WPAbstract or from a descendant of WPAbstract.

WPProgram This class is descended from WPAbstract and is used to represent pointers to executable programs. Note the difference between WPProgram objects and WPProgramFile objects. WPProgramFile objects are the actual file system .EXE programs, whereas WPProgram objects are abstract objects that point to program file objects and contain unique settings for the program.

WPShadow This class is descended from WPAbstract and is used to represent a short-cut method of reaching another object or to allow the user to have multiple ways of accessing a single object.

WPNetLink This class is descended from WPShadow. It is used to provide a persistent link to a shared directory object.

WPDisk This class is descended from WPAbstract and is used to represent the disk drives on a system.

WPFileSystem

This class is used for objects that are stored as files or directories on the local hard drives, on diskettes, on CD-ROM drives, or on remote drives.

This class uses extended attributes to store its persistent data. In particular, the .CLASSINFO extended attribute is used to store the buffer of data collected by _wpSaveState.

It implements many additional details columns and several new settings pages as well. The three file attribute pages are implemented here. These pages display information about the file, its attributes, and some of its extended attributes. The Menu page of a settings notebook is implemented here.

This class also implements methods for dealing with the file system attributes and for maintaining the relationship between the file name of the object and the title of the object.

The class itself provides some new methods, such as _wpclsQueryObjectFromPath, which, given any path, will find and awaken the object represented by that path.

In addition, this class provides virtual methods for _wpclsQueryInstanceType and _wpclsQueryInstanceFilter.

These two methods allow a class to specify that any files that are not already assigned to another specific class be given a class based on the value of the .TYPE EA or on the value of the extension.

Classes Descended from WPFileSystem

WPFolder and WPDataFile are both direct descendants of WPFileSystem. These classes are used most often for creating new object classes. Several other classes are descended from either WPFolder or WPDataFile.

WPFolder

This class is descended from WPFileSystem and is used to represent directories on the disk media. Custom object classes are often descended from this class.

This class implements several settings notebook pages, as follows:

- Background page
- Sort page
- Include page
- The three View pages—Icon, Tree, and Details

The most commonly overridden methods are _wpOpen and _wpPopulate.

The following describes the classes that descend from WPFolder:

WPDesktop The class of the desktop. It adds several settings pages, as well as several pop-up menu choices.

WPTemplateFolder	It is the template folder and is populated with the templates for each object class and a template for each type of data file.
WPDrives	It is populated with the WPDisk objects representing the disk drives available on the system.
WPNetgrp	It is contained within the WPNetwork folder. Objects of this class are folders containing the servers available on a particular network. It is populated with WPServer objects.
WPNetwork	It is visible only if the computer is connected to a network. It is populated with the WPNetgrp objects for the available networks.
WPProgramGroup	It is used to represent program groups as created by the PrfCreateGroup.
WPStartup	All folders of this class are kept track of in the OS2.INI file under the application name PM_Workplace:Startup, and all objects in all startup folders are opened automatically when the system is started.
WPMinWinViewer	Is the Minimized Window Viewer. It contains objects of the WPMinWindow class that represent minimized windows.
WPRootFolder	Is used to represent the root folder (directory) on a file system device. Note that there is a correspondence between WPRootFolder objects and WPDisk objects.
WPServer	Contained in folders of the WPNetgrp class. These objects represent network servers. These folders are populated with WPNetLink and WPRPrinter objects.

WPDataFile

This class is descended from WPFileSystem and is used to represent files. Custom object classes are often descended from this class. Indeed objects of this class can be placed onto diskettes, or a network server, or sent via a mail system to other users. Document classes are normally descended from this class.

This class adds the File Type settings page.

This class implements the link between programs that specified an .ASSOCTABLE extended attribute or that have been associated with certain types of files or extensions to the documents of that type.

WPProgramFile This class is descended from WPDataFile and is used to represent executable programs.

WPCommandFile This class is descended from WPProgramFile and is used to represent REXX command files or batch command files.

Workplace Shell Programming Interface

The programming interface provided by the Workplace Shell is very large, so only a small amount of detail is provided in this chapter. It is provided in terms of several cycles, or sequences of interrelated events.

A Workplace Shell Object

Each Workplace Shell object has a life cycle and can exist in a couple of different states or can be in transition from one state to another.

New objects are created when you invoke the _wpclsNew method against the class object for the kind of object that is desired. Invoking _wpclsNew against a class object, if successful, returns a pointer to the newly created object of the specified class.

Objects are destroyed by invoking the _wpFree method against the object to be destroyed. As soon as an object has been destroyed, the pointer representing that object should no longer be used for method invocations. Referencing an object pointer for an object that has already been freed is one of the most common errors that occur when programmers use the Workplace Shell methods.

An object can be in one of two states, either dormant or awake. It can be accessible in memory and available for method invocations against it, or it can be in a dormant state, not immediately available for method invocation but stored in a persistent format on the disk.

An object moves from the active in memory (or awake) state to the dormant state via the _wpMakeDormant method. You should not invoke the _wpMakeDormant method yourself. The system will call _wpMakeDormant when it believes that the active state of your object is no longer needed. More precisely, each object has a lock count associated with it, and the system will ask the object to go dormant whenever that lock count reaches zero.

An object moves from the persistent or dormant form to the active, awake state via the _wpclsMakeAwake method. Of course, just like the _wpclsNew method, the _wpclsMakeAwake method is invoked against the class object for the kind of object desired to be made awake. Again, you do not normally invoke or override the _wpclsMakeAwake method; instead, the system will invoke this method as a result of some other method call or event. For example, when a folder is opened, the system finds the persistent form of all objects in that folder and invokes the _wpclsMakeAwake method on them, moving them from the dormant state to the awake state.

As an object moves from the dormant state to the awake state, or as an object is newly created, it goes through a phase where it is being initialized but is not yet really completely ready. The method _wpObjectReady is invoked at the end of the initialization phase, and the _wpIsObjectReady method can be invoked to determine if this critical point in time has passed.

As changes are made to the state data of an object, it might be desirable for those state changes to be reflected in the persistent form of that object as well. The _wpSaveImmediate method can be invoked against an object and will not return to the caller until the persistent form of the object has been rewritten. However, because updating the persistent form of the object involves writing the data to disk, it is not usually desirable to have this call made on a thread with visible windows. So, an alternative method, _wpSaveDeferred, is provided. Invoking _wpSaveDeferred against an object will result in having a queued request for a later invocation of _wpSaveImmediate on a background thread.

Note that not all methods that change the state of an object result in having the state change made persistent. That is, sometimes, if you want the state changes saved, you are responsible for invoking _wpSaveDeferred or _wpSaveImmediate to have your changes made persistent. We will note in this chapter which methods result in calls to _wpSaveDeferred or _wpSaveImmediate.

It is also important that you understand that persistence of an object is an orthogonal concept to the awake or dormant state of the object. That is, when an object goes dormant, the system does not automatically invoke _wpSaveImmediate on the object. It is also important to understand that when the system is shut down, objects are not even asked to go dormant. Any outstanding _wpSaveDeferred requests are honored, the system flushes several different kinds and levels of cache, and stops.

Now, let us take a closer look at the implementation of object persistence for the Workplace Shell. When _wpSaveImmediate for an object is called, the Workplace Shell calls _wpBeginSave to acquire a buffer for storing the persistent object data and then calls _wpSaveState against the object. For each piece of data that is intended to be made persistent, the implementing of _wpSaveState will call _wpSaveLong, _wpSaveString, or _wpSaveData to write the information into the buffer acquired by _wpBeginSave. When _wpSaveState returns control back to _wpSaveImmediate, it will then store the persistent data, and then call _wpEndSave to free up the buffer.

Conversely, when an object is being made awake, via _wpclsMakeAwake, the system retrieves the stored persistent data and needs to set the instance data for the object being awakened using this information. Setting this instance is done by calling _wpBeginRestore to set the pointer to the buffer containing the saved information, and then _wpRestoreState, and each class retrieves its persistent data by calling _wpRestoreLong, _wpRestoreString, or _wpRestoreData in its override of _wpRestoreState. Note that it is important that each class's implementation of _wpRestoreState calls the parent method first, and then restores its state information.

Drag and Drop

When a user begins a drag operation by pointing to an object, holding mouse button 2, and dragging the object, the following sequence of events occurs:

1. Presentation Manager sends the container control window for the folder a WM_BEGINDRAG message.
2. The container control sends a WM_CONTROL, CN_INITDRAG message to the owner of the container control.
3. The Workplace Shell subclass window procedure for the container control's owner window receives the WM_CONTROL, CN_INITDRAG message and does the following:

a. Counts the number of items being dragged.

b. Allocates and initializes a draginfo structure for that many items.

c. Iterates through the objects to be dragged and invokes _wpFormatDragItem for each object being dragged.

d. Determines if the default operation should be DO_CREATE or DO_DEFAULT, based on whether or not templates are being dragged.

e. Puts together the drag image structure for the objects being dragged.

f. Calls DrgDrag.

g. After return from DrgDrag, cleans up as appropriate.

4. While DrgDrag is running, it will send WM_DRAGOVER messages to the windows beneath the mouse pointer.

   a. If a container control window receives a WM_DRAGOVER message, it forwards it on to its owner as a WM_CONTROL, CN_DRAGOVER message.

   b. If the container control's owner has been registered with the Workplace Shell via _wpRegisterView or if the container control has had objects inserted into it, then the Workplace Shell has subclassed the container control's owner window and will receive the WM_CONTROL, CN_DRAGOVER message.

   c. On receipt of the WM_CONTROL, CN_DRAGOVER message, the Workplace Shell's subclass window procedure will invoke the _wpDragOver method for the object that is underneath the mouse pointer.

5. When the user releases mouse button 2, a final WM_DRAGOVER message is sent, and if it returns indicating that the drop is acceptable, a WM_DROP message is sent to the window beneath the mouse pointer.

   a. If the window that the object was dropped on is a container, it will forward the WM_DROP message to its owner as a WM_CONTROL, CN_DROP message.

b. If the container control's owner has been subclassed by the Workplace Shell, then the subclass procedure will receive the WM_CONTROL, CN_DROP message and will in turn invoke the _wpDrop method against the object that is dropped on one or more times, depending on how many objects were being manipulated, and also depending on the response to the previous _wpDrop invocation.

A File System Look at the Workplace Shell

The information presented in this section is provided to facilitate a better understanding of the Workplace Shell. In addition, this information might prove to be useful to developers for debugging purposes. However, this information does not constitute an intended programming interface for the OS/2 system. IBM will likely change some of the details presented within this section, so programmers should not rely on this information for any purposes other than debugging. In the future, for example, much of this information might be moved into the system registry.

Information Stored in INI Files

Several different kinds of information are kept in the OS/2 user INI file and in the OS/2 system INI file:

- The list of registered classes and the DLLs that contain them
- The association between Object IDs and Object Handles
- The persistent form of abstract objects
- The association of abstract objects with the Object Handle of the containing folder
- The association of object handles with file system paths
- The list of replaced classes and the replacement classes

- The list of classes that should be loaded at IPL time
- The definition of the various color schemes
- Most of the information related to the objects in the System Setup folder
- The position and size of windows
- The list of objects to be restarted automatically
- The set of DLLs that should be loaded when Presentation Manager is initialized, both the first time and once per process

Information Stored in Extended Attributes

The OS/2 Workplace Shell stores the persistent information for files and folders (you will remember that folders map to directories on the file system) in extended attributes.

Extended attributes allow up to 64KB of additional information to be stored for each file or directory. This space is organized as a set of named streams of information. The system reserves all extended attribute names that begin with a period (.) for defining standard extended attributes. Several system-defined extended attributes are used by the OS/2 Workplace Shell.

The .ASSOCTABLE extended attribute is placed onto executable files, along with a .CHECKSUM extended attribute, by the resource compiler. A programmer specifies that the resource compiler is to place an .ASSOCTABLE extended attribute on a program by using the ASSOCTABLE keyword in the resource file for the program. This keyword allows programmers to define new types, to associate the program they are creating with data files of that type, and to specify a custom icon for the data files. In addition, the programmer can associate the program with data files based on file extension. When the pop-up menu is requested for a data file, and that data file is associated with a program that is available, the system places the associated program on the open cascade of the pop-up menu.

The information saved by _wpSaveState is stored in the .CLASSINFO extended attribute.

The position of all objects in a folder is stored in the .ICONPOS extended attribute.

The .TYPE extended attribute is intended to be used for many of the same purposes that extensions are used in DOS. That is, the .TYPE EA informs the system of the kind of data that is stored and, possibly, which programs are available to work on that data. It is possible to associate a specific type with a specific object class using _wpclsQueryInstanceType.

The .LONGNAME extended attribute is used to store the title associated with a file system object whenever the file-name conventions supported by the file system cannot directly store the title. For example, for titles longer than 8.3 characters on FAT file systems, or titles that contain special characters, such as backslashes, the .LONGNAME extended attribute is used.

The .HISTORY extended attribute is used to store information of an historical nature about a file. The Workplace Shell does not update this information but displays it on one of the File settings pages if it is available.

The .ICON extended attribute is used to store a custom icon for file system objects.

The .SUBJECT extended attribute is displayed and can be modified on one of the File settings pages.

The .COMMENTS extended attribute is displayed and can be modified on one of the File settings pages.

The .KEYPHRASES extended attribute is displayed and can be modified on one of the File settings pages.

So, as you can see, extended attributes play a vital role for the Workplace Shell. The Workplace Shell can work with file systems that do not support extended attributes, but many of the capabilities associated with file system objects are unusable on file systems that do not support extended attributes.

Networks

This chapter introduces the concept of a *network operating system* (NOS), consisting of client systems and server systems that have a *single system image*. It introduces you to IBM's Open Blueprint, which describes how to distribute function across a network using industry interfaces, protocols, and formats and still maintain that single system image. It also tells you how the principles of the Open Blueprint applied to the new microkernel-based operating system design will, some time in the future, result in a complete OS/2 Warp client and server solution. OS/2 Warp Connect (PowerPC Edition) is the client operating system, which together with a future, similarly architected server operating system, will provide a single system image of a network.

Introducing Network Operating Systems

In the early days, computer systems were self-contained. Software ran on mainframes to which were attached various peripheral devices, such as printers, plotters, tape units, dumb terminals, and so on, all driven by the mainframe. With the advent of personal computers, computer systems were still basically self-contained. But, dumb terminals were replaced with smart (personal computer) terminals and personal computers began to talk to each other. And PC networking was born. As long as a machine was connected to another machine that understood the same formats and protocols, everything was OK.

But that's not the way things work in the real world. There are *many* different hardware platforms with many different architectures and formats and protocols that would like to talk with each other, but can't. And what about the "Anytime, Anywhere Connectivity" vision for computing, where a "computer in every pocket" can tie into any home personal computer, as well as any supercomputer in a research center on another continent? Or where your computer, as you walk off a plane anywhere in the world, will automatically and instantly sync up with the local cellular LAN and connect you to all the things you were connected to the last time you had it opened?

Wouldn't it be nice if you didn't have to worry about whether or not the hardware and software you use will work with someone else's hardware and software?

Client/Server Computing

Single computer systems such as mainframes and personal computers own and manage their system resources (devices, files, DASD, memory, programs). They can have one or more users who share those resources.

Multiple systems linked in a computer network each have their own sets of resources that are managed by their respective system owners. Some resources, such as files and printers, can be designated as shared in a client/server relationship. A client application, as the representative of the user, makes a request for services (such as printing a file or sending mail) from servers (other software) that reside on the same local computer or on remote computers connected to a network.

A network is a set of systems physically connected to each other and organized into domains, where a domain represents a workgroup or specific set of services. There are three types of systems in a network:

- Personal systems (personal computers and technical workstations) are used by people for access to and manipulation of information and for collaboration with other people.

- Server systems are general-purpose systems that have been configured to perform a specific set of server tasks (file, database, security, directory, mail, and so on).

- Special-purpose systems are systems that have been designed, from a hardware point of view, to perform specific tasks, such as network functions (routers) and office functions (printers, faxes, plotters, and so on).

Server systems are designed primarily to hold and process information, rather than to support human interaction. While personal computers and technical workstations can (and often will) be used as server systems (especially in peer-to-peer configurations), server systems are designed for scale, availability, and unattended operations. Server systems are based on the same microprocessor architectures as personal systems but they are built to allow for "vertical" scaling of memory, DASD, and network bandwidth to meet a very large capacity range. Server software consists of continuous processes that wait for requests, perform services, return results, wait for another request, and so on.

Connection to a network is not transparent to a user. The user must understand the services provided by each machine in order to make a decision regarding the machines to connect to. The user must then establish a connection to those machines and explicitly log on to them. Having an understanding of the services provided by a particular machine, the user must then explicitly invoke those services by entering some kind of command. The user has to deal with each machine in the network, separately and individually.

Distributed systems, on the other hand, are networked systems that behave as if they were a single system. Resources can be shared by multiple users across multiple platforms. Users share data efficiently but are not bothered by the underlying mechanisms, because the system has the authority and flexibility it needs to manage all resources between all users across all platforms as it sees fit. As an example, distributed file systems, such as NFS and DFS, support files that physically reside on multiple systems. The physical location of files is transparent to the user. The user does not have to worry about the machine a particular file resides on. The user deals with the file, while the file system deals with the machine on which it resides. The file systems manage all file resources, moving and replicating them when needed for better performance.

A network operating system is made up of two or more systems that are separated from each other, yet connected to each other by a communications network. Just as an operating system provides the management of resources, such as files, databases, printers, transactions, and so on, on a single system, a network operating system provides for the management of the same types of resources across the network. A network operating system is a distributed operating system, where the network is "the computer."

A network operating system puts the user at the center of the computing universe. All information appears locally available to the user, regardless of whether it is located nearby or far away. Thus, the user has a *single system image* of the network. The entire network (all the services provided by all the machines) appears to be folded into the user's system.

IBM's Open Blueprint

The distribution of functions across a network, though, is not always easy, given different hardware driven by software that might have its own formats and protocols. In order to make hardware and software fit together easily and efficiently no matter what the platform or where the various elements are located in the overall network, the Open Blueprint offers a client/server solution that insulates users and software developers from the complexities inherent in using, managing, and connecting distributed systems. IBM's Open Blueprint describes how to distribute an operating system across a network using industry interfaces, protocols, and formats and still maintain that single system image.

The Open Blueprint defines a set of resource managers that manage and provide access to resources, such as data, applications, or presentations, that can be distributed and replicated across a variety of servers in a network. Resource managers provide:

- Network services, which provide protocols and functions for transporting information from one system to another.

- Communication services, which provide mechanisms for parts of a distributed application or resource manager to talk to each other.

- Object management services, which provide transparent access to local and remote objects.

- Data access services, which allow applications and resource managers to interact with various types of data.

- Presentation services, which define the interaction between applications and the user.

- Application services, which provide common services, such as mail, that are available for use by all applications.

- System Management services, which provide facilities for a system administrator to manage the network operating system.

- Local operating system services, which are used by a single system in a network to manage its memory or dispatch its work.

A resource manager that operates in a single system is a *local resource manager*. A *distributed resource manager* operates across multiple systems and includes *client* parts that support the interfaces that requesters use and *server* parts that perform functions, requested by the client part, on the resources. The client part might do some of the processing (for example, validation) and is responsible for determining which server part should handle the request. The client part supports multiple protocols as needed to deal with a heterogeneous environment. The client and server parts communicate through an agreed-to protocol.

The resource manager interfaces can be structured as a *framework*. Frameworks allow for different implementations of the resource manager. Resource manager implementations can be replaced without changes to the programs that use them. Currently, resource manager frameworks are based on traditional procedural interfaces, but they will evolve over time into object frameworks.

The client portion of resource manager frameworks that applications use must be on the same platform as the applications. Smaller systems, such as mobile computers or personal digital assistants (PDAs), could contain only a few resource manager frameworks and required communications support. The server portions of required distributed resource managers must be accessible somewhere in the distributed network.

The Open Blueprint is also based on standards for interfaces and protocols that allow systems from multiple vendors to participate equally in the network. These standards include:

- Network protocols such as IPX, NetBIOS, OSI, SNA, TCP/IP

- Transport interfaces such as Sockets from X/Open and POSIX

- Network interfaces based on Multiprotocol Transport Networking (MPTN) architecture.

- Directory and Naming, Security, and Time services from OSF's DCE and Transaction services from X/Open.

- Communication models such as peer-to-peer by SNA APPC and IBM's and X/Open's CPI-C, remote procedure call (RPC) from OSF's DCE and IBM's Message Queue Interface (MQI).

- Object management services provided by DSOM that conform to OMG's Common Object Request Broker Architecture (CORBA).

- File protocols such as Network File System (NFS) and Distributed File System (DFS).

- Database interfaces and architectures such as Structured Query Language (SQL), Distributed Relational Database Architecture (DRDA), and Remote Database Access (RDA).

The Open Blueprint promotes the integration of multivendor systems and simplifies the more cumbersome aspects of distributed computing, such as multiple logons, multiple passwords, and unique application directories for locating resources. Products that align with the Open Blueprint provide designated interfaces and protocols. Products that use resource managers defined within the Open Blueprint, rather than their own unique mechanisms, are truly integrated with the Open Blueprint. For example, if every application uses its own unique security facility, a user must present a unique password for each application. If applications and resource managers use the security services from the Open Blueprint, a single user password will suffice for the cooperating applications. This integration improves the single-system image of the distributed system as perceived by the user and application developer.

A Microkernel-Based Network Operating System

Microkernel-based operating systems provide the implementation of the Open Blueprint. The Open Blueprint describes resource managers to manage and provide access to resources distributed across a network. Microkernel-based operating systems have shared services that perform the same type of functions. Although each individual system does not necessarily contain these services *physically*, each individual system *logically* contains them. Resource managers are divided into a client part (which must reside on the client system) and a server part (which might reside on the client system or on another server system). Shared services (as well as operating system services) for microkernel-based operating systems consist of a client library and a server task. For OS/2 Warp Connect (PowerPC Edition), the client libraries and server tasks reside on the same system. Some time in the future, those server tasks might reside on a microkernel-based server system.

Frameworks (the client library interfaces) for shared services hide different implementations of the services from the application programmer (and, therefore, from the user). Application programmers make a request for a network service, for example, by calling the same network function regardless of what kind of network they are connected to. The frameworks resolve the request by routing it to the appropriate server. In this way, the application programmer has a single system image (that is, a consistent interface) of the system.

Shared services for microkernel-based operating systems can be scaled not only across systems of all sizes (embedded, palmtops, and so on) but also across networks of all sizes, from a single system to multiple, interconnected domains. Systems running in a microkernel-based NOS domain might include any combination of these. Some of those systems might not even be microkernel based. But because many of the elements of the microkernel-based NOS are derived from industry standards (both programming interfaces and protocols), non-microkernel-based systems, which utilize the same industry standards, can also participate in the microkernel-based NOS domain.

A microkernel-based NOS, then, will provide a way to deliver integrated, interoperable products and solutions.

- For *users*, integration with the NOS hides the complexities of the network and makes it appear as a single system.
- For *application developers*, standard interfaces enable a single system view of the network and allow for the development of interoperable applications that can run on many platforms.
- For *system administrators*, the architecture defines a consistent way to manage the network in order to hide the complexities from application developers and users.

The User's Model

There are four principal characteristics of the user's model for an OS/2 Warp NOS:

- Real-world object manipulation
- Network invisibility and scaling
- Workgroup collaboration
- User mobility

Real-World Object Manipulation

OS/2 users are already familiar with objects on the OS/2 Desktop (the Workplace Shell). The Desktop provides a uniform model for manipulating objects, performing actions, configuring properties, and so on.

Most objects that users manipulate will be provided by applications. The object-oriented programming model of a microkernel-based NOS will encourage applications to model information workflow in terms of real-world entities and to present a human-centric model to the users. The presentation might involve more than just graphical information and mouse manipulation; it might also include audio and video information and manipulation through speech commands, touch-sensitive screens, and pens. Applications will collaborate on the Desktop to provide real-world objects that model the users' work. Users do not really see applications but rather familiar objects on which can be performed familiar actions. It's a virtual reality in a sense; the object-oriented user interface presents, for users, an illusion that looks like their business.

Network Invisibility

From the user's perspective, a network does two things: it provides access to the information users need to do their jobs, and it connects people together.

A microkernel-based NOS is designed to do this invisibly. If systems in the network conform to the same microkernel-based architecture, users will not see any of the network topology. The physical network and the individual systems are hidden from users, along with all the complexity of the network. The network looks like a single system, an extension to the user's desktop. We call this *single system image* (see Figure 12-1). The single system image is part of the virtual reality. Moreover, for a particular user, the image is the same from any geographic location, whether the user walks up to another desktop or carries one around. The image is both mobile and ubiquitous.

The network needs only one definition of a user, and it defines the user in the context of a consistent security policy. The user is not confused by multiple platform-specific policies; the user performs only one logon (even across network boundaries). The definition of the user also contains all the user's preferences, as well as the active state of the desktop at the time the user suspends operation. All the user has to do is log on to be able to resume operating from the last point of suspension.

Figure 12-1. A User's Single System Image

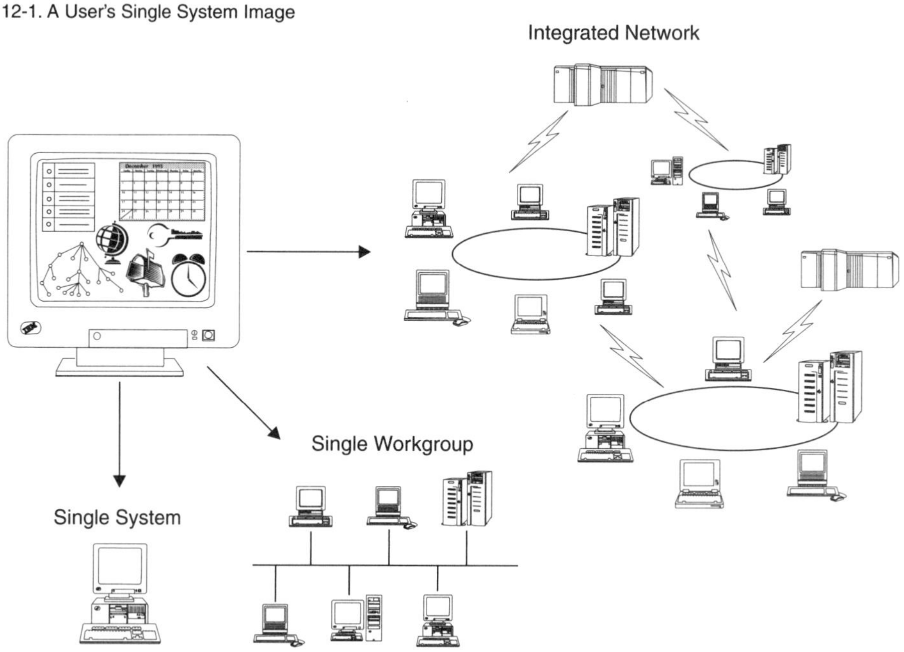

Because the user can see objects anywhere in the network, constrained only by the security policy, the model is sometimes referred to as a *sea of objects*. A single hierarchical name space is provided for these objects, and every user utters the same name for the same object. Utilities allow users to browse and search for information in the system either by name, by properties, or by content, and to view the information as objects that can be dragged onto the Desktop or into a compound document. As the scope of the network available to the user grows, the information retrieval facilities scale with the network so as to avoid overwhelming the user.

Workgroup Collaboration

Universal access to information is the principal enabler of human collaboration. If people have access to all the information they need, wherever they or the information is physically located, then it is possible to create ad hoc work groups that can collaborate on the rapid execution of a mission. The network can also be treated like a telephone system. Through multimedia and telephony facilities, a group of users anywhere in the network can connect to each other and conduct a video conference using the desktop as a shared "chalkboard." And, because they all have access to the same information, they can collaborate real-time on document updates and workflow.

One of the fundamental information models for a microkernel-based NOS is the compound document. A document can be composed of objects of almost any form (including audio and video information), and the objects provide their own built-in editing tools. It is simply sufficient to select an embedded object and use the editing tools that are part of the object. It is not necessary to launch different applications to deal with different forms of information. The objects embedded in a document can be shared by many documents, created by many people, and stored on many systems. These boundaries are not visible, or relevant, to the user of the document. But it allows for the collaboration of many users, across the network, on a particular document.

Mobile Users

Personal systems are not just stationary on the desktop. Some are designed to be mobile, either as portable notebooks with full human-centrics, or as palmtops with limited human-centrics. Both can get to the same information in the network, but it might be presented in different forms. Mobile notebook systems can tolerate both planned disconnection and temporary disconnection from the network, as well as movement. For planned disconnections (for example, the user decides to shut down the system), the system will allow the user to specify what objects to cache and can heuristically cache objects that the user has been manipulating recently. If the user performs updates to any cached objects, or sends messages, these will be temporarily stored on the mobile system and synchronized with the appropriate servers on reconnection to the network.

Travelling Users

Some users do not carry personal systems with them when they travel but might use whatever system is available at their destination. What they expect, however, is that the system should behave as much like their own system as possible. They should be able to log on to their home domain and access all the information they would normally have access to. They should also be able to receive mail normally and have the benefit of all their personal system configuration preferences. The owner of the system that the traveller uses expects that any private data remains private.

A microkernel-based NOS will capture all the characteristics of the user, including personal system configuration preferences, in the user object in the domain user registry (rather than in a local configuration file on the personal system). Each personal system might also be configured as a multiuser system to allow other users to log on while protecting the private information of the owner.

The Administrator's Model

First, it is important to distinguish what administration is and who administrators are. The network has a purpose, such as the operation of a company or an organization. Any work that the owner does to construct the network and to keep it operational is, by definition, administration. Programmers and engineers build system facilities and applications and service them. Administrators install them and keep them operational, and users use them to do their jobs. Some people wear many hats. Some domains employ professional administrators and, in some, users double as administrators. It is the goal of the administration model for a microkernel-based NOS to make resource administration simple enough so that a few professional administrators can manage a large domain and the users can manage small domains.

Many of the system management functions can be driven from a display of the topology of systems in the network that the administrator manages. The topology of the network of systems is discovered by a background process that builds a topology database that is used to construct its graphical representation. The graphical display allows the administrator to navigate through the topology and select a system on which to perform management functions. The functions are performed on the system's MIB (management information base), which includes the hardware and software inventory, the dynamic state of each subsystem, and the history logs of recent events.

The single system image of the network is primarily for the benefit of users and programmers. The topology of the network cannot be completely hidden from administrators. The goal, however, is that the administrator of a particular type of resource has to understand only the logical topology and administrative functions of these resources. Only a network administrator has to understand the physical topology of the network. Only a file system administrator has to understand what file resources are on what server, independent of the underlying network topology, protocols, and communication mechanisms.

The goal, also, is to provide administration mechanisms that are on-line and nondisruptive. That is, the resources of a subsystem can be administered (for example, moved from server to server to balance loads and replicated to other servers for availability) while they are in use and in a way that is transparent to the users. Resources should not have to be taken off-line in order to manage them, nor should an administrator have to be physically present at a server in order to manage its resources. All administration can be done remotely.

Domains

The network model for microkernel-based operating systems is one of inter-connected domains. A domain is the information technology owned by an organization—typically occupying a single geographic location (an office in a home, a small business in a single building, or a branch or division of a larger corporation on its own campus). Because a domain is as big (or small) as an organization wants it to be, the information technology must be scalable (up or down) to meet these diverse needs. In most cases, a domain is connected by a LAN (maybe several interconnected LANs), but increasingly, with mobile systems, it is connected through the public-switched network by some private wireless network (radio frequency or infrared).

The Information Technology resources in a domain are managed by a network operating system (NOS). Early network operating systems (such as NetWare 2.x and LAN Manager) provided simple file and printer sharing with just enough security and directory mechanisms to manage those services. They typically did not try to hide the existence of multiple servers in the domain. The user had to know what was on each server. The server name was part of the file or printer name. The file or printer could not be moved without the user needing to know. Other services could be added to the domain but not in any integrated way. Because the NOS did not provide general-purpose network services, the database servers and mail servers, for example, could not use the security or directory services of the NOS, so they had to provide their own.

Just as a good operating system presents a coherent abstract model of resources residing on a single system, a microkernel-based NOS presents a coherent model of resources residing in a domain. The domain itself can be heterogeneous with respect to physical media, hardware platforms, and local operating systems, but the NOS hides this heterogeneity. The overriding objective is to hide the complexity of the network from both the user and the application developer with a single system image. Network operating systems without a single system image are harder to use, harder to manage, harder to extend, and harder for the application developer to deal with.

A microkernel-based NOS is composed of a set of shared services running on the base operating systems in the domain. Each shared service manages a particular class of distributed resources. Shared services, with their client/server design providing transparent distribution of resource in the context of a single system image, can scale horizontally without limit, using whatever server systems provide the optimum price, performance, and availability for the job. Horizontal scaling simply means the ability to add new servers as the need for capacity and concurrent access increases, without disrupting either the users or the applications, and without having to take any system off-line. It should be a normal administrative operation. Resources can be moved or replicated to the new servers without any need to change names and while the resources are still in operation.

The client framework for a shared service provides the coherent model (both operational and administrative) of the resources. A framework is a shared library that presents a programming abstraction of the model in the form of object and procedural API (industry standard, where possible) that hides the differences between the various services that support it. A framework is an open structure that provides the means to allow third-party network services to plug in. The set of frameworks provided by the microkernel-based NOS is sometimes referred to as the *Universal Client*. It is the Universal Client that actually provides the single system image of the NOS.

The coherency of the single system image provided by the microkernel-based NOS is the result of all the services conforming to common architectures. In particular, they conform to:

- A common directory architecture that allows for the construction of a single hierarchical name space for the resources and objects in the domain
- A common model that specifies all the user's characteristics and preferences in a single object in the directory so that the network can treat the user in a uniform way
- A common security architecture that allows the domain administrators to construct a consistent security policy for the domain
- A common transaction architecture that allows resources and objects of all types to participate in a single distributed transaction
- A common system management architecture that provides consistent and comprehensive software administration, problem determination, and performance management facilities
- A common transport architecture that allows the customer a free choice of physical network and network protocols
- A common internationalization architecture (based on Unicode) that makes applications independent of the natural languages of the domain
- A common mobile architecture that allows the whole system to tolerate disconnection from the network and still perform sensibly for the user

An important consideration in the design of an NOS is its ability to scale across different types of environments, from very small LANs to integrated networks, such as:

- Peer-to-peer

  In a peer-to-peer environment, users casually share their desktop files, printers, and application objects. Users administer the resources on their own personal systems to allow their peers access to the objects, files, and printers they want to share (although it is possible to designate one particular user as the server).

- Workgroup

  A workgroup consists of client and server systems. It is large enough to have at least one server system that can support all the shared resources of the group and can assign administrative responsibility for the servers. People in a workgroup can still use the peer-to-peer casual sharing, and, in fact, treat the servers as peers.

- Enterprise

  These are client/server systems that can scale to large domains and can support a single system image that spans more than one domain.

However, neither the full power of the microkernel-based NOS nor the simplicity of its single system image will be materialized to the application programmer, or to the user, unless all the frameworks of the Universal Client are installed on the user's personal system. The model that the application programmer, the user, and the administrator see from a currently installed client will be whatever that particular client presents. It will be able to access only those resources of the NOS that its API and protocols allow, and the client will be manageable to the extent that its software supports the management protocols of the NOS.

A microkernel-based NOS will provide facilities that can be used to connect heterogeneous domains. Without change, two unlike domains will not be able to communicate, share information, or collaborate for any number (usually all) of the following reasons:

- They use different transport protocols (NetBIOS, IPX, TCP/IP, and so on).

- Services (such as files and print spooling) that they have in common use incompatible protocols.

- Their naming models (directory services) are so different that it is not possible for a user in one domain to even refer to a resource in the other domain.

- Their security mechanisms are sufficiently different that services in one domain cannot recognize users from the other domain.

- Their programming interfaces and distributed programming models (such as RPC and messaging) are different, so that client/server applications cannot span domains.

Even when they do have a protocol in common, it is likely that the protocol does not scale sufficiently well to provide acceptable service across two dispersed domains. Indeed, LAN-based protocols might, in fact, be so demanding on the network as to bring down WAN routers.

The microkernel-based NOS strategy for connecting unlike domains is to superimpose microkernel-based NOS services into both domains and to design the servers such that they can accept the protocols of multiple, well-known network operating systems that are likely to be in use in the local domains. This design allows both domains to continue their local operations unchanged, while being able to interoperate. It also allows them to migrate all their operations smoothly to the common microkernel-based NOS services over time.

The ability of the NOS frameworks to support multiple network service protocols transparently makes this all possible. Therefore, any client that wants to communicate across domains need only install the Universal Client together with the local domain services and NOS services. No more than two sets of network services need ever be deployed in a domain, and the NOS provides the common set of services on which they can both agree. Over time, the NOS client can be deployed pervasively across all systems in both domains.

Naming

The microkernel-based NOS will provide the facilities to construct a single global (worldwide) naming tree. The intent is to provide all resources and objects with unique, human-readable names. The intent, however, is not to force users to enter long character names into commands in order to use the objects. There will be graphical browsing tools for users to find and select objects, and there will be property-based and content-based searching tools for users to find objects. Objects contained in compound documents can be found using the normal editing tools available on the document. Once the object is found, the system can supply the name to the appropriate commands to perform whatever function the user directs. Users can, however, talk about the objects using the character names (taking advantage of contextual abbreviations).

The name space, which is a tree, is hierarchical (see Figure 12-2). The importance of this form is that it allows for the delegation of naming authority. The top of the global name space is decided by an independent group of administrators applying an international naming convention down to the root of each company's name space (so that the company has a unique name, or set of names). Each company can then manage its own name space. A large company, for example, can decide how many domains there should be, and whether they should be organized geographically or functionally. Under the company's root, each domain can be assigned its own globally unique name. The administrators in each domain are then free to organize the domain name space. Users can be assigned their own home directory in the file name space and can organize their own file name space independent of any changes in the overall name space.

There is a conventional structure for the domain name space. Each type of resource (such as files, objects, databases, printers, and users) forms a separate subtree under

Figure 12-2. Name Space for a Domain

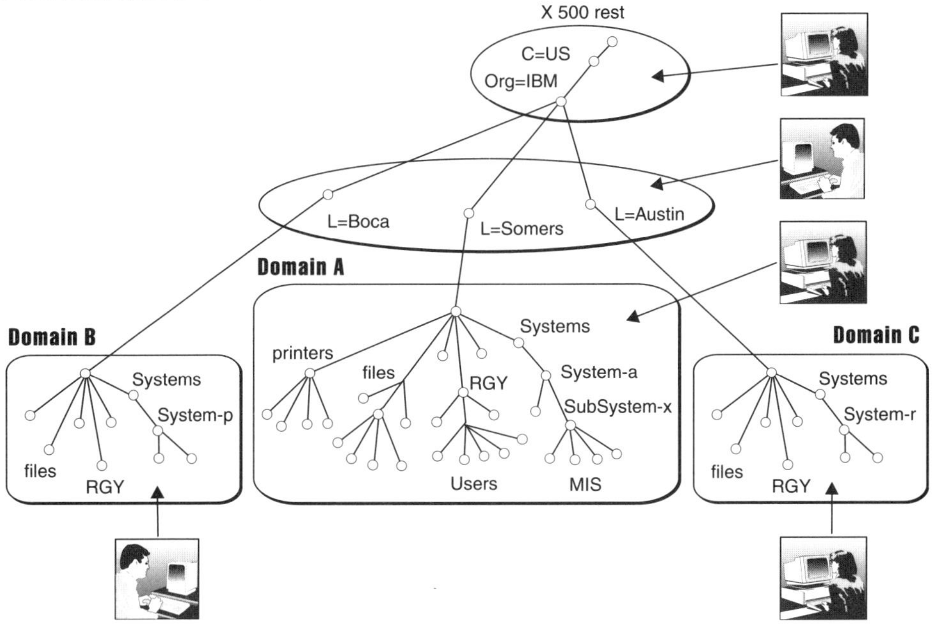

the domain root. Each subsystem supporting a particular type of resource provides its own administration mechanisms for constructing the subtree. (The file system provides an example of how the resources of a particular service can be administered and named.)

All the systems in the domain appear in a directory under a node usually named *host*. Each system is itself a directory, and all elements of the software and hardware inventory installed on a system appear in that system's directory. This subtree is constructed automatically as systems and subsystems are installed.

User Registry

One of the more important (and, today, more troublesome) resources to administer are users. With the microkernel-based NOS, it will never be necessary to define a user more than once, even if that user accesses resources in more than one domain. The user registry has an administration user interface for defining what the authentication architecture calls principals (generally speaking, these are users and servers). It also allows the definition of user groups. These principals and groups appear in subdirectories under the root of the user registry in the domain name space.

The user object in the registry defines all the characteristics and preferences of the user, including the security attributes. These characteristics and preferences are used whenever a subsystem needs information about the user (such as where to send mail, what telephone number to use, what user interface is preferred, and where to send printer output).

Generally speaking, all systems maintain their own registry of users to allow those users to log on and access local resources, even when the system is not connected to the network. (That same logon is good for network access when the system is connected to the network.) These local registries are derived from the central domain registry. Periodically and automatically, each system refreshes its registry from the domain's central registry. The central registry is designed to hold any attributes that are peculiar to the needs of heritage systems in the domain.

The security subsystem also provides an administrative user interface to allow two domains to establish a trust relationship, such that a logon by a user in one domain is trusted by the servers in the other domain. Access control lists associated with resources can contain the global name of users and groups to allow this cross-domain access.

Thus, when users are defined in the central registry of a domain, they have a single, global name. The user object contains the user's password, and a single logon by the user with this password provides access to all the resources in all the domains to which the user has been authorized.

File System Administration

The bytestream file system provides a good example of transparent administration. Using the OSF DFS (Distributed File System), the administrators manage logical file and DASD resources, independent of network complexity.

In setting up the file name space for a domain, the file administrators divide the naming tree into subtrees that make sense administratively, such as a subtree for bulletin boards, a subtree for software binaries, subtrees for shared data files of various kinds, and subtrees for the private files of each user in the domain (the user's home directory). New subtrees can be added later.

Initially, of course, this is just a skeleton tree (because the files do not yet exist), but it is sufficient enough to show its overall shape. Each subtree has a root (a file directory) and enough leaves to mount the subtrees together to form a single tree (the root of each subtree is mounted at a leaf of its parent subtree). The administrator assigns an owner (using the normal security access control mechanism) to each root subdirectory. That owner will then be able to grant suitable access to all the files and directories that are created in the subtree.

On a disk, these subtrees are stored as file sets. Each file set is assigned a disk space limit (this limit can be changed administratively). Any user trying to exceed this limit will be warned and will either have to manage the available space or go through the administrative procedure to increase the space limit assigned to the file set.

Once the file tree has been set up, the servers installed, and the file sets assigned to servers, the file system is operational.

It is important to note that users do not need to understand the concept of a file set. All the users see is a single file name tree for the domain, and they can perform the normal file operations under normal security access control. In particular, they can create files up to the limit of their file sets, which they see simply as space limitation.

Administratively, once the file tree is set up and operational, the administrators can perform all their administrative functions without any need to access the files. In fact, they might not be able to access the files, because they might have assigned other owners to the root directories of the subtrees. What administrators can do, however, is:

- Replicate file sets on multiple servers (there is always one master and many replicas).
- Move a file set to a different server (to balance load).
- Introduce new servers as the need arises.
- Use the built-in policy-driven mechanisms to establish backup procedures.
- Restore file sets as the need arises.
- Extend the file tree with new file sets (for example, to accommodate new users).

DFS also allows the administrators to mount the files of other file systems (for example, NFS and the LAN Server) as leaf subtrees in the domain's file naming tree.

The Programmer's Model

A microkernel-based NOS will provide a complete object environment for application developers consisting of:

- An underlying uniform, CORBA-compliant object model that provides a single system image for all objects, both transient and persistent
- A complete set of object frameworks for system services
- A compound document programming model for building interactive application components

The microkernel-based NOS will also support the well-known procedural distributed programming models (RPC, conversations, and messaging) and procedural interfaces to all the system services.

Object Programming

Objects are software entities made up of data structures and functions that perform operations on the data. Together, the data and the associated functions enable objects to model the characteristics (represented by the data) and behavior (represented by the functions) of almost any real-world entity.

Objects hide (or encapsulate) the internal structure of their data and the algorithms by which their functions work. Instead of exposing these implementation details, objects provide interfaces (known as methods) that represent their abstractions cleanly, with no extraneous information. By using the interfaces of an object, the programmer can concentrate on what the object does, not how it does it. This encapsulation also has the benefit that object implementations can change without affecting their clients.

All new microkernel-based NOS shared services will provide such object-oriented interfaces.

A microkernel-based NOS is grouped into subsystems, or shared services, that provide functions, such as multimedia, graphics, transaction processing, and so on. Each subsystem is composed of one or more frameworks into which the client/server network services fit. Each framework is a group of object classes that work together to provide an adaptable base, not only for using the subsystem but for extending it.

Subsystems fall into two basic categories: those designed to be extended and reused as the basis for application development (also called application frameworks), and those designed to be extended and reused by system service providers (also called system frameworks). OpenDoc is the prime example of the former; a security subsystem is an example of the latter. The Service Framework provides system services to both the application subsystems and the applications that fit into it.

In either case, the frameworks are designed to be extended, and the fundamental mechanisms for extension are the same. A subsystem's frameworks provide the architecture and design as well as a partial implementation, and all the extensions share, and benefit from, the reuse of the same overall architecture. This partial implementation can be extended by subclassing (deriving new object classes from those provided in the framework in which methods are added or replaced) and by providing implementations for abstract classes defined by the framework.

A framework is typically designed to be extended independently by multiple developers; yet, because these independent extensions are all built within the context of a single architecture, they work together seamlessly. It is precisely this seamless interoperation within the context of service frameworks that makes it possible to develop a single system image out of heterogeneous services.

The net result is that the application developers (or system developers) leverage and reuse the intellectual content invested in the design of the subsystem. This means that the developers can concentrate more of their time and energy on the application domain and build more widely-applicable solutions. In other words, they:

- Write less code, yet achieve more
- Produce more reliable and robust code because the frameworks have already been tested
- Produce applications that are more modular and consistent

Programming within a framework requires a change in perspective that can be expressed as "Don't call us, we'll call you." Because the programmer is developing components to fit into a predefined subsystem, the subsystem controls the flow of execution. It, therefore, calls the components. The developer must concentrate, not on flow of control, but on models—what the objects do, rather than when they should do it. The framework will take care of when they do it.

Fundamentally, the Universal Client provides the frameworks that allow applications to access information anywhere in the network, and it is they that provide the single system image to the programmer.

The System Object Model (SOM)

The object model for a microkernel-based NOS determines the general behavior common to all objects. It specifies how object interfaces are defined, how methods are called, and how objects can be made persistent and accessed concurrently by many processes throughout the network, and it provides the means to construct language-neutral class libraries.

The model is independent of the relative location of objects and independent of the mechanisms used to implement the model. Thus, the model provides for the transparent distribution of objects in the network. A client calls an object's methods in the same way no matter which system each resides on, as long as both systems support the model.

The object model is derived from (and conforms to) the OMG CORBA (Common Object Request Broker Architecture), and the services that form the model are implemented as a set of frameworks that allow multiple mechanisms to be hidden under the model. This set of frameworks, and their mechanisms, is called the SOM run time, sometimes called the ORB (Object Request Broker). The different mechanisms allow SOM to scale from a single system to a small LAN to an interenterprise network.

Language Neutrality

SOM provides the means to develop object libraries that are both language-neutral and binary reusable, even using languages that would otherwise be procedural. Language neutrality means that the clients of the library can be implemented in a different language than the library. Binary reuse means that objects can be derived from the library without access to the library's source code.

The facilities provided for this purpose are:

- A CORBA IDL (Interface Definition Language) for defining an object's interfaces, inheritance, and data members

- An IDL precompiler (the SOM compiler) and macros (bindings for a number of languages) that allow the programmer to refer to data members and call methods, while allowing SOM to hide the details of memory layout and method resolution

- A common object run time that creates and initializes objects, resolves method calls, and generally encapsulates an object's implementation

- A standard calling convention (the same that has been developed for procedural calls)

There are two mechanisms for creating such libraries—one using compilers that have no built-in knowledge of SOM, and the other using compilers that do.

In the first mechanism, the class developer creates a definition of the library using IDL. This definition is precompiled by the SOM compiler, which generates header files and a skeleton library implementation file for the designated language. The class developer then completes the implementation of the library in the chosen language (using the SOM macros to refer to data members and call methods) and compiles it with the native language compiler using the appropriate SOM compiler-generated header file as input.

In the second mechanism (which requires an object-oriented language, and is known as a direct-to-SOM, or DTS), the compiler understands both IDL and the SOM run time. In this case, the object interfaces can be defined in the native language. The native compiler will generate the necessary IDL header files for use by clients that want to call the library.

Clients that want to construct objects that use the library, or derive objects from (that is, inherit from) the library, can do so in either of the preceding two ways. It is simply necessary to include the appropriate library header file.

Persistent Objects

When an object is instantiated (that is, created), it can be made either transient or persistent. A transient object lives no longer than the process that creates it, while a persistent object can live longer and must be explicitly destroyed.

The essential characteristic of persistent objects is that they can be accessed concurrently by many processes throughout the network and, therefore, SOM must provide storage and retrieval, global naming, security, transaction, and locking models for them.

Only the object's data members are stored in the persistent object store. The methods are stored in an implementation repository, and class resolution binds a particular activation to a particular class implementation. It is an administration responsibility to make sure that the appropriate repository contains the appropriate class library version whenever (and wherever) the methods are called.

References and Names

Objects are instantiated by the SOM classNew() function. For transient objects, an active instantiation is created on the process's heap, and a reference to the new object is returned. This reference must be used on all subsequent method calls to identify the active instance. For persistent objects, the classNew() function is extended to allow the object's global name to be specified. In general, the global name of an object is structured hierarchically (like a file name), and is used to locate the object in the persistent object store.

Note: The syntax of file names allows for a number of contextual abbreviations: /... is the global root; /.: is the domain (cell) root; /: is the domain's file tree root. The global syntax also allows X.500 property-based names to appear in the domain name prefix. It would be possible to apply the same kind of abbreviations to object names and to invent an abbreviation for the root of the domain's object tree (or to even include objects in the file tree). Also, in designing the XFN naming framework for X/Open, the OSF members are defining further conventions (policies) to allow users and administrators to deal more easily with global names.

If a process wants to use an existing persistent object, it is necessary to activate it. If the process knows the name, the String_to_object() function can be used for the purpose. It takes the global name of the object and returns a reference to the most recent activation of the object in the process (creating an activation, if necessary).

If the application does not know the name of an object, it can, in conjunction with the user, take advantage of the browsing and query functions of the Name Services to locate a suitable object. Browsing involves the user walking the object naming tree looking for the object by name or appearance. Query involves the user supplying a set of properties that the desired object must possess. The properties that an object possesses in the Name Services are not part of its encapsulated state (no more than its name is). The Name Services can therefore browse and query without having to open all objects.

The Name Services return an opaque string identifying the selected object in a particular store. This opaque string can also be given to String_to_ref()—also known as open()—to activate the object.

Not all persistent objects are exported into the naming tree. Objects that form part of a composite object, and are not visible outside it, do not need a global name. The component object can be activated by the composite object using a memory pointer. How the composite object names and finds its components is encapsulated behavior.

A compound document (which is itself a persistent object) contains component objects that can be linked to by many other compound documents (it is thus an object store in its own right). The compound document provides its own name service for embedded objects and manages their name resolution. The compound document is a junction in the naming tree, and exports the name service interface.

Version Control

Because the instantiation of persistent objects can last for a long time, the class library might experience many modifications over the lifetime of any instance. These modifications might be incompatible with the instance (although this is a situation that can, and should, be avoided by the class developer). SOM maintains a version ID in both the class object and each instance (which is the version of the class from which the instance was created). Unfortunately, it is also possible (though also avoidable) to have multiple versions of a class in existence at the same time in the network.

When a persistent object is activated, and the version of the instance differs from that of the class to which it is to be bound, SOM can detect whether the class library is compatible with the activation (either a new class library that can deal with old objects, or a new object that is a compatible extension of the old version). If compatibility exists, the activation can be successfully created; otherwise the activation is created, but an exception is raised.

SOM also provides the means to update old instances to new versions. Given a reference to the activation of an old version that is bound to a newer version of the class, it is possible to call a method that can create a new instance to replace the old and to initialize it from the data members of the old version. The reference to the newly active instance can be substituted for the reference to the old activation.

Transactions and Concurrency Control

Because persistent objects are accessible concurrently by many processes throughout the network, it is necessary to provide both transactional control and concurrency control (locking) over them. SOM provides both.

Transactional control over objects (just like traditional transactional control) is intended to guarantee that a group of updates to a set of objects appears to be atomic from outside the transaction. That is, all the updates performed by a transaction appear to happen at the same time or not at all. The objects participating in the transaction are not confined to one system; they can be arbitrarily distributed around the network. SOM provides the methods to Start(), Commit(), or Backout() transactions and to deal with nested transactions. SOM also keeps track of all objects participating in the transaction as it spreads through the network and maintains a log of changes caused by the transaction on each system. If the transaction is committed, SOM commits all the changes using a two-phase commit protocol between the ORBs on the systems involved. Otherwise, all the objects are reset atomically to the state that existed at the start of the transaction. All persistent objects are inherently transactional; however, they do not have to inherit the behavior, nor do they have to understand logging or participate in the two-phase commit protocol.

Objects are locked for the same reason that data is locked, either to obtain consistent information or to achieve a consistent set of updates. SOM provides both implicit and explicit locking. SOM implicitly obtains an exclusive lock on a newly instantiated object. When a process attempts to create a new activation of an old persistent object, SOM tries to obtain a read lock on the object. The activation will be successful only if the lock can be obtained. SOM will upgrade the lock to an exclusive lock on a subsequent attempt to write to the object in the process. (Only one process in the network can hold an exclusive lock on an object at any given time; if the lock attempt fails, an exception is raised.) A client object can also explicitly lock and unlock a group of objects to preserve their consistency and to implement a strategy of deadlock avoidance (which generally requires the acquisition of locks in a prescribed order). Whenever a process unlocks a persistent object, it is deactivated and the reference invalidated.

If the activations are in the context of a transaction, any locks held are released (and the activations terminated) when the transaction terminates (commits or backs out).

Security

SOM provides a secure association between a client object and a server object. That is, when a client activates an object, the user (on whose behalf the client is executing, as identified by the process in which it is executing) is authenticated by SOM.

Note: The object store on which the persistent object resides is the identified principal that will act as the server in the three-party authentication scheme.

Each object can be protected by an Access Control List (ACL) (which SOM provides the means to construct) that grants specific access rights to some or all defined users. There are various types of masks that can be specified on a class basis, for example:

- Read, write, create, and destroy
- Yes, no
- User, admin, super
- Method1, method2, method3, and so on

Each class chooses the type of mask that applies to it and has a definition that indicates how to interpret the mask for each method (that is, what rights are required to invoke each method). SOM uses the authenticated UserID, the required rights mask, and the ACL to authorize the methods called on behalf of the user.

Persistent objects do not have to participate in the implementation of the security policy (because authentication and authorization are performed by SOM).

Object Export/Import

Today, a sophisticated editor uses a file to persistently store the internal representation of a document; any other editor would not be able to edit the document in this form. The editor provides a function to export the document in an interchangeable form.

The same applies to persistent objects; while an object is in the persistent store, it is bound to a particular class. However, the class can provide a method to export the object's data. The export() function takes parameters that specify the form of the exported data, and the global name of a container (such as a file, a database, and a Bento container). A class can also provide an import() function that allows an active instance of the class to be initialized from an exported object. The import() function takes a reference to the active instance (as always) and the name of the container from which it is to be initialized. The active instance can refuse to initialize itself if it does not recognize the data in the container.

Note: Bento is the architecture, agreed to for OpenDoc, to export and import application components. See Chapter 13, "OpenDoc" on page 273.

Procedural Programming Models for Distributing Function

Three procedural programming models are discussed in this section—RPC, conversations, and messaging.

RPC

RPC for microkernel-based NOS is a compatible extension of the OSF RPC model. It has some similarities with the object model. It is based on the call model but does not provide encapsulation. RPC can be used either to implement a remote subroutine library or as the foundation of a distributed resource manager. The subroutine library might need to execute on a particular system either because it is computationally intensive or because it requires special hardware (a vector processor, for example).

An RPC server can support many RPC libraries. An RPC library has an interface defined by a language (NIDL, Network Interface Definition Language) that is a syntactical extension of the way the C language defines procedures. It allows the library developer to specify a signature for all the entry points to the library, including specifying which are input and which are output parameters. These input and output parameters form the content of CALL and RETURN messages that flow between client and server. The messages are processed by stubs (on both client and server) generated by the NIDL precompiler. The client calls a client stub, which translates it into a CALL message that the RPC run time sends to the RPC server. The RPC run time on the server gives the message to the corresponding server stub, which translates it into a call to the appropriate interface. The return is the same in reverse. As the stubs process messages, they also deal with differences in the data and character representation on client and server systems. The RPC run time deals with the mutual authentication between client and server.

When a new RPC interface is developed, the NIDL compiler assigns it a globally unique ID. This ID is used to identify the interface at run time, no matter what system (or systems) it resides on. The ID is embedded in the client when it includes the interface. When the server exports the RPC interface to the name service, it does so through the RPC/NSI (RPC Name Service Interface). The entry in the name service for the interface contains all the communication protocol stack information necessary to send the CALL messages to the server. (This information is called the RPC binding.) The RPC run time, however, does not provide the means to automatically launch the server; this must be done either programmatically or administratively. The client uses the RPC/NSI, with the RPC interface ID, to find a server that supports the interface.

The RPC server can be a shared service. In this case, the shared service developer can also provide a client API (derived from the RPC interface) to allow a remote system to manipulate the resources. The server exports its resources into the name service along with the RPC binding information.

The requestor calls the client API with the name of a resource, and the client API library looks up the name of the resource in the name service to obtain the RPC binding. The client library binds to the server and translates subsequent API calls into RPC interface calls to the server. If the RPC client/server is an implementation of one of the microkernel-based NOS network services, the client API library can be embedded under the appropriate service framework.

Microkernel-based NOS RPC provides transactional extensions to the OSF RPC (in the form of NIDL extensions). The RPC allows a transaction context to be passed on the calls to a server acting as a recoverable resource manager and provides interfaces to the transaction service. The transaction service allows the RPC run time and the RPC server to register with the service for a particular distributed transaction.

Conversations

A conversation is a distributed programming model (based on LU6.2 semantics) that allows two programs, connected by an APPN network, to converse. The term was coined because originally a half-duplex discipline was imposed, which allowed only one party to talk at a time; now a full-duplex option is provided. The API used by both parties in the conversation is the common programming interface for communications (CPI-C, an X/Open standard).

The model can be used for client/server development because it allows one side (the client) to launch a transaction program (the server) on the other side and to create a session between them over which they can hold conversations. The session also provides the mutual authentication between the client and the server. The transaction program name is resolved by the APPN directory.

If conversations are the model of communications used by a shared service (an example is a database server using DRDA), then the shared service should define an API to allow its clients to manipulate the resources. The API is implemented as a client library that translates the API calls into conversations with the server. The server exports its resources through the name service along with the necessary transaction program name. The client library looks up the resource names in the name service and attaches to the corresponding transaction program. As with RPC, if the client/server is implementing one of the microkernel-based NOS network services, the client API library can be embedded into the appropriate service framework.

CPI-C has an option (syncpoint) that allows the transaction context to flow on the conversation from client to server, and both the conversation service and the resource manager can then use this information to include the resource managers in the distributed two-phase commit. The conversational model has no built-in mechanism (like NIDL or IDL) to deal with the heterogeneous data and character representation between client and server.

Messaging

The message model is based primarily on the MQI (Message Queuing Interface). The messaging model is based on the concept of time-independent execution triggered by messages (in queues). In that sense, it is the only connectionless model (apart from primitive datagrams). It is not necessary for the server to be up and running at the time a message is sent; indeed, it is not even necessary for the server system to be powered on. The model, therefore, adapts well to the mobile environment. Also, the decoupling of clients and servers using intermediate queues means that the model adapts well to parallel processing environments, with multiple servers able to process a queue of messages from multiple clients.

Each message sent by a client is, in a sense, a self-contained request to trigger a piece of work (for example, a transaction). The message is sent to a named destination, but the model can store the message at any number of intermediate points (including at the client) until the network/server is ready to accept it.

The model supports a number of classes of messages, from lightweight memory-based messages to fully recoverable messages within the scope of a transaction. The model is provided by a pluggable framework, allowing different technologies to be used for message delivery, such as different message stores, directories, and transport services.

The store and forward queuing mechanism is both secure and, optionally, can be fully recoverable, with once-only guaranteed delivery. The delivery nodes authenticate themselves and store the messages reliably. The client can also include the sending of a message as part of a broader transaction and commit (or back out) the message along with the rest of the transaction.

All the necessary information required for the target application to process the message is sent to the destination system. Any reply from the server is sent as an independent message back to the client and arrives in a queue on the client. The messages can also contain the sender's authenticated ID, which can be checked at the destination. There are plans to support a full IDL-like interface to allow the message model to deal with the automatic transformation of data and character information between client and server in a heterogeneous network.

The messaging support includes the ability to export services through the name service, along with the information that the model requires to find the destination queues.

OpenDoc

OpenDoc is an architecture for providing an advanced, component-oriented approach to compound documents for extending existing applications. This chapter introduces OpenDoc, describes compound documents, and provides information about SOM and the Open Scripting Architecture (OSA), which is used to communicate with components.

This chapter also describes Bento, which is used to store component data in interchangeable form, and seamless OLE, which provides interoperability between OpenDoc and Microsoft OLE 2.0.

Introducing OpenDoc

Many years ago, the electronics industry was producing console stereos. These units were more like furniture than they were like electronic devices. One large cabinet came complete with television, record player, speakers, and AM/FM radio. Consumers' choices were severely limited. If we didn't like the speakers, we had to live with them or buy a different model, but then maybe the record player wouldn't be up to our standards. There was no way to mix and match the pieces of the systems to match our needs, tastes, or budget. As if that weren't bad enough, when new technology arrived, we couldn't just add it to the box. For example, when color television became available, it wasn't possible to exchange our black and white unit for the color one. We had to scrap what we had and buy a complete, new package. But those days are long since gone.

Today, a trip to an electronics store means choices. We can mix and match components among various manufacturers. When a component with a new technology comes out, we are assured that it will plug into our home system and not require an upgrade to a newer version of stereo equipment. We are used to picking and choosing the speaker, tuners, turntables, VCRs, video monitors, and so on that we like and putting them together in any way to form our personal home entertainment system. We have complete freedom to choose from a large number of products from different manufacturers and from an ever-growing number of different technologies. And we need not worry that our home system will be instantly obsolete because of a new product we might want to buy next year. We are safe in assuming that the producers of consumer electronics will make sure that next year's products will "plug" into the home system purchased today.

This situation is great for both the producers and the consumers. The consumers have immense flexibility in configuring their electronic systems, and the producers have a bigger market in which to sell their technology. Making upgrades to existing systems is easy, so a modest advance in technology can be parlayed into a successful money-maker, and new technology can be introduced aggressively because the consumer no longer tends to wait until the console system "smokes" itself into oblivion before making the significant move of throwing it away and buying a new one.

Today's software industry is in many ways comparable to the electronics industry of yesteryear. Applications are monolithic, containing every possible function that users might need, whether or not they really want it, and they lock users into a way of working. New technology means new purchases. Finding a cooperative set of applications means buying into a "suite" of products, usually from a single manufacturer. There is no way to mix and match applications, no way to add new technology to an existing suite without purchasing an updated suite, and no easy way for users to build a "custom system."

The changes in the electronic industry, from console systems to component systems, were revolutionary. The changes in the software industry that will take us from suites to customer systems will be no less so. And the first step in that revolution is called OpenDoc!

The Alliance

On Tuesday, June 29, 1993, the IBM Corporation, Apple Computer, Inc., and WordPerfect/Novell joined with a host of other computer industry leaders in launching the OpenDoc program.

The *New York Business Wire* on that date described the OpenDoc program as follows:

> "OpenDoc is an open, cross-platform software architecture designed to simplify the sharing of complex documents in a multi-vendor environment.
>
> OpenDoc also provides users with a more natural and flexible way to create compound documents—documents that include information and media from many different applications."

Apple Computer

Apple Computer, Inc., had been working for some time on a way to introduce to the user community a radical new way of using computers. They had a vision of component software, a way of allowing software functions to be packaged into small chunks that the user could assemble in unique ways to solve problems instead of relying on huge programs that were at the same time loaded with function yet inflexible.

The so-called monolithic application of today has to have a full-range of capabilities to match the complete requirements of the user community. And, yet, any given user needs only some subset of those capabilities. But because the applications are not expandable, the vendor has no choice but to build the application with everything including the kitchen sink. The end user pays both with dollars, for functions never used, and with the loss of flexibility.

Component software, on the other hand, is completely flexible. Users pay only for the functions that they want when they purchase a software component. And vendors get a break too because they are relieved of the burden of supporting a full-set of functions in each and every offering. The savings can be passed on to the customer, which stimulates the market. The market can be further revitalized with add-on purchases that can be made for substantially less cost than a current upgrade to an application suite would cost. Users can mix and match components from different vendors seamlessly and without having to commit to one suite of applications (see Figure 13-1).

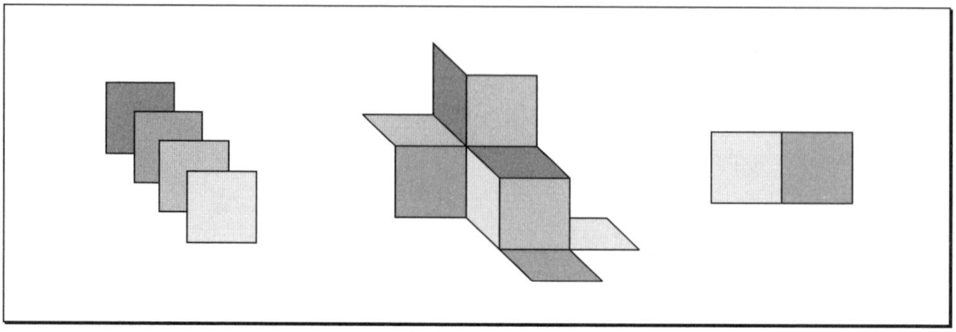

Figure 13-1. Components Make Using Software Easy

International Business Machines

At the same time that Apple was working on component software, IBM was pursuing object technology. Techniques for hiding data and treating program fragments as black boxes had been developed. Their use held much promise for the software industry. High on the list was the concept of reusability. A conventional program can be made reusable but to do so requires much effort on the part of the programmer to modify it to fit the intended use because it was built as a "custom unit" in the first place. A well-written program object is more like prefab sections used in the building industry. Compare the cost of building a house with all custom doors, windows, and so on versus using standard ones and you'll get an idea of the magnitude of the problem.

The goal of software reuse was proving to be elusive. While the existing programming languages allowed objects to be built, it was often difficult or impossible to get objects built with different tools from different sources to work together. Enter the System Object Model (SOM) developed by IBM.

SOM tackled the problems plaguing the fledgling software object industry in a language- and platform-neutral manner. Working with standards developed by an industry-wide committee, the OMG (Object Management Group), IBM developed SOM so that objects could work together no matter what tools, language, or platform was used to develop them. A further development, Distributed System Object Model (DSOM), enables objects to work together in a network. This latter capability will become more and more important as we enter the world of the information superhighway.

A marriage of the technologies was in order, with Apple providing the means to create component software and IBM enabling it across language, platform, and network boundaries.

WordPerfect/Novell

But new technologies are seldom borne in isolation. And so it is with OpenDoc. Microsoft's Object Linking and Embedding (OLE) technology precedes OpenDoc. It provides to Windows users similar capabilities but without being truly object-based, open, or network-enabled. In order to preserve the investment of vendors who have implemented products based on OLE and for the benefit of users with OLE-enabled products, WordPerfect Corporation has developed technology that allows OpenDoc and OLE documents and components to work together.

The Consortium

Keeping these technologies truly "open" required an impartial owner. CI Labs (Component Integration Labs) was founded to oversee OpenDoc's use, to distribute the base technologies (available in source form), and to certify that products developed for OpenDoc do indeed meet the level of compliance needed to work together seamlessly.

The Benefits of OpenDoc

OpenDoc is a set of architectures that will revolutionize the way software is built, sold, and used. Software manufacturers will be able to package their products more effectively because they can break up their large monolithic applications into smaller units, which can be purchased and used separately or assembled into larger custom packages.

Users of these OpenDoc "parts" will be freed from thinking in terms of what applications they are using; instead they can concentrate on the task at hand. The technologies underlying OpenDoc enable automation of parts through the use of "events" that can be sent between documents. The technology is distributed, which means that events can be delivered, even if the documents are on different computers, as long as there is an appropriate network between them. Indeed, the direction OpenDoc is taking will someday mean that documents can be created and shared in a network environment without regard to the type of computer in use and without the user knowing if the "parts" are local or remote.

Figure 13-2. OpenDoc Lets You Work the Way You Want

Component Software for Sale

To the software manufacturer, this is a great opportunity. It will be much easier to entice customers to make an addition to their software if it can be done at a reasonable price and without scrapping their existing investment. Freed from the necessity of putting every conceivable function into an application, software designers can concentrate on their chosen problem domain and produce a better solution for the user.

Document-Centric IS User-Centric

Along with the component revolution comes another equally profound change away from an application-centric view of computing to a document-centric one. The word "document" is used in this sense very loosely and is meant to denote a whole range of output from the classic printed document to a desktop. In a document-centric world, users think about the task at hand and not about the applications that they are going to use. The work progresses as users pick and choose from a "parts" bin, assembling their documents as they go.

Document-centric computing is a concept that aims to put the users' focus back on the content and layout of their documents. The idea is to start with an empty document "shell." The document grows as "parts" of various types and formats are added. During this growing process, the document designer can move and resize the parts until the desired layout is achieved. The user can change the parts without leaving the document and without having to stop and think about what application created the original.

But how will a user assemble the document? Templates are the answer.

Templates

OpenDoc code will be delivered to users NOT as discrete applications but rather as electronic "stationery" called *templates*, which are used to assemble a particular application or document that the user creates. Templates are represented on the Desktop as a pad or stack in order to communicate the metaphor graphically. For each part that is available in the system, there will be a corresponding pad of stationery representing that part-type. In order to add a part of that type to their document, users will simply "tear off" a piece of the stationery and drop it onto the document.

OpenDoc Features

Compound document architectures have been around for a long time now. OpenDoc was designed to overcome some of the limitations of the earlier technologies. A few of the more noteworthy ones are discussed below.

Scripting, Events, and Recordability

Scripting, events, and recordability are all advantages enjoyed by OpenDoc documents that are compliant with Open Scripting Architecture. Open Scripting Architecture, OSA for short, will give OpenDoc users a way of customizing their documents to an extent never before possible. Many power users of PC software will already be familiar with the many macro languages available for the more powerful spreadsheets, word processors, databases, and so forth on the market. These macro languages enable a user to customize an application. Sometimes they can be used to provide a record/playback facility, a way of automatically "remembering" a sequence of keystrokes and then "reexecuting" them as a single command. In the hands of an experienced user, a macro language can be used to create new functions to the point where the old application is almost unrecognizable.

The OpenDoc technology gives users the kind of flexibility and power that heretofore was only available to the programming professional. Semantic events replace UI events (such as mouse clicks) as the prime mover of the program. The events are standardized in a registry that is available to all developers, and so interoperability among documents is assured. Use of object specifiers gives users the freedom to use natural language to express their commands. And the use of pluggable script components means that a range of script language can be selected to suit the audience. An application can metamorphose with scripting and can be tailored with record/playback. New input devices will drive the OSA-compliant applications of today and the future.

Alternative Input

Programmers who support Open Events in their applications and factor them get a number of benefits (such as scriptability and recordability) for their efforts. But another benefit that they get for free is alternative input devices. Because the application is structured so that it operates entirely on the exchange of Open Events, its functions are independent of the source of the events. The events could have been generated by the standard user interface or by a scripting component. It doesn't matter. As long as the Open Events are constructed correctly, it all works. Alternative input devices, such as voice, pen, and touch-sensitive screens, can be built to generate Open Events, and they can be used to drive the application without the programmer having to change a single byte in the code!

User-Built Interfaces

In OpenDoc, a part can be as complex as a text editor or as simple as a graphic shape. So, it's easy to see how a set of user controls such as buttons and scroll bars could be built as OpenDoc parts. With the capability of attaching a script to a part, you have instant user-built interfaces.

Imagine you have a document that represents a real-estate listing. Because this is an OpenDoc document, you can drop a floor plan into the document and a video clip of a walk-through. Now with a simple button-part embedded into the various rooms in the floor plan, you can customize the walk-through. A script need only be attached to each button that sends an Open Event to the video part, telling it to play the part of the clip corresponding to the room in which the button is embedded. This idea can be extended to where users can visually build a user interface from scratch or modify an existing one.

Irregular Shapes

Graphic designers have often criticized the software available on most desktops as being too limiting. (You could create any shape you wanted as long as it was a rectangle! Further, the rectangles couldn't overlap.) For a graphic designer who wants full creative freedom, this is unacceptable.

A design goal from the very beginning of OpenDoc was to allow fully irregular shapes that can overlap in any way that the document user or graphic designer could want.

Concurrency

Modern operating systems, such as OS/2 Warp Connect (PowerPC Edition), allow concurrence of tasks.

In a compound document, that means that every part of a document can be "alive and kicking" at the same time. Thus video and audio parts can be playing while a clock and ticker tape continually update their view and while the user edits the document.

Linking

Sometimes data is used in more than one part of a document or indeed in multiple documents. Linking gives us a way to share this data.

- Intradocument linking, which allows data within a document that is embedded in multiple places to be stored once within the document.

- Interdocument linking (same place), which allows one copy of data to be shared in multiple documents.

- Network linking (homogeneous), which allows a copy of data to be shared among documents stored on a network of computers running the same operating system.

- Network linking (heterogeneous), which allows a copy of data to be shared on a network among computers running on different platforms (operating systems and hardware).

Cross-Platform Support (Future Version)

A prerequisite to linking in heterogeneous networks is cross-platform support. This support will allow documents to be shared across different OpenDoc implementations. For instance, a document created on an OS/2 system will be able to be displayed and edited on a Macintosh, UNIX, or Windows platform.

Distributed Processing

The ultimate goal of the OpenDoc technology is to allow full freedom of parts—that is to say, to allow a part of a document to reside anywhere in a network, on any platform, and to permit a user to compose, view, and edit a document from any workstation that supports OpenDoc. This vision would have "part bins" with collections of parts that can be used to create documents readily available to network users. The whereabouts of the parts and the platforms for which they were originally written will be details that are unimportant and transparent to the end user.

OpenDoc Technologies

OpenDoc can also be viewed as a set of related technologies donated by the members of CI Labs (Component Integration Laboratories), the nonprofit organization that owns the OpenDoc technology.

System Object Model

IBM donated the base object technology used by OpenDoc. As mentioned earlier in this book, SOM is based on an industry standard—Common Object Release Broker Architecture (CORBA). SOM was a natural choice for OpenDoc. Besides CORBA-compliance, SOM offers a solution for some basic problems that have beset object technology from the beginning and have hindered its widespread acceptance. SOM provides binary compatibility between objects and avoids the "fragile base class problem," a situation where the changing of the implementation of a parent class requires the complete rebuilding of any child classes that inherit from the parent.

Document Services

Apple Computer, Inc., developed a standard way to allow disparate parts to cooperate, coalescing into "compound documents." OpenDoc's document services provide a set of run-time subsystems, made up of cooperating objects or cliques, which

OpenDoc developers use to create OpenDoc components. The main goals of OpenDoc's document services were to allow a full range of data types within a document, without sacrificing fidelity when the document is viewed or printed.

Storage Services

As soon as the user has assembled a document from a diverse set of parts, it is reasonable to assume that the user will want a way to store the document and perhaps exchange the document with other users. It is not a trivial matter to store a document that contains an arbitrary number of parts with many data types. Bento, developed by Apple Computer, Inc., is the container technology used by OpenDoc. It provides efficient storage of multiple data types, which is crucial for compound documents. Bento is based on an architecture that is extensible, so any data type, even ones not invented yet, can be supported.

Insider's View: Bento: n. "Japanese" 1. A box lunch or picnic lunch. 2. A box or basket with multiple compartments, containing a collection of disparate elements arranged in an aesthetically pleasing manner.

Bento, borrowing its name from the Japanese lacquer box with many compartments—one for each food-type—provides the OpenDoc part with a black-box way of storing its data (see Figure 13-3). OpenDoc doesn't need to know anything about the data format that the part stores. Yet Bento keeps it all straight and contained within one file. The same storage system is used for all data transfers at a file level as well as in memory for clipboard, drag-drop, and link objects. Finally, Bento allows for multiple values for a data item to be stored together. As a result, a part can store data in a high-fidelity format as well as in more universal formats. For instance, a text part could store data in a proprietary and efficient format for its own use, the same data in rich text format for interchangeability with other text editors, and, finally, as straight ASCII to ensure that even the most unsophisticated accesses to the data can interpret it correctly.

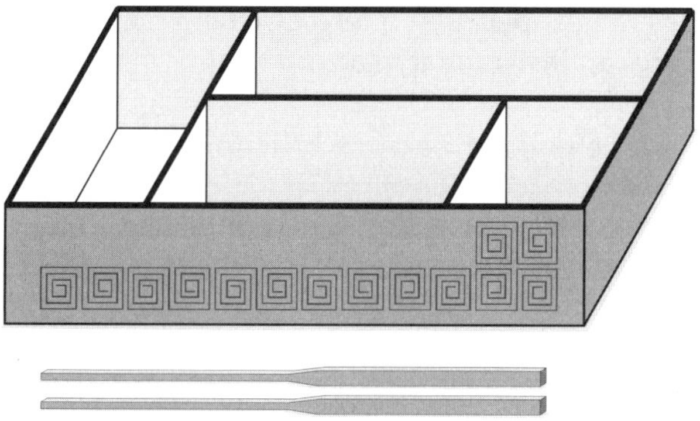

Figure 13-3. A Japanese Bento Box

Bento is designed to provide storage containers for multiple data types in an efficient and flexible way. OpenDoc uses Bento to provide multiple *drafts* in a document. As a user modifies a document, a new draft is created. This is an implicit archiving of the document that is very efficient in storage because only the changes from the previous draft are stored. The Bento system provides an easy way to create links to other parts in the document or even outside of the document. Users can create a piece of a document once and include it in any number of other documents using these links, even when the documents are on diverse nodes and platforms in a network. This capability is an important point because today's and tomorrow's computing environment is distributed. And the networks on which parts and documents will be found will most certainly be heterogeneous.

Open Scripting Architecture

Open Scripting Architecture's name belies its true power, which extends much beyond simple scripting. OSA is based on Open Events—coded messages between applications, parts, and documents.

OSA supports multiple script languages. Any language that can emit Open Events can be embraced by OSA. Because OSA communication happens through events, a listening application can record them for later playback. This sequence of events provides an instant macro record facility.

OSA defines the way in which documents and parts communicate with each other. The Open Event Registry is a standard that describes the verbs or commands passed within the event as well as the object classes on which the verbs operate. The Event Registry can be used by all part handlers to guarantee interoperability.

The Event Registry gives precise definitions on how to encode the verbs and the objects. The verbs are further organized into suites according to the type of applications that typically use them.

Some examples of the standard suites are:

Required	Defines the base set of functions that all compliant parts will need to support.
Core	Defines file and edit functions and basic scripting.

Text Defines basic text editing and formatting.

Table Defines commands used for table editing and formatting.

Each standard suite can define any of the following:

- Open Events (the verbs)
- Open Event object classes (the class of data or parameters operated on by the events, such as document, selection, or text)
- Descriptor types (the type of the data or parameter, such as record or Boolean)
- Primitive object classes (no properties and only one element, such as RGBColor or IntlText)
- Key forms (used to specify how to search for an object—by range, position, or ID)
- Comparison operators (such as contains, begins with, and equals)
- Constants

Object Specifiers

A very powerful concept of OSA is the *object specifier*. Object specifiers allow an application to provide a parameter by describing the data in relative terms. They are designed to make it easy to go from a natural language construct such as "the third word of the fourth line of paragraph one" to an object specifier encoded in an Open Event. The Object Services Library (OSL), an OSA component, is used by the application to encode the object specifier. The program calls OSL repeatedly to create a nested specifier, with the outermost container specified first. Each subsequent call uses the results of the previous call as its "container." At the other end, the process is reversed and the object specifier is decoded by the target application in a manner not unlike peeling an onion. The target application, which is OSA-compliant, has provided accessor functions for finding an object. As the object specifier is resolved, the appropriate accessor function is called. It returns a token understood internally to indicate the found object. Each subsequent step in resolving the specifier will use the previously generated tokens until the complete set of tokens has been generated for the object specified. The application will also provide callbacks that will be used for functions that only the application itself can perform, such as counting, comparing, or marking objects.

Scripts are very powerful and can create totally new applications by automating an existing program or by providing a way for two or more independent programs to operate as a unit with the script acting as the programming glue. OSA allows for scripts to be attached to an application or a document and executed every time the program is activated or the document is selected. In OpenDoc, it will be possible to attach scripts to documents or to the individual parts embedded in a document. There are many ways in which these scripts might be used. For instance, a script could be attached to a text part that invoked a spell checker (the user's favorite spell checker—not just the one included with the application) when executed. Or perhaps a graph part displaying stock information could have a script that accessed a dial-in service to get up-to-the-minute values of stock whenever the document is opened. The possibilities are limited only by the imaginations and ingenuity of the users—in other words, boundless!

As soon as OSA support has been incorporated into a part, scriptability, recordability, alternate input, and so on become a reality. Because the application is set up to respond to OSA Events, it's easy to write an application that monitors the event traffic and records events for later playback. Another advantage of factoring a part to be driven by OSA Events is that any component that can generate an OSA Event, such as the UI, a script language, voice, or pen, can drive the application.

Component Glue (OLE Interoperability)

WordPerfect/Novell is providing OpenDoc technology on all of the Windows platforms. As part of that effort, they are producing the component glue technology, which will allow OpenDoc documents to include OLE2 (Object Linking and Embedding, Version 2) objects. In turn, OLE2 containers will be able to embed OpenDoc objects. All this is accomplished through a series of special OpenDoc parts and document shells as well as OLE2 wrappers and specialized containers. The important thing to remember, though, is that, from the point of view of the creator and user of the document as well as the software provider, all is done under the covers (transparently to them).

OS/2, with its WIN-OS/2 technology, will fully support component glue. Furthermore, OS/2 will allow the OLE2 applications and OpenDoc for Windows parts to run in the WIN-OS2 full-screen or window session. These objects and parts will be able to coexist in a document created with OpenDoc.

The Components—Parts and Part Handlers

Key to the compound document architecture is the concept of a part. Parts are the individual components used to create a document. The most common part for a document would be a text part. It would provide the ability to embed and edit text into a document. Other part-types might include graphical, spreadsheet, multimedia (such as video and audio), graph, and spell-check parts. The list goes on and on because the OpenDoc architecture is designed to support ALL types of data, including data types that are not even invented yet!

OpenDoc developers will write software components called *part handlers*. A part handler implements all of the code needed to include a particular data type in a document. In particular, a part handler knows how to render the data to the screen or format it for printing. Part handlers come in two sorts:

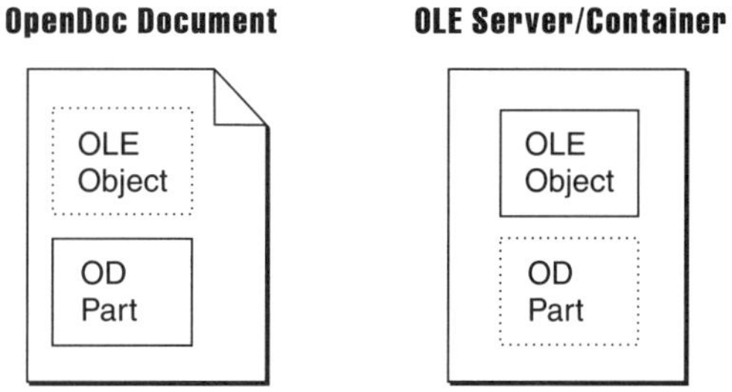

Figure 13-4. OpenDoc Is the Best Way to Build Components. It Works with Older Technologies Like OLE, Too!

Editors — Editors are full-function part handlers that can create new data and modify existing data. Part editors are the basic component that software producers will sell.

Viewers — In order to meet the goal of "full-fidelity" viewing and printing of a document on all platforms, part handlers that can be used for that purpose are expected to be produced by OpenDoc developers and freely licensed and distributed. The result is that part viewers for a wide-range of data types should be available on all platforms that support OpenDoc.

The Tools

This section describes how the developer can use the SOM compiler or direct-to-SOM compilers as well as subclassing techniques when creating part handlers.

SOM Compiler

As mentioned, OpenDoc is based on the CORBA-compliant object model, SOM (System Object Model), invented and developed by IBM. One of the advantages of SOM is its ability to support multiple languages. Thus we say the SOM is "language neutral." One of the main tools to enable this is the SOM compiler and its language bindings emitters.

Interfaces to OpenDoc are defined using an interface description language, or IDL, defined by CORBA. The IDL files are then processed by the SOM compiler, which produces, according to options selected by the application developer, a series of header files and template files to be used with the language chosen by the developer. Currently, the SOM compiler supports languages such as C and C++. The OpenDoc part writers create IDL descriptions of the part handlers that they are implementing. After the part handlers are run through the SOM compiler, the part writers can then edit the template files that were emitted to fill in the bulk of the code required. Finally, the resulting source files, along with header files supplied with the OpenDoc toolkit, are submitted to the normal compiler/linker used with their language.

Direct-to-SOM Compilers

While the SOM compiler and emitter development style allows any language to support SOM objects through bindings (for example, macros in the C language), it is inconvenient and unnecessary with a language such as C++ that already supports the notion of "objects." Direct-to-SOM compilers, DTS for short, have been developed to allow the C++ programmer to bypass the IDL writing stage and the SOM compilation and to eliminate the SOM bindings that are put into the template source files. C++ programmers can program directly in their (presumably) favorite language, compiling it directly into SOM code. In other words, the fact that SOM objects are being generated by the compiler instead of generic C++ objects is completely transparent to the developer. And, of course, because the developers are using SOM objects, their code will work correctly with any other SOM objects, including those generated with a non-object-oriented language and SOM bindings.

Subclassing Techniques

The ultimate goal of any OpenDoc part-handler developer is to implement an object of class "ODPart." ODPart is a pure virtual class, in C++ terms. That means that while all of the necessary methods of the object and its interfaces are defined, there is no implementation provided for those methods. It is up to the developer to subclass ODPart and override all of its methods, providing implementations that will enable all of its OpenDoc behaviors. That means code for about 60+ methods needs to be there at run time.

However, because we are using object-oriented technology, application developers can use an existing "base part" that provides default implementations for all of the ODPart methods. Thus, the task of writing a new part consists of subclassing the base part and overriding only those methods that need to be changed to provide the unique function of the new part. In this way, a minimal "hello world" part can be implemented by overriding only a few methods, mainly init and draw methods.

Human-Centered Computing

This chapter explains Human-Centered computing, describes some of the Human-Centered technologies currently offered by IBM, and discusses technologies we hope to see in the future.

Introducing Human-Centered Computing

Just ten years ago, very little focus was placed on the users of computers. Computer interfaces were not intuitive and components, such as keyboards, were not standardized. It was challenging for users to move from one computer system to another and make effective use of it without significant retraining.

Within the last ten years, the focus has changed to a more natural approach to computing in which users no longer need special training to use computers. This natural approach to computing is what Human-Centered computing is all about.

Human-Centered computing is accomplished in part through the use of human metaphors in user interfaces. These human metaphors encompass writing, listening, speaking, and gesturing, which are interactions we, as humans, practice and exercise every day. The goal is to use these metaphors to improve and enhance the advances already made in user interfaces until the interfaces become intuitive and special knowledge is no longer required. For example, in recent years, graphical user interfaces that employ drag-and-drop, folders, and icons have contributed to changes in the way computers are perceived and used. But, although users might be less intimidated by dragging a document icon and dropping it on a printer icon than they were by typing print commands at a prompt, this action is still not intuitive to a first-time user. To make this and all other computer interactions intuitive, Human-Centered computing utilizes emerging technologies, some of which are still in their infancy.

Human-Centered Computing Today

Today's Human-Centered technologies include but are not limited to:

- Speech recognition
- Pen-based technologies such as handwriting recognition
- Groupware or collaborative computing that enables a group of users to produce work together using a computer
- Multimedia solutions that combine text, text-to-speech, audio, video, and animation
- Visual recognition systems that recognize gestures
- Intelligent agents that perform tasks for you or assist you with tasks you want to do yourself
- Virtual reality technologies that utilize 3-D graphics, animation, and rendering
- Artificial intelligence
- Voice signature recognition

These individual technologies already exhaust the capabilities of desktop systems. The demands of combining these CPU-intensive technologies and drawing upon them simultaneously seems an almost insurmountable hardware resource issue. But the power and speed of the processor can make the difference between high-quality, real-time sound and movement and low-quality, choppy sound and movement. New processors, like the PowerPC 603 and PowerPC 604, provide the processing power and speed to support these Human-Centered, CPU-intensive technologies. And the hardware configuration of PowerPC systems means that Human-Centered applications written for OS/2 will not require the use of special, additional hardware. For example, tasks requiring special processors and dedicated adapters in the past are today being satisfied by the host PowerPC processors.

OS/2 Warp Connect (PowerPC Edition) already makes use of many of these technologies, including speech with intelligent agents, pen, groupware, and multimedia. The sections that follow describe these technologies and identify technologies that we hope to see in the future.

Speech

Today's speech technology includes the ability of the computer to interpret a user's spoken word and to carry out an action. We already have the ability to direct machines and computers with voice commands. For example, we can program our phone system to associate a phone number with a name and location so that we can call home by simply picking up the phone and saying "call home." We can use our computers as dictation devices, much like we use a Dictaphone or a voice-activated tape recorder. Or, we can give a series of instructions to our computers that we would normally have to enter via mouse or keyboard.

For example, let's suppose that you have sent me E-mail about coming into town and meeting me for lunch the second Tuesday of next month. To mark my calendar with this event, I would tell my computer to:

```
Open my calendar and show me the agenda for the

second Tuesday of next month.

Mark my calendar for lunch.
```

If my lunch hour is not free, I would send a note to my secretary to reschedule whatever meeting is on the agenda.

I would instruct my computer to:

```
Compose a memo

Send To:  My secretary

Subject:  Lunch meeting scheduled for second Tues-
day of next month.

Begin memo:  Please reschedule at earliest time
mutually convenient for all attendees.  End memo.

Send memo.
```

I might also have my computer help me make a reservation for us at the Best Restaurant in Town by telling it to:

```
Open my electronic Yellow Pages.

Look up the number for the Best Restaurant in Town.

Dial the number for me.
```

The benefits of speech technology can be applied to various types of applications, especially those designed for users who are unable to use their hands because of the hands-on requirements of their jobs (such as auto mechanics) or because of special needs.

Speech technology is further enhanced by the use of agents.

Speech and Conversational Agents

Agents are types of programs that perform tasks for users, with each task assigned to its own agent. Their level of "intelligence" can be measured by how much they can do without having to be guided step-by-step. Agents are supported by devices and subsystems for basic I/O technologies (such as pen, touch, audio, video, and so on). Speech and conversational agents help to further the recognition and conversational language interpretation performed by the computer.

In our previous example, an agent could further the functions carried out by the computer so that all I would have to do is TELL my computer to block my time for you and make a lunch reservation for us. Then, my computer would automatically reschedule the meeting based on the electronic calendars of the attendees. My computer would also know where I like to take my special friends to lunch, automatically look up the number, call it, and request a reservation for two in my name for lunch for that day.

In fact, as agent technology advances, someday my computer wouldn't have to wait for me to tell it to make these arrangements, but would automatically do it when it received my E-mail. It would know you were important to me and that I would want to have lunch with you, so it would go ahead and do it!

Not only will users get to know their agents as personal assistants but they can personalize the agent by selecting an actor—a synthesized voice, a human face, or combination of a voice and face—to represent the agent.

Speech Support in OS/2 Warp Connect (PowerPC Edition)

The speech support for OS/2 Warp Connect (PowerPC Edition) is available in the Human Center, a conversational interface that uses speech and conversational agents. And, because it is running on the PowerPC, it does not require a speech adapter card. The Human Center has several components:

Office Assistants

The Human Center office assistants let you use speech to accomplish your daily office tasks, much like the ones we accomplished in the preceding example. They supply services such as general calendar information, time of day, and meeting reminders. And, they include a mail agent to assist with electronic mail tasks and a telephone agent to help you make phone calls.

Speech Recognition

The Human Center's speech recognition support includes speech dictation and command and control technologies, all of which can be run without the use of an accelerator card. The speech dictation support involves training the system to recognize your specific speech patterns so that you can dictate documents such as memos. The speech command and control technologies enable you to navigate the Desktop using day-to-day English language and reduce, if not eliminate, the need for a mouse or keyboard.

Future Enhancements

The discussion that follows identifies some new features envisioned for later versions of OS/2. Although no promises for support are being made here, it is likely that these features will soon be a reality.

Text-to-Speech

Text-to-speech is a quickly maturing technology. The interpretation of the written word and translation to audio by a computer is an area where great strides are being made. As a human metaphor, this technology holds the promise of breaking down some of the computer-to-human interface barriers, by making interfaces seem more natural and friendlier.

This technology is already used to provide the actors' voices in the Human Center.

Enhanced Dictation

In the future, the vocabularies for dictation will be decreased and the training requirements will be lessened.

Pen

A pen is a natural pointing device and is an ideal technology for furthering the development of Human-Centered computing. Little instruction must be given to users in order for them to use a pen. As a pointing device, a pen has more dimensions than a mouse device. A pen device can point, select, and drag, but it can also make use of pressure, angle, and height to provide instructions to the computer.

Pen technology relies upon a pen device, a pen digitizer or touch-sensitive screen, and "electronic ink." The electronic ink flows from the tip of the pen and can be displayed as drawings and annotations or interpreted as handwriting or gestural commands. A variety of applications can be enhanced or implemented by this technology including those for graphic design, annotations in groupware applications, handwritten diaries, electronic forms, and shared electronic chalkboards. These applications are especially useful in mobile computing environments, such as those used by sales people, repair people, and people in the health-care industry, in which the transportable computers or devices are small and applications involve filling out forms.

Pen Support in OS/2 Warp Connect (PowerPC Edition)

Pen for OS/2 is IBM's pen product for OS/2. Currently, this product is available in a version for Intel-based systems. But, it is hoped it will be developed to use the PowerPC platform in the near future.

Pen for OS/2 is an extension to the OS/2 operating system that enables users to write text through handwriting recognition, initiate commands through gestures, and draw sketches through the use of a sketch pad.

Handwriting Recognition

The handwriting recognition component of Pen for OS/2 enables users to write and edit alphanumeric characters in any window that normally accepts keyboard input (such as the window of a text editor, a command prompt window, or a settings notebook), regardless of whether the application running in the window is designed for pen technology. This capability provides almost unlimited use of handwriting recognition.

Pen for OS/2 also includes a Handwriting Pad, which users can write on instead of a window, and a Pop-Up Keyboard, which users can tap on to create text. They can then send the text from the pad or keyboard to the active window.

Gestures

System commands are assigned to pen actions and gestures—symbolic strokes users draw on the screen. By using gestures, users can initiate the same commands they could by using a mouse, but gestures also provide a short-cut for telling programs and the operating system what to do.

Drawing

The Pen for OS/2 Sketch Pad can be used to draw and capture images. Users can copy or cut and paste these drawings and images into memos or other documents.

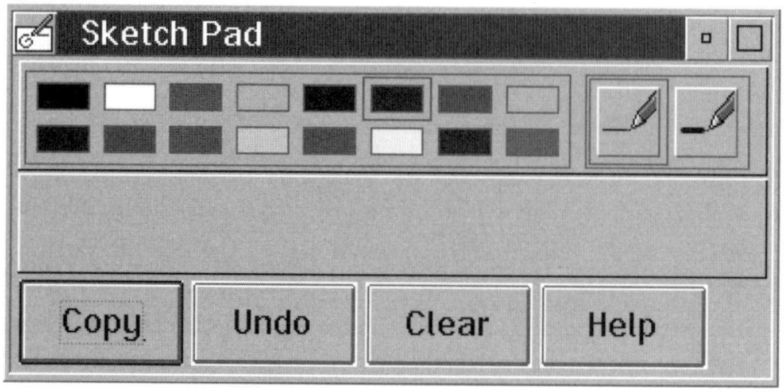

Groupware

Groupware is a name for applications that are meant to be shared by a group of people working on the same project. Just as Human-Centered computing has enhanced other computer applications, it has made groupware applications intuitive, and it has made it easier for groups to produce work together. Most types of groupware applications include features that allow for the annotation and viewing of a document by multiple people in multiple places at the same time. Human-Centered technologies have helped extend these features by enabling a document or project to be created to contain multiple types of media (audio, video, text, and graphics) that are produced by numerous types of applications in varying formats.

As a result, groups can focus on the task at hand rather than the applications and the formats the applications produce.

Groupware Support in OS/2 Warp Connect (PowerPC Edition)

Examples of groupware applications available for current or future releases of OS/2 Warp Connect (PowerPC Edition) are Person to Person and HC Markup.

Person to Person (P2P)

Person to Person enables people and computers connected by a network or modems to share information in the forms of data, files, graphics, images, video, or application screens. The information can be placed on a shared "chalkboard" that can be viewed by everyone connected. Each person sees the same information at the same time and can annotate it and discuss it in real time.

HC Markup

HC Markup is part of the Human Center, available for OS/2 Warp Connect (PowerPC Edition). HC Markup is a document markup program that enables users to bring in documents created by word processing programs, such as Lotus Notes or WordPerfect, annotate them with synchronized audio, video, highlighting, or other text markings, and then send them to a co-worker. HC Markup can also be employed to create documents using Human-Centered technologies or just to annotate those created under some other application.

The features of HC Markup enable users to produce work together without holding multiple meetings and distributing hardcopy.

Future Enhancements

In the future, we can expect groupware programs to take advantage of other Human-Centered technologies, such as OpenDoc, by which users create documents using part handlers instead of applications.

Multimedia

Various forms of media surround us continuously. Newspapers, radio, billboards, and textbooks all convey important and necessary information to us daily. Each of these media forms conveys the data using a single medium and involves a single sense, such as sight or sound. For this reason, none of these qualifies as multimedia.

Consider instead television and motion pictures where, in addition to seeing the information unfold, we can hear and understand the thoughts and beliefs of the authors. Music can heighten or camouflage the events about to unfold. Here, sight and sound are incorporated to raise the awareness and involvement of the viewer.

The benefits of multimedia are believed to be related to this heightened awareness and user involvement. Multimedia designers and developers contend that by involving more of the senses and incorporating video and audio, text and graphics, and various levels of interactivity, improved absorption of the material results. Retention and understanding are enhanced and, specifically in the area of education, attention levels are raised and sustained for extended periods of time. A new level of reality exists; seeing, hearing, and experiencing is believing.

Demands of Multimedia on Hardware and Software

This impressive technology has its price. The storage of audio and video data consumes enormous disk resources, whether on a hard drive or CD-ROM. These large amounts of data require systems with higher file system throughput. The movement and manipulation of this data require processors with higher bandwidths and faster processors with multiple instruction paths. In addition, memory subsystems need to be enhanced; typically 8MB or 16MB of memory might be required. Video subsystems are stressed to the limit and, in many cases, expensive video adapters with hardware-assisted video acceleration are needed. An audio adapter is now a new necessity, as is a CD-ROM drive. The PowerPC platform eases these demands and has the following advantages:

- Handles processor-intensive operations
- Has multiple pipes
- Is good for implementing CODECs in software instruction preprocessing

Multimedia utilizes the features of the underlying operating system to the limit. In the simplest of cases, multimedia consists of a producer and consumer of data; for example, playing an audio WAVE file consists of moving data from the disk (the source or producer) to an audio adapter (target or consumer).

The challenges of a strong multimedia platform come from the quantity of data to be moved, the efficiency of the system moving it, and the flexibility and adaptability to different formats and data types. In a multitasking operating system like OS/2, these demands are further complicated by the quality of service demanded by applications, other than multimedia, that might be running simultaneously and competing for system services. Add to this the demands and complications of moving multimedia data across LAN services in client/server environments, or while communicating across the Internet, or meeting the demands of supplying LAN services for other applications that might be running.

Multimedia Support in OS/2 Warp Connect (PowerPC Edition)

The multimedia platform offered by OS/2 Warp for both Intel-based systems and PowerPC platforms has never been more extensive or mature. As a development platform, the API has never been more stable. As for supported function, it surpasses all previous releases where audio and video formats are concerned. Extensions for animation have been added. Extensions for game developers have been added. And system requirements have been reduced through improvements in performance, lowered memory footprint, and enhanced image quality.

Developer's Tip: OS/2 Warp Connect (PowerPC Edition) enables applications to be ported from an Intel-based system to the PowerPC platform. Initial efforts expended to aid in the porting effort indicate that, in most instances, successful ports of multimedia applications take from 3 hours to 40 hours.

This is an extremely powerful statement and a very important message for independent software vendors. Although it is envisioned that there will be exceptions to this rule, the ease of the porting exercise should allow for a wide variety of applications to be available on the PowerPC platform in a very short timeframe. In addition, applications on the Intel Intel-based system should require minimal testing expense.

The first exposure users have to multimedia in OS/2 Warp (if they aren't knocked out of their seats by a system sound on startup) is the presence of the Multimedia folder on the Desktop. Users can find assorted icons in the folder for configuring multimedia, setting the system master volume, and controlling and configuring system sounds,as well as icons for a compact disc player, a digital audio editor, a MIDI player, a digital video player (also used for playing animations), multimedia REXX support, a multimedia data converter, and assorted sound bites and movie samples. These icons represent some fairly sophisticated sample tools provided so users can begin to explore the multimedia capabilities supported by OS/2 Multimedia.

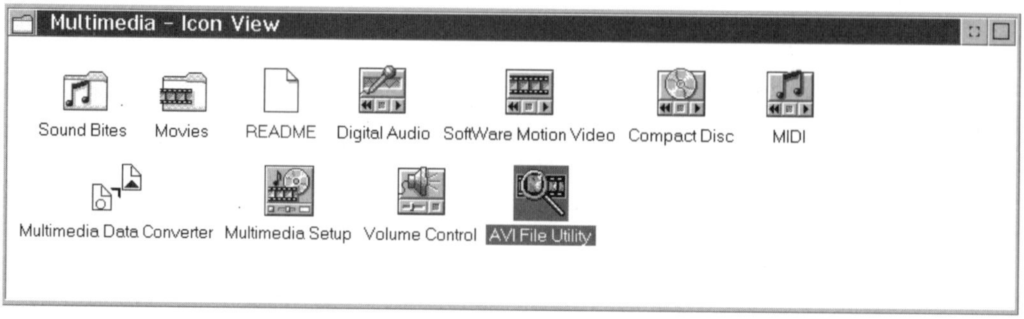

OS/2 Multimedia is designed to allow for a considerable amount of device independent control. This means that certain commands are supported by all devices. Because some devices have special capabilities, unique extensions are available to exploit these special features.

The media player is written to take advantage of this device independence and, therefore, can be utilized to control MIDI, WAVE, CD-ROM, or digital video devices among others. The media player can also be used to demo some of the capabilities of OS/2 Multimedia when used with command line options /s and /a. When the /s option is specified as a parameter with a file name, the Play command is issued immediately after the file is loaded. This parameter effects a sort of auto-start mode. The second parameter that can be specified is /a. This parameter effects an auto-repeat mode (which, when used with the MACAW.AVI, causes members of the multimedia development team to cringe). These two options are often used at shows and demos when highlighting the impressive multitasking ability of OS/2 and the device sharing and resource management of OS/2 Multimedia.

The following are brief descriptions of the icons in the Multimedia folder.

Multimedia Setup

The Multimedia Setup Utility program enables users to set work paths and default devices, associate file types with devices, and select MIDI support. The MIDI selection can be made on the Software Synth pages of the Settings notebook.

Software Synth represents MIDI synthesis, which is new for the PowerPC platform and is not found on Intel-based systems as yet. The advantage of Software Synth to users is free MIDI support whether the audio adapter supports it or not. In systems

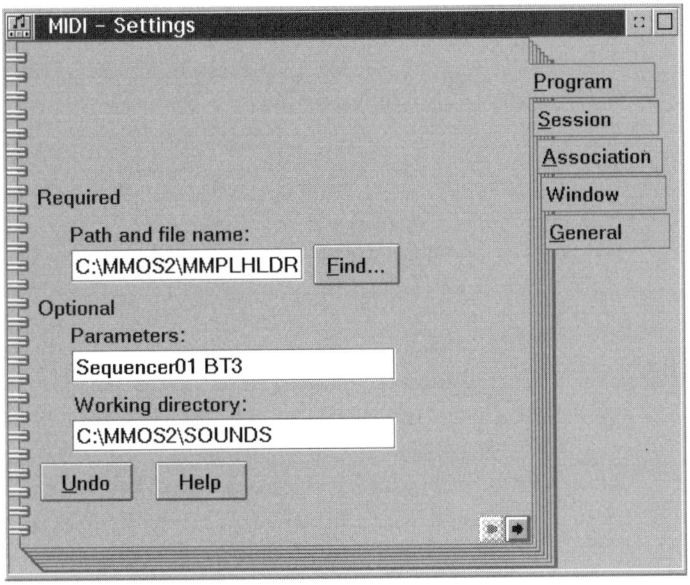

not configured for hardware MIDI, the PowerPC processor's performance and speed allow OS/2 Multimedia software to translate MIDI notes into sampled WAVE data that is then fed to the audio device. In configurations where MIDI hardware is available, MIDI Software Synth will not be selected as the default MIDI device, reserving the processor's bandwidth for other applications. Note that MIDI Software Synth is treated as a WAVE audio device, so that when you play MIDI in this manner, support for audio WAVE playback might not be available. A second setup page allowing file association is available as it is for other devices, but exclusive to MIDI is the third setup page titled Options. This page enables users to access the MIDI mapper, a list of check boxes that enable or disable individual MIDI tracks. Typically, each MIDI track can represent a particular instrument. Depending on the selection to be played, the perceived quality can be improved when you deselect certain tracks. After tracks have been deselected, it's important to remember to restore these settings before playing other tracks. Failure to do so might cause these other tracks to sound strange or not play completely.

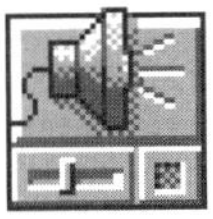

Volume Control

The multimedia system's master volume control enables users to adjust the overall volume of the devices in the system.

System Sounds

System Sounds enables users to control and manage sounds that provide audio feedback representing system events. Sample sounds are located in the MMOS2\SOUNDS directory. Users can record new sounds using the digital audio player.

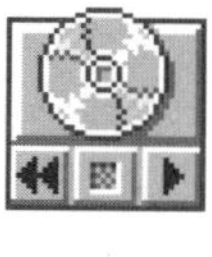

Compact Disc

The Compact Disc player enables users to play audio CDs and control the CD from the desktop.

Digital Audio Player

The Digital Audio Player enables uses to play or create audio files including .WAV, .IFF, .AU, .SND, .MOD, and others.

MIDI

MIDI stands for Musical Instrument Digital Interface and is a unique form of compression developed to meet the special needs of the music industry. Briefly, instead of storing the sampled WAVE audio content as heard from the instruments, the actual notes, as played by the artist, are recorded. Additional information is also stored as necessary to accurately reproduce the artist's original interpretation of the music, but the end result is a much reduced file storage requirement. These well-defined notes (time stamps and so on) can then be played back in their original sequence.

The MIDI player (MPPM.EXE with a sequencer01 parameter) enables users to play MIDI files.

Software Motion Video

Software motion video refers to the reproduction of video content implemented strictly through software. Alternatively, video playback can utilize hardware through special adapters designed to do so. Although offloading this processor-intensive task to adapters frees up the system for other work, this is at the expense of the added, often costly, hardware. A software solution provides the capability to display video content to all users, independent of the system configuration. In industrial and commercial applications of multimedia, the savings can be significant. The savings are illustrated by considering the cost of applying multimedia in environments such as a network of hundreds of kiosks in malls and the lobbies of large office complexes, corporate just-in-time training systems, or on-line encyclopedias and interactive educational tools in our school systems.

OS/2 Multimedia offers one of the best software implementations of software motion video and support for various hardware adapters in the industry today. Support exists for playback of a multitude of content types including IBM Ultimotion technology, Intel Indeo 2.1, 3.1, and 3.2 algorithms, and AutoDesk FLC and FLI animation technology. This support for industry content types is growing and is made available through OS/2 Multimedia's support of installable CODECs (compressors/decompressors). In addition to the support provided by IBM, shareware CODECs are available through bulletin boards and Internet sources for support of other industry-standard video compression and decompression schemes. In some instances, a decompressor might be available without a companion compressor. In these cases, playback of the video data type is supported but authoring or recording might not be.

Digital Video Player

The Digital Video Player enables users to play .AVI, .FLI, and .FLC files.

One of the true tests of the robustness and quality of a multimedia system is its ability to reproduce synchronized video and audio. Few systems, if any, can match the synchronization technology offered by OS/2 Multimedia. The ability of OS/2 Multimedia to play back multimedia content that incorporates video and audio where lip-sync or video events are tied to audio sounds is unparalleled. To stress the significance of this statement, start two or more Digital Video Players simultaneously and watch the impressive ability OS/2 Multimedia has to remain synchronized in each of the instances. To truly appreciate this capability, multiple audio adapters are recommended.

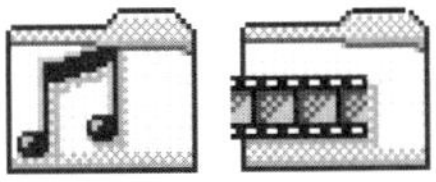

Sound Bites and Movies

These folders contain audio and video samples. Their Workplace Shell associations enable users to double-click on the icons for the samples and have the system load the appropriate media player.

Multimedia with REXX

Multimedia with REXX provides support so that REXX programs can exploit the OS/2 Multimedia capabilities.

Multimedia Data Converter

The Multimedia Data Converter enables users to convert images and audio files from one format to another.

Audio Data and File Formats

The following chart illustrates the audio file formats supported by OS/2 Warp (for Intel-based systems) and OS/2 Warp Connect (PowerPC Edition).

File Format	File Extensions	Intel-based		PowerPC		Comments
		Today	Future	Today	Future	
RIFF	.WAV	Y		Y		
AIFF	.AIF	Y		Y		
IFF	.IFF	Y		Y		Amiga IFF
SND	.SND	Y		Y		UNIX
VOC	.VOC	Y		Y		Creative Labs Voice File
AVC	._AU, ._AD	Y				IBM Audio/Video Connection
MIDI	.MID	Y		Y		General MIDI type 0
MIDI	.MID	Y		Y		General MIDI type 1

The following chart illustrates the audio CODECs and data types supported by OS/2 Warp (for Intel-based systems) and OS/2 Warp Connect (PowerPC Edition).

Audio Type	Intel-based		PowerPC		Comments
	Today	Future	Today	Future	
Linear PCM	H		H		.WAV, ._AU, .IFF, AIFF
Alaw	H	S/H	S/H		.WAV, ._AU
MUlaw	H	S/H	S/H		.WAV, ._AU
IBM Alaw	H	S/H	S/H		.WAV, ._AU

Audio Type	Intel-based		PowerPC		Comments
	Today	Future	Today	Future	
IBM MUlaw	H	S/H	S/H		.WAV, ._AU
OKI ADPCM	H				.WAV, need OKI hardware and device driver
IMA ADPCM, DVI ADPCM	S/H		S/H		.WAV
Microsoft ADPCM	S/H		S		.WAV
IBM Digispeech					.WAV standard
IBM Speech Viewer					.WAV
IBM AVC ADPCM	H				.WAV, ._AU, ._AD, Audio Video Connection, ADPCM
Creative Labs ADPCM	H				.WAV, ._AU
AVC MIDI					Standard MIDI
General MIDI	H	S/H	S/H		
MT32	S		S		Software MIDI mapper

Legend

S Software support. The data type is processed in software and is converted to a more commonly understood format. In the instances where the system recognizes that hardware support exists for the data type, the hardware support is utilized in the interest of conserving system processor utilization.

H Hardware support. The data type is generally processed by hardware adapters.

Video Data and File Formats

One of the unique requirements of video is the need and importance of synchronized audio. This requirement becomes a critical issue when playing movies or animations. Because the delivery mechanism for this multimedia content is typically through the file system, off of CD-ROM, or across the LAN, timely access to the video data and respective audio data is mandatory. This requirement has facilitated the development of interleaved file formats. To illustrate this, imagine a scenario in which one file exists containing video content and a second file, elsewhere on the hard disk, contains the related audio data. In this situation, reading the video content leaves the hard disk's read head positioned near the video content. Numerous seeks are then required to locate the file system directory information for the corresponding audio. The head needs to be repositioned in the vicinity of the audio content, the information needs to be read, and then the process repeated to retrieve additional video information. On a CD-ROM, where seek times and read times are excessive, synchronized video and audio would be unrealistic. To simplify this problem, video content is typically stored as a frame with the corresponding audio data for that frame. A single read could thereby load the video and audio data together making the content simultaneously available. Some video types do not support the synchronous playback of audio however. Such is the case with FLC and FLI data types. In this instance, OS/2 Multimedia allows the user to add audio to these clips through an enhancement. To implement this, the user needs only to store the audio content desired in the same directory as the video content with the same name and a .WAV extension. If the audio content is recognized, playback of the animation content will be accompanied by the audio that the user provided.

The following chart illustrates the video file formats supported by OS/2 Warp (for Intel-based systems) and OS/2 Warp Connect (PowerPC Edition).

File Format	File Extensions	Intel-based		PowerPC		Comments
		Today	Future	Today	Future	
AVI	.AVI	Y		Y		
FLC/FLI Files	.FLC, .FLI	Y		Y		FLC/FLI Animation
MPEG	.MPG	Y		Y		MPEG 1
MOV	.MOV		Y		Y	

The following chart illustrates the video CODECs supported by OS/2 Warp (for Intel-based systems) and OS/2 Warp Connect (PowerPC Edition).

Video	**Intel-based**		**PowerPC**		
Type	**Today**	**Future**	**Today**	**Future**	**Comments**
RAW	SP/SC		SP	SP/SC	.AVI
Ultimotion	SP/SC		SP	SP/SC	.AVI
Indeo 2.1	SP/SC	SP			.AVI
Indeo 3.1	SP/SC	SP			.AVI
Indeo 3.2	SP	SP			.AVI
Indeo 4.0					.AVI
AutoDesk FLC/FLI	SP		SP		.FLC, .FLI
MJPEG					.AVI
MPEG-1	HP	SP		SP	.MPG, .VBS, .DAT
MPEG-2		HP		HP	.MPG, .VBS, .DAT
Cinepak		SHP			.AVI,.MOV
Microsoft Video1		SHP			.AVI

Legend

SP Software playback support (decompressor)

SC Software capture support (compressor)

HP Hardware playback support (requires decompressor on hardware adapter)

SHP Shareware playback decompressors are available

Image Data and File Formats

The following chart illustrates the image file formats supported by OS/2 Warp (for Intel-based systems) and OS/2 Warp Connect (PowerPC Edition).

File Format	File Extensions	Intel-based		PowerPC		Comments
		Today	Future	Today	Future	
DIB	.DIB, .RDI	Y		Y		
Bit map	.BMP	Y		Y		
PCX	.PCX	Y		Y		
TIFF	.TIF	Y		Y		
GIF	.GIF	Y		Y		
TARGA	.TGA	Y		Y		
PhotoCD	.PCD	Y		Y		Kodak PhotoCD
MMotion	.VID	Y		Y		

The following chart illustrates the image CODECs supported by OS/2 Warp (for Intel-based systems) and OS/2 Warp Connect (PowerPC Edition).

Image Type	Intel-based		PowerPC		Comments
	Today	Future	Today	Future	
AVC Image					
MMotion Image					._IM
JPEG		S		S	
Kodak PhotoCD	S		S		.PCD

Legend

S Software support

Current Audio and Video Enhancements

The following are OS/2 Multimedia enhancements for OS/2 Warp Connect (PowerPC Edition).

MIDI Synthesis

New to OS/2 Warp Connect (PowerPC Edition) and not presently available in OS/2 Warp for Intel-based systems is PowerPC-hosted software MIDI. Two forms of MIDI are commonly found on today's Intel-based systems—MIDI synthesis and sampled MIDI. The difference between these two methods for translating MIDI data to audible instruments is that MIDI synthesis involves the translation of the MIDI data to an algorithmically generated simulation of the instrument. Sampled MIDI involves a sort of library of sampled MIDI notes played by the respective instruments and stored as .WAV data. The data is subsequently looked up and played as required.

Both of these instances are typically implemented on audio hardware using components such as the OPL3 chip or downloaded patch tables. The distinction between these existing implementations and PowerPC-hosted software MIDI is that, independent of whether specific MIDI hardware exists, the PowerPC processor can be utilized to translate the MIDI data to sample MIDI WAVE data that is then passed on to the audio hardware. If the hardware support exists, however, the software technique is abandoned in favor of the hardware solution, leaving PowerPC processor bandwidth for other applications that may be running.

EnDIVE Support

One of the more aggressive enhancements to OS/2 Multimedia in video playback is the Enhanced Direct Interface to Video Extension (EnDIVE). EnDIVE supplies a robust set of high-performance and highly efficient functions for moving video content. Used by the multimedia subsystem and available to game writers and multimedia developers, EnDIVE allows developers to display video content that users can then move and stretch as desired. Implemented as self-modifying code, EnDIVE regenerates and alters its assembly language instructions as the user drags and adjusts the video display window. The performance of EnDIVE accounts for the extremely high frame rates achievable on the OS/2 Multimedia platform. EnDIVE also determines whether hardware acceleration exists and can be utilized to enhance video playback. This determination removes the burden that developers have to support various hardware platforms. Other extensions to EnDIVE might be available soon, supporting features such as transparent blitting (bit block transfer) and special full-screen modes.

Future Enhancements

The discussion that follows identifies some new features envisioned for OS/2 Multimedia audio and video. Although no promises for support are being made here, it is likely that these features will soon be a reality.

High-Speed Audio Interfaces

Similar in nature to the efforts discussed in the EnDIVE section, high-speed audio interfaces to better support game developers and speech-recognition systems will probably be forthcoming.

Real-Time MIDI

High-speed interfaces for accurate MIDI playback and eventually MIDI recording will probably be available soon.

Flexible Audio Connections

One-to-many and many-to-one-type subsystem connections might be supported soon. The nature of this support will enable the use of applications that involve DSPs, subsystem mixing and splitting, distributed multimedia, and multiple language audio track support.

MPEG Support

Fast becoming the industry standard for video content, MPEG I and MPEG II will probably be supported. Although MPEG I is currently supported on hardware such as the Sigma Design ReelMagic adapter, software support is probably forthcoming.

CODECs

Efforts are underway to support additional video and audio CODECs.

Future Human-Centered Technologies

Human-Centered technologies are some of the fastest growing technologies in the computer industry today. Ideas for new technologies are as limitless as one's imagination and can be implemented as quickly as new hardware is developed on which to use them. In the future, we can expect to see further enhancements to the technologies we have today and new technologies that we haven't thought of yet.

Speech, multimedia, pen, and groupware technologies will be combined with visual recognition systems, 3-D graphics, animation, and artificial intelligence to make computers more intuitive, easier, and fun to use.

Assisted by intelligent agents, who have human faces and voices, and SMART technologies that address physiological and social factors as well as artistic and cultural differences, users will be more productive. These future agents will, upon recognizing you by your face or your voice, automatically pull up the files you use or your customized desktop, or automatically save your work when you shut down your system. They will also enhance intelligent information systems of the future that will adapt information to the user's level of experience, based on prior interaction patterns, and will display help messages proactively, by sensing when the user needs assistance with the current task.

Human-Centered technologies will also contribute to the availability of applications that are fully "aware" (that is, applications that can interpret the new types of data from various media in their own context). These technologies will also enhance the evolution of the desktop.

In the future, thanks to Human-Centered computing, we will see a world in which no one is afraid to use a computer because it will be natural or second nature to use. Users will no longer need to be trained to use their computers because computers will train themselves to recognize and anticipate the needs of their users.

Information and Help

This chapter describes the information and help system for OS/2 Warp Connect (PowerPC Edition) from the user's perspective, as well as from the author's perspective. It tells you how you can be creative and customize your information with action, sight, and sound. It also tells you how you can save time and money by using tools that help you locate the information you need faster and easier. Finally, this chapter introduces you to an Integrated On-line Information system that we all can look forward to in the future.

Introducing Information and Help

Information, like all other technologies, has come a long way: from the prehistoric version of multimedia (stone on stone, smoke signals, and animal calls) to pen on parchment, printing presses, telegraph, telephone, radio, and television. Today, many of us have the capability to record and play back audio and video in full stereo and color in the comfort of our homes. With graphic and text processors readily available for personal computers, many of us also have the potential to *create* our own audio and video. Travelling the information superhighway, we also have the ability to tap into and download all types of information from databases virtually anywhere on and off the planet.

But, it's still not all that easy, much less effortless, to have information *anytime, anywhere.* My desktop has on-line information presented in a manner consistent with the software I am using. It is stored on my machine in a certain format that is understood, or viewable, by the system installed on my machine. It has its own *look and feel*; it's presented in windows of text and graphics, maybe with some accompanying audio and video. I can do a certain set of things with it: I can cut and paste and move it and maybe even add my own notes to it. On the other hand, your system connected to mine on the same LAN might have information that looks entirely different. Without the viewer to understand it, I might not even be able to look at it.

Wouldn't it be nice if our systems automatically searched whatever they are connected to (a LAN, the World Wide Web) to find whatever we need to know and return it to us in a form we can understand and use?

A Good Foundation with IPF

OS/2 Warp today, for both Intel-based systems and PowerPC systems, has a powerful information system and set of supporting tools. The current function will become even more powerful, seamless, and elegant in the future.

In OS/2 Warp Connect (for Intel-based systems and, now, for the first release of the PowerPC Edition), on-line information is supported by the OS/2 Information Presentation Facility (IPF).

IPF consists of:

- An authoring language to create script files that contain the text for the information, as well as tags that define how the text appears on the screen.
- A compiler (IPFC) that takes the script files, formats the information, and builds binary files that contain viewable help panels (HLPs) or on-line books (INFs).
- A help engine that creates and manages help windows (frame windows, also known as *coverpages*) in which all on-line information (helps or books) is displayed. IPF help windows provide a consistent user interface to on-line information.
- A programming interface to the help engine that programmers can use to create and customize help windows for their applications.

- A viewer (VIEW1.EXE) that displays on-line HLPs or INFs in a help window.

Help panels provide information associated with objects on the screen. Help panels are displayed when a user requests help by pressing F1 or by selecting an item from a **Help** menu. You create help panels by:

1. Using a text editor to create an IPF script file with IPF authoring tags that describe each help panel: what information is to be displayed (that is, the content), how it is to be displayed (for example, in paragraphs, lists, split-windows, and so on), and other things you might do with it (such as hypertext to other topics). Each help panel has a unique ID or resource number defined in the heading tag.
2. Compiling the script file with IPFC to format the information and create a binary .HLP file.

HELPTABLEs and HELPSUBTABLEs associate IDs for help panels with the objects they describe. You can define HELPTABLEs and HELPSUBTABLEs in memory or as application resources (.RC files) that are bound to the application's executable file or placed in a separate dynamic link library (DLL).

An .HLP file (also referred to as a help library) contains the help panels for all visual objects (windows, fields, and so on) associated with an application. It can also contain help information that is *not* associated with a particular field or window (for example, general information on completing a task). As shown in Figure 15-1, you can get to this information by selecting **Contents** on the **Options** pull-down menu for the Help window.

An on-line book consists of panels of information that correspond to topics or headings that you would find in a hardcopy book. The title of the book appears as the title of the help window. An on-line book has a Table of Contents, an Index, and other elements of a typical hardcopy book. An on-line book is created in the same way help libraries are created, with the following exceptions:

- IDs associated with heading tags are not associated with HELPTABLEs or HELPSUBTABLEs.

- The /INF option for IPFC is used to compile the tagged source file.

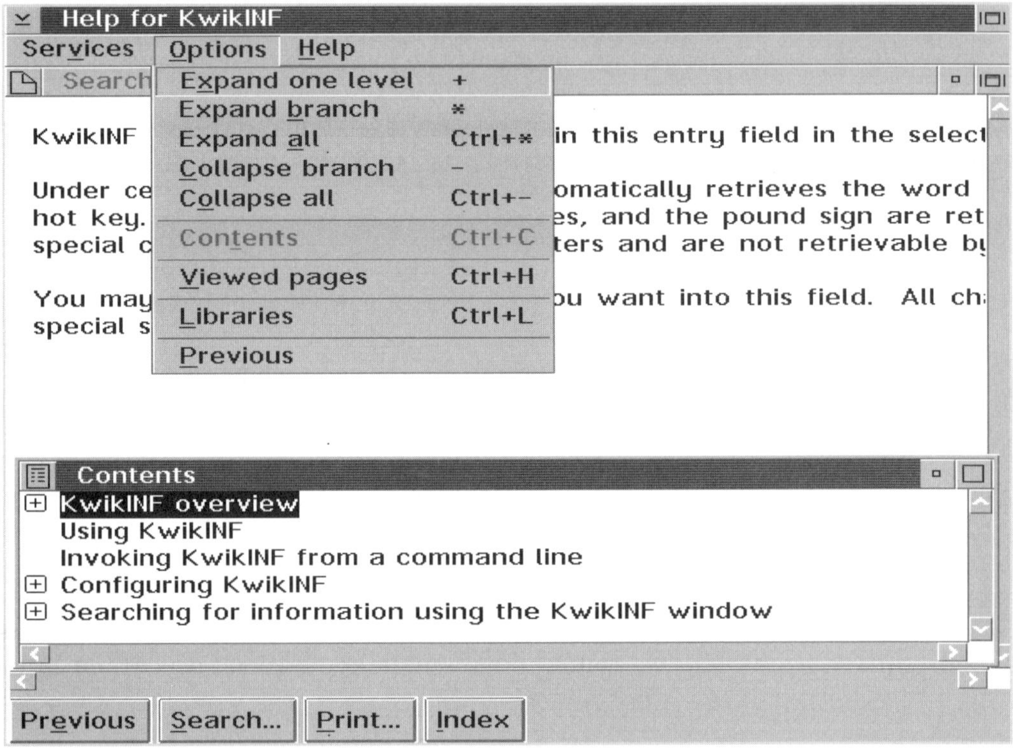

Figure 15-1. Getting to All Application Information through the Contents Option

You open an on-line book by starting VIEW1.EXE from an OS/2 command prompt or by double-clicking on a program object that bears the name of the on-line book title.

Developer's Tip: You can also design and create on-line information for OS/2 by using the Hyperwise WYSIWYG-like authoring tool. Hyperwise, which comes with the Developer's Toolkit for OS/2, creates HLPs and INFs for you without your having to create IPF script files. Hyperwise also provides an environment in which you can view your information, while you are developing it, as your users will view it.

IPF Features

The IPF user interface provides:

- Support for graphics, as well as text with different fonts and colors
- Push-button controls (Previous, Back, Next, and so on) for better navigation

- Hypertext and hypergraphic links that connect panels of related information, giving users faster paths to more complete information on a topic

- The ability to customize information so that it can be presented in a variety of ways (for example, in a split screen or in multiple windows) to allow for easier navigation

- A robust Search facility, which gives users an easier means of finding information they are looking for

Other significant features are described in the following sections:

Cut and Paste

You can copy IPF on-line information fairly easily into other applications. You can, for example, use it to construct skeleton code from examples imbedded in help panels. You copy the contents of a help window (or one of its child windows):

- To other windowed applications via the clipboard. (You select **Copy** from the **Services** menu of the help window.)

- To other non-windowed applications via a file, TEXT.TMP, in the current directory. (You select **Copy to file** from the **Services** menu of the help window.)

Although IPF does not provide the user with a "mark text" function, authors can design information so that help windows contain discrete sets of information that the user might typically want to cut and paste. The on-line Programming References found in the Developer's Toolkit provide an example of this. Detailed descriptions of OS/2 programming functions are divided into modules that are then displayed in their own child windows. The syntax description is displayed in its own child window, as is example code. You can "copy" the contents of either child window and then use the paste function of an editor to place the contents into your application source code.

Application-Controlled Viewports

The windows in which on-line information is displayed are sometimes referred to as *viewports*. The client window of the help frame window (or coverpage) can have child windows. The client window and each of its child windows can be separate viewports for information.

Most viewports are *IPF-controlled*: An author uses IPF tags (in a script file) to describe a viewport (its size, position, and relationship to other viewports), along with what the information is and how it is displayed on the screen. When a user views the information, IPF creates the viewport, displays the information in the viewport, and provides the PM controls for the viewport.

Viewports can also be *application-controlled*: An author can use the :acviewport tag to describe a viewport (its size, position, and relationship to other viewports) and give control over that viewport to application code residing in a dynamic link library (DLL). This gives an author a great deal of flexibility: function simulation, animation, and audio, video, and user interactive presentations can be used to customize and greatly enhance on-line information. Anything that you can do within the realm of the OS/2 Presentation Manager you can do within your on-line information.

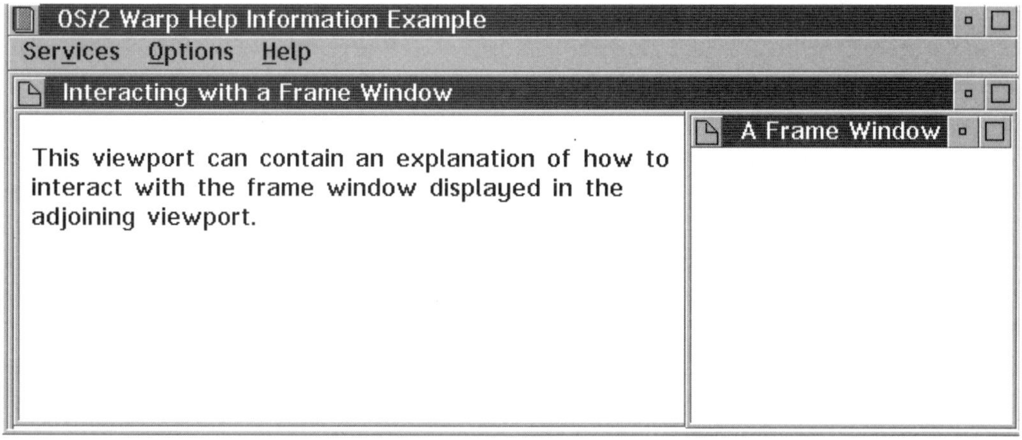

Figure 15-2. IPF-Controlled and Application-Controlled Viewports

```
.*
.*  Define a help panel as a composite of an IPF-controlled and
.*  an author-controlled viewport.
.*
:h1 scroll=none.Interacting with a Frame Window
.*
.*  Define the IPF-controlled viewport:  IPF displays it in the left
.*  half of the help window.  Its contents are defined in the panel
.*  that has an id=mytext.
.*
:link reftype=hd refid=mytext vpx=left vpy=bottom vpcx=50% vpcy=100%
titlebar=none scroll=none auto child.
.*
.*  Define an application-controlled viewport:  IPF displays it in the right
.*  half of the help window.  Its contents are defined and controlled by
.*  the code object MyObject that resides in MyDLL.  When IPF calls
.*  MyObject, it passes the objectid and objectinfo attributes to MyObject.
.*  In this example, these attributes are placeholders and are not used by
.*  MyObject.
.*
:acviewport dll='MyDLL' objectname='MyObject'
objectid=1 objectinfo='optional'
vpx=right vpy=bottom vpcx=50% vpcy=100%.
:h2 hide id=mytext.How to Interact with a Frame Window
:p.This viewport can contain an explanation of how to interact with the frame
window displayed in the adjoining viewport.
```

Figure 15-3. Hooking Application Code into On-line Information

Communication Links with IPF

You can modify the overall appearance or behavior of a help window, or any of its child windows, by hooking code into the script file for your help library or on-line book. The code (residing in a DLL) establishes a communication link with IPF.

How and what you want to affect within a help window determine how you hook the code (that is, load the DLL and call the code entry point) into your script file:

- If you want to make a modification that will affect the help window and ALL its child windows (for example, change the coverpage size), you specify the names of the DLL and code entry point on the :docprof tag.

- If you want to make a modification that will affect only a specific child window, you specify the names of the DLL and code entry point on the :acviewport tag (you are providing code to control a specific window).

When a user views your on-line information, IPF processes the .HLP or .INF file and, when it encounters the :docprof or :acviewport tag, IPF loads the specified DLL and calls the specified entry point in the DLL. Your DLL creates a communication window to establish a communication link with IPF and any IPF window for which you can get a window handle. Your communication window basically receives and responds to messages from IPF and other IPF windows. You can then orchestrate events (that is, what appears in your help window and when it appears in your help window) driven by your code from your script file. You do this by using IPF tags and attributes that cause IPF to generate messages to its windows.

For example, the following tags

```
:link reftype=inform res=100 auto.
```

cause IPF to send an HM_INFORM message to its windows. If you specify within your script file a DLL that creates a communication window, that communication window will receive this message, along with the resource number specified on the :link tag. The code associated with the communication window can then take a specific action associated with the HM_INFORM message and its resource number. Figure 15-4 outlines the general scenario for this example.

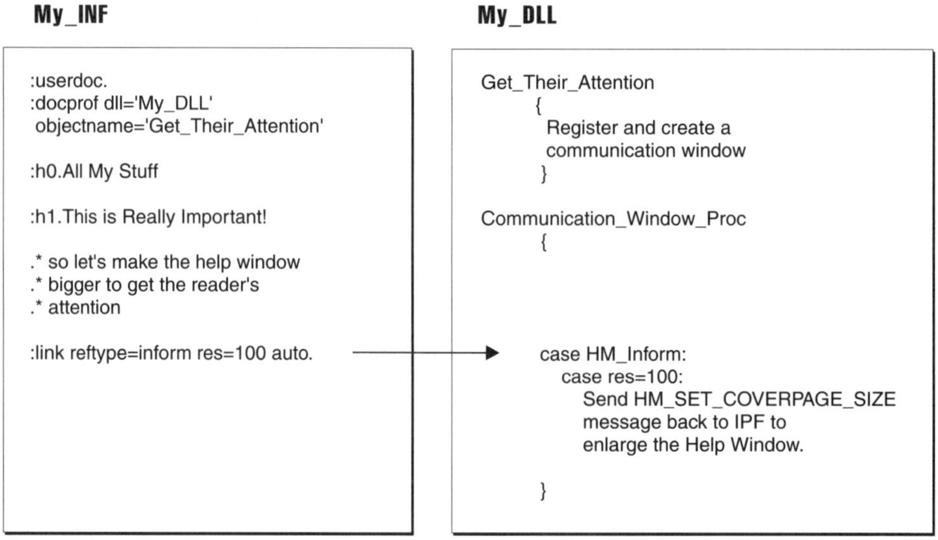

Figure 15-4. Using Communication Windows to Change the Size of the Help Window

Dynamic Data

You can also hook data that resides outside your .HLP and .INF files into your online information at run time. This means that you can use IPF as a user interface for any data your system has access to.

You do this by opening a communication window via the :docprof tag. The window procedure for this window handles requests for data (HM_QUERY_DDF_DATA) that are generated by IPF when IPF encounters a :ddf tag within a script file. The resource number attribute for the :ddf tag provides more details for the HM_QUERY_DDF_DATA request.

For example, suppose you have header files associated with a programming interface that you have created. You want to provide an on-line book that contains descriptions of that interface for your customers. The header files provide the latest, greatest, and most accurate information on each function you have defined. You construct a well-ordered header file that can be easily parsed. You also create a DLL that parses the header file and, based on resource numbers, locates specific information in the header file. Your DLL then uses DDF functions to buffer the information in the header file for IPF to display on the screen. This scenario, as illustrated in Figure 15-5, allows you to take advantage of the true source of your information. Your on-line information is always guaranteed to match your header files and is as accurate as they are.

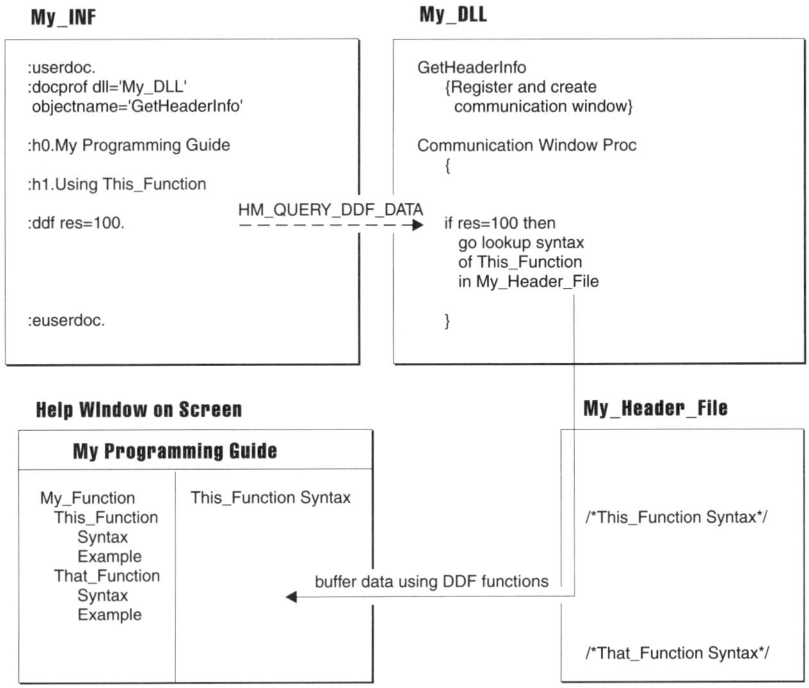

Figure 15-5. Providing a Viewer into Header Files

Significant New Features of IPF

The following list describes the new features of IPF for OS/2 Warp Connect (PowerPC Edition):

- Enhanced NLS support—for any code page that the system recognizes in conjunction with a country code.
- Search enhancements
  - The scope of IPF searches has been broadened to include headings, as well as index, sections, and libraries.
  - IPF searches are now done on separate threads, so that you can leave the help window and do other things.
- VIEW1.EXE enhancements
  - VIEW1.EXE can now be used to view .HLP files (online help libraries), as well as INFs (on-line books).
  - In the future, VIEW1.EXE will give users access at all times to the Table of Contents for an on-line document. This means better navigation: you need fewer keystrokes to choose another topic, and you can always determine where you are within a document. As shown in Figure 15-6, you will be able to use this feature to create "premarked" text for cutting and pasting just as you now do with a multiple-windowed information design. Instead of creating a child window for a topic with a menu of hypertext links into other child windows for subtopics, you create simple headings that can be expanded into other simple subheadings, any of which can be viewed within a single window.

Information Tools to Save You Time and Money

This section describes some tools that help you save time and money when you create and use on-line information.

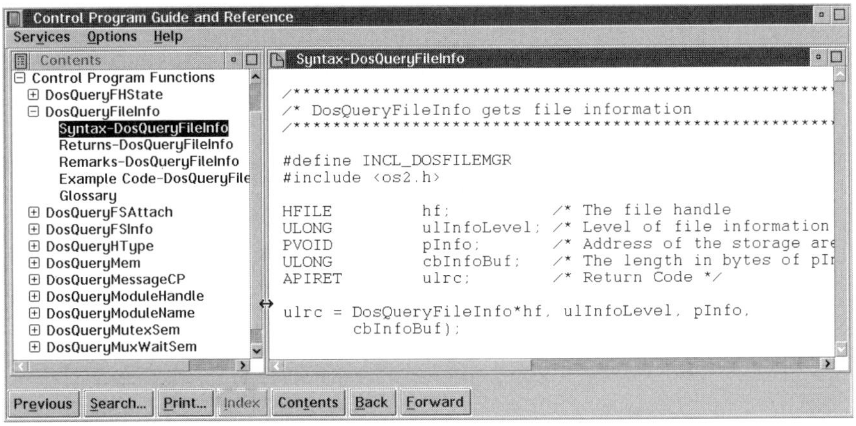

Figure 15-6. Viewable Table of Contents

Getting You Started with the OS/2 Warp Tutorial

To get everyone up and running on OS/2 Warp as soon as possible, OS/2 Warp comes with a built-in Tutorial, designed to meet a variety of needs in an interesting, as well as meaningful, way.

For the novice user unfamiliar with GUIs, the Tutorial offers a *kernel of knowledge* (also known as OS/2 Basics), a description of the things you need to know to get started using OS/2. So that novices don't have far to look, the icon for the Tutorial is visible on the Desktop's toolbar, instead of hidden within a folder.

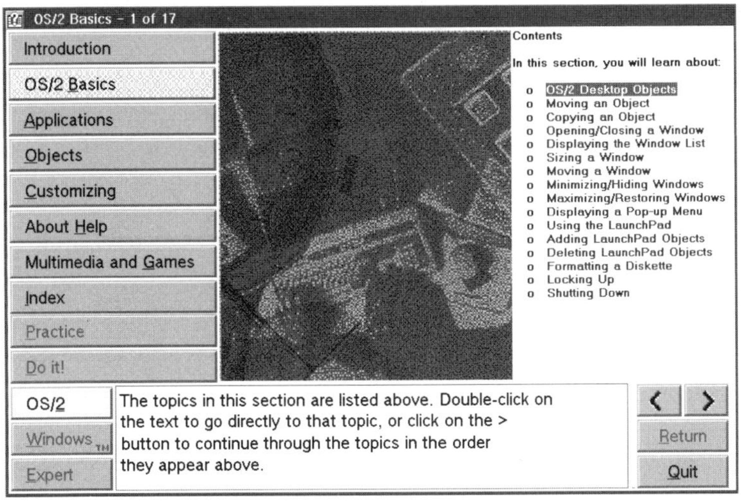

Figure 15-7. OS/2 Basics: The Kernel of Knowledge

Windows users can select the **Windows** push button to see how OS/2 functionality and terminology relate to the Windows environment.

Intermediate and power users can select the **Expert** push button to get expert tips and more technical details.

Users can learn about OS/2 and then immediately apply what they've learned through two built-in interactive mechanisms:

- **Practice**, in which the Tutorial guides you step-by-step through a task while you perform each step on the actual Desktop.

- **Do It!**, in which the Tutorial performs the steps for you.

So that users have no confusion over where to find all OS/2 educational materials, the OS/2 Tutorial offers a single point of entry to all tutorials on the OS/2 Desktop. From the front entry panel, users can launch tutorials on Networking and so on. So that users can progress through the information at their own pace, the OS/2 Tutorial offers navigational choices:

- *Linear* navigation, in which you progress straightforward from beginning to end.

- *Exploratory* navigation, in which you can get to any major topic at any time.

- *Selective* navigation, in which you can browse the Index for a topic you are interested in.

Getting Help Faster with the Master Help Index

All objects on the Desktop have helps associated with them. You look at these helps by single-clicking the right mouse button and selecting **Help** from the object's pop-up menu. Object helps provide general information on objects: what they are, what you can do with them, and how you use them. Object helps, like application helps, reside in .HLP files created with IPF.

As long as you have some idea what object you need to use in order to perform a task, you can rely on this technique to get more information on what to do next. But if you are not sure what object you need to use, this technique becomes a tedious and time-consuming process:

1. Move the mouse pointer over an object on the Desktop.
2. Single-click the right mouse button to display the object's pop-up menu.
3. Select **Help**.
4. Read the contents of the object's help window.
5. If the information doesn't address the task, close the help window and start all over again with another object on the Desktop.

This is not the most productive way to find information you need. And so we have a Master Help Index that provides a fast path to information for all objects on the Desktop.

The Master Help Index is represented by an object on the Desktop. The Master Help Index is an instance of a special class (MINDEX) of user objects provided with the Workplace Shell. The MINDEX class of objects has a built-in viewer that gives the tabbed, notebook-like presentation of index entries into object helps.

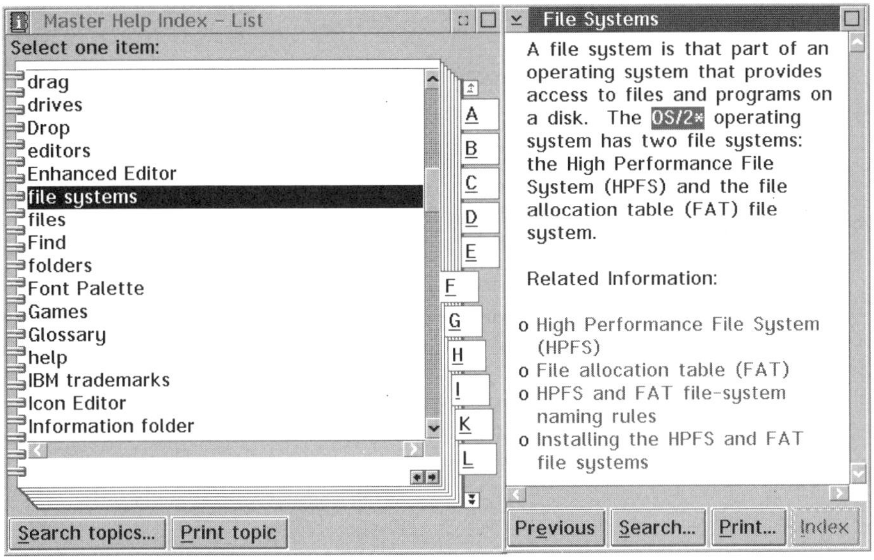

Figure 15-9. A Fast Path to Information for All Objects on the Desktop

The primary window for the Master Help Index contains a tabbed list of high-level topics associated with the objects on the Desktop. You can search this topic list by selecting the **Search topic** push button. Or you can scroll the list until you find the topic you are looking for.

By selecting a topic from this list, you can get a more detailed explanation of the task associated with the topic, as well as the opportunity to link to other related information (such as opening online books or the tutorial to the appropriate topic). This information is displayed in a secondary window, alongside the primary topic list. By selecting the **Search** push button in this window, you can invoke a more granular search for items that might not appear in the primary topic list. For example, the primary topic list contains an entry for environment variables. The description of environment variables contains a list of environment variables (such as PATH, DPATH, and so on). You can link directly from this list to the detailed descriptions in the *OS/2 Command Reference*. The specific environment variables are not listed in the primary topic list; thus, a **Search topics** for the PATH environment variable will come up empty.

Entries in MINDEX objects consist of .HLP file index entries with global attributes. The settings notebook for a MINDEX user object defines the scope of the object (that is, the set of help libraries whose global attributes are included in it). The HELP environment variable in CONFIG.SYS identifies the location (subdirectories) of .HLP files.

You can create your own Help Index by first creating an instance of the MINDEX class and then associating the .HLP files with the object through the object's settings notebook. You can also add an index entry for your application to the system's Master Help Index by using the global attribute on the index tag for your .HLP files and then placing your .HLP files in the HELP environment.

Developer's Tip: The Master Help Index for the OS/2 Desktop is not meant to contain ALL index entries from ALL help libraries for ALL applications installed. Rather, the Master Help Index should be viewed as a means to give your users an opportunity to get information on your application without actually launching it. With this in mind, you should mark **only one** index entry in your application .HLP file with the global attribute. This index entry should be imbedded in an information panel that provides a very brief overview of your application (what it is and what it does), links to other information within the application's help library, and a push button from which to launch the application.

Finding Information at the Touch of a Key with KwikINF

KwikINF is a highly configurable utility that provides a single point of entry, via a hot key, into all on-line books in the OS/2 BOOKSHELF, at any time, from anywhere on the Desktop, with the exception of DOS or WIN-OS/2 sessions.

Note: The BOOKSHELF is an environment variable, set in CONFIG.SYS, that contains a list of subdirectories containing IPF on-line documents (that is, viewable .INF files). On-line documents for OS/2 (for example, the *OS/2 Command Reference*) are stored in the \OS2\BOOK subdirectory of the drive on which OS/2 is installed. On-line documents for the Developer's Toolkit for OS/2 (for example, the OS/2 Programming References) are stored in the \TOOLKTxx\BOOK subdirectory of the drive specified during installation of the on-line programming information. After installation of OS/2 and the Developer's Toolkit, the BOOKSHELF environment variable is set as follows:

```
SET  BOOKSHELF = C:\OS2\BOOK;C:\TOOLKTxx\BOOK;
```

KwikINF comes with the Developer's Toolkit. You invoke it from its program object icon in the Toolkit Information folder. It is a background application that uses character device monitors and system hooks to poll your keyboard input for a hot key that you can select. When you first install KwikINF, the default hot key is Alt+Q. When you press this hot key, a window is displayed on your screen. Through this window, you can locate a topic in any book in the BOOKSHELF and open the book to that page. KwikINF has a rapid-search mechanism by which it uses index files, as defined with the HELPNDX variable in CONFIG.SYS, to quickly locate the book in which a topic can be found.

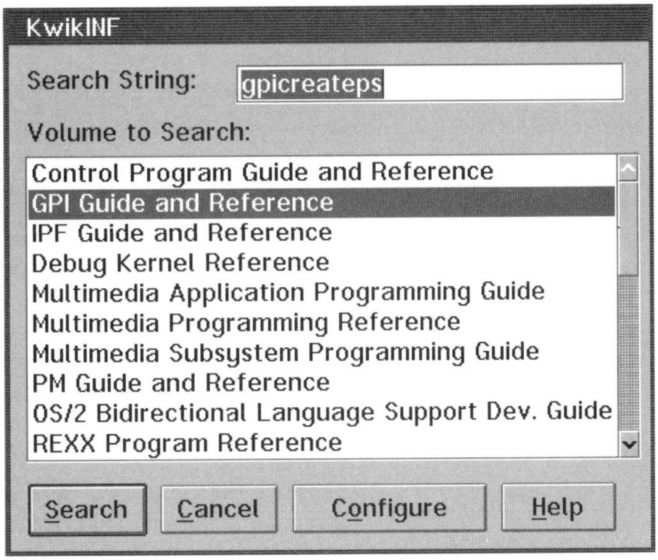

Figure 15-10. Finding a Topic in Any Book in the OS/2 BOOKSHELF with KwikINF

You can enable any on-line document for KwikINF by:

1. Creating the on-line document as a viewable .INF file using the Information Presentation Facility (IPF).
2. Adding the name of the subdirectory where it is stored to the PATH statement in CONFIG.SYS.
3. Appending the name of the subdirectory where it is stored to the BOOKSHELF in CONFIG.SYS.
4. Creating an index file to support the KwikINF rapid-search mechanism, storing it in the BOOKSHELF, and adding it to the HELPNDX variable in CONFIG.SYS.

For more detailed information on KwikINF, select **Contents** on the **Options** pull-down menu for the KwikINF help window.

Information Is a Single Click Away on the Desktop's Toolbar

Like a suitcase, the Desktop's toolbar (previously referred to as the LaunchPad) offers you the convenience of dragging all of your own personal "baggage," in one tidy package, along with you across your workspaces. The "baggage," of course, consists of the objects you most frequently use. (These things are stuffed into compartments, or drawers, on the toolbar itself.)

- The Tutorial, which gets you started and helps you when you're not sure what to do next
- An OS/2 window in which to run your applications
- An external diskette drive (A) from which to load new applications or back up data
- A printer to send your output to
- A shredder to discard the things you no longer need

The "baggage" also consists of tasks you most frequently perform. (These things are accessible through push buttons on the toolbar.)

- A way to find objects on the Desktop
- A view of the Window list of all windows for open objects and active programs
- The key to secure, or lock up, your system
- The procedure to shut down your system in an orderly way, allowing OS/2 to save object states, do clean up, and so on.

As shown in Figure 15-11, you can make sure that your information is just a single click away by placing shadows of your Master Help Index, KwikINF, and other on-line information on the Desktop's toolbar, or in one of its drawers.

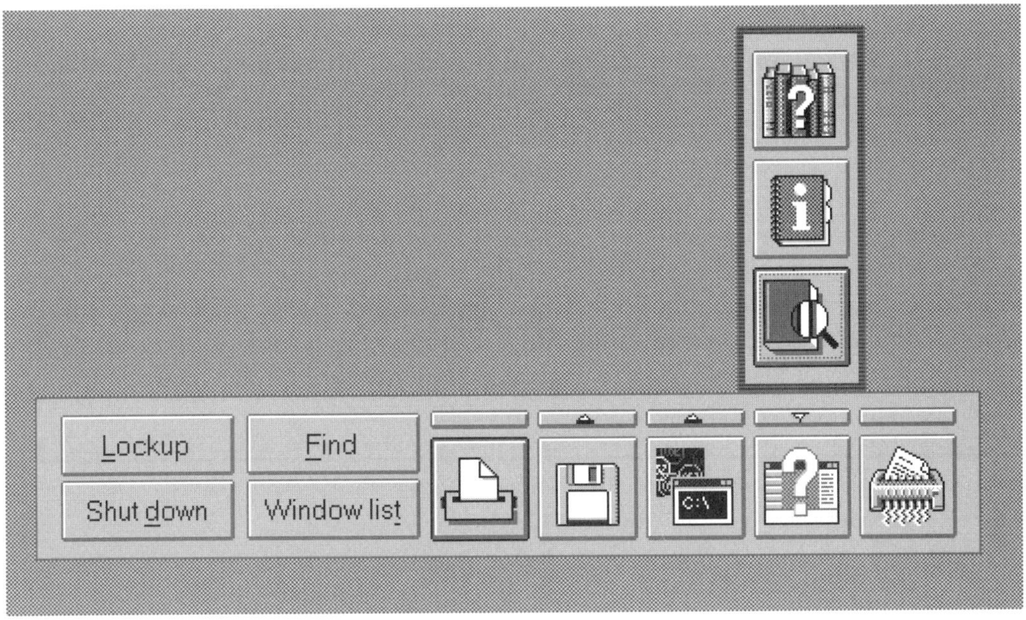

Figure 15-11. Information Is a Single Click Away on the Desktop's Toolbar

Where Do We Go from Here?

As we look ahead to where an information system should evolve, we need to consider a number of things.

Customer Trends

You can now get information anytime, anywhere. Customer environments are increasingly more portable and mobile. You can take your notebook anywhere (on a plane, on the golf course, at the beach, on safari, in the jungle) and then take it back to your office and dock it with your workstation. Your palmtop can send and retrieve information from any electronic facility anywhere in the world and then slide back into your pocket or briefcase. Information comes to you in compact places: in devices you can hold in your hand.

Everyone wants the latest information *here and now*. When a major event breaks out, television and radio networks respond instantly by interrupting programs to bring us the latest news bulletins. And if an event is ongoing, we get a "blow-by-blow" account. We are wired into anything that's happening, while it's happening. And so we expect that any information we see, on television, in newspapers, as well as on our desktop, does indeed represent the latest and greatest.

Information is everywhere for everyone. Over time, more and more information will go on-line. Home pages on the World Wide Web provide anyone access to information that has been traditionally inaccessible. The Information Superhighway is no longer just a hobby or a toy, but serious stuff. We don't just use it for E-mail among friends. We use it to talk to our favorite movie stars and the astronauts on board the space shuttle circling the earth, to look at art in the Louvre in Paris, to read the St. Petersburg Press in Russia, and to knock at the doors of the CIA and FBI.

Finally, as travelling the Information Superhighway becomes faster and cheaper, information will be distributed in ways not traditionally associated with computers. On-line versions of books, as well as video games and music, will be rented in much the same way that you now pay your local cable TV company to view special events and recently released movies. Instead of driving to your local video store or bookstore, you will access their services through their Home Pages on the Web.

The bottom line to all this is that we are a seamless and integrated society that demands equally seamless and integrated information solutions for our small planet: our Desktops should be windows to the world.

Customer Requirements

To make our desktops windows to the world, we have to change the foundations of our information structures.

Information needs to be *modular*. Smaller chunks of information can be more easily managed. They can be *reused* in many places. For example, the kernel of knowledge for OS/2 consists of a subset of all information on OS/2. As a module, the kernel of knowledge is accessible from the OS/2 tutorial, as well as from the OS/2 on-line help facility. Because smaller chunks of information can be used in different places, information can be more easily *scaled* to the environment. For example, your notebook might contain a subset of function available to you on your workstation. When using your notebook, you only need information for objects you use on your notebook. Smaller chunks of information can also be more easily *customized* for the user. For example, an object on the Desktop might have different helps for different levels of user expertise. You see the helps appropriate for your level of expertise with each object.

Information needs to be *open and customizable*. No matter how great the information you supply your customers, it can be even better if you give them the ability to make their own adjustments. This goes beyond the notion of letting them change colors or backgrounds. This includes letting them add their own personal comments, as well as integrating their own modules of information.

Information needs to be *portable*. If I have information related to functions available on many different systems, it would be nice if I could reuse information from one system on another. This means that the format of my information needs to transcend system requirements. For example, a LAN for OS/2 and a LAN for AIX might have a lot of information in common. But OS/2 information comes in an IPF form while AIX information comes in the form of manpages.

Information needs to be *smart and intuitive*. Good structure and good writing are important. But information loses its worth without a good user interface. A user interface needs to be easy to use—simple, but not simple-minded. It also needs to be responsive to the user.

Industry Directions

So what kind of information technology do we have to build this foundation on?

First of all, we already have technologies that cross system boundaries:

- Object technologies such as SOM and OpenDoc
- Industry-standard authoring languages such as HTML and SGML
- Information models from the Information Superhighway, such as Home Pages on the World Wide Web

We also have a robust set of multimedia technologies that enhance the kinds of information that we can present: audio, video, 3-D graphics, animation.

We already see these technologies used in highly interactive video games and information systems and more fully developed virtual reality applications.

Finally, sophisticated information tools are making our systems and how we create them more information-driven. Visual tools such as Visual Basic let developers design new user interfaces without having to write new code. Authoring tools let developers create and integrate information without having to write code to make audio sync up with video or to imbed graphics generated from one application into text generated from another.

Information System Objectives

If we meet customer requirements and utilize current technology, what else do we have to do to make our information system competitive?

First of all, users need to get to information from a single point. From the perspective of the World Wide Web and a LAN, that single point is a Desktop. From the perspective of the Desktop, that single point is the underlying help system.

Second, the information system must be flexible: easy to navigate, user-centric and customizable (adaptive and proactive), and extendable for future software (such as agents and virtual reality).

Third, the information system, like the rest of an operating system, must support the heritage.

Finally, an authoring environment should be provided to make the creation and integration of information as effortless and seamless as possible.

A Future with Integrated On-line Information

In order to meet and surpass objectives for an information system, we have to change the way we build one.

In our traditional OS/2 information system, the presentation (how it is perceived), structure (how it is organized), and content (what it consists of) of information are all interwoven and interlocked.

As shown in Figure 15-12, an author creates an IPF script file for OS/2 information using a word processor or the Hyperwise authoring tool. The author then uses the IPF compiler to generate HLP or INF binary files from the IPF tagged source. (Hyperwise will do this for you.) The HLP and INF files are interpreted by the Help Manager (IPF) and displayed on the screen in help windows. It's a simple enough process, but one that results in a single IPF presentation style and an IPF information structure based on headings imbedded in the content of the information. Using some of the features of IPF that we have already discussed at the beginning of this chapter, an author can

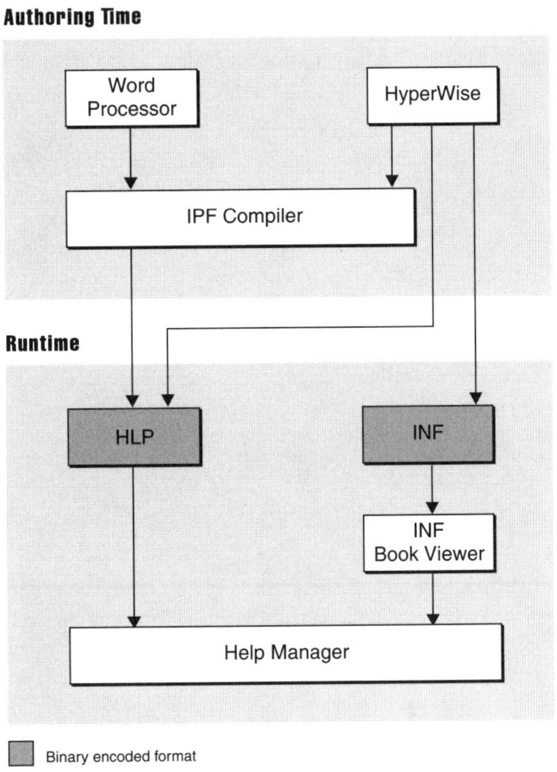

Figure 15-12. OS/2 Information Delivery Today

effect some changes and improvements, but not without writing some code or restructuring headings throughout the entire tagged source for the information. Conversely, changes to IPF, such as new interfaces (author tags) for a different style or presentation, might require changes to the information source as well.

But if we make presentation and structure and content all independent of each other, many new possibilities present themselves. Selectable presentation and navigational styles can be readily available without restructuring and rebuilding information script files and without writing additional code.

And that brings us to Integrated On-line Information (IOI), the future information delivery system for IBM's microkernel-based operating systems (see Figure 15-13).

Figure 15-13. IOI Shared Service Components

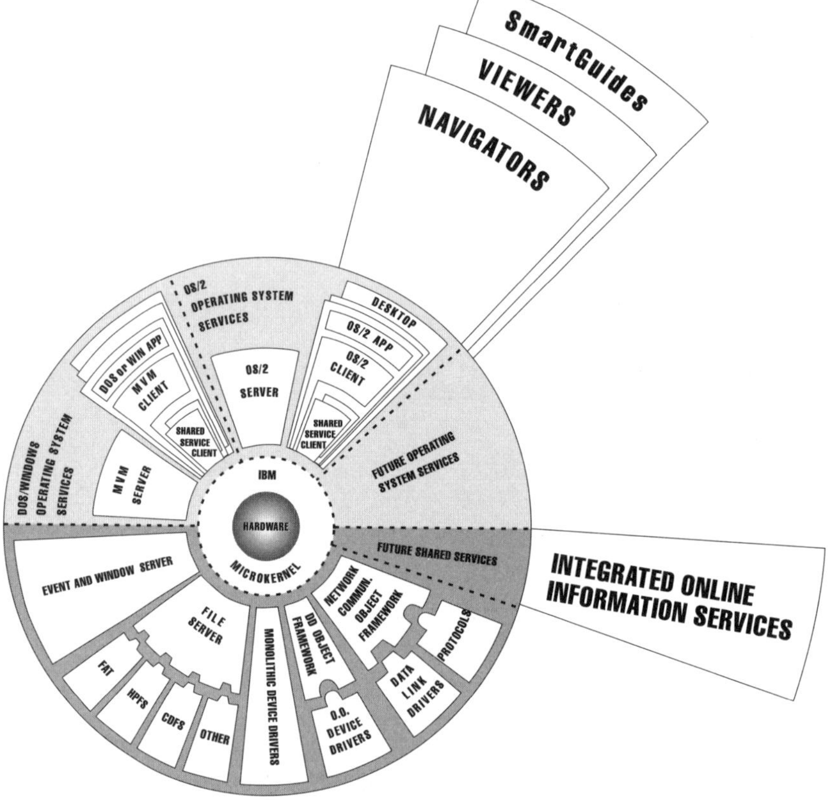

IOI is a shared service, consisting of a client library that handles requests for information services from an object-oriented server. As a shared service, IOI offers you all the advantages provided by the microkernel-based architecture:

- Portability across hardware and software platforms
- Information that can be shared via a consistent user interface across operating system services running on the IBM Microkernel
- Support for heritage function (DDF) and information (HLPs and INFs)

Because the IOI user interface is independent of the information it displays, it offers a very high level of flexibility. The IOI UI is *open*, consisting of *pluggable* metaphors that can be superimposed on top of or mapped into the information without affecting the information or the system itself. This means that IOI can address the widest variety of customer requirements and needs.

As shown in Figure 15-14, IOI Services will provide seamless access to information, no matter where it is located. IOI Services are both LAN-aware and WEB-aware. This means that the view of the world from your desktop includes your local information, information on the LAN you are connected to, and information on the World Wide Web when you are connected to the Internet. If information can be found, IOI Services will find it for you, regardless of where it is.

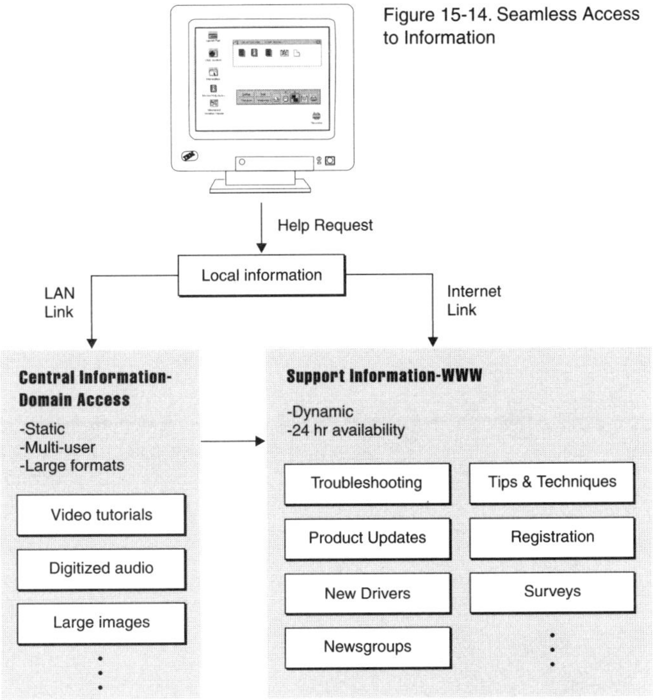

Figure 15-14. Seamless Access to Information

Application Development

This chapter provides information about developing applications and migrating existing applications. In addition, this chapter provides information about tools and resources available from IBM and other vendors that are of interest to application developers.

Programmers might rightly face a new platform with some trepidation—after all, there's a new hardware architecture to understand, different APIs to master, and new tools to learn. Typically, programmers might find this a daunting process and one from which they might not expect to emerge for several months.

However, you can put your mind at ease. OS/2 Warp Connect (PowerPC Edition) might be running on blazing new hardware and there might be a lot of new code inside, but at the level of the application programming interface (the API), the place where programs (and programmers) live and breathe, this *is* OS/2! This means that your OS/2 programs will feel right at home and the underlying system will respond as you expect.

The development tools will also seem quite familiar. There are, to be sure, some essential differences but, overall, the development process is the same—you use PowerPC versions of the tools you've used for the version of OS/2 for Intel-based systems.

What's New, What's Not?

That said, what are the differences, or more positively—what's new? One major new capability is the option to do cross-system development. For the first time, you have the choice of using your current Intel-based OS/2 Warp system as a "host-system" and your OS/2 Warp Connect (PowerPC Edition) system as a "target-system." This capability is important because it lets you continue to use current hardware and software to do things such as accessing code libraries, editing files, and compiling and building your application. When it's built, the application can be transferred to the PowerPC system for testing and debugging.

Why is this useful? Well, for one thing, it means that your current hardware and system software configuration for writing and building code can remain unchanged. Just add the OS/2 Warp Connect (PowerPC Edition) development tools, add the PowerPC hardware to your LAN (Token Ring or Ethernet), and you're ready to begin. All of your usual programming tasks, including debugging, will remain focused on the Intel-based OS/2 Warp environment while your application program runs on the PowerPC, the "target system." For example, the remote version of the C Set++ debugger will present the debugging information on your Intel-based OS/2 Warp system while controlling the program under test on the PowerPC system.

There are some definite benefits to this arrangement and also a drawback. The drawback is that you now have twice as much hardware in your office—but, as a trade-off, there is minimal unwanted interaction between the debugger and the program being debugged (most of the debugger is running on the host system), and you can use a lot of screen "real estate" for the debugger (on the Intel-based system) while having an unobstructed view of the program being tested on the PowerPC-based system.

Of course, if having a lot of hardware in your office is a big drawback for you, you can still use a "native" development environment (that is, use the PowerPC-based OS/2 Warp Connect system as both the host system and the target system). A complete set of native development tools is also available.

What Do I Need to Learn?

If you're reading this chapter, chances are good that you already have the skills you need. What are they?

First, you should be an OS/2 programmer. Familiarity with a standard suite of OS/2 development tools will help you greatly.

Second, an acquaintance with the basics of the PowerPC architecture would be useful. The architectural overview given in this book might very well be all you'll ever need. Almost all programming for OS/2 is done in C, C++, or a language even further removed from the details of the hardware (such as PL/I, COBOL, REXX, or Smalltalk). Assembler language is definitely not recommended for serious application programming, even though it has its uses. However, if you do want to go deeper, consult one of the many books on the PowerPC platform making their way to the bookstores.

Where Do I Begin?

Begin by obtaining a set of development tools for OS/2 Warp Connect (PowerPC Edition). As this is being written, not all of the tool developers who will be creating products for the PowerPC have made their plans known. For simplicity, this chapter describes the products available from IBM, although there will be several other development houses with products in this arena. By the time you are reading this, it should be obvious whether your own favorite compiler vendor has an OS/2 Warp Connect (PowerPC Edition) version on the market.

What If I Have to Migrate My Application from Another System?

Most developers will not be starting from scratch but, rather, will have an existing application that they want to move over to OS/2 Warp Connect (PowerPC Edition). It's likely you have a 32-bit OS/2 Warp application, in which case things are going to be very straightforward. But perhaps you have a 16-bit application originally written for Microsoft Windows or OS/2 Version 1.3. In this case, there is some actual code migration and porting to take into account, and IBM supplies programming tools to make this job a bit easier. The primary tool to help out in this area is called SMART—Source Migration Analysis Reporting Tool. This is a tool suite that analyzes source code and can, in many cases, actually migrate code for you. A thorough overview of SMART can be found in the section on Application Migration further on in this chapter.

How Long Will It Take to Migrate an Existing Application?

One of the benefits of using SMART is that the analysis tool can provide a rough estimate of the cost (in time and effort) of porting the code to OS/2. This estimate can be very useful in planning the activity. Of course, if you're recompiling a program that started life on OS/2 Warp, you'll find that this is very fast, indeed.

Where Do I Get More Information?

Your best source of information and tools is *The Developer Connection for OS/2*, a quarterly subscription service that includes a newsletter and programming tools on a CD-ROM. You can subscribe to *The Developer Connection for OS/2* by calling 1-800-6DEVCON (1-800-633-8266) in the United States. Refer to the following list for information on how to order if you live outside the US:

- Canada: 1-800-561-5293
- Mexico: 91-800-00639
- Mexico City: 627-2444
- Brazil: 0800-111205
- Asia/Pacific: 61-2-354-7684
- Europe (Order from IBM SPC in Denmark. Operators speak the following languages):
  - Dutch: 45-4-810-1400
  - English: 45-4-810-1500
  - French: 45-4-810-1200
  - German: 45-4-810-1000
  - Italian: 45-4-810-1600

- Scandinavian Languages: 45-4-810-1300
- Spanish: 45-4-810-1100

The Development Environment

Let's look at a development environment with all the tools and hardware required. Our development environment example is a common development environment: an Intel-based OS/2 host machine tied to a PowerPC-based target machine via a LAN connection. Here's what you'll need:

Hardware

You will require either:

- A PowerPC Common Hardware Reference Platform (CHRP) conforming system with appropriate LAN hardware and connectivity.
- An Intel-based PC with LAN hardware and connectivity and, naturally, a respectable amount of RAM and disk space—this is a development system, after all, and more is definitely better and faster.

System Software

The Intel-based machine should be running OS/2 2.11, OS/2 Warp Version 3 with LAN Requester, or OS/2 Warp Connect.

The PowerPC will be preloaded with OS/2 Warp Connect (PowerPC Edition) and the required LAN software.

Development Software

At the time of this writing, the PowerPC development software is distributed as a Developer's Toolkit—a beta-level package that combines all the development tools in one CD-ROM via The Developer Connection for OS/2 and that is being updated in each quarterly release. The latest release includes compilers and tools from MetaWare (a cross-hosted compiler, assembler, linker, and archiver) and IBM (equivalent to the latest release of VisualAge C++ retargeted to generate code for the PowerPC).

The following basic tools are provided:

- A Cross-compiler (Intel-hosted, PowerPC-targeting)

  The native compilers (PowerPC-hosted and targeted) will probably have arrived by the time you read this.

- A PowerPC assembler

  Besides the odd task or two that programmers might want to do with an assembler, it serves (at least in the earlier kits) as the final stage of the compiler.

  That is, the compiler does not emit object code; rather it emits assembler source and the assembler turns it into object code for the linker. This is purely a design strategy on the part of the compiler writers. Some compilers for OS/2 Warp Connect (PowerPC Edition) will use the assembler as the final stage, and some will not, preferring instead to generate their own object code.

- A linker

  Simply stated, the linker combines the separate object files produced by the compiler or assembler into one or more executable files (.EXE or .DLL) that can be loaded for execution by the OS/2 system loader. It also dynamically links the appropriate dynamic link libraries (.DLL) to the executable so that they can be found at load or execution time. This latter step is very important because essentially all OS/2 system services are provided to the application in the form of entry points in dynamic link libraries.

  On OS/2 Warp Connect (PowerPC Edition), the linker has the additional task of linking the resource files into the executable if necessary. This job is done by the Resource Compiler on the version of OS/2 for Intel-based systems, but here the resource compiler creates the resource object files that the linker adds to the .EXE or .DLL.

  The linker for OS/2 Warp Connect (PowerPC Edition) is a powerful 32-bit linker for Executable and Linkable Format (ELF) objects and creates ELF executables, which, conveniently enough, are exactly what the OS/2 system loader needs in order to create an in-storage executable image of the program.

- NMAKE

  This utility is unchanged in the kit provided for cross-development work but is recompiled to run on the PowerPC for native development.

- The MTools: MultiLib, MultiRes, and MultiAnalysis

  This is actually a family of tools built around a common set of functions. (You'll see MServer on your system. All of these tools will call it at one time or another.)

  MultiLib (MLIB.EXE) is the OS/2 system librarian. The librarian groups object files emitted by the compiler or assembler into "libraries" that can be used to group related files into one convenient package. MLIB also is used to maintain these libraries, adding and deleting object files as requested. MLIB supports the AR (archive) library format as well as the LIB format. The latter is the preferred format because it allows extensions required by OS/2.

  MultiRes (MRES.EXE) is the Resource Compiler. In contrast to the version of OS/2 for Intel-based systems, MRES can combine resource files and generate resource object (.OBJ) files, but it cannot link them into the executable; the linker must do that.

  The following are considerations to keep in mind when using MultiRes:

  – When you are working with resources on the version of OS/2 for Intel-based systems, it is acceptable to group resources together with the copy command (for example, copy A+B+C D.RES). This is not acceptable when dealing with OS/2 Warp Connect (PowerPC Edition), and you should use MultiRes to combine resource files.

  – Because the linker must be used to bind resource files into the executable, the content of some makefiles might have to be changed to make the link step the last operation. MultiAnalysis (MASYS.EXE) is the "analyzer" or browser for OS/2 Warp Connect (PowerPC Edition) binaries. If you'd like to have a look at object files (.OBJ), load modules (.EXE or .DLL), libraries (.LIB), or resource files, this tool will help you decode the ELF formatting and show you what's inside.

- The Debugger

  OS/2 programmers who use the IBM C/C++ compilers (C Set++ and now VisualAge C++) are familiar with the powerful debugger supplied with these products. The Debugger is an interactive, Presentation Manager tool with great power and flexibility. With the OS/2 Warp Connect (PowerPC Edition) Developer's Toolkit, a new remote capability is added to IPMD. With this capability, the visual front-end of the debugger can run on a system different from the one where the program being debugged (and some debugger code called the *back-end*) is run. The front- and back-ends of the debugger communicate across a network connecting the two computers—typically Token-Ring or Ethernet. This flexibility permits the debugger to operate as a cross-system tool or as a native tool, as the situation warrants or the programmer desires.

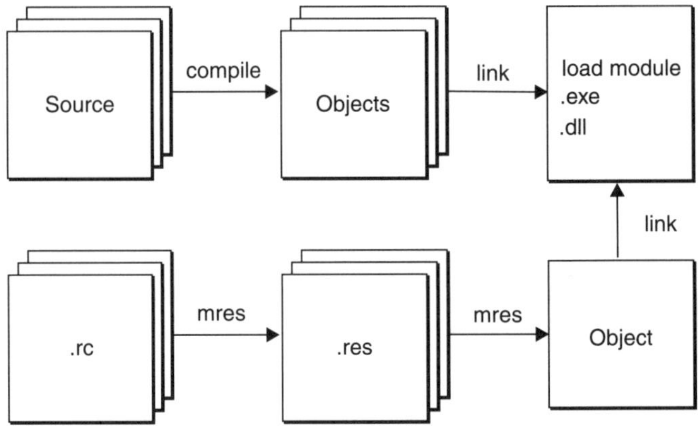

Figure 16-1. Development Flow through the Tools from Source to Executable

The OS/2 API

The OS/2 Application Programming Interface (API) is the means by which programs (and programmers) communicate requests for service to the system. Much of the design effort on OS/2 Warp Connect (PowerPC Edition) entailed enhancing and maintaining compatibility with the OS/2 API that programmers have been using on OS/2 Warp. It is important to realize that, while there certainly have been changes, in all ways, the 32-bit API is fully applicable to both the version of OS/2 for Intel-based systems and the PowerPC version of OS/2. In addition, it is our intent that there will be no "undocumented" interfaces—everything will be appropriately documented.

Two places will serve as good sources of API information—the Programming References distributed with the Developer's Toolkit for OS/2 Warp and the *OS/2 Warp Connect (PowerPC Edition) API Addendum*, which contains additional functions and information useful for programming for OS/2 Warp Connect (PowerPC Edition).

So, What's Different?

Well, let's talk about what is not there first. Most important, there are no 16-bit API calls. When OS/2 moved from OS/2 1.3 into the 32-bit world with OS/2 2.0, the API was extended and reworked to create a new, portable 32-bit API that would carry OS/2 into the future. For reasons of compatibility, the 16-bit API was retained even in the latest versions of OS/2 Warp. This permits both 16-bit and 32-bit OS/2 programs to run on OS/2 Warp and, in fact, even permits the creation of mixed-mode programs whose executable units can contain modules running 16-bit or 32-bit code. This made life convenient for programmers moving to 32-bit OS/2, but there was clear warning that the writing was on the wall for the 16-bit API—at some point, there were going to be OS/2 systems that would not support 16-bit code. At the same time, the 32-bit API was declared the "official" API that would move into the future. Well, the future is now, and the 32-bit API has moved to OS/2 Warp Connect (PowerPC Edition). The constraints of designing a 32-bit operating system to run on pure 32-bit hardware have necessitated that only a 32-bit API be supported.

Similarly, the Installable File System (IFS) functions are not included. There are two reasons for this. First, IFS is also a 16-bit API and an undocumented one. Additionally, the architecture of OS/2 Warp Connect (PowerPC Edition) is, at the kernel level, different from that of OS/2 Warp. File systems are designed, not as kernel extensions, but as shared services that are implemented as IBM Microkernel tasks.

Any functions that relate to ABIOS have been removed as there are no ABIOS functions on PowerPC systems.

DosAllocThreadLocalMemory() and DosFreeThreadLocalMemory() have been removed in favor of equivalent functions in the newly supplied dynamic C run-time support.

So, That's What's Gone—Now, What's New?

Remember the statement made earlier in this chapter—"at the level of the API, this *is* OS/2"? To a programmer, OS/2 *is* the API. However, there certainly are some additions, which are mainly designed to make life easier for those moving applications to the platform.

First, many programmers have been concerned that, as they moved their 16-bit programs from OS/2 1.3 to OS/2 2.1 or OS/2 Warp, they've been unable to use 32-bit equivalents of the text-oriented Keyboard, Mouse, and Video API set (KBDxxx, MOUxxx, and VIOxxx). This has led to the creation of mixed-mode programs, which will not easily port to OS/2 Warp Connect (PowerPC Edition) without some reworking. To ease this situation, some additional functions have been defined that are essentially 32-bit equivalents of the 16-bit Mouse, Video, and Keyboard functions of OS/2 1.x. These functions are included in the API set of OS/2 Warp Connect (PowerPC Edition) and are available, as well as a set of headers and LIBS that can be used to retrofit mixed-mode programs that run on the version of OS/2 for Intel-based systems. This allows for easy porting of these programs and for the creation of a single source base for text-mode applications running on Intel-based systems and PowerPC systems.

Second, OS/2 Warp Connect (PowerPC Edition) supports Unicode, and there is a complete set of functions for creating Unicode-enabled applications. See Appendix B, "Creating Applications for the World" on page 385.

Additionally, several new features are provided that have programming interfaces, including a new RAM semaphore, and a logging and tracing facility that can be accessed by applications.

Lastly, the C language run time, which had been provided by compilers and included with applications on prior versions of OS/2, will now be provided by the system. This provides the opportunity to deliver smaller applications (the run time doesn't have to be included) and a smaller overall footprint for the entire application set (only one run-time image need exist for the entire system).

Migrating Windows Applications

As discussed earlier in this chapter, the primary tool to help migrate and port applications is SMART.

Overview of SMART

SMART is the Source Migration Analysis Reporting Toolset, developed by One Up Corporation. IBM distributes this development tool with The Developer Connection for OS/2. SMART works with the source code of Windows 16-bit and 32-bit applications and source code of OS/2 16-bit applications. SMART gives you porting assistance and migrates a large portion of application source code to OS/2 Warp Connect (PowerPC Edition).

SMART has a main engine that uses migration dictionaries or migration tables to migrate the application source code. SMART uses these dictionaries to identify, in the source code, items and keywords that will require migration. SMART groups these migration items or keywords in the source code into categories. The SMART categories are based on the level of difficulty required to migrate the items. SMART defines the following areas of difficulty:

- 000 Informational only

  An exact match of the keyword exists in OS/2 Warp Connect (PowerPC Edition). There might be a change in the size or type (for example, short to long).

- 010 Literal replacement

  An equivalent definition exists in OS/2 Warp Connect (PowerPC Edition). A literal change in the keyword is required (for example, LPSTR to PSZ).

- 020 Replacement with parameter changes

  The equivalent function exists in OS/2 Warp Connect (PowerPC Edition), but parameters or fields of a structure differ slightly from the source platform definition. This category also includes some of the parameters that are not applicable or required in OS/2 Warp Connect (PowerPC Edition).

- 030 Change with more/fewer API calls

  The equivalent function exists in OS/2 Warp Connect (PowerPC Edition), but the function must be implemented with more, or sometimes fewer, function calls. This category also includes items that map to one of several choices depending upon the type of parameter used.

- 040 Logic changes required

  Similar function exists in OS/2 Warp Connect (PowerPC Edition), but the logic required to do the function must be reworked.

- 050 Functionality does not exist

  The function is not available on OS/2 Warp Connect (PowerPC Edition). This category includes, among other items, items that are not functionally needed under OS/2 Warp Connect (PowerPC Edition) and items that could be developed as an extension to OS/2 Warp Connect (PowerPC Edition).

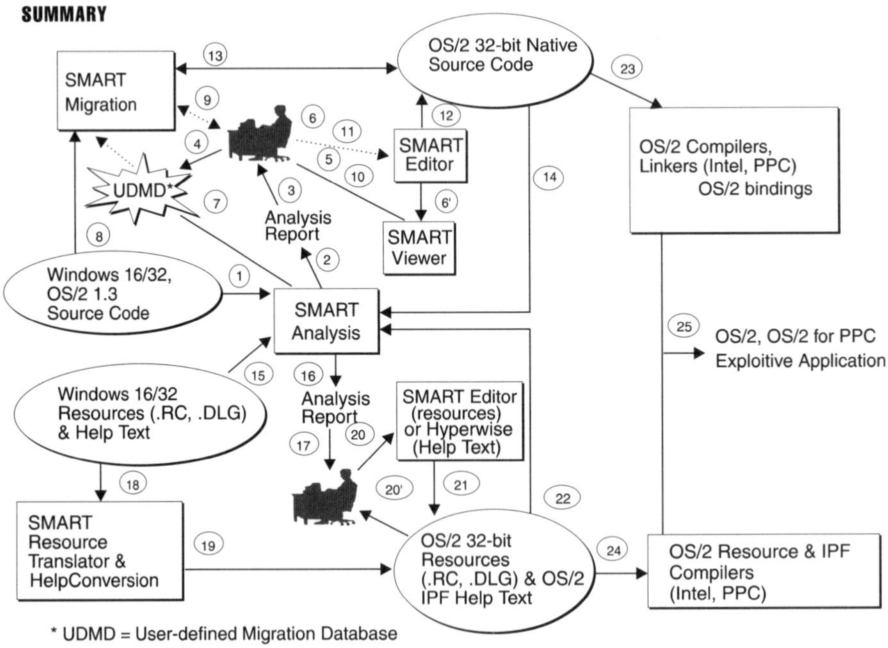

Figure 16-2. SMART Source Code Analysis Process

- 999 Dictionary entry not defined

  The SMART dictionary does not currently have a complete description for the migration of the keyword.

SMART Migration Process

The SMART migration process is a multistep process as shown in Figure 16-2.

The process begins with the source code analysis. You can use the SMART Source Code Analysis tool to obtain an analysis of the level of difficulty or the effort you will face in migrating your source code from 16-bit and 32-bit Windows and from 16-bit OS/2 to OS/2 Warp Connect (PowerPC Edition). The source code analysis will give you a level of understanding of the changes to be made in migrating your application to OS/2 Warp Connect (PowerPC Edition). The source code analysis will guide you into taking different actions in migrating your source code. For several instances, SMART can automatically migrate the source code for you. For other instances, you might need to invest in additional development. Some of that development might have you making manual modification in migrating your source code. Another type of development might be creating a SMART User-Defined Migration Database (UDMD). The development of a SMART UDMD is the next step in the SMART Migration Process.

UDMD is a SMART function that lets you tell SMART which items in your source code need to be changed and what they should be changed to when migrating to OS/2 Warp Connect (PowerPC Edition). A UDMD is basically a method used to expand or override the list of migration entries in the SMART tables. The SMART UDMD function and the UDMD development are discussed in more detail later on in this chapter. For now, you should know that the development of a UDMD is another step in the SMART Migration Process and that it is one that is optional. The next step in the SMART Migration Process is the source code migration. In this step, you simply make use of SMART and any UDMD you have created to migrate your source code to OS/2.

This step is iterative and can involve analyzing your source code at key points. This step can also include additional manual development. Before your application can be completely migrated to OS/2 Warp Connect (PowerPC Edition), you will need to migrate your menu, dialog boxes, help, and any resources used by your application.

For this step in the migration process, you can use the SMART Resource Translation utility to first analyze the effort to translate the resources and then to do the actual translation of the resources. For more information on the utility, see page 363.

SMART Options

SMART provides the following operating options. You can use SMART to generate automatic OS/2 source code. You can also use SMART to generate in-line comments. When you use SMART to migrate your source code and use in-line comments, you can select the type of comments you would like used in the source code.

When you use SMART to migrate your source code to OS/2, the source generated will have no requirements on proprietary vendor run-time modules.

Source Code Analysis

The SMART Analysis and Reporting Tool analyzes your source code and resources and provides reports on the level of difficulty required to migrate source code from Windows to OS/2.

The SMART Analysis and Reporting Tool generates three types of reports:

- Analysis Summary Report
- File Detail Report
- Keyword Detail Report

To obtain a SMART Analysis Report, you select files that contain source code using SMART. You then run the SMART Analyze option from the SMART main menu. The SMART reports are generated and can be optionally sent to the SMART Editor if the editor is installed on your system. When the SMART Analysis Reports show that there are items in your source code that cannot be automatically migrated by the SMART base migration databases, you can use the SMART Viewer to obtain additional porting information. When SMART generates the Analysis Reports, you can choose the option in SMART that generates hyperlinks to your source code. If you choose this option, you can use the SMART Editor in combination with the SMART Analysis Reports to find the exact line of source in your source code that requires migration.

Analysis Summary Report

The SMART analysis of a sample application source code provides the Analysis Summary Report shown in Figure 16-3.

The Total File Count, Total File Size (Bytes), Total Source Lines, and Total Code Lines in the SMART Analysis Summary Report specify the number of files analyzed, the total size of the files in bytes, the total lines in the source files, and the total lines of source code, respectively.

```
Total File Count                                          1
Total File Size (Bytes)                               5,105

Total Source Lines                                      147
Total Code Lines                                        121

Total Category 000 Hits                                   6
Total Category 010 Hits                                  27
Total Category 020 Hits                                  10
Total Category 030 Hits                                   7
Total Category 040 Hits                                   5
Total Category 050 Hits                                   1
Total Migration Hits                                     56

Total Cat 000 & 010 Hits Auto Migrated                   33
Total Hits MiCL Processed                                 0
Total Hits Processed with UDMD                            0
Total Hits Excluded                                       0

Total Migration Keyword Instances                        38

Estimated Migration Effort Without SMART               19.8
Savings from SMART Base Migration                       2.3

Savings from Cat 010 Auto Migrate                       5.8
Savings from Keyword Exclusions                          .0

** Net Migration Effort **                             11.7
Percent Effort Reduction using SMART                   40.9 %
```

Figure 16-3. Example of a SMART Analysis Summary Report

SMART identifies items or keywords in the source code that will require migration to OS/2. As explained earlier in this chapter, SMART groups these migration items or keywords in the source code into categories. The SMART categories are based on the level of difficulty required to migrate the items to OS/2. The "Total Category Hits" lines in Figure 16-3, as you might guess, are the number of migration items by category.

The "Total Migration Hits" line in Figure 16-3 shows the total number of items that must be migrated to OS/2 Warp Connect (PowerPC Edition) in order to port the sample application to OS/2.

The "Total Cat 000 & 010 Hits Auto Migrated" line gives you the number of items that SMART will migrate automatically to OS/2. SMART will migrate automatically to OS/2 all CATEGORY 000 and 010 items. For this sample program, the SMART Analysis Summary Report indicates that, of the 56 Total Migration Items, SMART will automatically migrate 33 of the items (or 59% of the items needing to be migrated to OS/2).

SMART Version 2 includes a Migration Command Language (MiCL) that allows you to program the migration process for each keyword affected. Through the use of SMART MiCL commands, you can program SMART to prompt for data or processing options when an occurrence of a migration keyword is detected. The SMART MiCL commands provide you with the capability of extending SMART to be more interactive, as you need it. You can use the SMART MiCL commands within the SMART User-Defined Migration Database (UDMD), which is explained later in this chapter. The "Total Hits MiCL Processed" in the SMART Analysis Summary Report is the number of MiCL commands processed. This first SMART Analysis Summary Report does not make use of a UDMD or MiCL commands. Therefore, the "Total Hits MiCL Processed" is 0 in the SMART Analysis Summary Report for this sample program.

SMART also includes a User-Defined Migration Database (UDMD) function that provides you with the capability to create your own migration tables and databases. You can analyze and migrate your source modules by specifying the use of your UDMD and a SMART table (for example, Windows 3.1 to OS/2) or by specifying the use of one or the other (that is, a UDMD or the SMART table).

With a UDMD you can override equivalent migration items or keyword entries in the SMART tables. You can also use a UDMD to expand the list of migration items or keywords SMART will convert for you automatically. This allows you to define a keyword mapping from the Windows platform to OS/2 once; then with SMART, you can use the UDMD to make the mapping or migration for multiple instances of the keyword in your source code. The "Total Hits Processed with UDMD," in the SMART Analysis Summary Report shown in Figure 16-3, is the number of keywords processed for which the mapping or migration is specified in the UDMD. For this sample program, this value is 0 because a UDMD was not used when this SMART Analysis Summary Report was created.

SMART uses keywords listed in an Exclude file to override both the SMART table and a UDMD to omit processing of keywords. The "Total Hits Excluded" is the number of keywords that were not processed because they appear in the Exclude file list. Examples of items or keywords that you would include in the Exclude file are simple API functions that you might have implemented for OS/2 on your own. The min and max functions are good examples.

The SMART Analysis Summary Report, shown in Figure 16-3, also gives you the "Total Migration Keyword Instances." This indicates the total number of unique ways an item or keyword is used in the source code.

The "Estimated Migration Effort without SMART," shown in Figure 16-3, is the approximate effort (in many cases, this value is the approximate number of hours) it might take to manually migrate the source code to OS/2.

The "Savings from SMART Base Migration" and the "Savings from Cat 010 Auto Migrate" indicate the effort saved from the category 000 and 010 items, which are automatically migrated by SMART.

The "Savings from Keyword Exclusions" is basically the migration effort saved by having SMART ignore the keywords or migration items in the Exclude file.

The "Savings from SMART Base Migration," the "Savings from Cat 010 Auto Migrate," and the "Savings from Keyword Exclusions" are subtracted from the "Estimated Migration Effort Without SMART" to provide the "Net Migration Effort." The "Net Migration Effort" is the net approximate effort it might take you to migrate this sample program to OS/2. Again, in many cases, this number is the approximate number of hours. However, the migration effort is based on your programming experience in both Windows and OS/2. To obtain a better indication of what this number means, you should migrate one or two source code modules and compare the effort indicated by SMART to the time you actually spend using SMART and making any manual changes required to fully migrate those modules to OS/2. That exercise should give you an indication of the "Effort Modifier." You can enter the "Effort Modifier" at the SMART Source Code Analysis dialog box during the SMART analysis process to obtain effort numbers that are based on your Windows and OS/2 programming experience. As you can guess, the migration and analysis process is iterative.

The "Percent Effort Reduction Using SMART" is computed by taking the percentage of the total of all the savings of the SMART migration from the "Estimated Migration Effort Without SMART" (for example, (2.3 + 5.8)/19.8 * 100 = 40.9%). When "User-Defined Migration Data Base Development" is discussed, you will see how you can improve on this number by investing some time in UDMD development.

Analysis File Detail Report

The SMART Analysis File Detail Report presents a detailed analysis of each source file. The SMART analysis of this sample program generates the File Detail Report shown in Figure 16-4.

PATH/FILENAME	SIZE	LINES	CODE	HITS	PCT HITS	INSTS PCT	INST	EFFORT	CAT 000	CAT 010	CAT 020	CAT 030	CAT 040	CAT 050	CAT 999
C:\FILEDIR\FILENAME.C															
	5,105	147	121	56	46.3	38	31.4	12.7	6	27	10	7	5	1	0
SubTotal (1)	5,105	147	121	56	46.3			12.7	6	27	10	7	5	1	0
Total (1)	5,105	147	121	56	46.3	38	31.4	12.7	6	27	10	7	5	1	0

Figure 16-4. SMART Analysis File Detail Report

SMART gives you most of the same information in both the SMART File Detail Report and the SMART Analysis Summary Report. The "SIZE," "LINES," and "CODE" columns give you the size of the file in bytes, the lines in the file, and actual lines of code in the file, respectively. The "HITS" are the number of keywords or migration items in the source code module. The "PCT HITS" represent the percentage of hits based on the lines of source code ("CODE"). "INSTS" is the number of instances or unique ways the keywords or migration items have been used within the source code. The "EFFORT," as in the SMART Analysis Summary Report, is the approximate effort (in many cases, this value is the approximate number of hours) it would take to migrate the items or keywords in the source module to OS/2. Figure 16-4 also shows the HITS (migration items or keywords) by SMART Category. This gives you an indication of which source modules contain the items that are most difficult to migrate.

Keyword Detail Report

The SMART Analysis Keyword Detail Report gives you a breakdown of the keywords identified during the analysis. SMART presents this data to you as shown in Figure 16-5.

Example of a SMART Analysis Keyword Detail Report (Sample report sections only)

ITEMS	HITS	PCT HITS	FILES	INSTS	PCT INSTS	EFFORT
CATEGORIES						
000 Informational only	6	10.7	1	2	5.3	.0
010 Literal replacement	27	48.2	1	16	42.1	.0
020 Replacement with parameter changes	10	17.9	1	8	21.1	1.8
030 Change with more or less API calls	7	12.5	1	6	15.8	3.3
040 Logic changes required	5	8.9	1	5	13.2	5.0
050 Functionality does not exist	1	1.8	1	1	2.6	1.6
*** Category Totals	56	100.0	1	38	100.0	11.7
TYPES						
010 Function	18	32.1	1	16	42.1	7.8
020 Message	5	8.9	1	4	10.5	1.5
030 Symbol	18	32.1	1	12	31.6	1.6
040 typedef	15	26.8	1	6	15.8	.8
AREAS						
060 Resource-Management	2	3.6	1	2	5.3	2.0
200 Message	8	14.3	1	7	18.4	2.6
210 Window-Creation	7	12.5	1	6	15.8	1.7
220 Display and Movement	1	1.8	1	1	2.6	.5
230 Input	8	14.3	1	6	15.8	2.0
260 Dialogs	4	7.1	1	4	10.5	1.8
280 Menu	1	1.8	1	1	2.6	.5
300 System	1	1.8	1	1	2.6	.0
320 Error	2	3.6	1	1	2.6	.3
340 Cursor	1	1.8	1	1	2.6	.0
940 Variable Typedefines	21	37.5	1	8	21.1	.3
KEYWORDS (by Category and Hits)						
050 Functionality does not exist						
DLGWINDOWEXTRA	1	1.8	1			1.6
040 Logic changes required						
WinMain	1	1.8	1			1.0
SetFocus	1	1.8	1			1.0
RegisterClass	1	1.8	1			1.0
LoadCursor	1	1.8	1			1.0
030 Change with more or less API calls						
SendMessage	2	3.6	1			.8
WNDCLASS	1	1.8	1			.5
WM_CHAR	1	1.8	1			.5
ShowWindow	1	1.8	1			.5
020 Replacement with parameter changes						
MessageBeep	2	3.6	1			.3
HANDLE	2	3.6	1			.3
TranslateMessage	1	1.8	1			.2
GetMessage	1	1.8	1			.2
DefWindowProc	1	1.8	1			.2
CreateDialog	1	1.8	1			.2
010 Literal replacement						
DWORD	5	8.9	1			.0
PASCAL	3	5.4	1			.0
VK_ESCAPE	2	3.6	1			.0
000 Informational only						
NULL	5	8.9	1			.0
BOOL	1	1.8	1			.0

Figure 16-5. Example of a SMART Analysis Keyword Detail Report

The data is broken down by:

- Keyword by SMART category
- Keyword by the types of the keywords
- Keyword by functional area
- Individual keyword

You can use the SMART Keyword Detail Report to determine exactly which migration items SMART will automatically migrate for you. You can also use the SMART Keyword Detail Report to determine if you should develop a UDMD to enhance the SMART migration.

User-Defined Migration Database Development

The SMART UDMD function lets you tailor the SMART migration. To develop UDMDs, you can use the SMART Viewer, which will help you find additional migration information on keywords.

The SMART Viewer

The SMART Keyword Detail Report shows that there are a few migration items that are not automatically migrated by SMART. To analyze these items, you can use the SMART Viewer tool. The SMART Viewer is installed in the SMART folder. You can invoke the SMART Viewer directly from the SMART folder. You can also invoke the SMART Viewer directly from the SMART Editor through a REXX macro provided with the SMART package.

The SMART Viewer provides context-sensitive, on-line help to the SMART migration. You can use the SMART Viewer to search on a topic name. The information on that topic will be displayed in a SMART Viewer window. The SMART Viewer also gives you "Template," "Prototype," "Example," and "References" for a migration keyword.

For example, we've used the SMART Viewer to look at the information provided for some of the SMART category 020 items. Again, these category 020 items are migration items for which an equivalent function exists in OS/2 but parameters or fields of a structure differ slightly from the Microsoft Windows definition. This category also includes some of the parameters that are not applicable or required in OS/2. By using the SMART Viewer to analyze the information provided for these category 020 items, you can determine if you can expand the SMART knowledge base by writing a UDMD that will automatically migrate these category 020 items.

The SMART Viewer gives you the following information for MessageBeep:

```
Cat:020   Type:010   Area:320

Replace with WinAlarm.
```

Note that there are a number of additional alarm values available in OS/2.

The SMART Viewer also gives you the following "WinAlarm" sample information, prototype, and template:

```
SAMPLE
Windows:
MessageBeep (MB_OK);
OS/2:
WinAlarm (HWND_DESKTOP, WA_WARNING);
PROTOTYPE
BOOL APIENTRY WinAlarm(HWND hwndDesktop, ULONG
rgfType);
TEMPLATE
WinAlarm (HWND_DESKTOP, );
```

You can use the information provided by the SMART Viewer to create a UDMD that will migrate the MessageBeep call to the WinAlarm call for all instances of MessageBeep in a program or set of programs. You can use the same analysis process to create a UDMD that will convert all of the category 020 items in the source code of your applications to category 010 items. SMART can then migrate automatically for you all those category 010 items.

The UDMD and Migration Command Language (MiCL)

UDMDs are ASCII text files containing format tags and data. You can use one database created from a UDMD with a SMART Migration Database. You can use the utility function under **Tables, Create User UDMD** under the main menu of SMART to convert the UDMD (text file) into a SMART Migration Database format and tables. The ASCII text file looks as shown in Figure 16-6.

```
.Notice  =A Copyright statement can be placed here
.Table   =This is the place to give this table a title
.Version =Table version number
.Date    =Date the table was created

.Keyword =010 010 200 MessageBeep
.SComment=Replace MessageBeep with WinAlarm
.LComment=Replace MessageBeep with WinAlarm.  The first parameter
         =to WinAlarm can be the window handle to the desktop.  The
         =second parameter to WinAlarm can usually be the first
         =parameter to the MessageBeep Windows call.
.Sample  =Windows:
         =   MessageBeep (MB_OK);
         =OS/2:
         =   WinAlarm (HWND_DESKTOP, WA_WARNING);
.Prototyp=BOOL WinAlarm (HWND hwndDeskTop, ULONG flStyle);
.Template=WinAlarm( HWND_DESKTOP, $P1 );
.Command =/* Replace source code for MessageBeep, Cat. 20 */
         =IF $P1 = "0" THEN $P1 = "WA_ERROR"
         =SmRemove( LINE )
         =SmOutputLine( $T1 )
```

Figure 16-6. UDMD and MiCL Example

A UDMD consists of format tags starting with a period in the first column. An equal sign appears in column 10. The data for each table element begins in column 11. A colon found in column 11 will cause SMART to ignore the record. This is useful in creating comments. Each UDMD input file must contain the table header data at the beginning of the file. The ".Notice," ".Table," ".Version," and ".Date" tags have been briefly defined in the above example UDMD. The ".Keyword" tag is a compound statement that consists of the following parameters:

Type Code	3 characters, column 11-13 (for example, 010)
Category Code	3 characters, column 15-17 (for example, 010)
Functional Area Code	3 characters, column 19-21 (for example, 200)
Keyword Name	Column 23 (for example, MessageBeep)

The "Type Code," "Category Code," and "Functional Area Code" are values that must match the valid codes specified in the SMART Migration Database. You can obtain this information through the SMART Viewer.

The ".SComment" tag is a short, one-line comment for the migration keyword. The ".LComment" tag is a one-line or multiple-line comment for the migration keyword. The ".Sample" tag is a one-line or multiple-line example source code that shows how to implement the keyword. The ".Prototype" tag is a one-line or multiple-line source code that specifies the formal function prototype for the migrated keyword. The ".Template" tag is the specification for the code generated for the SMART Migration.

The SMART Migration Command Language (MiCL) can be used to create a migration command using the template. The SMART MiCL predefines a number of variables. The predefined variables begin with a dollar sign ($). Variables that are within $P1–$P99 contain the argument string of an API keyword. In the template shown in Figure 16-6, the $P1 stands for the first parameter in the MessageBeep call.

SMART includes several built-in functions that can be invoked from within the SMART UDMD ".Command" lines. SmRemove and SmOutputLine are examples of these SMART built-in functions. The SmRemove built-in function will remove either the keyword, the source code line in which the keyword is found, or the complete statement block in which the keyword is found. The type of removal is indicated with the following parameter types, which are self-explanatory:

- KEYWORD
- LINE
- BLOCK

You can use the SmRemove along with the SmOutputLine built-in function to replace source code with new output source code as in the example UDMD in Figure 16-6. The parameter to the SmOutputLine can be a variable, as in the example, or a literal string. In the example UDMD, the value of the parameter $T1 is evaluated as the first template string. As you might have noticed, you can implement some amount of logic through IF/THEN/ELSE clauses in the UDMD MiCL commands.

The example UDMD simply states that, for each MessageBeep keyword found, the keyword should be treated as a category 010 migration item during both the SMART analysis and migration. In addition, when the keyword is migrated, the first parameter of the MessageBeep Windows function (the only parameter in this case) is to be used in place of the second parameter in the WinAlarm OS/2 Warp function. This replacement is to be done only if the value of that first parameter ($P1) is not equal to 0, in which case the value of $P1 is set to WA_ERROR. In either case, the original source code line containing the MessageBeep call is to be replaced with an equivalent line that replaces the MessageBeep for the WinAlarm call.

You probably noticed that the SMART Keyword Detail Report, shown in Figure 16-5, indicates that there are only two hits for the MessageBeep keyword and similar numbers of hits for the rest of the category 020 items found in the sample program. Larger applications with several additional lines of source code would obtain more benefit from the analysis of the MessageBeep information above and, therefore, from a UDMD that would automatically migrate keywords such as MessageBeep and the rest of the category 020 items found in the source code. The amount of time spent in expanding the SMART knowledge base with UDMDs can actually be an investment and savings in additional migration effort for a large application. For additional details on developing SMART UDMDs and MiCL commands, please refer to the *SMART Programming Guide*, an on-line book, which is installed in the SMART folder when you install SMART on your system.

For this sample application, we spent approximately two hours creating a UDMD that was of use and were able to increase the "Percent Effort Reduction Using SMART" to 75.5%. The SMART Analysis Report Summary produced after adding the use of the UDMD to the SMART migration is shown in Figure 16-7.

Migration Analysis Report Summary Using a UDMD to Assist the Migration

Total File Count	1
Total File Size (Bytes)	5,105
Total Source Lines	147
Total Code Lines	121
Total Category 000 Hits	6
Total Category 010 Hits	47
Total Category 040 Hits	2
Total Category 050 Hits	1
Total Migration Hits	56
Total Cat 000 & 010 Hits Auto Migrated	53
Total Hits MiCL Processed	21
Total Hits Processed with UDMD	22
Total Hits Excluded	0
Total Migration Keyword Instances	38
Estimated Migration Effort Without SMART	14.7
Savings from SMART Base Migration	2.3
Savings from Cat 010 Auto Migrate	8.8
Savings from Keyword Exclusions	.0
** Net Migration Effort **	3.6
Percent Effort Reduction using SMART	75.5 %

Figure 16-7. Migration Analysis Report Summary Using a UDMD to Assist the Migration

Notice that the lines "Total Hits MiCL Processed" and "Total Hits Processed with UDMD" now indicate that there were hits or migration items processed with MiCL commands and UDMDs. The "Net Migration Effort" was also reduced to 3.6, or approximately 3.6 hours as explained earlier. Notice also that the "Total Category 010 Hits" was increased from 27 to 47 and that there are now no category 020 items reported. That is because the UDMD that was created converted all category 020 items to category 010 items. The UDMD also converted all of the category 030 items and three of the category 040 items to category 010 items. Remember that all of the category 010 items are automatically migrated by SMART.

The SMART Editor

You can make use of the SMART Editor to hyperlink to each type of change and make the changes you have decided to make across all source files. The SMART Editor is useful in finding all occurrences of a structure or function. In many cases, you might want to do this before you make a change to a field or parameter to understand its use. The SMART Editor is very valuable in making global replacements for a number of strings in all source files. The SMART Editor gives you context-sensitive access to the on-line help for the IBM development help facility.

SMART Resource Analysis and Translation

To build your complete OS/2 application after migrating the source code with SMART, you will need to also migrate your Microsoft Windows application resources to the OS/2 resources. When you migrate OS/2 16-bit source code to OS/2 32-bit code, your resources are common (for both the 16-bit and 32-bit platforms), and migration of resources is not needed.

Resource Conversion

To migrate your Microsoft Windows application resources to OS/2 resources, you use the SMART Windows-to-OS/2 Resource Conversion utility (SMARTRC.EXE). This tool gives you source-to-source conversion of Microsoft Windows resource definition files to OS/2 resource definition files.

This utility will convert the following types of statements:

ACCELERATORS	CURSOR	POPUP
AUTOCHECKSTATE	DEFPUSHBUTTON	PUSHBUTTON
AUTORADIOBUTTON	DIALOG	RADIOBUTTON
AUTO3CHECKSTATE	EDITTEXT	RCDATA
BITMAP	FONT	RTEXT
CAPTION	GROUPBOX	SCROLLBAR
CHECKBOX	ICON	SEPARATOR
CLASS	LISTBOX	STATE3
COMBOBOX	LTEXT	STRINGTABLE
CONTROL	MENU	STYLE
CTEXT	MENUITEM	USERBUTTON

The SMART Resource Conversion utility also recognizes and processes the following preprocessor directives:

- #define
- #elseif
- #else
- #endif
- #if
- #ifdef
- #ifndef
- #include
- #undef
- rcinclude

The SMART Resource Conversion utility:

- Reformats all Microsoft Windows resource definition statements to the equivalent OS/2 format
- Generates alternative accelerator key sequences
- Reformats strings contained in RCDATA to produce equivalent binary representation in the RES file
- Converts mnemonic characters
- Scales and recalculates OS/2 dialog units from Microsoft Windows dialog units
- Remaps Microsoft Windows dialog control styles to OS/2 dialog control styles
- Remaps common dialog control identifiers to equivalent OS/2 common dialog control identifiers
- Detects named resources and generates the header file to assign integer identifiers
- Provides optional dialog font mapping from Microsoft Windows font name and point size to OS/2 font name and point size
- Performs code-page conversion of text strings from the Microsoft Windows code page to the OS/2 code page

The SMART Resource Conversion utility will convert any Microsoft Windows resource with equivalent function to the OS/2 resource. It will identify all resource statements and will point out those that might result in slightly different functionality in OS/2.

The SMART Resource Translation utility is invoked through **Translate Resources** from the SMART Resource menu item. It can be run from a command line or embedded in a batch command file. When the SMART Resource Converter encounters a problem during the conversion process, it will output information, warning, or error messages. Detailed explanations of these messages are available in the help files for the SMART Editor.

The SMART Resource Converter has many run-time options. You can simply specify the resource file name without options to process your resource files with the system default parameters.

Graphical Resource Conversion

The SMART Windows-to-OS/2 Graphical Resource Conversion utility (SMARTCVT.EXE) converts your binary Microsoft Windows resources such as icon, cursor, and bit-map files to OS/2 pointer files and bit-map files, respectively. Icon and cursor files are referred to as pointer files in OS/2. The graphical format of Microsoft Windows icons and cursors is significantly different from OS/2 pointer files.

The SMARTCVT utility can be executed from SMART through the interface dialog panel associated with **Convert Graphical Resources** from the Resources menu item. It can be run from a command line or embedded in a batch command file. If the Graphical Resource Converter encounters a problem during the conversion process, it will output information, warning, or error messages.

SMART Help Conversion

To complete the automatic migration of your application to OS/2, you will need to convert your Microsoft Windows help files to OS/2 help files. You use the Windows-to-OS/2 Help Conversion Utility (SMARTHLP.EXE) to convert the files.

You can invoke the SMART Help Conversion Utility from the SMART interface, from the command line, or a command file.

You convert your Microsoft Windows help to an OS/2 .HLP file using this utility by specifying the .HPJ file, which is your Microsoft Windows help file. If you invoke the SMART Help Conversion Utility without specifying any options, SMART processes your help conversion with the default options.

The Microsoft Windows .HPJ file is not much more than a list of Rich Text Format (.RTF) files and bit-map (.BMP) files. SMARTHLP processes the .RTF files directly but calls the graphical conversion utility program, SMARTCVT, to process the .BMP files. All of these Microsoft Windows help components are then combined to make an .IPF file. The .IPF file created by SMARTHLP is passed to the IPF compiler (IPFC), which produces an OS/2 help file that can be accessed by the OS/2 Help Manager facility.

The System Object Model

As mentioned earlier in this book, OS/2 Warp Connect (PowerPC Edition) supports the IBM System Object Model (SOM). SOM on OS/2 Warp (for Intel-based systems) is SOM Version 2, a highly tuned and high-performance implementation. OS/2 Warp Connect (PowerPC Edition) contains the same advanced version of SOM as OS/2 Warp (for Intel-based systems). This means that any applications or facilities that run on OS/2 Warp (for Intel-based systems) that are SOM-based will port to the PowerPC system quite easily.

With the advent of Direct-to-SOM (DTS) compilers, writing SOM code in C++ will be made easier, and the advantages of SOM (release-to-release binary compatibility and elimination of the fragile base class problem) will be more widely available.

SOM experienced some growing pains between the first release and the version on OS/2 Warp. In particular, becoming fully CORBA-compliant meant the Object Interface Definition Language (OIDL) used by SOM initially has now been replaced by the Interface Definition Language (IDL). So, in a few words: If you have SOM code running on OS/2 Warp, it will port to OS/2 Warp Connect (PowerPC Edition) quickly and easily. Code running on older releases will need to be updated to IDL. With the appearance of DTS compilers, the issue of writing IDL becomes a moot point.

Commercial Tool Offerings

The following provides information about application development tools. This section provides information about IBM and vendor products.

VisualAge C++

The version of this product for OS/2 Warp (on Intel-based systems), the next generation of C Set++ compiler from IBM, is a good model of what the PowerPC version might contain. Of course, there is some speculation here because the PowerPC version of VisualAge C++ hasn't been announced as of this writing. However, let's look at what's in the new version for Intel-based systems:

- A new visual builder tool that enables the construction of applications from composite parts. This feature enables Rapid Application Development (RAD) in C++. The visual builder is based on the same parts construction technology as IBM's well-known VisualAge Smalltalk product—a very successful client/server RAD tool. However, rather than generating Smalltalk code, this visual builder generates C++ code built around the IBM Open Class Library.

- Enhancements to the IBM Open Class Library, including classes that directly support database access and classes designed for enhanced application support. The Open Class Library is both rich in function (containing over 400 classes and 4,000 member functions) and open in the sense of being portable across a variety of IBM and non-IBM platforms.

  Many of the classes in IBM Open Class Library have been implemented as parts that are accessible from the VisualAge C++ visual builder—making development more efficient than previously possible.

- New Direct-to-SOM binary support for the IBM System Object Model. This support enables you to write C++ classes and compile directly to SOM binaries without the need for IDL or the SOM compiler.

- Enhanced development environment, including:

  - A new live-parsing syntax highlighting editor.

  - Improved class browser, performance analyzer, and debugger.

- Support for multiple platforms, including OS/2, AIX, MVS, and Sun Solaris.

The last feature set should give you a clue as to what is possible from a PowerPC implementation of VisualAge C++. IBM has made POWER-architecture compilers available for quite a while now (on the AIX operating system). In addition, the TOBEY back-end technology, a product of IBM Toronto and IBM Research in Yorktown Heights, NY, is considered the state of the art in RISC optimizing compiler technology. In fact, the IBM research project that invented the RISC architecture simultaneously built the first RISC optimizing compilers.

Metaware High C/C++ for PowerPC

MetaWare, Inc., of Santa Cruz, California, plans to deliver their portable High C/C++ family of compilers targeting OS/2 Warp Connect (PowerPC Edition). They expect their compiler to support cross- as well as native-compilation. MetaWare offers Tool Interface Standards (TIS) compliance and delivers the compiler complete with a class library (Rogue Wave, Inc.), assembler, linker, archiver, and debugger.

MetaWare, Inc. is located at 2161 Delaware Avenue; Santa Cruz, CA 95060.

Watcom Products for OS/2 Warp Connect (PowerPC Edition)

Watcom International Corporation of Canada plans to introduce versions of their Watcom C/C++ and VX-REXX products to support OS/2 Warp Connect (PowerPC Edition).

The Watcom C/C++ development system combines a state-of-the-art compiler, with an easy-to-use, integrated development environment and toolset to enable the creation of sophisticated, multiplatform applications.

Watcom VX-REXX is a powerful visual development system for rapidly building applications that exploit the strengths of OS/2—graphical user interface, multithreading, and multiprocessing. VX-REXX is also available in a Client/Server Edition that adds powerful capabilities for connection, query, and chart accesses to a variety of database systems.

Watcom International Corporation is located at 415 Phillip Street, Waterloo, Ontario, Canada N2L 3X2.

Reference Material for Developers

The following provides information about additional books and magazines that might be of interest to OS/2 Warp Connect (PowerPC Edition) application developers:

- The OS/2 Redbooks

  IBM publishes a series of books on practical aspects of OS/2 programming in different areas. Some of the current titles include:

  - *Control Program*, #GG24-3730
  - *DOS and Windows Environment*, #GG24-3731
  - *Presentation Manager and Workplace Shell*, #GG24-3732
  - *Application Development*, #GG24-3774
  - *Printing*, #GG24-3775

- The OS/2 Technical Library

  The OS/2 Technical Library is the documentation provided by IBM to accompany the Developer's Toolkit for OS/2 Warp and, of course, it is applicable to OS/2 Warp Connect (PowerPC Edition). It contains about 17 volumes at last count and covers various areas of programming for OS/2 in great detail. However, if you would prefer the information on-line, the entire set of books (and more) is available on the CD-ROMs that accompany a subscription to The Developer Connection for OS/2. (See page 342 for more information.)

- *OS/2 Developer Magazine* - published by Miller-Freeman, Inc.

Building Development Tools

If you are a programmer who builds, as well as uses, development tools, you often need to be aware of internal details of the operating system that are not generally important to programmers who build application programs.

Issues such as the precise content of registers when processes are started, the layout of parameters in registers and storage on function calls, the responsibilities assigned to programs that call other programs versus those that are called, the definition of which architected CPU instructions can (or more importantly, cannot) be used by a valid program, the format of the data emitted by a compiler so that the linker can properly build a running program, and the format of the program emitted by the linker so that the OS/2 loader can construct an executable image in storage and allow it to execute—all these and more fall within the definition of the *OS/2 Application Binary Interface for PowerPC*. A document by this name is central to the design of OS/2 Warp Connect (PowerPC Edition) and is available with the Developer's Toolkit. In the section that follows, a few of these interfaces are described, and the reasons for the interfaces are discussed.

Standards and Binary Interfaces

Early in the design cycle, it was decided that OS/2 Warp Connect (PowerPC Edition) was going to be a system that followed open standards. To this effect, when possible, new standards were not invented when existing ones would do, and when necessary, code was changed to support existing standards or extend existing standards in a compatible and standards-conforming manner. One of the ways IBM has supported this direction was to join (as a charter member, in fact) the Tool Interface Standards (TIS) Committee—a cross-industry committee of systems, tools, and application vendors whose goal is to agree on standards whose adoption would aid the industry as a whole.

The Tool Interface Standards Committee

The TIS Committee's membership quickly established as its first goals selecting a portable object format and executable format. After a series of debates, the committee selected ELF (Executable and Linkable Format) as the answer to both questions. The *object format* defines the general structure of objects generated by compilers and acted upon by linkers. The *executable format* defines the structure of objects that can be taken in by a linker or loaded for execution by the system's loader. There is some benefit that accrues by having the same format for objects and executables, but there is more benefit to having a standard format, because now there is a reasonable expectation that an application programmer can mix and match development tools to create the most efficient development environment for the task at hand.

The OS/2 Application Binary Interface for the PowerPC uses ELF for these purposes and defines some OS/2-specific and PowerPC-specific information for ELF objects and executables.

The Application Binary Interface

In addition to the object and executable formats, the Application Binary Interface also defines some critical behaviors that all programs must be aware of. For example:

There are 32 general-purpose registers in the PowerPC register file (each 32-bits wide), and there are 32 floating-point registers (each 64-bits wide). According to the PowerPC architecture, these general-purpose registers are truly general purpose and can be used freely by the application programs. However, the system can be made to operate much more efficiently if there are standard ways of dealing with some of the general purpose registers in a system-wide manner. Toward this end, the Application Binary Interface defines the general-purpose registers as shown in Figure 16-8.

Register Usage

Register	Purpose
r1	Stack frame pointer
r2	Thread Information Block pointer
r3 - r10	Parameter passing and return values
r14 - r31	Non-volatile
r0, r11 - r13	Volatile
f1 - f8	Parameter passing and return values
f14 - f31	Non-volatile
f0, f9 - f13	Volatile

Figure 16-8. General Purpose Registers

This definition thus creates a "standard" for the way each program must behave within the system. Besides creating a standard interface between called and calling programs, the ABI enforces the most efficient modes of operation for all programs.

If you are interested in learning more, start by reading the *OS/2 Application Binary Interface for PowerPC* document that is included in the Developer's Toolkit.

Frequently Asked Questions

What Happened to the Workplace?

In the beginning, IBM called this product the Workplace or Workplace OS. Then at the end of last year, IBM no longer referred to it as such. What happened to the Workplace?

Workplace was originally used as a code name to describe a family of technologies that IBM is incorporating into all of its operating system products. Workplace OS was used to refer to the operating system based on the IBM Microkernel architecture. This operating system is now called OS/2 Warp Connect (PowerPC Edition).

The Workplace architecture really began with OS/2 2.0. The Workplace Shell, an award-winning, object-oriented user interface, was the first deliverable of that architecture. The microkernel-based version of OS/2 Warp Connect extends this object-oriented paradigm to the very heart of the operating system, the kernel.

IBM abandoned the name Workplace but did *not* abandon the technologies or products. The name Workplace was confusing to our customers. Many people thought Workplace was a replacement for OS/2 Warp. This notion had some heavy implications for them: a different software base that might make the OS/2 applications they were currently developing obsolete before the applications were finished and in the marketplace.

It was much simpler to explain that the Workplace OS is just OS/2, except that it runs on the PowerPC instead of Intel-based computers. It was also important to make it clear that applications currently running on or being developed for OS/2 Warp on Intel-based systems are only a compile away from running on the PowerPC version.

Why Name the Product OS/2 Warp Connect (PowerPC Edition)?

There's a lot of confusion over OS/2 Warp, OS/2 Warp Connect, OS/2 for the PowerPC, and OS/2 Warp Connect (PowerPC Edition). What's the difference?

OS/2 Warp is a desktop operating system and the flagship of the OS/2 family of products. It runs OS/2, DOS, and Windows applications at the same time, with as little as 4MB of memory. For Windows users, it comes in two flavors: one uses the Microsoft Windows software you already have installed on your system; the other provides Windows application support (via WIN-OS/2) when you do not have Windows software already installed. OS/2 Crash Protection means that a problem with one application does not affect other applications running on your Desktop. OS/2 Warp has a high-performance, 32-bit application programming interface (API), as well as an object-oriented user interface (the Workplace Shell). And finally, OS/2 Warp comes with a BonusPak, productivity and online connection software that includes:

- IBM Works
- FaxWorks
- IBM Person to Person
- IBM Internet Connection, with IBM Gopher and IBM WebExplorer
- Multimedia tools such as Video IN and Multimedia Viewer

OS/2 Warp Connect is a client operating system for Intel-based computers that, together with OS/2 LAN Server 4.0, offers a complete connectivity solution for today's client/server environments in small businesses, workgroups, and large enterprises. OS/2 Warp Connect has all the advantages and features of OS/2 Warp: the same high-performance 32-bit API, multitasking with Crash Protection, the Workplace Shell user interface, and integrated productivity applications (the BonusPak).

It also provides programs you need to communicate and share resources with co-workers on a LAN, including:

- IBM Peer for OS/2, for peer networking without a dedicated server
- LAN Server Requester, NetWare Client for OS/2, LAN Distance Remote for OS/2, and Network SignON Coordinator, for networking with a dedicated server
- TCP/IP for OS/2, for network communications and Internet connectivity
- Lotus Notes Express, for collaborative computing

OS/2 for the PowerPC is the name IBM applied to the Workplace OS product from the Fall of 1994 through the early Summer of 1995 when it was officially named OS/2 Warp Connect (PowerPC Edition).

OS/2 Warp Connect (PowerPC Edition) is IBM's "super" client operating system for PowerPC computers. Like OS/2 Warp Connect for Intel-based computers, it has the look and feel of the Workplace Shell and preserves the heritage of applications that run on OS/2. But because of the PowerPC microprocessor, it can handle a new range of applications that allow users to work freely, intuitively, conversationally, and co-operatively. OS/2 Warp Connect (PowerPC Edition) has network and connectivity features similar to its counterpart for Intel-based systems. Because it has a microkernel-based architecture, it is open, extendable, and highly flexible. It is, for example, designed to use a variety of networking protocols to connect to multivendor network servers. This means that you can choose the best products for your business from different vendors.

Why PowerPC?

Why put OS/2 Warp Connect on PowerPC computers?

PowerPC-based systems are the first marriage between the RISC and PC worlds. Until now, RISC has represented powerful performance and industrial-strength applications typically associated with workstations. RISC, which stands for reduced instruction-set computing, is a technology invented by IBM, as was the POWER Architecture. Together with Motorola and Apple, IBM developed the PowerPC microprocessor, which makes workstation power affordable on the desktop.

PowerPC computers offer next-generation performance for demanding client/server environments. PowerPC chips provide the processing power to deliver a new breed of applications without sacrificing performance:

- Intelligent user interfaces that make use of speech recognition, multimedia, and so on.

- High-end workstation applications such as engineering and scientific modeling, simulation, imaging, and Computer-Aided Design/Computer-Aided Manufacturing (CAD/CAM).

- Communication applications that create online, collaborative business environments.

Therefore, OS/2 Warp Connect running on PowerPC computers greatly broadens the scope of the OS/2 family.

Why the IBM Microkernel?

Wouldn't it have been easier to just port OS/2 for Intel-based systems to the PowerPC?

OS/2 for Intel-based systems is heavily customized for the Intel architecture. It would certainly have been possible to port it to PowerPC computers. However, IBM decided to make OS/2 Warp truly portable to today's PowerPC computers, as well as to tomorrow's new computers. The new microkernel-based architecture is the best way to achieve this. In the future, IBM can easily and quickly port OS/2 to new hardware platforms by rebuilding only those relatively small, hardware-specific portions of the OS/2 Operating System Services and the IBM Microkernel.

What are the benefits of microkernel-based architecture?

The microkernel-based architecture is:

- *Scalable*, from embedded systems to clients to servers, such that users can access applications across multiple classes of systems

- *Modular,* such that individual components can be easily upgraded or replaced without affecting other components of the system
- *Portable* to future platforms while preserving hardware and software investments
- *Client/Server,* allowing applications to be easily distributed across multiple platforms
- *Open* and fully licensable, both in binary form for use on supported hardware platforms and in source form for porting to new hardware platforms

What Applications Run on OS/2 Warp Connect (PowerPC Edition)?

Do applications written for OS/2 Warp (for Intel-based systems) run on OS/2 Warp Connect (PowerPC Edition)? What about DOS and Windows applications?

OS/2 Warp Connect (PowerPC Edition) best exploits the capabilities of the PowerPC processor when applications run in native mode (that is, are pure 32-bit). Pure 32-bit OS/2 applications are source portable to PowerPC OS/2 systems (that is, they need only be recompiled). Mixed 16-bit and 32-bit OS/2 applications can be easily made pure 32-bit applications that can be recompiled for OS/2 Warp Connect (PowerPC Edition).

DOS and Windows 3.x applications, with the exception of specialized DOS applications that are device-dependent, run unaltered on OS/2 Warp Connect (PowerPC Edition). This is accomplished via an Instruction Set Translator (IST) that, using the WIN-OS/2 technology, dynamically translates a DOS or Windows application into the Intel instructions for DOS or Windows applications into PowerPC instructions.

How are 16-bit and mixed 16-bit and 32-bit applications made pure 32-bit applications that can be recompiled for the PowerPC?

New migration and development tools, such as One-Up Corporation's SMART (Source Migration Analysis Reporting Toolset), are available to assist with the conversion of 16-bit code to OS/2 32-bit code. Once 16-bit OS/2 or Windows code is converted to OS/2 32-bit code, the source code can be recompiled for either the Intel or PowerPC versions of OS/2 Warp.

Conversely, one of the cornerstones of the architecture for OS/2 Warp Connect (PowerPC Edition) is API compatibility with OS/2 Warp for Intel-based systems. API compatibility libraries make new applications developed with 32-bit API for OS/2 Warp Connect (PowerPC Edition) source-code-compatible with versions of OS/2 Warp for Intel-based systems. This means that new applications developed for OS/2 Warp Connect (PowerPC Edition) are also a compile away from running on those versions of OS/2 Warp.

What about Device Drivers?

Do existing OS/2 Warp device drivers work on OS/2 Warp Connect (PowerPC Edition)?

Presentation Manager (PM) printer drivers are source-compatible between the x86 OS/2 Warp family and OS/2 Warp Connect (PowerPC Edition).

IBM has re-architected the graphics subsystem and provided a new graphics display driver model for OS/2 Warp Connect (PowerPC Edition) to make the job of writing PM graphics display drivers significantly easier. This new, layered model requires only about 5000-8000 lines of device-specific code for a device, making driver development and distribution a far simpler task for third-party OEMs. And, the new-model device drivers will be portable to a later release of OS/2 Warp.

For base device drivers (SCSI, CD-ROM, Multimedia, and so on), the 16-bit ADD model for OS/2 today has proven to be a very flexible approach, and third-party OEMs have readily adapted it for their own devices. IBM is building a new, fully 32-bit device driver model for OS/2 Warp Connect (PowerPC Edition). This new model, based on device driver frameworks, will provide even more flexibility than the current 16-bit OS/2 model. It is our intent to allow these new 32-bit device drivers to run on later releases of OS/2 Warp.

What are the benefits of a device driver framework?

A device driver framework provides a significant reduction in the amount of code that device driver writers need to create. It also offers a rich set of system services (for example, configuration management). Because device drivers will be easier to write, more drivers will be available, and they will be available more rapidly and at lower cost, giving end users more device drivers and hardware options.

What about Shared Services?

When do I write an application as a shared service?

Shared services are generally equivalent to what you commonly know as subsystems. They typically have no user interface. These services include database engines, file systems, and device drivers. Shared services provide system functions that can be used by other shared services, as well as multiple operating system services. Because of the new microkernel-based architecture of OS/2 Warp Connect (PowerPC Edition), shared services can be updated or replaced and new shared services can be added to the operating system without disrupting the system.

Shared services typically consist of two parts: a client library and a services task (server). A client library consists of the programming interface for client tasks that want to use the service. Client libraries are typically written as sets of shared (DLL) code that are linked into the client task address space. The service task contains the worker routines, that is, the code that actually performs the service that has been requested. The service task executes within its own address space, separated from the client task that requests the service. The client library, on behalf of the client task, communicates with the server task through the IBM Microkernel Interprocess Communication (IPC) or Remote Procedure Call (RPC) facilities.

What about the Performance of OS/2 Warp Connect (PowerPC Edition)?

What kind of performance improvements can be expected in applications recompiled for the PowerPC?

The PowerPC chip is built for performance. The scalar performance rivals that of Intel's Pentium chip, and the floating-point performance far exceeds the Pentium's performance. Consequently, native 32-bit applications should perform better on a PowerPC processor than on an Intel processor. On the PowerPC, CPU instructions run equal to or better than on a Pentium due to the chip's processing elements. The video runs much faster, as do floating-point instructions. Applications that perform a high percentage of floating-point calculations and are video-intensive, such as CAD/CAM applications, will show significant performance improvements. Also, applications based on interprocess communication (IPC), such as client/server applications, will run faster.

What about the Size of OS/2 Warp Connect (PowerPC Edition)?

How much memory will I need to run OS/2 Warp Connect (PowerPC Edition)?

Because RISC code is inherently larger than x86 code, it is not reasonable to compare the memory and DASD resource requirements for the PowerPC with that of an x86-architected system. Compared to a RISC-based system running a UNIX-type operating system, OS/2 Warp Connect (PowerPC Edition) has much lower hardware requirements for similar RISC benefits. The actual amount of RAM required for good performance will be different in each installation and will be determined by the suite of applications that the customer wants to run.

So Why Should I Want OS/2 Warp Connect (PowerPC Edition)?

How large is the application base for OS/2 Warp Connect (PowerPC Edition)?

OS/2 Warp Connect (PowerPC Edition), supporting the OS/2 Warp heritage, will be translated into 22 languages. It will be available as a preload offering on the IBM Power Series systems. It will also be available as a shrink-wrapped product. The OS/2 Warp heritage includes more than 2500 native OS/2 applications that are a compile away from running on the PowerPC Edition, as well as the large volume of existing x86 DOS and Windows 3.x applications. In addition to this heritage, a full range of applications is being developed by other software vendors, as well as by IBM. These applications include:

- Networking products
- System management tools
- Data management products
- Workgroup products
- Development tools
- Human-centered applications

What are the compelling reasons to buy OS/2 Warp Connect (PowerPC Edition)?

OS/2 Warp Connect (PowerPC Edition) is the world's *best* PC super-client operating system on the hottest new platform in the industry.

The PowerPC microprocessor currently represents the most exciting, fastest growing platform in the industry today. PowerPC systems support two classes of operating systems: PC operating systems and workstation operating systems. Not only is OS/2 Warp the highest volume 32-bit PC operating system today, it is the only PC operating system being offered on the PowerPC platform. The remaining alternatives, AIX, Windows NT Workstation, and Solaris, are all workstation operating systems. Finally, the connectivity elements of OS/2 Warp Connect and the new range of applications made possible by the PowerPC microprocessor make OS/2 Warp Connect (PowerPC Edition) a super PC client operating system. OS/2 Warp Connect is *the* solution for PC users moving to the PowerPC platform.

OS/2 Warp Connect (PowerPC Edition) is *the* foundation for next-generation software being developed today.

Today there is a demand for a whole new breed of applications—applications that perform much more complex tasks than the applications many people use today. Development and deployment of these new applications require systems that offer more complex services and capabilities than the operating systems commonly used in the past. OS/2 Warp Connect (PowerPC Edition) combines the benefits of OS/2 Warp with a new foundation that allows development of these applications to begin today.

OS/2 Warp Connect (PowerPC Edition) *protects* your hardware and software investment.

Companies and consumers alike have made, and will continue to make, significant investments in both software and training. OS/2 Warp Connect (PowerPC Edition) continues IBM's long-standing commitment to protecting these investments. IBM has shown many times that it understands the importance of heritage. An investment in OS/2 Warp Connect (PowerPC Edition) is an investment that, today and in the future, you can count on.

How Does OS/2 Warp Connect (PowerPC Edition) Stack Up against Its Competition, Windows NT?

- User Interfaces
  - Windows NT: The Windows NT user interface is a multi-threaded version of the Windows 3.x GUI. It does not yet include the new object-oriented Explorer interface for Windows 95.

- OS/2 Warp Connect (PowerPC Edition): The OS/2 Warp object-oriented Desktop (the Workplace Shell) provides a single, consistent user interface across the entire family of products.

- Object Technology
  - Windows NT: Microsoft's object technology, including OLE and COM, is object-based (supporting encapsulation but not inheritance or polymorphism) rather than object-oriented, and it is based on a proprietary architecture. (COM uses the industry-standard CORBA as a transport only.)
  - OS/2 Warp Connect (PowerPC Edition): IBM's System Object Model (SOM) is both object-oriented and CORBA-compliant.

- Connectivity
  - Windows NT: Windows NT 3.5 Workstation ships with a NetWare client that connects to a NetWare LAN.
  - OS/2 Warp Connect (PowerPC Edition): IBM's support of open standards is reflected in its any-client-to-any-server strategy. Built-in LAN requesters seamlessly link desktop systems to each other and to all major network operating systems, including OS/2 LAN Server, Novell NetWare, NT Server, Lotus Notes, and a variety of Internet servers.

- Application Programming Interfaces
  - Windows NT: Multiple sets of APIs (Win16, Win32, Win32s, and Win32c) are inconsistent across the various Windows products.
  - OS/2 Warp Connect (PowerPC Edition): A single 32-bit OS/2 API set across the entire OS/2 Warp family provides significant advantages to application developers.

- Symmetrical Multiprocessor (SMP) support
  - Windows NT: NT SMP support is designed to support 32 processors but is not designed to dynamically assign processes to the available processors. Users assign processes to specific processors.

  - OS/2 Warp Connect (PowerPC Edition): OS/2 Warp SMP is designed to support 1024 processors and dynamically assign processes to available processors for maximum efficiency.

- Application Compatibility
  - Windows NT: Windows NT 3.5 is not compatible with existing DOS TSR programs and device drivers and relies on emulation to support Windows 3.x 16-bit applications.
  - OS/2 Warp Connect (PowerPC Edition): OS/2 Warp's backward compatibility is designed to protect your current investment in DOS and Windows 16-bit applications, while not relying on emulation.

Where Can I Get More Information?

The best place to look for the latest and greatest information on OS/2 Warp Connect (PowerPC Edition) is on the World Wide Web:

- The IBM Home Page:

  http://www.ibm.com

- The Developer Connection Home Page:

  http://www.austin.ibm.com/developer/programs/DevCon.html

- Solution Developer Operations Home Page:

  http://www.austin.ibm.com/developer

Creating Applications for the World

This appendix describes National Language Support and the considerations for writing applications for a worldwide audience.

There are three major aspects to National Language Support (NLS):

- Keyboard input and displayed or printed output of information
- Country-specific, or national conventions for currency, date and time, and data manipulation
- Information that is integrated into an operating system and its applications (also known as machine readable information, or MRI)

A fourth aspect, linguistic support, is emerging with new technologies for speech recognition and speech synthesis.

The first two aspects of NLS center around sets of characters and how they are manipulated. This functionality has been provided and, historically, has been limited by code within an application or the operating system. Keyboard layouts and fonts that provide a system's input and output mechanisms are based on *code pages* that map sets of characters to unique single-byte numbers. These are referred to as single-byte character sets (SBCS). There is at least one code page for each national language, and there are special-purpose code pages that include special-purpose characters. Code pages are set via the CODEPAGE statement in CONFIG.SYS or the CHCP command.

Code pages support only 256 characters at a time. This character limit is sufficient for languages such as English, French, Spanish, and German. However, it is not sufficient for languages such as Japanese, Chinese, and Korean that have thousands of characters. Double-byte character sets (DBCS), where each character is represented as two bytes, provide a code-page solution for these languages. But DBCS code pages require DBCS-enablement of the code that manipulates the information. This requirement means that the code for SBCS and DBCS-enabled applications and operating systems are different.

As global computer networks expand and become more distributed, multilingual and multinational support will take on a much larger meaning. Programs written today in one country often fail to work correctly when run in another country because of character-set or code-page differences. This results in different versions of programs for different countries and different languages. But what happens when a French customer and a Chinese customer try to run (share) the same program distributed over the network to which they are both attached? The French customer will want to see the French version; the Chinese customer will want to see the Chinese version. Different language versions of the same code will no longer make sense if they are to truly share code and data (which is the purpose of distributed networks).

The solution lies in *internationalized* applications and operating systems. These are written so that text data is manipulated in a language-neutral manner. In other words, we need to remove all the code-page information from our code.

For IBM's microkernel-based operating systems, the solution is based on the XPG notion of *locales*, the Universal Character Set, or Unicode, and the Universal Language Support (ULS) API functions.

A locale is a collection of modules and data that define country-specific and cultural preferences for units of money, date and time formatting, numeric systems, file I/O and code-page conversions, MRI handling, language-sensitive string handling, and so on. Unicode is an ISO-standard, large character set containing 16-bit representations for all of the world's publishable characters (256x256 bytes). The ULS API provides the means by which internationalized applications manipulate and handle Unicode data.

ULS functions are provided with the Developer's Toolkit so that new applications written for the operating system can be internationalized. Over time, the OS/2 Warp Connect (PowerPC Edition) operating system itself will be fully internationalized.

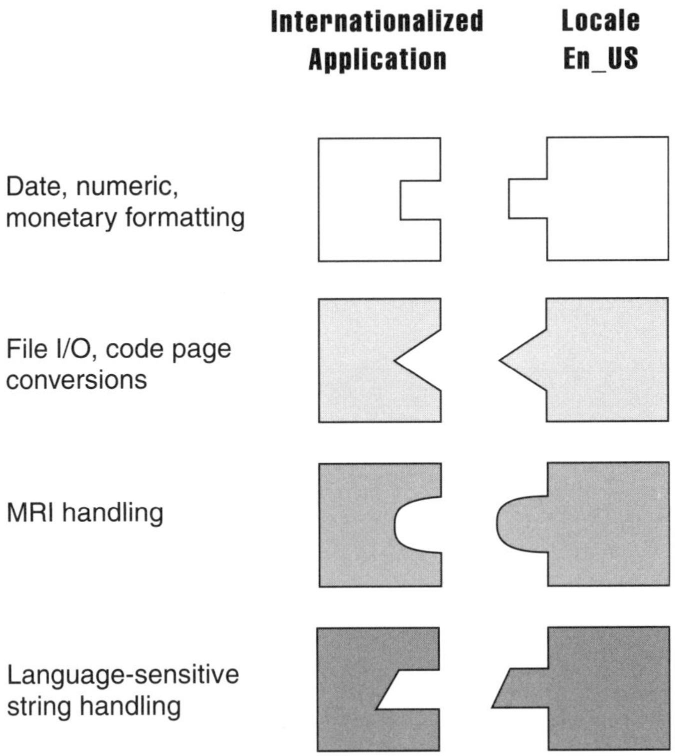

Figure B-1. Relationship between an Internationalized Application and a Locale

Examples of Workplace Shell Objects

In this appendix, two examples of objects will be presented, along with a discussion of what methods are being overridden, and why. The examples are intended to be fairly simplistic, in order that the complexity of the example not hinder understanding.

We are going to create two classes of objects. The first class will be a LedgerEntry class. It will represent entries into a ledger book. This class will be descended from WPDataFile. Note that using a data file for a ledger might be a little heavy, but it will allow us to demonstrate much of the programming detail desired.

The second class will be Ledger. It will be descended from WPFolder and will represent a ledger book. Its default view will be Details, and it will present the details of a ledger entry.

Interface Definition List for the Two Classes

We will begin by looking at the Interface Definition List (IDL) file for the ledger entry class.

```
#ifndef LedgerEntry_idl
#define LedgerEntry_idl

#include <wpdataf.idl>
#include <somcls.idl>

interface M_LedgerEntry;
interface LedgerEntry : WPDataFile

{
   implementation
   {
      externalstem = ldge;
      local;
      externalprefix = ldge_;
      majorversion = 1;
      minorversion = 2;
      filestem = ledgere;
      metaclass = M_LedgerEntry;
      callstyle = oidl;
      dllname = "ledgere.dll";

      ULONG  ulDebit;
      ULONG  ulCredit;
      PSZ    pszDescription;
      CDATE  cDate;

      somDefaultInit: override;
      somDestruct: override;
      wpOpen: override;
      wpPrintObject: override;
      wpQueryDetailsData: override;
      wpRestoreState: override;
      wpSaveState: override;
      wpSetupOnce: override;
   };
};
```

```
interface M_LedgerEntry: M_WPDataFile
{
   implementation
   {
      externalstem = ldge;
      local;
      externalprefix = ldgeM_;
      majorversion = 1;
      minorversion = 2;
      filestem = ledgere;
      callstyle = oidl;
      dllname = "ledgere.dll";

      wpclsCreateDefaultTemplates: override;
      wpclsInitData: override;
      wpclsQueryDefaultHelp: override;
      wpclsQueryDefaultView: override;
      wpclsQueryDetailsInfo: override;
      wpclsQueryIconData: override;
      wpclsQueryInstanceFilter: override;
      wpclsQueryInstanceType: override;
      wpclsQueryTitle: override;
   };
};
#endif
```

Next, we will examine the IDL file for the ledger class.

```
#ifndef LedgerFolder_idl
#define LedgerFolder_idl

#include <wpfolder.idl>
#include <somcls.idl>

interface M_LedgerFolder;

interface LedgerFolder : WPFolder
{
   implementation
   {
      externalstem = ldgf;
      local;
      externalprefix = ldgf_;
      majorversion = 1;
      minorversion = 2;
```

```
        filestem = ledgerf;
        metaclass = M_LedgerFolder;
        callstyle = oidl;
        dllname = "ledgerf.dll";

        somDefaultInit: override;
        somDestruct: override;
        wpDragOver: override;
        wpOpen: override;
        wpPrintObject: override;
        wpSetupOnce: override;
    };
};

interface M_LedgerFolder: M_WPFolder

{
    implementation
    {
        externalstem = ldgf;
        local;
        externalprefix = ldgfM_;
        majorversion = 1;
        minorversion = 2;
        filestem = ledgerf;
        callstyle = oidl;
        dllname = "ledgerf.dll";

        wpclsCreateDefaultTemplates: override;
        wpclsQueryDefaultHelp: override;
        wpclsQueryDefaultView: override;
        wpclsQueryIconData: override;
        wpclsQueryInstanceFilter: override;
        wpclsQueryInstanceType: override;
        wpclsQueryTitle: override;
    };
};
#endif
```

Rationale for IDL

Next, we will examine each of the methods and method overrides defined for each class and the rationale for overriding or providing each method.

Instance methods for the ledger entry:

- wpSetupOnce

  The wpSetType method is called to specify the .TYPE extended attribute.

- wpFormatDragItem

  We modify the rendering format to indicate that it is <DRM_OS2FILE,DRF_LEDGER>

- somDefaultInit
- somDestruct
- wpCopiedFromTemplate

  This method is invoked to put up a dialog asking for the initial information for this ledger entry. Now, good ledgers do not allow deletion or modification of ledger entries. If you make a mistake, you make a new ledger entry to correct the mistake. The dialog is put up as a non-modal dialog and is passed the object's pointer when it is created.

- wpSaveState
- wpRestoreState

Class methods for the ledger entry:

- wpclsQueryInstanceType
- wpclsInitData
- wpclsQueryTitle
- wpclsQueryDefaultHelp

- wpclsQueryIconData
- wpclsQueryDetails
- wpclsQueryDetailsInfo
- wpclsQueryDetailsData
- wpclsCreateDefaultTemplates

Instance methods for the ledger:

- wpDragOver
- wpDrop
- wpSetupOnce

  Here, we specify that the details class to be displayed is the ledger entry details class and that the normal file system details are not visible.

  - wpSetFldrDetailsClass
  - wpSetDetailsColumnVisibility

- wpAddSettingsPage

Class methods for the ledger:

- wpclsInitData
- wpclsQueryDefaultView

  Here, we specify that the Details view is the default view.

- wpclsQueryTitle

  Here, we specify that the default ledger name is "Ledger."

- wpclsQueryDefaultHelp

- wpclsQueryIconData
- wpclsCreateDefaultTemplates

Class Implementation

The following example is the code for the ledger entry class:

```
/*
 *  This file was generated by the SOM Compiler and Emitter Framework.
 *   Generated using:
 *      SOM Emitter emitctm: 2.42
 */

#ifndef SOM_Module_ledgere_Source
#define SOM_Module_ledgere_Source
#endif
#define LedgerEntry_Class_Source
#define M_LedgerEntry_Class_Source
#define INCL_PM

#include <os2.h>
#include <som.h>
#include "ledgere.ih"
#include "ledgered.h"

/* Our module handle is stored as a global, given to us for free
 * by the system when our dll is loaded...
 */

HMODULE vhmod = NULLHANDLE;

/* NUM_DETAILS_COLUMNS is the number of variables defined in the
 * ENTRY_DETAILS structure just below
 */

#define NUM_DETAILS_COLUMNS 4

typedef struct {
   CDATE  cDate;
   PSZ    pszDescription;
   ULONG  ulCredit;
   ULONG  ulDebit;
   } ENTRY_DETAILS;
```

```
CLASSFIELDINFO MyColumnDescriptions NUM_DETAILS_COLUMNS;

MPARAM EXPENTRY EntryDlgProc(HWND hwnd,ULONG msg,MPARAM mp1, MPARAM mp2);

SOM_Scope void SOMLINK ldge_somDefaultInit(LedgerEntry *somSelf,
                                           somInitCtrl* ctrl)
{
    LedgerEntryData *somThis; /* set in BeginInitializer */
    somInitCtrl globalCtrl;
    somBooleanVector myMask;
    LedgerEntryMethodDebug("LedgerEntry","somDefaultInit");

    LedgerEntry_BeginInitializer_somDefaultInit;

    LedgerEntry_Init_WPDataFile_somDefaultInit(somSelf, ctrl);

    /*
     * local LedgerEntry initialization code added by programmer
     */
}

SOM_Scope void SOMLINK ldge_somDestruct(LedgerEntry *somSelf,octet
                                  doFree, somDestructCtrl* ctrl)
{
    LedgerEntryData *somThis; /* set in BeginDestructor */
    somDestructCtrl globalCtrl;
    somBooleanVector myMask;
    LedgerEntryMethodDebug("LedgerEntry","ldge_somDestruct");
    LedgerEntry_BeginDestructor;

    /*
     * local LedgerEntry deinitialization code added by programmer
     */

    LedgerEntry_EndDestructor;
}

SOM_Scope HWND  SOMLINK ldge_wpOpen(LedgerEntry *somSelf, HWND hwndCnr,
                                  ULONG ulView, ULONG param)
{
    HWND hwndFrame;

    /* LedgerEntryData *somThis = LedgerEntryGetData(somSelf); */

    LedgerEntryMethodDebug("LedgerEntry","ldge_wpOpen");
```

```
    if (ulView == IDD_LEDGERENTRY)
    {
       hwndFrame = WinLoadDlg(HWND_DESKTOP, HWND_DESKTOP, EntryDlgProc,
                              vhmod,IDD_LEDGERENTRY,somSelf);
    }
    else
    {
       hwndFrame = LedgerEntry_parent_WPDataFile_wpOpen(somSelf,
                                        hwndCnr, ulView, param);
    }
    return hwndFrame;
}

SOM_Scope BOOL  SOMLINK ldge_wpPrintObject(LedgerEntry *somSelf,
                        PPRINTDEST pPrintDest, ULONG ulReserved)
{
    /* LedgerEntryData *somThis = LedgerEntryGetData(somSelf); */

    LedgerEntryMethodDebug("LedgerEntry","ldge_wpPrintObject");

    return (LedgerEntry_parent_WPDataFile_wpPrintObject(somSelf,
            pPrintDest, ulReserved));
}

SOM_Scope ULONG  SOMLINK ldge_wpQueryDetailsData(LedgerEntry *somSelf,
                                PVOID* ppDetailsData, PULONG pcp)
{
    ENTRY_DETAILS *pDetails;

    LedgerEntryData *somThis = LedgerEntryGetData(somSelf);

    LedgerEntryMethodDebug("LedgerEntry","ldge_wpQueryDetailsData");
    LedgerEntry_parent_WPDataFile_wpQueryDetailsData(somSelf,
                                        ppDetailsData, pcp);
    if (ppDetailsData)
    {
       pDetails = (ENTRY_DETAILS *)*ppDetailsData;
       pDetails->cDate.day = _cDate.day;
       pDetails->cDate.month = _cDate.month;
       pDetails->cDate.year = _cDate.year;
       pDetails->ulDebit = _ulDebit;
       pDetails->ulCredit = _ulCredit;
       pDetails->pszDescription = _pszDescription;
    }
    *pcp += sizeof(ENTRY_DETAILS);
    return (TRUE);
```

```
}

SOM_Scope BOOL  SOMLINK ldge_wpRestoreState(LedgerEntry *somSelf,
                                              ULONG ulReserved)
{
    DATETIME DateTime;

    LedgerEntryData *somThis = LedgerEntryGetData(somSelf);
    LedgerEntryMethodDebug("LedgerEntry","ldge_wpRestoreState");

    _ulDebit = 10;
    _ulCredit = 20;
    DosGetDateTime(&DateTime);
    _cDate.day = DateTime.day;
    _cDate.month = DateTime.month;
    _cDate.year = DateTime.year;
    _pszDescription = "Testing, testing, testing...";

    return (LedgerEntry_parent_WPDataFile_wpRestoreState(somSelf,
             ulReserved));
}

SOM_Scope BOOL  SOMLINK ldge_wpSaveState(LedgerEntry *somSelf)
{
    LedgerEntryData *somThis = LedgerEntryGetData(somSelf);
    LedgerEntryMethodDebug("LedgerEntry","ldge_wpSaveState");
    return (LedgerEntry_parent_WPDataFile_wpSaveState(somSelf));
}

SOM_Scope BOOL  SOMLINK ldge_wpSetupOnce(LedgerEntry *somSelf,
                                           PSZ pszSetupString)
{
    /* LedgerEntryData *somThis = LedgerEntryGetData(somSelf); */
    LedgerEntryMethodDebug("LedgerEntry","ldge_wpSetupOnce");

    return (LedgerEntry_parent_WPDataFile_wpSetupOnce(somSelf,
             pszSetupString));
}

SOM_Scope BOOL  SOMLINK ldgeM_wpclsCreateDefaultTemplates(M_LedgerEntry
                                    *somSelf, WPObject* Folder)
{
    /* M_LedgerEntryData *somThis = M_LedgerEntryGetData(somSelf); */
      M_LedgerEntryMethodDebug("M_LedgerEntry",
                              "ldgeM_wpclsCreateDefaultTemplates");
#ifdef LATER
```

```
    /* Let us create our template, and give it an objectid so that we
     * can find our template at a later date...
     */

     _wpclsNew(somSelf,
               NULL,
               "TEMPLATE=YES;OBJECTID=<LEDGERE_TEMPLATE>",
               Folder,
               TRUE);
#endif

     return TRUE;
}

SOM_Scope void  SOMLINK ldgeM_wpclsInitData(M_LedgerEntry *somSelf)
{
    /*  M_LedgerEntryData *somThis = M_LedgerEntryGetData(somSelf);*/

        M_LedgerEntryMethodDebug("M_LedgerEntry","ldgeM_wpclsInitData");

        M_LedgerEntry_parent_M_WPDataFile_wpclsInitData(somSelf);

    /*  Set up our column descriptions for the wpclsQueryDetailsInfo
        method */

    memset((PBYTE)&MyColumnDescriptions,0,sizeof(MyColumnDescriptions));
    MyColumnDescriptions[0].cb = sizeof(CLASSFIELDINFO);
    MyColumnDescriptions[0].flData = CFA_DATE | CFA_RIGHT | CFA_SEPARATOR;
    MyColumnDescriptions[0].flTitle = CFA_STRING | CFA_CENTER |
              CFA_FITITLEREADONLY;
    MyColumnDescriptions[0].pTitleData = "Date";
    MyColumnDescriptions[0].pNextFieldInfo = &MyColumnDescriptions[1];
    MyColumnDescriptions[0].offFieldData = 0;
    MyColumnDescriptions[0].ulLenFieldData = sizeof(CDATE);
    MyColumnDescriptions[0].flCompare = COMPARE_SUPPORTED | SORTBY_SUPPORTED;
    MyColumnDescriptions[1].cb = sizeof(CLASSFIELDINFO);
    MyColumnDescriptions[1].flData = CFA_STRING | CFA_RIGHT | CFA_FIREADONLY
              |CFA_SEPARATOR;
    MyColumnDescriptions[1].flTitle = CFA_STRING | CFA_CENTER |
              CFA_FITITLEREADONLY;
    MyColumnDescriptions[1].pTitleData = "Description";
    MyColumnDescriptions[1].pNextFieldInfo = &MyColumnDescriptions[2];
    MyColumnDescriptions[1].offFieldData = 4;
    MyColumnDescriptions[1].ulLenFieldData = sizeof(PSZ);
    MyColumnDescriptions[1].flCompare = COMPARE_SUPPORTED |SORTBY_SUPPORTED;
    MyColumnDescriptions[2].cb = sizeof(CLASSFIELDINFO);
```

```
    MyColumnDescriptions[2].flData = CFA_ULONG | CFA_RIGHT | CFA_SEPARATOR;
    MyColumnDescriptions[2].flTitle = CFA_STRING | CFA_CENTER |
            CFA_FITITLEREADONLY;
    MyColumnDescriptions[2].pTitleData = "Debit";
    MyColumnDescriptions[2].pNextFieldInfo = &MyColumnDescriptions[3];
    MyColumnDescriptions[2].offFieldData = 8;
    MyColumnDescriptions[2].ulLenFieldData = sizeof(ULONG);
    MyColumnDescriptions[2].flCompare = COMPARE_SUPPORTED | SORTBY_SUPPORTED;
    MyColumnDescriptions[3].cb = sizeof(CLASSFIELDINFO);
    MyColumnDescriptions[3].flData = CFA_ULONG | CFA_RIGHT | CFA_SEPARATOR;
    MyColumnDescriptions[3].flTitle = CFA_STRING | CFA_CENTER |
            CFA_FITITLEREADONLY;
    MyColumnDescriptions[3].pTitleData = "Credit";
    MyColumnDescriptions[3].pNextFieldInfo = NULL;
    MyColumnDescriptions[3].offFieldData = 12;
    MyColumnDescriptions[3].ulLenFieldData = sizeof(ULONG);
    MyColumnDescriptions[3].flCompare = COMPARE_SUPPORTED | SORTBY_SUPPORTED;
}

SOM_Scope BOOL  SOMLINK ldgeM_wpclsQueryDefaultHelp(M_LedgerEntry
         *somSelf, PULONG pHelpPanelId, PSZ pszHelpLibrary)
{
    /* M_LedgerEntryData *somThis = M_LedgerEntryGetData(somSelf);*/
    M_LedgerEntryMethodDebug("M_LedgerEntry",
                             "ldgeM_wpclsQueryDefaultHelp");
    return (M_LedgerEntry_parent_M_WPDataFile_wpclsQueryDefaultHelp
        (somSelf, pHelpPanelId, pszHelpLibrary));
}

SOM_Scope ULONG  SOMLINK ldgeM_wpclsQueryDefaultView(M_LedgerEntry
                                                        *somSelf)
{
    /* M_LedgerEntryData *somThis = M_LedgerEntryGetData(somSelf);*/
        M_LedgerEntryMethodDebug("M_LedgerEntry",
                                "ldgeM_wpclsQueryDefaultView");
    return IDD_LEDGERENTRY;
}

SOM_Scope ULONG  SOMLINK ldgeM_wpclsQueryDetailsInfo(M_LedgerEntry
        *somSelf, PCLASSFIELDINFO* ppClassFieldInfo, PULONG pSize)
{

    PCLASSFIELDINFO pClassFieldInfo;
    ULONG ulParentCols;
```

```
ULONG i;

/* M_LedgerEntryData *somThis = M_LedgerEntryGetData(somSelf); */
   M_LedgerEntryMethodDebug("M_LedgerEntry",
                              "ldgeM_wpclsQueryDetailsInfo");
/* Let the ancestor classes put in their two cents worth...*/

 ulParentCols = parent_wpclsQueryDetailsInfo(somSelf,
                                   ppClassFieldInfo, pSize);
 if (pSize)

 {
     *pSize += sizeof(ENTRY_DETAILS);
 }

 /* Is the request just to get the size of the detail data so the
  * shell can allocate the storage for an instance, or does the
  * shell really want the completed structures?
  */

 if (ppClassFieldInfo)

 {
    pClassFieldInfo = *ppClassFieldInfo;
    /* Find the place where we are to chain our class details.  */

     for (i = 0; i < ulParentCols ; i++)

     {
        /* Only visible columns should be mine...*/
        pClassFieldInfo->flData |= CFA_INVISIBLE;
        pClassFieldInfo->flCompare &= ~(COMPARE_SUPPORTED |
                                        SORTBY_SUPPORTED);
        if (!pClassFieldInfo->pNextFieldInfo)
{
           break;
        }

        pClassFieldInfo = pClassFieldInfo->pNextFieldInfo;
     }

    /* Link in our details.  Note that the MyColumnDescriptions array
     * was initialized when the class was initialized.
     */
     pClassFieldInfo->pNextFieldInfo = MyColumnDescriptions;
  }
```

```
    return (ulParentCols + NUM_DETAILS_COLUMNS);
}

SOM_Scope ULONG  SOMLINK ldgeM_wpclsQueryIconData(M_LedgerEntry
                              *somSelf, PICONINFO pIconInfo)
{

    /* M_LedgerEntryData *somThis = M_LedgerEntryGetData(somSelf); */
   M_LedgerEntryMethodDebug("M_LedgerEntry",
                                    "ldgeM_wpclsQueryIconData");

    if (pIconInfo)

    {
        pIconInfo->fFormat = ICON_RESOURCE;
        pIconInfo->hmod = vhmod;
        pIconInfo->resid = IDP_LEDGERE;
    }

    return sizeof(ICONINFO);
}

SOM_Scope PSZ  SOMLINK ldgeM_wpclsQueryInstanceFilter(M_LedgerEntry
                                                   *somSelf)
{
    /* M_LedgerEntryData *somThis = M_LedgerEntryGetData(somSelf);*/
   M_LedgerEntryMethodDebug("M_LedgerEntry",
                              "ldgeM_wpclsQueryInstanceFilter");

    return "*.LGE";
}

SOM_Scope PSZ  SOMLINK ldgeM_wpclsQueryInstanceType(M_LedgerEntry
                                              *somSelf)
{

   /* M_LedgerEntryData *somThis = M_LedgerEntryGetData(somSelf);*/
   M_LedgerEntryMethodDebug("M_LedgerEntry",
                              "ldgeM_wpclsQueryInstanceType");
    return "LedgerEntry";
}

SOM_Scope PSZ  SOMLINK ldgeM_wpclsQueryTitle(M_LedgerEntry *somSelf)
```

```
{
    /* M_LedgerEntryData *somThis = M_LedgerEntryGetData(somSelf); */
    M_LedgerEntryMethodDebug("M_LedgerEntry", "ldgeM_wpclsQueryTitle");
    return "Ledger Entry";
}

MPARAM EXPENTRY EntryDlgProc(HWND hwnd,ULONG msg,MPARAM mp1, MPARAM mp2)
{
   MRESULT mr;

   switch(msg)
   {
       case WM_INITDLG:
          mr = WinDefDlgProc(hwnd,msg,mp1,mp2);

          WinSetFocus(HWND_DESKTOP, WinWindowFromID(hwnd,
                      DID_DESCRIPTION));
          break;

       case WM_CLOSE:
          DosBeep(100,100);
          mr = WinDefDlgProc(hwnd,msg,mp1,mp2);
          break;

       default:
          mr = WinDefDlgProc(hwnd,msg,mp1,mp2);
   }

   return mr;
}

unsigned long EXPENTRY _DLL_InitTerm(unsigned long modhandle,
                                     unsigned long flag)
{
   if (flag == 0)
   {
       vhmod = (HMODULE)modhandle;
   }

   return 1;
}
```

The following example is the code for the ledger class:

```
/*
 *  This file was generated by the SOM Compiler and Emitter Framework.
 *  Generated using:
 *  SOM Emitter emitctm: 2.42
 */

#ifndef SOM_Module_ledgerf_Source
#define SOM_Module_ledgerf_Source
#endif
#define LedgerFolder_Class_Source
#define M_LedgerFolder_Class_Source

#define INCL_PM
#include <os2.h>
#include <som.h>
#include "ledgerf.ih"
#define IDP_LEDGERF 1

/* Our module handle is stored as a global, given to us for free
 * by the system when our dll is loaded...
 */

HMODULE vhmod = NULLHANDLE;

SOM_Scope void SOMLINK ldgf_somDefaultInit(LedgerFolder *somSelf,
                                             somInitCtrl* ctrl)
{
    LedgerFolderData *somThis; /* set in BeginInitializer */
    somInitCtrl globalCtrl;
    somBooleanVector myMask;
    LedgerFolderMethodDebug("LedgerFolder","somDefaultInit");
    LedgerFolder_BeginInitializer_somDefaultInit;
    LedgerFolder_Init_WPFolder_somDefaultInit(somSelf, ctrl);

    /*
     * local LedgerFolder initialization code added by programmer
     */
}

SOM_Scope void SOMLINK ldgf_somDestruct(LedgerFolder *somSelf, octet
                                  doFree, somDestructCtrl* ctrl)
{
    LedgerFolderData *somThis; /* set in BeginDestructor */
```

```
    somDestructCtrl globalCtrl;
    somBooleanVector myMask;
    LedgerFolderMethodDebug("LedgerFolder","ldgf_somDestruct");
    LedgerFolder_BeginDestructor;

    /*
     * local LedgerFolder deinitialization code added by programmer
     */

    LedgerFolder_EndDestructor;
}

SOM_Scope MRESULT  SOMLINK ldgf_wpDragOver(LedgerFolder *somSelf,
HWND hwndCnr, PDRAGINFO pdrgInfo)

{
    ULONG     ulCount;
    ULONG     i;
    PDRAGITEM pdItem;
    USHORT    usDropInd = DOR_DROP;
    MRESULT   mr;
    PSZ       pszClassName;
    WPObject  *Object;

    /* LedgerFolderData *somThis = LedgerFolderGetData(somSelf); */
    LedgerFolderMethodDebug("LedgerFolder","ldgf_wpDragOver");

   /* Only allow LedgerEntry objects into this folder */

    ulCount = DrgQueryDragitemCount(pdrgInfo);
    for (i = 0; i < ulCount ; i++)
    {
        pdItem = DrgQueryDragitemPtr(pdrgInfo,i);
        if (DrgVerifyRMF(pdItem,"DRM_OBJECT","DRF_OBJECT"))
        {
           Object = OBJECT_FROM_PREC(pdItem->ulItemID);
           pszClassName = _somGetClassName(Object);
           if (strcmp(pszClassName,"LedgerEntry"))
           {
               usDropInd = DOR_NEVERDROP;
               break;
           }
        }
        else
        {
```

```
                usDropInd = DOR_NEVERDROP;
                break;
            }
        }
        if (usDropInd == DOR_DROP)
        {
            mr = LedgerFolder_parent_WPFolder_wpDragOver(somSelf,
                                                    hwndCnr, pdrgInfo);
        }
        else
        {
            mr = MRFROM2SHORT(DOR_NEVERDROP,DO_DEFAULT);
        }
        return mr;
}

SOM_Scope HWND  SOMLINK ldgf_wpOpen(LedgerFolder *somSelf, HWND
                                hwndCnr, ULONG ulView, ULONG param)
{
    HWND  hwndFrame;
    HWND  hwndClientCnr;
    CNRINFO cnrinfo;
    PFIELDINFO pFieldInfo;

    /* LedgerFolderData *somThis = LedgerFolderGetData(somSelf); */

    LedgerFolderMethodDebug("LedgerFolder","ldgf_wpOpen");

    hwndFrame = parent_wpOpen(somSelf, hwndCnr, ulView, param);

    hwndClientCnr = WinWindowFromID(hwndFrame,FID_CLIENT);

    /* look at the field info structures to find the one we want
     * to be the last on the left side, and set up the structure
     * accordingly.
     *
     * This should have been provided somehow, as either a method,
     * or as an attribute for one of the columns returned by
     * _wpclsQueryDetailsFieldInfo; however, this much-needed
     * function is currently missing from the Workplace Shell.
     */

    cnrinfo.pFieldInfoLast = NULL;
    pFieldInfo = WinSendMsg(hwndClientCnr,CM_QUERYDETAILFIELDINFO,
```

```
    MPFROMP(NULL),MPFROMSHORT(CMA_FIRST));
    while (pFieldInfo > 0)

    {
        if (!(pFieldInfo->flTitle & CFA_BITMAPORICON))
        {
           DosBeep(300,300);
           cnrinfo.pFieldInfoLast = pFieldInfo;
           break;
        }
        pFieldInfo = WinSendMsg(hwndClientCnr,
                 CM_QUERYDETAILFIELDINFO, MPFROMP(pFieldInfo),
                 MPFROMSHORT(CMA_NEXT));
    }
    WinSendMsg(hwndCnr,CM_SETCNRINFO,MPFROMP(&cnrinfo),
                 MPFROMLONG(CMA_PFIELDINFOLAST));
    return hwndFrame;
}

SOM_Scope BOOL  SOMLINK ldgf_wpPrintObject(LedgerFolder *somSelf,
                        PPRINTDEST pPrintDest, ULONG ulReserved)
{
    /* LedgerFolderData *somThis = LedgerFolderGetData(somSelf); */

    LedgerFolderMethodDebug("LedgerFolder", "ldgf_wpPrintObject");

    return (LedgerFolder_parent_WPFolder_wpPrintObject(somSelf,
                                    pPrintDest, ulReserved));
}

SOM_Scope BOOL  SOMLINK ldgf_wpSetupOnce(LedgerFolder *somSelf, PSZ
                                         pszSetupString)

{
    SOMClass *Class;
    somId    Id;
    BOOL     fSetup;

    /* LedgerFolderData *somThis = LedgerFolderGetData(somSelf); */
    LedgerFolderMethodDebug("LedgerFolder","ldgf_wpSetupOnce");

    fSetup = LedgerFolder_parent_WPFolder_wpSetupOnce(somSelf,
                                                pszSetupString);
    /* Now, set up some special stuff for our folder*/
```

```
    if (fSetup)
    {
        _wpSetDefaultView(somSelf,OPEN_DETAILS);

        Id = SOM_IdFromString("LedgerEntry");
        if (Id)
        {
            Class = _somFindClass( SOMClassMgrObject, Id, 1, 1);
            if (Class)
            {
                _wpSetFldrDetailsClass(somSelf,Class);
                _wpSetFldrSortClass(somSelf,Class);
            }

            SOMFree(Id);
        }
    }

    return fSetup;
}

SOM_Scope BOOL  SOMLINK ldgfM_wpclsCreateDefaultTemplates(M_LedgerFolder
                                      *somSelf, WPObject* Folder)
{
    /* M_LedgerFolderData *somThis = M_LedgerFolderGetData(somSelf);*/
    M_LedgerFolderMethodDebug("M_LedgerFolder",
                              "ldgfM_wpclsCreateDefaultTemplates");
    return (M_LedgerFolder_parent_M_WPFolder_wpclsCreateDefaultTemplates
           (somSelf, Folder));
}

SOM_Scope BOOL  SOMLINK ldgfM_wpclsQueryDefaultHelp(M_LedgerFolder
          *somSelf, PULONG pHelpPanelId, PSZ pszHelpLibrary)
{
    /* M_LedgerFolderData *somThis = M_LedgerFolderGetData(somSelf);*/
    M_LedgerFolderMethodDebug("M_LedgerFolder",
                              "ldgfM_wpclsQueryDefaultHelp");
    return (M_LedgerFolder_parent_M_WPFolder_wpclsQueryDefaultHelp(somSelf,
                                      pHelpPanelId, pszHelpLibrary));
}

SOM_Scope ULONG  SOMLINK ldgfM_wpclsQueryDefaultView(M_LedgerFolder
                                                      *somSelf)
{
    /*  M_LedgerFolderData *somThis = M_LedgerFolderGetData(somSelf); */
```

```
    M_LedgerFolderMethodDebug("M_LedgerFolder",
                                     "ldgfM_wpclsQueryDefaultView");
    return (M_LedgerFolder_parent_M_WPFolder_wpclsQueryDefaultView(somSelf));
}

SOM_Scope ULONG  SOMLINK ldgfM_wpclsQueryIconData(M_LedgerFolder
                                     *somSelf, PICONINFO pIconInfo)
{
    /* M_LedgerFolderData *somThis = M_LedgerFolderGetData(somSelf);*/
    M_LedgerFolderMethodDebug("M_LedgerFolder",
                               "ldgfM_wpclsQueryIconData");
     if (pIconInfo)
     {
         pIconInfo->fFormat = ICON_RESOURCE;
         pIconInfo->hmod = vhmod;
         pIconInfo->resid = IDP_LEDGERF;
     }
     return sizeof(ICONINFO);
}

SOM_Scope PSZ  SOMLINK ldgfM_wpclsQueryInstanceFilter(M_LedgerFolder
                                                      *somSelf)
{
    /* M_LedgerFolderData *somThis = M_LedgerFolderGetData(somSelf);*/
    M_LedgerFolderMethodDebug("M_LedgerFolder",
                               "ldgfM_wpclsQueryInstanceFilter");
    return "*.LDG";
}

SOM_Scope PSZ  SOMLINK ldgfM_wpclsQueryInstanceType(M_LedgerFolder
                                                      *somSelf)
{
    /* M_LedgerFolderData *somThis = M_LedgerFolderGetData(somSelf);*/
    M_LedgerFolderMethodDebug("M_LedgerFolder",
                               "ldgfM_wpclsQueryInstanceType");
    return "Ledger";
}

SOM_Scope PSZ  SOMLINK ldgfM_wpclsQueryTitle(M_LedgerFolder
                                         *somSelf)
{
    /* M_LedgerFolderData *somThis = M_LedgerFolderGetData(somSelf);*/
    M_LedgerFolderMethodDebug("M_LedgerFolder", "ldgfM_wpclsQueryTitle");
    return "Ledger";
}
```

```
unsigned long EXPENTRY _DLL_InitTerm(unsigned long modhandle,
                                     unsigned long flag)
{
   if (flag == 0)
   {
      vhmod = (HMODULE)modhandle;
   }
   return 1;
}
```

These two classes will be implemented in two different DLLs, so DEF files and resource files are needed for each.

```
#define IDP_LEDGERF 1

ICON IDP_LEDGERF LEDGERF.ICO

#include "ledgered.h"
#include "os2.h"

ICON IDP_LEDGERE LEDGERE.ICO

DLGTEMPLATE IDD_LEDGERENTRY LOADONCALL MOVEABLE DISCARDABLE
BEGIN
    DIALOG  "Ledger Entry", IDD_LEDGERENTRY, 28, 30, 214, 88,
WS_VISIBLE, FCF_SYSMENU | FCF_TITLEBAR
    BEGIN
        LTEXT               "Date Entered:", -1, 0, 79, 65, 8
        LTEXT               "Description", -1, 0, 71, 67, 8
        COMBOBOX            "", 102, 0, 36, 214, 35, WS_GROUP
        GROUPBOX            "Type", 103, 0, 0, 48, 36, NOT
                                  WS_VISIBLE
        AUTORADIOBUTTON     "Debit", DID_DEBIT, 2, 17, 39, 10,
                                  WS_TABSTOP
        AUTORADIOBUTTON     "Credit", DID_CREDIT, 1, 4, 39, 10,
                                  WS_TABSTOP
        GROUPBOX            "Amount", 107, 50, 0, 163, 36
        LTEXT               "", DID_DATE, 61, 79, 153, 8
        CONTROL             "", DID_AMOUNT, 55, 10, 153, 12,
                                  WC_SPINBUTTON,
        SPBS_ALLCHARACTERS | SPBS_NUMERICONLY | SPBS_MASTER |
        SPBS_SERVANT | SPBS_JUSTDEFAULT | SPBS_JUSTRIGHT |
        SPBS_FASTSPIN | WS_GROUP | WS_TABSTOP | WS_VISIBLE
    END
```

```
END


;  This file was generated by the SOM Compiler.
;  FileName: ledgerf.def.
;  Generated using:
;      SOM Precompiler somipc: 2.29.1.7
;      SOM Emitter emitdef: 2.42
LIBRARY ledgerf INITINSTANCE
DESCRIPTION 'LedgerFolder Class Library'
PROTMODE
DATA MULTIPLE NONSHARED LOADONCALL
EXPORTS
   LedgerFolderCClassData
   LedgerFolderClassData
   LedgerFolderNewClass
   M_LedgerFolderCClassData
   M_LedgerFolderClassData
   M_LedgerFolderNewClass

;  This file was generated by the SOM Compiler.
;  FileName: ledgere.def.
;  Generated using:
;      SOM Precompiler somipc: 2.29.1.7
;      SOM Emitter emitdef: 2.42
LIBRARY ledgere INITINSTANCE
DESCRIPTION 'LedgerEntry Class Library'
PROTMODE
DATA MULTIPLE NONSHARED LOADONCALL
EXPORTS
   LedgerEntryCClassData
   LedgerEntryClassData
   LedgerEntryNewClass
   M_LedgerEntryCClassData
   M_LedgerEntryClassData
   M_LedgerEntryNewClass

/* REXX */

Call RxFuncAdd 'SysLoadFuncs', 'REXXUTIL', 'SysLoadFuncs';
Call SysLoadFuncs;

/* Get system DLL directory path */
system_dll=FileSpec('Drive',Value('SYSTEM_INI',,'OS2ENVIRONMENT'))||'\OS2\DLL';
```

```
rc=SysDeregisterObjectClass('LedgerEntry');
say "rc" rc "from deregistering LedgerEntry"

rc=SysDeregisterObjectClass('LedgerFolder');
say "rc" rc "from deregistering LedgerFolder"

Address CMD 'ERASE 'system_dll'\LEDGERF.DLL 2>NUL';
Address CMD 'ERASE 'system_dll'\LEDGERE.DLL 2>NUL';
Address CMD 'COPY LEDGERF.DLL 'system_dll;
Address CMD 'COPY LEDGERE.DLL 'system_dll;

rc=SysRegisterObjectClass('LedgerFolder',system_dll||'\LEDGERF.DLL');

If rc <> 1
   Then Do;
     Say  "Could not register LedgerFolder class, rc="rc".";
     Exit;
     End;

rc=SysRegisterObjectClass('LedgerEntry',system_dll||'\LEDGERE.DLL');

If rc <> 1
   Then Do;
     Say  "Could not register LedgerEntry class, rc="rc".";
     Exit;
     End;

/* Now create object on Desktop */

rc=SysCreateObject('LedgerFolder', 'Accounts Receivable',
             '<WP_DESKTOP>', ,'OJECTID=<AR_LEDGER>;','replace');
Say "Object Handle for ledger folder is" rc

rc=SysCreateObject('LedgerEntry','New Entry', '<WP_DESKTOP>',
                                                 'TEMPLATE=YES');
Say "Object Handle for ledger entry template is" rc

.SUFFIXES: .idl .c

SCFLAGS = -mnoqualifytypes -maddstar -S128000 -C128000 -mnoint -v

CFLAGS  = -Q -Ss -Rn -C+ -Mp -Gd+e- -Yp+

LFLAGS  = /noi /map /nol /exepack:2 /packcode /packdata /align:4 /noe /nod
.idl.ih:
```

```
   sc $(SCFLAGS) -s "ih;h;c;hh;def" $(@B).idl
.c.obj:
   icc $(CFLAGS) $(@B).c
all: ledgerf.ih ledgerf.obj ledgerf.dll ledgere.ih ledgere.obj ledgere.dll

ledgerf.h: ledgerf.ih
ledgerf.c: ledgerf.ih
ledgerf.def: ledgerf.ih

ledgere.h: ledgere.ih
ledgere.c: ledgere.ih
ledgere.def: ledgere.ih

ledgerf.dll: ledgerf.obj makefile ledgerf.def ledgerf.rc
   ilink /NOFREE @<<
$(LFLAGS) +
$(@B).obj
$@
$(@B).map
os2386.lib+cppon30.lib+somtk.lib
$(@B).def
<<
   rc $(@B).rc $@
   mapsym $(@B)

ledgere.dll: ledgere.obj makefile ledgere.def ledgere.rc ledgered.h
   ilink /NOFREE @<<
$(LFLAGS) +
$(@B).obj
$@
$(@B).map
os2386.lib+cppon30.lib+somtk.lib
$(@B).def
<<
   rc $(@B).rc $@
   mapsym $(@B)
```

Glossary of Terms

This glossary includes terms and definitions from:

- The *IBM Dictionary of Computing*, New York: McGraw-Hill, copyright 1994 by International Business Machines Corporation.
- The *American National Dictionary for Information Systems*, ANSI X3.172-1990, copyright 1990 by the American National Standards Institute (ANSI). Copies may be purchased from the American National Standards Institute, 11 West 42 Street, New York, New York 10036. Definitions are identified by the symbol (A) after the definition.
- The *Information Technology Vocabulary*, developed by Subcommittee 1, Joint Technical Committee 1, of the International Organization for Standardization and the International Electrotechnical Commission (ISO/IEC JTC1/SC1). Definitions of published parts of this vocabulary are identified by the symbol (I) after the definition; definitions from draft international standards, committee drafts, and working papers being developed by ISO/IEC JTC1/SC1 are identified by the symbol (T) after the definition, indicating that final agreement has not yet been reached among the participating National Bodies of SC1.

A

ABI
Application binary interface.

abstract class
A class that defines common characteristics and behaviors for descendent classes. An abstract class is never instantiated. Compare with concrete class.

access control list (ACL)
A list of the access privileges assigned to users for an object. It identifies who can access the object and how the object can be accessed (for example, read-only or write-only access).

ACL
Access control list.

actors
Audio-visual entities that converse with users, thereby providing a Human-Centered computer interface. These entities might be voices only or human faces on the screen that talk to you.

adapter devise driver (ADD) architecture
The new device driver model for OS/2 Warp Connect (PowerPC Edition) that uses frameworks to abstract adapter hardware.

ADC
Analog-to-digital converter.

ADD
Adapter devise driver architecture.

address space
(1) The range of addresses available to a program. (A) (2) The area of virtual storage available for a particular job.

Advanced Interactive Executive (AIX)
IBM's implementation of the UNIX operating system. The RISC System/6000, among others, runs the AIX operating system.

Advanced Peer-to-Peer Networking (APPN)
An extension to SNA featuring (a) greater distributed network control that avoids critical hierarchical dependencies, thereby isolating the effects of single points of failure; (b) dynamic exchange of network topology information to foster ease of connection, reconfiguration, and adaptive route selection; (c) dynamic definition of network resources; and (d) automated resource registration and directory lookup. APPN extends the LU6.2 peer orientation for end-user services to network control and supports multiple logical unit (LU) types, including LU 2, LU 3, and LU 6.2.

Advanced Program-to-Program Communication (APPC)
The general facility characterizing the LU 6.2 architecture and its various implementations in products. Sometimes used to refer to the LU 6.2 architecture and its product implementations as a whole, or to an LU 6.2 product feature in particular, such as an APPC application programming interface.

agent
An entity that performs tasks for the user.

AIX
Advanced Interactive Executive.

all points addressable (APA)
In computer graphics, pertaining to the ability to address and display or not display each picture element (pel) on a display surface.

American National Standard Code for Information Interchange (ASCII)
The standard code, using a coded character set consisting of 7-bit coded characters (8 bits including parity check), that is used for information interchange among data processing systems, data communication systems, and associated equipment. The ASCII set consists of control characters and graphic characters.

Note: IBM has defined an extension to ASCII code (characters 128-255).

American National Standards Institute (ANSI)
An organization consisting of producers, consumers, and general interest groups, that establishes the procedures by which accredited organizations create and maintain voluntary industry standards in the United States.

analog
Pertaining to data consisting of continuously variable physical quantities. (T) Contrast with digital.

analog-to-digital converter (ADC)
A functional unit that converts data from an analog representation to a digital representation.

ANSI
American National Standards Institute.

APA
All points addressable.

API
Application programming interface.

APPC
Advanced Program-to-Program Communication.

application
A collection of software components used to perform specific types of user-oriented work on a computer; for example, a payroll application, an airline reservation application, a network application. See also application component.

application binary interface (ABI)
An interface consisting of linkage conventions for a particular microprocessor. (These conventions define how registers are used, how they are saved and destroyed across calls, how parameters are passed, and so on.)

application component
An OpenDoc component that the user employs to create, edit, or view document parts. Part editors and part viewers are application components; they replace the function of conventional applications.

application programming interface (API)
A functional interface supplied by the operating system or by a separately orderable licensed program that allows an application program written in a high-level language to use specific data or functions of the operating system or the licensed program.

APPN
Advanced Peer-to-Peer Networking.

arbitrator
An OpenDoc object that manages negotiation among parts about ownership of shared resources. Examples of such resources are the menu focus, selection focus, keystroke focus, and the serial ports.

ASCII
American National Standard Code for Information Interchange.

ASCIIZ
A string of ASCII characters that is terminated with a byte containing the value 0.

asymmetric multiprocessing
Unequal distribution of tasks across multiple processors.

ASYNC
Asynchronous.

asynchronous (ASYNC)
(1) Pertaining to two or more processes that do not depend upon the occurrence of specific events such as common timing signals. (T) (2) Without regular time relationship; unexpected or unpredictable with respect to the execution of program instructions. See also synchronous.

asynchronous I/O
A series of input/output operations that are being done separately from the job that requested them.

attach
(1) In programming, to create a task that can be executed asynchronously with the execution of the mainline code. (2) To connect a device to a ring network.

audio
Pertaining to the portion of recorded information that can be heard.

audio synthesizer
A device that produces and controls electronically generated sounds.

audiovisual
Pertaining to experiences, equipment, and materials used for communication that make use of both hearing and sight.

authentication
In computer security, verification of the identity of a user or the user's eligibility to access an object; verification that a message has not been altered or corrupted.

authentication server
Part of the trusted security base; a server responsible for authenticating identities of clients. Maintains passwords and group membership information for users.

B

background task
A task that is running even though the user is not currently interacting with it. Contrast with foreground task.

base part
A code module that contains default implementations for all of the methods defined for an OpenDoc part. The base part is provided to developers to use as a parent class, thereby freeing them from writing routine implementation code when the default behavior of the base part will suffice.

basic input/output system (BIOS)
In an IBM personal computer, microcode that controls basic hardware operations, such as interactions with diskette drives, hard disk drives, and the keyboard.

Bento
A format for persistent object storage. Developed and maintained by CI Labs, Bento allows OpenDoc to store and exchange compound documents and multimedia.

Big Endian
A format for storage or transmission of binary data in which the most significant bit (or byte) is placed first. Contrast with Little Endian.

binding
(1) In programming, an association between a variable and a value for that variable that holds within a defined scope. The scope may be that of a rule, a function call, or a procedure invocation. (T) (2) In OpenDoc, the process of selecting an executable code module based on type information.

BIOS
Basic input/output system.

bit map
A representation of an image by an array of bits.

block device
A storage device that performs I/O operations on blocks of data called sectors. Data on block devices can be randomly accessed. Block devices are designated by a drive letter (for example, C).

BOOKSHELF
An environment variable, set in CONFIG.SYS, that contains a list of subdirectories where IPF on-line books are located.

boot
To prepare a computer system for operation by loading an operating system.

bootstrap
(1) A sequence of instructions whose execution causes additional instructions to be loaded and executed until the complete computer program is in storage. (T) (2) A technique or device designed to bring itself into a desired state by means of its own action; for example, a machine routine whose first few instructions are sufficient to bring the rest of itself into the computer from an input device. (A) (3) A small program that loads larger programs during system initialization. (4) To execute a bootstrap. The term bootstrapping is also used for translating a compiler by using the compiler or a previous version as the translator. (T) See also bootstrap loader.

bootstrap loader
An input routine in which preset computer operations are used to load a bootstrap. (I) (A) See also bootstrap.

breakpoint
(1) A point in a computer program where execution may be halted. A breakpoint is usually at the beginning of an instruction where halts, caused by external intervention, are convenient for resuming execution. (T) (2) A place in a program, specified by a command or a condition, where the system halts execution and gives control to the workstation user or to a specified program.

bridge
A functional unit that interconnects two local area networks that use the same logical link control protocol but may use different medium access control protocols. (T) Contrast with gateway and router.

buffer
(1) A portion of storage used to hold input or output data temporarily. (2) To allocate and schedule the user of buffers.

bus
(1) A facility for transferring data between several devices located between two end points, only one device being able to transmit at a given moment. (T) (2) A computer configuration in which processors are interconnected in series.

byte
(1) A string that consists of a number of bits, treated as a unit, and representing a single byte character. (T) (2) A binary character operated upon as a unit and usually shorter than a computer word. (A) (3) A group of 8 adjacent binary digits that represent one EBCDIC character.

byte ordering
The arrangement of bytes under specific machine architectures. Two common methods of byte ordering are Big Endian and Little Endian.

C

cache
(1) A special-purpose buffer storage, smaller and faster than main storage, used to hold a copy of instructions and data obtained from main storage and likely to be needed next by the processor. (T) (2) A high-speed buffer storage that contains frequently accessed instructions and data; it is used to reduce access time.

cached micro presentation space
A presentation space from a Presentation-Manager-owned store of micro presentation spaces. It can be used for drawing to a window only, and must be returned to the store when the task is complete.

CDFS
CD-ROM File System.

character device
A device that performs I/O operations on one character at a time. Because character devices view data as a stream of bytes, character-device data cannot be randomly accessed. Character devices include the keyboard, mouse, and printer, and are referred to by name.

character set
A group of characters used for a specific reason; for example, the set of characters a printer can print.

child class
See subclass.

child process
In the OS/2 operating system, a process started by a parent process, that shares the resources of the parent process. Contrast with parent process.

child window
A window that appears within the border of its parent window (either a primary window or another child window). When the parent window is resized, moved, or destroyed, the child window also is resized, moved, or destroyed; however, the child window can be moved or resized independently from the parent window, within the boundaries of the parent window. Contrast with parent window.

CI Labs
Component Integration Laboratories.

CID
Configuration, installation, and distribution.

CISC
Complex instruction set computing.

class
In object-oriented design or programming, a group of objects that share a common definition and that therefore share common properties, operations, and behaviors. Members of the group are called instances of the class.

class hierarchy
The structure by which classes are related through inheritance.

class method
In System Object Model, an action that can be performed on a class object. Also known as factory methods.

class object
In System Object Model, the run-time implementation of a class.

class style
The set of properties that apply to every window in a window class.

client
(1) A functional unit that receives shared services from a server. (T) (2) In a distributed system environment, a system that is dependent on a server to provide it with programs or access to programs. (3) Synonymous with requester.

client library
A collection of executable code and data that is bound to an application and provides the API of a shared service to applications. The library can handle the service request or will route the request to a server or microkernel service. See also shared library.

client/server
(1) A model for operating systems in which a small group of services (servers) at the system layer support requests for services from a large group of users (clients) at the application layer. (2) The relationship between the microkernel, operating system services, and shared services in a microkernel-based operating system such as OS/2 Warp Connect (PowerPC Edition).

clustered multiprocessing
Distribution of tasks across sets of multiple processors.

code page
An assignment of graphic characters and control function meanings to all code points; for example, assignment of characters and meanings to 256 code points for an 8-bit code.

code point
A 1-byte code representing one of 256 potential characters.

CODEC
Compressor/decompressor.

Common Object Request Broker Architecture (CORBA)
The industry standard architecture that allows objects from different vendors and from different platforms to interact with each other. Defined by the OMG.

Common Programming Interface (CPI)
Definitions of those application development languages and services that have, or are intended to have, implementations on and a high degree of commonality across the SAA environments. One of the three SAA architectural areas. See also Common User Access architecture.

Common Programming Interface for Communications (CPI-C)
A common interface for the implementation of the conversational model of IBM's Open Blueprint for distributed computing on all its major platforms. CPI-C provides access to interprogram services such as (a) sending and receiving data, (b) synchronizing processing between programs, and (c) notifying a partner of error in the communication.

Common User Access (CUA) architecture
Guidelines for the dialog between a human and a workstation or terminal. One of the three SAA architectural areas. See also Common Programming Interface.

component
The unit manipulated by the user in OpenDoc. Documents are built by components selected by the user. Synonymous with part.

component glue
The OpenDoc technology that allows OLE objects and OpenDoc parts to coexist in a document.

compound document
A document that contains linked or embedded information created by other applications. A compound document is made up of parts.

Component Integration Laboratories (CI Labs)
An organization formed by a consortium of industry leaders including IBM and WordPerfect to standardize the OpenDoc, Bento, SOM, and OSA technologies and license them to the rest of the industry.

compressor/decompressor (CODEC)
An algorithm, implemented either in hardware or software, that can either compress or decompress a data object. For example, a CODEC can compress raw digital images into a smaller form so that they use less storage space. When used in the context of playing motion video, decompressors reconstruct the original image from the compressed data. This is done at a high rate of speed to simulate motion.

concrete class
A class designed to be instantiated. Compare with abstract class.

configuration file
A file that specifies the characteristics of a system device or network.

Configuration, Installation, and Distribution (CID)
An IBM architecture used to automate installation and customization for OS/2 Warp Connect (PowerPC Edition) and other products. CID enables LAN-connected machines to be installed and maintained remotely.

container
In SAA Common User Access architecture, an object that holds other objects. A folder is an example of a container object.

container application
An application program that has been modified to support embedding of OpenDoc parts. A container application functions as both document shell and part editor for the root part.

container suite
A set of OpenDoc classes that implement persistent storage. The container suite consists of containers, documents, drafts, and storage units.

containing part
The part that immediately contains an embedded part. Each embedded part has one containing part; each containing part has one or more embedded parts.

containment
A relationship between objects wherein an object of one class contains a reference to an object of another class. Compare with inheritance.

contextual help
Help information about the specific choice or object that the cursor is on. The help is contextual because it provides information about the item in its current context.

control program
A computer program designed to schedule and to supervise the execution of programs of a computer system. (I) (A)

CORBA
Common Object Request Broker Architecture.

coverpage
Help frame window.

CPI-C
Common Programming Interface for Communications.

D

DAC
Digital-to-analog converter.

DASD
Direct access storage device.

Data Capture Interface (DCI)
A framework for performance monitoring. A proposed X/Open standard.

data link
In SNA, synonym for link.

database
A collection of data with a given structure for accepting, storing, and providing on demand data for multiple users. (T)

DBCS
Double-byte character set.

DCE
Distributed Computing Environment.

DCI
Data Capture Interface.

DDE
Dynamic data exchange.

DDF
Dynamic data formatting.

Desktop
In the OS/2 operating system, a folder that fills the entire screen and holds the objects that enable a user to interact with and perform operations on the system.

Desktop Management Interface (DMI)
An industry standard that provides a local operating system framework that links network management protocol agents to hardware and software components running on the system.

device driver
Software that enables a computer to communicate with a specific peripheral device, such as a pen, videodisc player, or CD-ROM drive. Device driver code typically resides in the most privileged level of the operating system, that is, the kernel. Device drivers for microkernel-based operating systems, such as OS/2 Warp Connect (PowerPC Edition), are shared services, running at the application level. They are built using device driver frameworks that can be quickly and easily customized for new devices as they become available.

device-independent
Pertaining to a function that can be accomplished without regard for the characteristics of particular types of devices.

DFS
Distributed file system.

digital
Pertaining to data in digits. (A) Contrast with analog.

digital signal processor (DSP)
A microprocessor designed specifically for high-speed processing of streams of nondigital information, such as speech.

digital-to-analog converter (DAC)
A functional unit that converts data from a digital representation to an analog representation.

digitizer
An electronic device that transmits coordinate data to software running on a computer.

direct access storage device (DASD)
A device in which the access time is effectively independent of the location of the data.

direct manipulation
The use of a pointing device to work with objects, rather than through menus.

direct memory access (DMA)
The system facility that allows a device on the Micro Channel bus to get direct access to the system or bus memory without the intervention of the system processor.

Direct to SOM (DTS)
Pertaining to a compiler that can create SOM objects directly from its native source, as in the C++ DTS compiler.

distributed computing
A method of computing in which a user works with data and functions that physically reside on more than one computer in a communication network.

Distributed Computing Environment (DCE)
A set of standards governed by the Open Software Foundation (OSF) for open computing in distributed systems.

distributed file system (DFS)
A file system composed of files or directories that physically reside on more than one computer in a communication network.

Distributed Relational Database Architecture (DRDA)
An architecture that defines how client applications access data stored at remote relational database management systems.

Distributed SOM (DSOM)
Distributed System Object Model. A version of SOM that provides remote access to SOM objects in a transparent way that insulates client programmers from having to know the location or platform type where a target object will be instantiated. DSOM allows programmers to use the same object model independently of whether the objects they access are in the same process, in another process on the same machine, or across distributed networks.

DLL
Dynamic link library.

DMA
Direct memory access.

DMI
Desktop Management Interface.

document
Visual components of a task. In OpenDoc the concept of document is very flexible; for example the desktop can be considered a document with the objects on the desktop as OpenDoc components.

domain
(1) That part of a computer network in which the resources are under common control. (T) (2) In Open Systems Interconnection (OSI), a part of a distributed system or set of managed objects to which a common policy applies.

DOS
Disk Operating System. (The original operating system used with IBM-compatible personal computers.)

DOS Protect Mode Interface (DPMI)
A programming interface for DOS applications that use real-mode operations (such as direct hardware access or interrupts) but are not permitted in a protect-mode task.

double-byte character set (DBCS)
A set of characters in which each character is represented by 2 bytes. Languages such as Japanese, Chinese, and Korean, which contain more symbols than can be represented by 256 code points, require double-byte character sets. Because each character requires 2 bytes, the typing, display, and printing of DBCS characters require hardware and software that support DBCS. Contrast with single-byte character set.

DPMI
DOS Protect Mode Interface.

draft
In OpenDoc, a version of a document.

drag-drop
A technique for operating a computer based on the manipulation of objects, which are moved (that is, dragged and dropped) over other objects with which to work. For example, in OpenDoc, parts are dragged from a parts bin and dropped onto a document.

DRDA
Distributed Relational Database Architecture.

DSOM
Distributed SOM.

DTS
Direct to SOM.

dynamic
(1) Pertaining to an operation that occurs at the time it is needed rather than at a predetermined or fixed time. (2) In programming, properties that can only be established during the execution of a program.

dynamic data exchange (DDE)
A messaging protocol that allows Presentation Manager applications to exchange data via shared memory. DDE transactions always take place between a client application and a server application. The client initiates a dialog with the server by requesting data from the server. The server responds by providing the requested data to the client.

dynamic data formatting (DDF)
A formatting procedure that enables users to incorporate text, bit maps, or metafiles in an IPF window.

dynamic link library (DLL)
A file containing executable code and data bound to a program at load time or run time, rather than during linking. The code and data in a dynamic link library can be shared by several applications simultaneously. DLLs can be interchanged without recompiling or relinking the applications that use them.

E

EA
Extended attribute.

EBCDIC
Extended binary-coded decimal interchange code. A coded character set of 256 8-bit characters.

editor
Software that creates or modifies data in a document.

ELF
Executable and linkable format.

embedded operating system (EOS)
An operating system that consists of minimum function that controls such things as appliances.

EMMI
External memory manager interface (of the IBM Microkernel product).

EMS
Expanded memory specification.

emulation
The use of a data processing system to imitate another data processing system so that the imitating system accepts the same data, runs the same programs, and achieves the same results as the imitated system. Emulation is usually achieved by means of hardware or firmware. (T)

encapsulation
The private, or internal, view of an object that describes how data and methods are actually implemented. Not accessible to other objects.

Endian
The addressing model that determines the byte ordering of both data and instructions that are stored in computer memory. The Big Endian model assigns the lowest address to the highest-order or most significant byte of a multibyte scalar data item. The Little Endian model assigns the lowest address to the lowest-order or least significant byte of a multibyte scalar data item.

EOS
Embedded operating system.

Ethernet
A 10-megabit baseband local area network that allows multiple stations to access the transmission medium at will without prior coordination, avoids contention by using carrier sense and deference, and resolves contention by using collision detection and delayed retransmission. Ethernet uses carrier sense multiple access with collision detection.

event and window services (EWS)
A shared service for microkernel-based operating systems that provides the mechanism for sharing the console device among operating system services and applications. It also provides services for the management of events and windows.

event manager
The OSA component responsible for accepting OpenEvents and delivering them to the target (such as another document, part, program, and so on.)

event semaphore
A semaphore that enables a thread to signal a waiting thread or threads that an event has occurred or that a task has been completed. The waiting threads can then perform an action that is dependent on the completion of the signaled event.

exception
An abnormal condition such as an I/O error encountered during processing of a file or execution of a program.

executable and linkable format (ELF)
In the microkernel-based architecture, the object module format.

exit list
In the OS/2 operating system, a list of subroutines that receive control when a particular process ends, either normally or abnormally.

expanded memory specification (EMS)
A memory specification that enables DOS applications to access memory above the 1MB real mode addressing limit.

extended attribute (EA)
Additional information, such as comments, history, or author's name, that a system or program associates with a file. The information contained in EAs is more comprehensive and varied than the information displayed by the DIR command. EAs are not part of a file and are maintained by the file system.

F

factored
An application that is split between the user interface portion and the main engine. Communication between the two is achieved through the use of OpenEvents.

FAT
File allocation table.

FEVSH menu system
File, Edit, View, Selected, Help menu system.

FFST
First Failure Support Technology.

FIFO
First-in-first-out. A queuing technique in which the next item to be retrieved is the item that has been in the queue the longest amount of time.

file allocation table (FAT)
In IBM personal computers, a table used by DOS to allocate space on a disk for a file and to locate and chain together parts of the file that may be scattered on different sectors so that the file can be used in a random or sequential manner. In contrast with High Performance File System (HPFS), which will perform faster on a large disk with less fragmentation.

File Services
A shared service for microkernel-based operating systems that provides a framework for multiple logical and physical file systems.

file system
Software that supports storing data on storage devices, such as hard disks and floppy disks. File systems manage the physical locations of data on the storage devices for applications and control the format of stored data.

File, Edit, View, Selected, Help (FEVSH) menu system
Selectable menu items found at the top of a window.

First Failure Support Technology (FFST)
A set of functions that applications can use for problem determination. FFST functions include logging and displaying errors and messages, formatting and routing generic alerts, and generating data dumps.

folder
A container used to organize objects.

foreground task
The task with which the user is interacting. Contrast with background task.

frame
The unit of transmission in some local area networks, including the IBM Token-Ring Network. It includes delimiters, control characters, information, and checking characters.

framework
Objects and object-oriented application interfaces (API) that provide a consistent set of functions or services that perform a specific task. In a framework, classes of objects are organized to work together so that they provide a rich set of default behavior. If the default behavior is acceptable, it need not be changed. If it is not acceptable, the behavior can be changed by subclassing existing classes in the framework. Frameworks allow programmers to program by exception, or customize an implementation for a particular situation. This means that code is highly reusable and development cycle time can be greatly reduced.

framework service provider
Code that performs the functions the applications associate with a set of service provider interfaces (SPIs). A framework exports an API to client applications. It translates to a service provider interface (SPI) that can be supported by multiple service providers. This translation enables applications to work with service providers from multiple vendors and frees programmers from the need to use a different set of interfaces each time a new product of a given class is introduced.

front panel
A container that "follows" the user from work area to work area; holds objects and actions that need to be accessed across work areas (printer, shredder, Shut Down, Lockup).

fully qualified path
A path specification that begins with either a drive specifier (x:) or a path separator character (\) preceded by zero, one, or two periods.

G

gateway
A functional unit that interconnects two computer networks with different network architectures. A gateway connects networks or systems of different architectures. A bridge interconnects networks or systems with the same or similar architectures. (T)

gesture
A hand-drawn symbol or uppercase letter which, when recognized by the system, invokes an action or a series of actions. Gestures denote an action and a target for the action.

GPI
Graphics programming interface.

GRADD
Graphics Adapter Device Driver.

graphical user interface (GUI)
In SAA Common User Access architecture, a type of user interface that takes advantage of high-resolution graphics. In common usage, a graphical user interface includes a combination of graphics, the object-action paradigm, the use of pointing devices, menu bars and other menus, overlapping windows, and icons.

Graphics Adapter Device Driver (GRADD)
The new model for video display device drivers for OS/2 Warp Connect (PowerPC Edition).

graphics engine
The drawing engine for the system. It manages display resources, such as color maps and bit maps, and serves as the interface between the graphics transportation protocols and the presentation (display) and printer device drivers.

graphics programming interface (GPI)
Programming interface defined for service provider response to system requests for presentation device services. The mechanism by which applications, controls, and the desktop access the graphics engine in order to display characters on a screen or printer.

graphics transportation protocols
The method by which graphics data is communicated between a client (application) and a server (graphics engine).

GUI
Graphical User Interface.

H

Hardware Resource Manager (HRM)
Part of the IBM Microkernel that provides services for configuration, access, and management of hardware to user level device drivers in the Microkernel Services run-time environment.

hashing
(1) A method of transforming a search key into an address for the purpose of storing and retrieving items of data. The method is often designed to minimize the search time. (T) (2) The application of an algorithm to the records in a data set to obtain a symmetric grouping of the records. Synonymous with key folding. (3) In an indexed data set, the process of transforming a record key into an index value for storing and retrieving a record.

header file
Synonym for include file.

help panel
Information displayed by a system in response to a help request from a user.

hierarchical inheritance
The relationship between parent and child classes. Inheritance between classes is hierarchical: A class that is lower in the inheritance hierarchy (that is, a child class of a parent or ancestor) inherits all the characteristics and behaviors of the (ancestor) classes above it in the hierarchy.

High Performance File System (HPFS)
In the OS/2 operating system, an installable file system that uses high-speed buffer storage, know as a cache, to provide extremely fast access to very large disk volumes. HPFS supports long file names; file names can have as many as 254 characters. On larger disks, HPFS will outperform FAT, with less fragmentation.

HLP
The binary file generated by the IPF compiler containing help panels that are displayed when the user requests help from a menu or via the F1 key.

HPFS
High Performance File System.

HRM
Hardware Resource Manager.

HTML
Hypertext Markup Language Specification.

human-centered
Pertaining to software interfaces that are more intuitive for people to use.

hypermedia
A method of presenting information in discrete units, or nodes, that are connected by links. The information may be presented using a variety of media such as text, graphics, audio, video, animation, image, or executable documentation.

Hypertext Markup Language (HTML) Specification
The language of the Internet. A simple SGML-like markup language used to create hypertext documents that are not constrained by information format (they don't require the application that created them to view them) or by hardware platform (they are viewable from any machine that can get to them).

I

IAB
Internet Architecture Board.

IAC
Interapplication communication.

IBM Microkernel Product
The IBM implementation of microkernel technology. It includes the microkernel and a set of Microkernel Services that can be used to create operating system services and other services that execute on the microkernel.

IDL
Interface Definition Language; a language defined by the OMG as a universal way of specifying objects and their methods.

IFI
Intelligent Font Interface.

IFS
Installable file system.

INF file
The binary file, generated by the IPF compiler, containing an on-line book. INFs are displayed via IPF's VIEW utility.

Information Presentation Facility (IPF)
The OS/2 component that supports on-line information; also referred to as the OS/2 Help Manager. IPF consists of an authoring language, a compiler, a help engine, a programming interface, and a viewer.

inheritance
Result of derivation of new classes of objects from existing classes of objects. Child classes inherit methods of parent and ancestor classes.

i-node
The internal structure that describes the individual files in the operating system; there is one i-node for each file. An i-node contains the node, type, owner, and location of a file. A table of i-nodes is stored near the beginning of a file system. Synonymous with file index. See also v-node.

input focus
The position, indicated on the screen, where a user's interaction with the keyboard will appear.

Input-output privilege level (IOPL)
In the OS/2 operating system, a statement in the CONFIG.SYS file that enables certain application programs to communicate directly with I/O devices.

installable file system (IFS)
A file system that is installed when the operating system is started.

instance method
Actions that can be performed on instance objects.

instance object
An object belonging to a certain class.

Instruction Set Translator (IST)
Emulation technology for executing Intel binaries for DOS and Windows applications on OS/2 Warp Connect (PowerPC Edition).

Integrated On-line Information (IOI)
The future OS/2 help system, consisting of a shared service and a set of UI applications.

Intelligent Font Interface (IFI)
The mechanism that allows the graphics engine to communicate with whatever font drivers are available in the system.

interactive
Pertaining to a program or system that alternately accepts input and then responds. An interactive system is conversational; that is, a continuous dialog exists between user and system.

interapplication communication (IAC)
Information transfer between applications, such as DDE and OLE.

interface
A shared boundary between two functional units, defined by functional characteristics, signal characteristics, or other characteristics, as appropriate. (T)

International Organization for Standardization (ISO)
An international organization established to promote development of standards to facilitate international exchange of goods and services and develop cooperation in intellectual, scientific, technological, and economic activity.

internationalization
National language support.

Internet
The internet administered by the Internet Architecture Board (IAB), consisting of large national backbone networks and many regional and campus networks all over the world.

internet
A collection of networks interconnected by a set of routers that allow them to function as a single, large network.

Internet Architecture Board (IAB)
The technical body that oversees the development of the Internet suite of protocols that are known as TCP/IP.

Internet Protocol (IP)
A connectionless protocol that routes data through a network or interconnected networks. IP acts as an intermediary between the higher protocol layers and the physical network. However, this protocol does not provide error recovery and flow control and does not guarantee the reliability of the physical network.

Internetwork Packet Exchange (IPX)
The network protocol used to connect Novell's servers, or any workstation or router that implements IPX, with other workstations. Although similar to the Internet Protocol (IP), IPX uses different packet formats and terminology.

interoperability
The capability to communicate, execute programs, or transfer data among various functional units in a way that requires the user to have little or no knowledge of the unique characteristics of those units. (T)

interprocess communication (IPC)
(1) In the OS/2 operating system, the exchange of information between processes or threads through semaphores, queues, and shared memory. (2) In microkernel-based operating systems, the asynchronous messaging facility for cooperating subsystems to communicate through ports. The basis for the client/server system model.

interrupt
A suspension of a process, such as execution of a computer program caused by an external event, and performed in such a way that the process can be resumed. To stop a process in such a way that it can be resumed. (A)

IOCtl
Input/output control.

IOI
Integrated On-line Information.

IOPL
Input-output privilege level.

IP
Internet Protocol.

IPC
Interprocess communication.

IPF
Information Presentation Facility.

IPX
Internetwork Packet Exchange.

ISO
International Organization for Standardization.

IST
Instruction Set Translator.

ITV
Interactive television.

J

JFS
Journal File System.

Journal File System
A file system that logs file system operations. In the event of a system failure, this log is replayed when the system is restarted, and the appropriate transactions are completed or backed out.

K

kernel
The set of basic operating-system services that runs at the highest priority level. The part of an operating system that performs basic functions such as allocating hardware resources.

KwikINF
A utility, represented by an object in the Developer's Toolkit, that provides a single point of entry, via a hot key, into all on-line books in the OS/2 BOOKSHELF. KwikINF can be used at any time, from anywhere on the Desktop, with the exception of DOS or WIN-OS/2 sessions.

L

LAN
Local area network.

large media extended partition (LMEP)
An architecture that supports large partitions (greater than one gigabyte) and is a superset of the current disk architecture.

lazy drag
A mouse action in which a user can pick up a set of objects and carry those objects around on the pointer without having to hold the mouse button down.

LFS
Logical file system.

LIFO
Last-in-first-out. A queuing technique in which the next item to be retrieved is the item most recently placed in the queue.

linear executable format (LX)
The object module format used by OS/2 on Intel-based systems.

link
To interconnect items of data or portions of one or more computer programs: for example, the linking of object programs by a linkage editor, linking of data items by pointers. (T)

linking
A data sharing technique that allows a document or parts of documents to share one copy of the data while displaying several copies. One document provides the source of the data while the other documents or parts maintain a connection to the original for updates.

Little Endian
A format for storage or transmission of binary data in which the least significant bit (or byte) is placed first. Contrast with Big Endian.

LMEP
Large media extended partition.

local
Pertaining to a device accessed directly without use of a telecommunication line. Contrast with remote.

local area network (LAN)
A computer network located on a user's premises within a limited geographical area. Communication within a LAN is not subject to external regulations; however, communication across the LAN boundary may be subject to some form of regulation. (T) Contrast with wide area network.

locale
A collection of modules and data that define country-specific and cultural preferences for units of money, formatting dates and times, numeric systems, file I/O and code page conversions, MRI handling, language-sensitive string handling, and so on.

localization
An architecture in which or a design by which a language and cultural differences are absorbed by the product. Localization is referred to by an abbreviation, L10N, because there are ten letters between the first L and the last N.

lock
The means by which integrity of data is ensured by preventing more than one user from accessing or changing the same data or object at the same time.

logical device
(1) A file for conducting input or output with a physical device. (2) A file for mapping user I/O between virtual and real devices.

logical drive
A portion of a physical drive.

logical file system (LFS)
A file services component that provides a consistent view of multiple physical file systems. The logical file system provides path resolution and other services that are independent of the on-disk format of data.

logical unit (LU)
A type of network accessible unit that enables end users to gain access to network resources and communicate with each other.

LU
Logical unit.

LU type
The classification of a logical unit (LU) in terms of the specific subset of SNA protocols and options it supports for a given session, namely:

- The mandatory and optional values allowed in the session activation request.
- The usage of data stream controls, function management headers (FMHs), request unit parameters, and sense data values.
- Presentation services protocols such as those associated with FMH usage.

LU types 0, 1, 2, 3, 4, 6.1, 6.2, and 7 are defined.

LU 6.2
A type of logical unit that supports general communication between programs in a distributed processing environment. LU 6.2 is characterized by (a) peer relationship between session partners, (b) efficient utilization of a session for multiple transactions, (c) comprehensive end-to-end error processing, and (d) a generic application programming interface (API) consisting of structured verbs that are mapped into a product implementation.

LVM
Logical Volume Management.

LX
Linear executable format.

M

Mach
An operating system kernel developed at Carnegie-Mellon University to support distributed and parallel computation.

machine-readable information (MRI)
All textual information presented to or received from a user interacting with a system. This information includes menus, prompts, messages, report headings, commands, and responses. MRI may appear on printers or on display panels.

macro language
An application-specific language, often ad hoc, which allows some level of automation and programmability to the user of the application.

MAN
Metropolitan area network.

Master Help Index
A utility, represented by an object on the OS/2 Desktop, that provides a fast path to information for all objects on the Desktop.

Message Interface Generator (MIG)
A developer's tool that generates low-level remote procedure calls between a client and server process using the microkernel IPC mechanism. The code that is generated includes routines to pack and unpack the messages used to communicate between processes.

Message Queue Interface (MQI)
An IBM standard interface for interprocess communication. One of three models for IBM's Open Blueprint for distributed computing.

metafile
A file containing a series of attributes that set color, shape and size, usually of a picture or a drawing. Using a program that can interpret these attributes, a user can view the assembled image.

method
An action that can be performed on an object.

method override
Polymorphism in SOM; child classes can override the implementation of methods inherited from parent and ancestor classes.

metropolitan area network (MAN)
A network formed by the interconnection of two or more networks which may operate at higher speed than those networks, may cross administrative boundaries, and may use multiple access methods. (T) Contrast with local area network and wide area network.

MiCL
Migration Command Language. See also SMART.

Micro Channel architecture
The rules that define how subsystems and adapters use the Micro Channel bus in a computer. The architecture defines the services that each subsystem can or must provide.

microkernel
The part of the IBM Microkernel product that runs in the most privileged state of the computer and controls the basic operation of the computer. It includes only those functions required to provide a set of abstract processing environments and to permit applications to work together as clients and servers. These are IPC, ports, tasks, threads, and virtual memory management.

microkernel services
The system services provided with the IBM Microkernel product. There are three classes of services: Kernel Services, which control the basic operation of the machine; Microkernel Shared Services, which run on the microkernel and provide boot, default pager, and root name services; and Device Services, which include device and I/O management services.

MIDI
Musical Instrument Digital Interface.

MIG
Message Interface Generator.

MINDEX
A special class of user objects provided with the Workplace Shell. The Master Help Index is an instance of the MINDEX class.

MMPM/2
Multimedia Presentation Manager/2.

MPTN
Multiprotocol Transport Networking.

MQI
Message Queue Interface.

MRI
Machine-readable information.

multimedia
Material presented in a combination of text, graphics, video, image, animation, and sound.

multiprocessor
(1) A computer including two or more processors that have common access to a main storage. (2) A system of two or more processing units, or processors, that can communicate without manual intervention.

multiprotocol Transport Networking (MPTN)
A networking architecture that provides a common view of network protocols through common transport semantics so that, for example, application programs designed to operate over a particular transport network such as TCP/IP run over additional networks such as OSI or NetBIOS.

multitasking
A mode of operation that provides for concurrent performance, or interleaved execution of two or more tasks. (I) (A)

multiuser
Pertaining to two or more people who use the services of a processor within a given period of time; usage is normally serial unless otherwise specified.

Musical Instrument Digital Interface (MIDI)
A protocol that allows a synthesizer to send signals to another synthesizer or to a computer, or a computer to a musical instrument, or a computer to another computer.

mutex (mutual exclusion) semaphore
A semaphore that enables threads to serialize their access to resources. Only the thread that currently owns the mutex semaphore can gain access to the resource, thus preventing one thread from interrupting operations being performed by another.

muxwait (multiple wait) semaphore
A semaphore that enables a thread to wait either for multiple event semaphores to be posted or for multiple mutex semaphores to be released. Alternatively, a muxwait semaphore can be set to enable a thread to wait for any ONE of the event or mutex semaphores in the muxwait semaphore's list to be posted or released.

MVM
Multiple virtual machine.

MVM Server
The server that manages the collection of virtual x86 machines. It provides DOS/Windows/DPMI program compatibility on a PowerPC. It manages and supports execution of multiple x86 DOS and Windows programs (in real mode and protect mode) each in its own virtual x86 machine.

N

Name Services
A core shared service that provides a programming interface for its clients to store and access transient or persistent systems and state information in the global name space. It exports APIs to its clients and defines SPIs for name service providers.

name space
A hierarchical (tree) structure of nodes, with one distinguished node called the root. Each node is labeled by a distinct, nonempty string of characters called a component name. Nodes are directories or leaves (for example, terminal nodes that represent an entity identified by a port: file, device, root of a file set, and user name). Each node may have a list of attributes and access control. A name space is assigned naming rules during creation.

named pipe
A named buffer that provides client-to-server, server-to-client, or full duplex communication between unrelated processes. Contrast with unnamed pipe.

national language support (NLS)
The modification or conversion of a United States English product to conform to the requirements of another language or country. This can include the enabling or retrofitting of a product and the translation of nomenclature, MRI, or documentation of a product. NLS is also known as internationalization.

NetBIOS
Network Basic Input/Output System. A standard PC interface on LANs that provides message, print-server, and file-server functions.

network
A configuration of data processing devices and software connected for information interchange.

Network File System (NFS)
A protocol developed by Sun Microsystems, Inc., that allows any host in a network to mount another host's file directories. Once mounted, the file directory appears to reside on the local host.

NFS
Network File System.

NLS
National language support.

notebook
A graphical representation that resembles a spiral-bound notebook that contains pages separated into sections by tabbed divider-pages. A user can turn the pages of a notebook to move from one section to another.

O

object
An abstraction of data and the operations associated with that data.

object linking and embedding (OLE)
An application protocol developed by Microsoft Corporation that allows objects created by one application to be linked to or embedded in objects created by another application.

Object Management Group (OMG)
An industry coalition for the promotion and use of object technology standards.

object module
A binary executable or data component, or both, resulting from source assembly or compilation, or from secondary linkage of such object modules.

object module format
A set of instructions in machine language produced by a compiler from a source program.

object-oriented
(1) Pertaining to a user interface in which a user works with objects rather than applications, to perform tasks. (2) Pertaining to programming, a method for structuring applications as hierarchically organized classes describing objects that may interact with other objects.

Object request broker (ORB)
An interface for building requests and saving references to distributed objects.

object specifier
A token or set of tokens that describes the object upon which a semantic event operates, for example, "the third word of the second line of paragraph two in document 3."

OIDL
Object Interface Definition Language; specification language for SOM classes.

OLE
Object linking and embedding.

OMF
Object module format.

OMG
Object Management Group.

Open Blueprint
IBM's strategy for distributed computing.

OpenDoc
(1) A set of standard technologies for creating compound documents, building storage containing multiple data types, object creation and control, and scripting. (2) The compound document technology developed by Apple and donated to CI Labs as part of the OpenDoc set.

OpenEvent Standard Suites
A registry of semantic events and the objects upon which they can act. These events are broken up into suites covering various application types. CI Labs owns the registry and is responsible for maintaining and distributing it as a standard.

OpenEvents
The set of semantic events described in the OpenEvent Standard Suites. A direct descendent of Apple events.

OpenGL
An industry standard, 3-D graphics engine and API.

Open Scripting Architecture (OSA)
The standard that defines how semantic events are defined, generated, delivered, and executed between cooperating parts of documents and applications. OSA defines an interface that allows scripting components to be attached to documents and parts and executed by the user.

Open Software Foundation (OSF)
A nonprofit research and development organization whose goals are (a) to develop specifications and software for use in an open software environment and (b) to make the specifications and software available to information technology vendors.

Open Systems Interconnection (OSI)
The interconnection of open systems in accordance with standards of the International Organization for Standardization (ISO) for the exchange of information. OSI architecture establishes a framework for coordinating the development of current and future standards for the interconnection of computer systems. Network functions are divided into layers, with each layer representing a group of related data processing and communication functions that can be carried out in a standard way to support different applications.

operating system (OS)
Software that controls the execution of programs and that may provide services such as resource allocation, scheduling, input/output controls, and data management. Although operating systems are predominately software, partial hardware implementations are possible. (T)

operating system service
A key element of a microkernel-based operating system. Operating system services provide functions specific to an operating system, such as the application programming interface, the user interface, system policies, and semantics.

optical disc
A disc with a plastic coating on which information (such as sound or visual images) is recorded digitally as tiny pits and read using a laser. The three categories of optical discs are CD-ROM, WORM, and erasable.

ORB
Object request broker.

OSA
Open Scripting Architecture.

OSF
Open Software Foundation.

OSI
Open Systems Interconnection.

OSL
Object Services Library. The OSA component that builds and decodes objects specifiers for use in OpenEvents.

P

parallel port
An access point through which a computer transmits or receives data that consists of several bits sent simultaneously on separate wires. Contrast with serial port.

parent class
A class from which another class inherits. See also inheritance.

parent process
A process that creates other processes. Contrast with child process.

parent window
In the OS/2 operating system, a window that creates a child window. The child window is drawn within the parent window. If the parent window is moved, resized, or destroyed, the child window will also be moved, resized or destroyed. However, the child window can be moved and resized independently from the parent window, within the boundaries of the parent window.

part bins
Folders that contain collections of parts as templates. Users drag parts from their respective templates as they assemble their document.

parts
Programmatic units written by OpenDoc developers. The parts are then assembled at will by the user to create unique solutions.

path resolution
The resolution of a path to the correct file services entity (directory or file).

PC Card
A credit-card-sized adapter used to add memory, storage, or I/O capabilities to a personal computer, personal communicator, or other electronic device. The standards for PC cards are established by the PCMCIA.

PCMCIA
Personal Computer Memory Card International Association.

PDA
Personal Digital Assistant.

pen
A pointing and input device used with a touch-sensitive device.

persistence
An attribute of an object that characterizes its lifespan. An object that remains in effect across time is said to have persistence.

Personal Computer Memory Card International Association (PCMCIA)
A nonprofit organization of companies that manufacture hardware, software, semiconductor components, connectors, and computer peripherals. This organization was established to promote the interchangeability of Integrated Circuit Cards (IC Cards) among a variety of computer and other electronic products.

Personal Digital Assistant (PDA)
A small portable computer that acts on modules of code and can be used to store data such as phone numbers.

PFS
Physical file system.

Physical File System (PFS)
A shared service that manages the on-disk storage, indexing, mounting, and recovery of data. The File Services framework supports the installation of multiple Physical File Systems. Examples of Physical File Systems include FAT, HPFS, and CDROM.

pipe
To direct data so that the output from one process becomes the input to another process.

PM
Presentation Manager.

polymorphism
Different implementations of the same method for two or more classes of objects.

port
(1) A connector on a device to which cables for other devices such as displays and printers are attached. (2) In a microkernel-based architecture, a unidirectional asynchronous communication channel between a client and a server. A port has a single receiver and may have multiple senders. If a reply is provided to a service request a second port must be used. (3) Synonymous with socket.

Portable Operating System Interfaces for Computer Environments (POSIX)
An IEEE standard for operating systems closely related to the UNIX system. A standards body that sets standards for API that are approved by X/Open to ensure that a POSIX-approved code will run consistently on any POSIX compile platform.

POSIX
Portable Operating System Interfaces for Computer Environments.

power management
A software subsystem that extends battery life in portable computer systems and conserves electrical energy (in compliance with the EPA's Energy Star guidelines) for all non-battery powered systems.

presentation device drivers
Device drivers that process the high-level function calls to the Presentation Manager interface and communicate with the physical devices or the display hardware.

Presentation Manager (PM)
The graphics-based windowed interface of the OS/2 operating system.

privilege level
A method of protection that allows only certain program instructions to be used by certain programs.

procedural
Pertaining to a programming system design that allows interactions between subsystems through direct calls. Contrast with object-oriented designs that require messaging facilities for such interactions.

process
Any operation or combination of operations on data.

processor
In a computer, a functional unit that interprets and executes instructions. A processor consists of at least an instruction control unit and an arithmetic and logic unit. (T)

program
A sequence of instructions suitable for processing by a computer. (I)

protect mode
A method of program operation that limits or prevents access to certain instructions or areas of storage. Contrast with real mode.

protocol
A set of semantic and syntactic rules that determine the behavior of functional units in achieving communications. (I)

PTDA
Per-Task Data Area.

Q

queue
A list of items waiting to be processed; for example, work to be done or messages to be displayed.

R

RAM semaphore
In the OS/2 operating system, a semaphore used to serialize different threads of a single process. Contrast with system semaphore.

raster graphics
Computer graphics in which a display image is composed of an array of pels arranged in rows and columns. (I) (A)

real mode
A method of program operation that does not limit or prevent access to any instructions or areas of storage. The operating system loads the entire program into storage and gives the program access to all system resources. Contrast with protect mode.

recordability
A property of an application, document or part that allows its operation to be stored as OSAEvents for generating scripts, or later playback, or both.

recursion
The performance of an operation in several steps, with each step using the output of the preceding step.

redirect
To define or use a logical device name as a reference to another device or file that may be local or remote.

reduced instruction set computer (RISC)
A computer that uses a small, simplified set of frequently used instructions for rapid execution.

reentrant
The attribute of a program or routine that allows the same copy of the program or routine to be used concurrently by two or more tasks.

registry
(1) Document that contains the standard suites defined by OSA. The registry defines the verbs and objects that are used by OSA compliant documents, parts, and applications. (2) A system facility for the use of each framework and its service providers. It provides a programming interface, allowing its clients to access status and control over each framework and its services. It is implemented as a general purpose data store.

remote
Pertaining to a system, program, or device that is accessed through a telecommunication line. Contrast with local.

remote initial program load (RIPL)
(1) The initial program load of a remote requester by a server on which the appropriate information is located. (2) Supplies a remote requester with the data and programs required to boot the remote requester with an operating system. The data and programs are located on and supplied by a server. The operating system can be DOS or OS/2.

remote procedure call (RPC)
A facility that a client uses to request the execution of a procedure call from a server.

requester
Synonym for client.

resolution
(1) In computer graphics, a measure of the sharpness of an image, expressed as the number of lines and columns on the display screen or the number of pels per unit of area. (2) The number of lines in an image that an imaging system (for example, a telescope, the human eye, a camera, and so on) can resolve. A higher resolution makes text and graphics appear clearer.

resource
Any facility of a computing system or operating system required by a job or task, and including main storage, input/output devices, the processing unit, data sets, and control or processing programs.

resource interchange file format (RIFF)
A tagged file format framework intended to be the basis for defining new file formats.

response file
A file that contains a set of predefined answers to questions asked by a program and that is used in place of user dialog.

REXX/2
Restructured extended executor programming language for OS/2. A general-purpose programming language for command procedures, application front-ends, and user-defined macros, or subcommands. REXX programs are executed by a language processor (interpreter); that is, the program is executed line-by-line and word-by-word, without first being translated to another form (compiled).

RIFF
Resource interchange file format.

RIPL
Remote initial program load.

RISC
Reduced Instruction Set Computer.

Root Name Server
A microkernel service that controls the first level of the name space. It does not support persistent information, and implements a subset of the Name Services API.

router
An attaching device that connects two LAN segments, which use similar or different architectures. In OSI terminology, a function that determines a path by which an entity can be reached. In TCP/IP, synonymous with gateway. Contrast with bridge.

RPC
Remote procedure call.

S

SAA
Systems Application Architecture.

SBCS
Single-byte character set.

script
A set of commands that can be used to automate a program. In OSA, script components are pluggable and generate OpenEvents.

scriptability
A property of an application, document, or part that allows it to respond to OSAEvents sent by a scripting component.

SCSI
Small computer system interface.

security policy facility (SPF)
The security object that makes security access decisions. The interface to this facility is a series of APIs defined in the security documents. The SPF centralizes security access decisions for ease of security evaluation and auditing.

semantic event
An event that expresses the intent of the user; a command such as Open, Print, Select, and Close.

semaphore
An entity used to control access to system resources.

serial port
An access point through which a computer transmits or receives data, one bit at a time. Contrast with parallel port.

server
(1) A functional unit that provides shared services to workstations over a network; for example, a file server, a print server, a mail server. (T) (2) In a network, a data station that provides facilities to other stations; for example, a file server, a print server, a mail server. (A) (3) In the AIX operating system, an application program that usually runs in the background and is controlled by the system program controller. (4) In AIX Enhanced X-Windows, a program that provides the basic windowing mechanism. It handles interprocess communication (IPC) connections from clients, demultiplexes graphics requests onto screens, and multiplexes input back to clients. (5) In TCP/IP, a system in a network that handles the requests of a system at another site, called a client-server.

service
A managed set of useful functions intended for use by multiple clients. The Registry Manager is an example of a service.

service manager
Installation programs, remote administrators, or other types of clients that can interact with (get and put) the state of frameworks and service providers through the Name Services.

service provider
See framework service provider.

service provider interface (SPI)
An interface defined by a framework for service providers. See also framework service provider.

session
In the OS/2 operating system, one instance of a started program or command prompt. Each session is separate from all other sessions that might be running on the computer. The operating system is responsible for coordinating the resources that each session uses, such as computer memory, allocation of processor time, and windows on the screen.

settings notebook
A control window that is used to display the settings for an object and enable the user to change them.

SGML
Standard Generalized Markup Language.

shared library
See client library.

shared service
A software component that provides support to other software components in a microkernel-based operating system. A shared service provides higher level system function, such as file systems and networks. Shared services are defined as client/server application tasks.

shell
A software interface between a user and the operating system of a computer. Shell programs interpret commands and user interactions on devices such as keyboards, pointing devices, and touch-sensitive screens, and communicate them to the operating system.

shutdown
The procedure required before turning off the computer to ensure that data and configuration information are not lost.

single-byte character set (SBCS)
A character set whose character codes are represented by one-byte code. Contrast with double-byte character set.

single input queue
The system queue that receives input events such as keystrokes and mouse clicks.

small computer system interface (SCSI)
A standard hardware interface that enables a variety of peripheral devices to communicate with one another.

SMART
Source Migration, Analysis and Reporting Tool.

SMP
Symmetric multiprocessing.

SNA
Systems Network Architecture.

socket
An endpoint for communication between processes or application programs. Synonym for port.

SOFTDRAW
A full software rasterizer that provides support for many functions that, in the past, presentation driver writers had to provide themselves.

software motion video
Reproduction of video content strictly through software.

SOM
System Object Model.

Source Migration, Analysis and Reporting Tool (SMART)
Software development tool created by One Up Corporation and distributed with The Developer Connection. SMART helps you port your Windows 16-bit and 32-bit applications and your OS/2 16-bit applications to OS/2 Warp Connect (PowerPC Edition).

SPF
Security Policy Facility.

SPI
Server Provider Interface.

spooler
A program that intercepts the data going to printer devices and writes it to disk. The data is printed or plotted when it is complete and the required device is available. The spooler prevents output from different sources from being intermixed.

SQL
Structured Query Language.

Standard Generalized Markup Language (SGML)
An ISO standard created by IBM. A generic encoding of information; a metalanguage that provides a grammar or set of rules by which a document interchange technology can be constructed.

stanza file
A type of control file that has an internal script that defines devices and the order of their processing. A stanza consists of a paragraph descriptor, paragraph attributes, and a terminator.

stroke
In pen systems, the collection of points between the point where the pen touches a touch-sensitive surface and the point where the pen is removed from the surface.

Structured Query Language (SQL)
A standard interface for accessing relational data. Originally developed by IBM, SQL has been accepted by ISO and X/Open as the standardized language for defining and manipulating data in a relational database.

stub
A program module that transfers remote procedure calls (RPCs) and responses between a client and a server.

subclass
A child class that defines new behavior in terms of new methods not inherited from parent or ancestor classes.

subsystem
A secondary or subordinate system, usually capable of operating independently of, or asynchronously with, a controlling system. (T) Subsystems are implemented as shared services in microkernel-based operating systems.

symmetric multiprocessing (SMP)
Equal distribution of tasks across multiple processors.

synchronous
Pertaining to two or more processes that depend upon the occurrence of specific events, such as common timing signals. (T) Contrast with asynchronous.

synthesizer
See audio synthesizer.

system
A collection of people, machines, and methods organized to accomplish a set of specific functions. (I) (A)

System Object Model (SOM)
A mechanism for language-neutral, object-oriented programming in the OS/2 environment. SOM is a CORBA-compliant, industry standard technology.

system semaphore
In the OS/2 operating system, a signal mechanism providing control between threads of multiple processes that do not share memory. Contrast with RAM semaphore.

Systems Application Architecture (SAA)
A set of IBM software interfaces, conventions, and protocols that provide a framework for designing and developing applications that are consistent across systems.

Systems Network Architecture (SNA)
The description of the logical structure, formats, protocols, and operational sequences for transmitting information units through, and controlling the configuration and operation of, networks. The layered structured of SNA allows the ultimate origins and destinations of information, that is, the end users, to be independent of and unaffected by the specific SNA network services and facilities used for information interchange.

T

task
In a multiprogramming or multiprocessing environment, one or more sequences of instructions treated by a control program as an element of work to be accomplished by a computer. (I) (A)

TCB
Trusted computing base.

TCP/IP
Transmission Control Protocol/Internet Protocol.

template
An object that creates a copy of itself when dragged and dropped by the user. OpenDoc parts are usually delivered as templates and stored in folders called part bins.

terminal
A device, usually equipped with a keyboard and a display device, that is capable of sending and receiving information.

thread
In the OS/2 operating system, the smallest unit of operation to be performed within a process.

timeout
A time interval allotted for certain operations to occur.

tinkerability
A property of an application, document, or part that indicates that it allows a user to attach scripts to various functions and controls such as buttons and menus. In this way a user can easily alter the application by writing or modifying scripts.

title bar
The area at the top of each window that contains the system-menu symbol, a small icon, a window title, and the maximize, minimize, and restore buttons.

token
In a local area network, the symbol of authority passed successively from one data station to another to indicate the station temporarily in control of the transmission medium. A token is a particular message or bit pattern that signifies permission to transmit. (T) When the token has data appended to it, it becomes a frame.

token-ring network
A ring network that allows unidirectional data transmission between data stations, by a token passing procedure, such that the transmitted data returns to the transmitting station. (T)

topology
In communications, the physical or logical arrangement of nodes in a network, especially the relationships among nodes and the links between them.

Transmission Control Protocol/Internet Protocol (TCP/IP)
A set of communication protocols that supports peer-to-peer connectivity functions for both local and wide-area networks.

trusted computing base (TCB)
In computer security, all of the protection mechanisms within a computer system, including hardware, software, and firmware, the combination of which enforces a security policy. It creates a basic protection environment and provides additional user services required for a trusted computer system.

U

UDMD
User-Defined Migration Database, generated by the SMART tool.

UI
User interface.

UI event
An event describing an action by the user, such as a button click, mouse movement, or a keystroke.

ULDD
User Level Device Driver.

Unicode
Code that is independent of language and culture, and supports multiple simultaneous character sets.

UNIX operating system
An operating system developed by Bell Laboratories that features multiprogramming in a multiuser environment. The UNIX operating system was originally developed for use on minicomputers but has been adapted for mainframes and microcomputers.

unnamed pipe
A circular buffer, created in memory, used by related processes to communicate with one another. Contrast with named pipe.

V

VFS
Virtual file system.

viewers
Part handlers whose only function is to render or print a part. Viewers cannot create new data or modify old data. They are offered freely by software producers allowing full-fidelity rendering of OpenDoc documents anywhere that a viewer exists.

viewport
Term applied to a help window.

virtual file system (VFS)
A remote file system that has been mounted so that it is accessible to the local user.

virtual machine (VM)
A virtual data processing system that appears to be at the exclusive disposal of a particular user, but whose functions are accomplished by sharing the resources of a real data processing system. (T)

vital product data (VPD)
A framework within which to characterize the software and hardware components that reside on the system.

VMAN
Video manager.

v-node
Virtual i-node. An object in a file system that represents a file. Unlike an i-node, there is no one-to-one correspondence between a v-node and the file system; multiple v-nodes can refer to a single file. A v-node is used to communicate between the upper half of the file system and the file system representations.

volume
The largest file system unit, a volume represents all the available storage on a logical drive. Volumes, identified by a volume name, are subdivided into directories, which contain files and other subdirectories. Each volume has a root directory.

VPD
Vital product data.

W

wide area network (WAN)
A network that provides communication services to a geographic area larger than that served by a local area network or a metropolitan area network, and that may use or provide public communication facilities. (T) Contrast with local area network and metropolitan area network.

WIN-OS/2
A feature of OS/2 that enables OS/2 to run supported Windows programs.

window
(1) A portion of a display surface in which display images pertaining to a particular application can be presented. Different applications can be displayed simultaneously in different windows. (A) (2) An area of the screen with visible boundaries within which information is displayed. A window can be smaller than, or the same size as, the screen. (3) A division of a screen in which one of several programs being executed concurrently can display information.

Workplace Shell interface
The object-oriented, graphical user interface of OS/2 2.0 and later versions of the operating system.

write once/read many (WORM)
An optical disc that, once written to, cannot be overwritten.

WYSIWYG
What-you-see-is-what-you-get. A capability of a text editor to continually display pages exactly as they will be printed.

Index

Symbols

A

B

C

D

E

F

G

H

I

J

K

L

M

N

O

P

Q

R

S

U

V

W

X

Y

Z

IDG BOOKS WORLDWIDE REGISTRATION CARD

RETURN THIS REGISTRATION CARD FOR FREE CATALOG

Title of this book: IBM's Official OS/2 Warp Connect, Power PC Edition: Operating in the New Frontier

My overall rating of this book: ❑ Very good [1] ❑ Good [2] ❑ Satisfactory [3] ❑ Fair [4] ❑ Poor [5]

How I first heard about this book:

❑ Found in bookstore; name: [6] ____

❑ Book review: [7] ____

❑ Advertisement: [8] ____

❑ Catalog: [9] ____

❑ Word of mouth; heard about book from friend, co-worker, etc.: [10] ____

❑ Other: [11] ____

What I liked most about this book: ____

What I would change, add, delete, etc., in future editions of this book: ____

Other comments: ____

Number of computer books I purchase in a year: ❑ 1 [12] ❑ 2-5 [13] ❑ 6-10 [14] ❑ More than 10 [15]

I would characterize my computer skills as: ❑ Beginner [16] ❑ Intermediate [17] ❑ Advanced [18] ❑ Professional [19]

I use ❑ DOS [20] ❑ Windows [21] ❑ OS/2 [22] ❑ Unix [23] ❑ Macintosh [24] ❑ Other: [25] ____ (please specify)

I would be interested in new books on the following subjects:
(please check all that apply, and use the spaces provided to identify specific software)

❑ Word processing: [26] ____

❑ Spreadsheets: [27] ____

❑ Data bases: [28] ____

❑ Desktop publishing: [29] ____

❑ File Utilities: [30] ____

❑ Money management: [31] ____

❑ Networking: [32] ____

❑ Programming languages: [33] ____

❑ Other: [34] ____

I use a PC at (please check all that apply): ❑ home [35] ❑ work [36] ❑ school [37] ❑ other: [38] ____

The disks I prefer to use are ❑ 5.25 [39] ❑ 3.5 [40] ❑ other: [41] ____

I have a CD ROM: ❑ yes [42] ❑ no [43]

I plan to buy or upgrade computer hardware this year: ❑ yes [44] ❑ no [45]

I plan to buy or upgrade computer software this year: ❑ yes [46] ❑ no [47]

Name: ____ Business title: [48] ____ Type of Business: [49] ____

Address (❑ home [50] ❑ work [51]/Company name: ____)

Street/Suite# ____

City [52]/State [53]/Zipcode [54]: ____ Country [55] ____

❑ **I liked this book!** You may quote me by name in future IDG Books Worldwide promotional materials.

My daytime phone number is ____

IDG BOOKS
THE WORLD OF COMPUTER KNOWLEDGE

❑ YES!

Please keep me informed about IDG's World of Computer Knowledge. Send me the latest IDG Books catalog.

SECRETS™

...FOR DUMMIES™
COMPUTER BOOK SERIES FROM IDG

MACWORLD MW AUTHORIZED EDITION

AUTHORIZED PC WORLD EDITION

NO POSTAGE NECESSARY IF MAILED IN THE UNITED STATES

BUSINESS REPLY MAIL

FIRST CLASS MAIL PERMIT NO. 2605 FOSTER CITY, CALIFORNIA

IDG Books Worldwide
919 E Hillsdale Blvd, STE 400
Foster City, CA 94404-9691